Praise for *Mr. and Mrs. Madison's War*

"Hugh Howard has turned the least known and least understood war in American history into a Technicolor, wide-screen epic of thrilling naval battles, brutal backwoods skirmishes, villainous intrigues, and stirring heroism. *Mr. and Mrs. Madison's War* moves smoothly between the White House, New Orleans, the Great Lakes, the Chesapeake, and the waters off New England. Thanks to Howard's prodigious research, fine eye for the telling detail, and vivid prose, the War of 1812 seems as contemporary and compelling as yesterday's battlefield dispatches from the Middle East."

—Thurston Clarke, *New York Times* bestselling author of *The Last Campaign: Robert F. Kennedy and 82 Days that Inspired America*

"An entertaining look at the forgotten war, the burning of Washington, and the fourth president's none-too-effective efforts to command the military."

—Military History Quarterly Magazine

"Hugh Howard tackles the history of a war that is incomprehensible in the modern sense of warfare and renders it understandable, giving a fascinating and engaging account of the people and events involved in America's first war. *Mr. and Mrs. Madison's War* will add enormously to public understanding of the War of 1812."

—Michael Quinn, president of James Madison's Montpelier

"*Mr. and Mrs. Madison's War* has a wonderful visual quality that allowed me to feel I was standing on the deck [of] the HMS *Confiance* as Captain Downie was struck by a cannon barrel and mingling with members of Congress at one of Dolley Madison's Wednesday gatherings."

—Patricia O'Sullivan, *Historical Novel Society*

"An engrossing narrative history of a conflict that few today know much about. Howard ranges widely, as the war did, from the Great Lakes to New Orleans to the Mid-Atlantic Coast. His descriptions of the human carnage during the naval battles are particularly dramatic and moving . . .

It was a struggle of memorable personalities and phrases: 'Don't give up the ship.' 'We have met the enemy and they are ours.' 'Oh, say does that star-spangled banner yet wave.' Howard reminds us of the gumption and bravery behind those words." **—Anne Bartlett, *BookPage.com***

"A thorough account of the War of 1812 that's both action-packed and intimate." ***—Shelf Awareness***

"Howard's meticulous research and wonderful storytelling ability truly paints a detailed portrait of the unthinkable result of the British invasion . . . *Mr. and Mrs. Madison's War* is a wonderful book about an overlooked chapter in history that featured one of this country's darkest moments." **—Anthony Bergen, *AND Magazine***

"Howard presents detailed accounts of James and Dolley Madison's significant roles during [the War of 1812] . . . [his] research has produced incisive portraits of significant figures during the war."
—Ted Odenwald, *The Oakland Journal* (Oakland, NJ)

"Howard makes the history come to life by adding in the details that most people consider unimportant. Because of this *Mr. and Mrs. Madison's War* is more memorable and a fun read." **—*Baltimore Reads* blog**

"The author delivers a skillful history of the war itself . . . Howard provides illuminating asides about [Dolley Madison's] activities as Washington's premier hostess and a far more colorful correspondent than her husband. An entertaining portrait of the era's first couple and the social life of the young nation's elite." ***—Kirkus Reviews***

"Hugh Howard provides us with vividly written accounts of some of the more dramatic highlights of the War of 1812. Readers with particular interests in the Chesapeake Bay campaigns of 1814 will find much to enjoy here."
—Professor J.C.A. Stagg, editor of
The Papers of James Madison

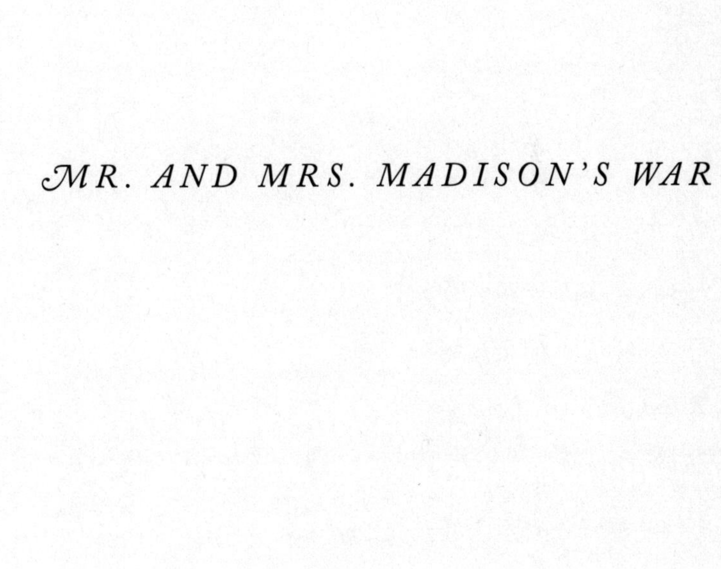

MR. AND MRS. MADISON'S WAR

OTHER BOOKS BY HUGH HOWARD

The Painter's Chair

Houses of the Founding Fathers

Dr. Kimball and Mr. Jefferson

Thomas Jefferson, Architect

House-Dreams

The Preservationist's Progress

MR. AND MRS. MADISON'S WAR

America's First Couple and the War of 1812

HUGH HOWARD

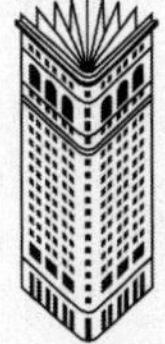

BLOOMSBURY PRESS
New York • London • New Delhi • Sydney

To Presidents

—then and now—

bewildered by unwinnable wars

Maps drawn by Moacir de Sá Pereira based on public domain originals

Published by Bloomsbury Press, New York
Bloomsbury is a trademark of Bloomsbury Publishing Plc

All papers used by Bloomsbury Press are natural, recyclable products
made from wood grown in well-managed forests. The manufacturing processes
conform to the environmental regulations of the country of origin.

LIBRARY OF CONGRESS CATALOGING-IN-PUBLICATION DATA

Howard, Hugh, 1952–
Mr. and Mrs. Madison's war : America's first couple and the second war of independence / Hugh Howard.—1st U.S. ed.
p. cm.
ISBN-13: 978-1-60819-071-3
ISBN-10: 1-60819-071-4
1. United States—History—War of 1812. 2. Madison, James, 1751–1836. 3. Madison, Dolley, 1768–1849. I. Title.
E354.H78 2012
973.5'2—dc23
2011017429

First U.S. edition published 2012
This paperback edition published 2014

Paperback ISBN: 978-1-60819-393-6

3 5 7 9 10 8 6 4 2

Typeset by Westchester Book Group
Printed and bound in the U.S.A. by Thomson-Shore Inc., Dexter, Michigan

AUTHOR'S NOTE

PICTURE A PRESIDENT looking morosely at the ruin of two of his nation's most iconic buildings. He mourns their loss, burned as they were in an act of international terrorism. A war declaration is in the air, one based on false intelligence; there's the promise, as well, of an easily accomplished victory. Unfortunately, the conflict will turn into a long slog that divides the country, empties its treasury, and leaves none of the warring parties feeling triumphant.

Now consider that the president was James Madison, the buildings the Capitol and the President's house, and the year 1814.

As a narrative historian, I seek story lines—and the so-called Second War of Independence offers many extraordinary stories. Some have assumed the status of legend, as the war left us with "Don't Give Up the Ship," *Old Ironsides*, "The Star-Spangled Banner," the sack of Washington, and, of course, Dolley Madison saving the big portrait of George Washington.

The American navy came of age in 1812 and 1813; a nation of coastal communities saw its economic, political, and demographic center of gravity shift westward. The next generation of presidents all played roles in this war, among them James Monroe, John Quincy Adams, Andrew Jackson, William Henry Harrison, and Zachary Taylor. The world, especially the community of European nations, began to pay new attention to the United States.

Yet as the bicentennial of the War of 1812 approaches, the conflict stands as perhaps the least understood of America's wars. In part, *Mr. and Mrs. Madison's War* is intended to be a corrective to that.

This book observes civilization's most essential tension at work—that is, the equilibrium of peace versus the chaos of war—as the most mild-mannered and meditative of American presidents becomes the first to declare war. The small stage of the Federal era offers good sightlines for viewing a rather opaque president along with the compelling Dolley Madison. She was a principal actor in the events that unfolded between the war declaration in June 1812 and the Treaty of Ghent, word of which arrived in Washington City in February 1815.

The War of 1812 has been cast and recast by historians and presidents alike. To some it was a coda to the War of Independence, a reprise that settled the issue once and for all. To others, it was a war that resolved nothing. To Henry Adams in his magisterial history of the era, published in 1890, it was a parable on a failed presidency; another Massachusetts boy, John F. Kennedy, regarded Madison, whose eight years in office were dominated by the rumors, acts, and residue of war, as "our most underrated president."

My purpose is neither to shape a parable nor to teach a lesson. Instead, *Mr. and Mrs. Madison's War* offers a view of events at first hand, being a reconstruction based upon contemporary primary sources including countless letters, journals, ledgers, newspaper reports, government records, memoirs, and other documents.

A moment from the past can no more be restored to a seamless whole than a broken mirror can, but the account that follows is as true as my researches could make it. That said, I acknowledge my reconstructed looking glass certainly has its imperfections.

—H.H.
Hayes Hill, New York

CONTENTS

Book II: The Guns of August 1814 *113*

Book III: Washington Regained *223*

THE PLAYERS

FRIENDS AND FAMILY

James Madison, *President of the United States*
Dolley Payne Todd Madison, *"Presidentess"*
John Payne Todd, *son of Mrs. Madison*
Anna and Congressman Richard Cutts, *Mrs. Madison's sister and brother-in-law*
Edward Coles, *Secretary to Mr. Madison and cousin of Mrs. Madison*
Lucy and Justice Thomas Todd, *Mrs. Madison's youngest sister and brother-in-law*
Paul Jennings, *Mr. Madison's personal slave and valet*
Sukey, *Mrs. Madison's personal slave and maid*
Jean-Pierre Sioussat, *Majordomo at the President's house*
Sarah Coles, *younger cousin and sometime companion of Dolley*

THE MEN OF THE GOVERNMENT

Richard Rush, *Attorney General*
Thomas Jefferson, *former President*
James Monroe, *Secretary of State*
Elbridge Gerry, *Vice President*
Henry Clay, *Speaker of the House of Representatives and Minister Plenipotentiary at Ghent*
Albert Gallatin, *Secretary of the Treasury and Minister Plenipotentiary at Ghent*
Paul Hamilton, *Secretary of the Navy*
William Jones, *Hamilton's successor as Secretary of the Navy*
John Armstrong, *Secretary of War*
John Quincy Adams, *Minister Plenipotentiary at Ghent*
James Bayard, *Minister Plenipotentiary at Ghent*
Jonathan Russell, *Minister Plenipotentiary at Ghent*
George Washington Campbell, *Gallatin's successor as Secretary of the Treasury*
Robert Stuart Skinner, *Agent for Prisoners of War*

WASHINGTON SOCIETY

Albert and Hannah Nicholson Gallatin, *friends and confidants of the Madisons*
Louis Sérurier, *French Minister Plenipotentiary*
Dr. William Thornton and Anna Maria Thornton, *Superintendent of Patents and diarist*
Samuel Harrison Smith and Margaret Bayard Smith, *former editor of the* National Intelligencer *and his wife, writers, both*
Daniel Webster, *Congressman of New Hampshire*
Elbridge Gerry Jr., *son of the Vice President*

John and Anne Ogle Tayloe, *Washington City's wealthiest couple*
Major Charles Carroll, *a gentleman of Washington City and a militia officer*
Benjamin Henry and Mary Hazelhurst Latrobe, *Architect of the Public Buildings and his wife, a childhood friend of Mrs. Madison*
Jacob Barker, *merchant and banker*
Francis Scott Key, *Georgetown barrister*
William Wirt, *Richmond lawyer and member of the Virginia militia*
George Ticknor, *visitor from Boston*
James Paulding, *Navy clerk and wit from New York*
Charles Jared Ingersoll, *Congressman from Pennsylvania*

THE MILITARY MEN

James Barron, *Captain of the USS* Chesapeake
William Henry Harrison, *Brigadier General and Commander of the North-Western Army*
Andrew Jackson, *former Senator and Major General*
William Hull, *Brigadier General and Governor of the Michigan Territory*
Isaac Hull, *Captain of the USS* Constitution
Stephen Decatur, *Captain of the USS* United States
Zebulon Pike Jr., *Brigadier General on the Canadian front*
James Lawrence, *Captain of the USS* Chesapeake
Isaac Chauncey, *Captain and Commander of forces on the Great Lakes*
Oliver Hazard Perry, *Master Commandant of the fleet on Lake Erie*
Joshua Barney, *Commodore of the fleet of Chesapeake galleys*
William Winder, *Brigadier General and Commander of the Tenth Military District*
Samuel Smith, *U.S. Senator and Major General of the Maryland Militia*
Thomas Macdonough, *Master Commandant and Commander of the Champlain fleet*

THE BRITISH

Augustus John Foster, *Minister Plenipotentiary*
Robert Stewart, *Viscount Castlereagh, Foreign Secretary*
Salusbury Pryce Humphreys, *Captain of the HMS* Leopard
James Dacres, *Captain of the HMS* Guerrière
Phillip Bowes Vere Broke, *Captain of the HMS* Shannon
George Cockburn, *Rear Admiral and Commander of the Chesapeake district*
Robert Barclay, *Commander of the British fleet on Lake Erie*
Robert Ross, *Major General and Field Commander*
George Downie, *Captain and Commander of the Champlain forces*
Edward Pakenham, *Major General and Field Commander*

PROLOGUE

Rumors of War

Peace . . . has been our principle, peace is our interest, and peace has saved to the world this only plant of free and rational government now existing in it.[1]
—Thomas Jefferson to Tadeusz Kosciuszko, April 13, 1811

1.

Midday, June 18, 1812 . . . The British Legation . . . Washington City

THE BRITISH AMBASSADOR KNEW something was about to happen. The *National Intelligencer* had suggested as much a week earlier, with a cryptic hint buried in one of the paper's tightly packed columns. "[S]ome measure of a decisive character has passed the House," the nation's most widely read paper reported, "and has been sent to the Senate for concurrence."[2] The sense of portent in the city, whose inhabitants were always attuned to events on Capitol Hill, had been intensified by the decision of both houses of Congress to spend much of the preceding two weeks in secret session.

British Minister Plenipotentiary Augustus John Foster had refused to put any stock in the predictions of war offered him weeks earlier by

Speaker of the House Henry Clay. Since then the rumors had grown warmer, and, though he remained dubious, Foster knew where to go to hear the latest reports. Since this was Wednesday, everyone in Washington City understood that even if the portals at Congress were sealed, Mrs. Madison's doors would soon be open. Foster needed only to wait for the line of carriages to form on Pennsylvania Avenue, as everyone who was anyone in Washington City would be making his way to the largest and finest house in town.

Dolley Madison's Drawing Rooms had come to be called *squeezes* because as many as five hundred people wedged themselves into the public rooms at the President's house. These gatherings amounted to more than social events. Everybody came, Democratic-Republicans and Federalists alike, and, as one young congressional wife observed, "Mrs. Madison . . . won golden opinions from all, and she possessed an influence so decided with her little Man that She was the worshiped of all the idol Mongers."[3] She was unquestionably the city's first hostess, a woman who was, as Foster himself conceded in his diary, "so perfectly good-tempered and good-humored that she rendered her husband's house as far as depended on her agreeable to all parties." She was very much her husband's partner; even before Madison's swearing-in five years earlier, she was called "Lady President" and "the Presidentess."[4]

The British minister could be certain that many of those in attendance would know more of the status of the deliberations in Congress than he did, not least Mr. Madison himself ("a gentleman in manners," in Foster's estimation, "a man of public virtue").[5] Foster wanted to believe that the Americans wished to avoid war, and had recently reported as much to Robert Stewart, Viscount Castlereagh, the British Foreign Secretary. "My hopes of a favorable issue," Foster had written, "continue to increase."[6]

Yet as a veteran observer of the American scene, he also understood better than most Britons the vestigial anger many Americans felt when reminded of three booming broadsides fired five years earlier. News of the British attack upon the USS *Chesapeake* had spread with surprising speed across the country, and Foster, though then a mere secretary to the British minister, had had to disguise himself. Afraid for his own safety, he had traveled incognito back to the Federal City. His concern had been well placed as, even without his being present, an angry mob in New York had threatened to throw his English curricle and horses into a river.[7]

Deny it though he might when writing to Castlereagh in 1812, Foster knew in his bones that the one-sided sea battle between the HMS *Leopard* and the USS *Chesapeake* in June 1807 had tilted the topography of history.

A FINE MIDSUMMER DAY FAVORED THE AMERICAN FRIGATE as a southeast wind filled her sails. Her rigging freshly overhauled and guns refitted, the USS *Chesapeake* was bound for the Mediterranean to relieve her sister ship, the USS *Constitution*, patrolling the Barbary Coast.

As they departed the harbor at Hampton Roads, Virginia, on June 22, 1807, the crew of the 38-gun warship observed a British squadron anchored in a nearby bay. The sighting surprised no one, as British warships were often in the waters of the Virginia capes and even within the confines of the Norfolk Navy Yard, where Royal Navy vessels sometimes docked for repairs. American Commodore James Barron saw nothing amiss when one of the ships, the HMS *Leopard*, weighed anchor and set sail. At least one of the British vessels could usually be observed cruising the coastline seeking French merchant ships, but the British were at war with Napoleon, not with their former colonies.

The *Leopard* appeared to be shadowing the American frigate, but the sight of the 50-gun British ship to larboard did not particularly worry Barron as he ate his two o'clock dinner in his cabin with his officers. Also at table was a State Department consul, who, along with his wife and three children, was on his way to a Mediterranean posting. When the *Leopard* closed within a cable length and its captain hailed, asking to send a boat with dispatches for the Americans, the explanation seemed at hand. Barron called back agreement, his voice amplified by a hailing trumpet.

With the ships broadside to one another, a boat was lowered from the *Leopard.* A junior officer was rowed across the two hundred feet that separated the vessels. On coming aboard, British Lieutenant John Meade saw dozens of ailing seamen on the upper deck; the *Chesapeake*'s doctor had ordered them to take the air and sun to speed their recovery. Though this was a ship of war, its captain believed it to be in safe waters, and the gun deck looked like an oversized storeroom with canvas partitions and an array of unstowed gear and foodstuffs. The weeks required to make the crossing would provide ample time to get everything shipshape.

Commodore Barron received Lieutenant Meade in his cabin a few minutes before four o'clock. The Briton handed the American officer not a bundle of letters but a single dispatch. To Barron's surprise, he found on reading it that Captain Salusbury Pryce Humphreys of the *Leopard* demanded to search the *Chesapeake.* According to Captain Humphreys, the American ship carried "some deserters . . . now serving as part of the crew."[8] The British lieutenant presented Barron with a second sheet, this one containing Humphreys's orders from his superior, Vice Admiral George Berkeley, commander of British ships on the North American station. Barron recognized its key assertion: "[M]any seamen, subject of His Britannic Majesty . . . while at anchor in the Chesapeake, deserted and entered on board the United States frigate called the 'Chesapeake,' and openly paraded the streets of Norfolk, in sight of their officers, under the American flag."[9]

Barron knew full well that some of his men were British citizens. That was neither new nor surprising, as British deserters often joined the rolls on American ships. Perhaps one in four sailors on vessels of American registry was British-born, lured by the higher wages paid by American paymasters, which typically quadrupled their earnings from thirty to thirty-five shillings a month (about seven dollars) to thirty dollars or more.[10] The working conditions were better, and American sailors knew, too, they would be free men after an agreed-upon term of service (the Crown, in comparison, regarded indefinite compulsory service in the Royal Navy as its prerogative).[11] At a time when American shipping was booming, an experienced British sailor had no difficulty finding a place to hang his hammock on an American ship.

One tar in particular, a tough-talking former tailor born Jenkin Ratford, had made himself notorious. Under the cover of a sudden squall, he and four other seamen had rowed quickly away from their ship, the sloop HMS *Halifax*. Having then signed on as an ordinary seaman on the *Chesapeake*, he was known to Barron by the name John Wilson. Days earlier, however, when confronted on a Norfolk street, Ratford had boldly refused to return to the *Halifax*, contemptuously informing a British navy officer that he was "in the land of liberty."[12]

Regardless of how many "John Wilsons" were on his rolls, Commodore Barron could never agree to a search of his ship. His honor as an officer and a gentleman—and an American—would not permit it.

EVERY CHILD AT PLAY ON A CITY WHARF knew the dangers of going to sea. Ports were peopled with orphans and widows, living evidence that some departing ships never returned. But for American sailors, the Royal Navy added to the risks.

Impressment required no explanation to the average American. Many merchant seamen on American ships were taken prisoner on the high seas or in neutral ports and forced to serve in His Majesty's Navy. Some were men who had recently deserted as Londoner Jenkin Ratford had done; others were British-born sailors who years earlier had chosen to become naturalized American citizens. Still others were American-born men on whom the press gang had no legal claim whatever but who happened to be in the wrong place at the wrong moment. One British seaman described "the Press" in matter-of-fact terms. "Being in want of men, we resorted to the press-gang, which was made up of our most loyal men, armed to the teeth; by their aid we obtained our full numbers. Amongst them were a few Americans. . . . The press-gang usually went ashore on the night previous to our going to sea; so that before [the impressed sailors] were missed they were beyond protection."[13]

For a British captain in the service of the King, the issue was a simple matter of arithmetic. The ranks of the Royal Navy had expanded greatly from the beginning of the French wars; sixteen thousand bluejackets in 1792 had grown to well over one hundred thousand seamen. With better than one in ten of Britain's adult male citizens already in military service, press gangs were essential to ensuring British ships sailed with a sufficiency of able-bodied men. At home, press gangs routinely made the rounds of English ports to collar merchant seamen into service to the Crown, while in American waters, British boarding parties seized sailors off the decks of merchantmen. By 1807, the number of impressed Americans in the British navy neared three thousand men. There was outrage aplenty beyond the docks, too. Senator John Quincy Adams called it "kidnapping upon the ocean," and former President John Adams railed at "the barbarous THEFTS OF AMERICAN CITIZENS!"[14]

The Press came to represent more than an infringement upon individual rights. As Commodore James Barron was acutely aware, the demand to board his ship made a mockery of the new nation's sovereignty. All levels of American society found it unacceptable that Britain's representatives thought they could behave with impunity even in American territorial waters. Many impressments took place along the coast, often within the three-mile limit.

The outrage on this day was compounded by the fact the USS *Chesapeake* was a military vessel. The British Navy was indisputably the most powerful in the world, as Admiral Nelson's decisive victory over the combined fleets of France and Spain at the Battle of Trafalgar in 1805 showed. That made Commodore Barron's refusal to permit the British to search the *Chesapeake* all the more dangerous.

WITH LIEUTENANT MEADE IN ATTENDANCE, Commodore Barron took up pen and paper. "I am . . . instructed never to permit the crew of any ship that I command to be mustered by any but their own officers," he replied to Humphreys. In a close interpretation of Captain Humphreys's meaning—though aware of deserters on board from other British ships, he could name none of those specifically mentioned in Vice Admiral Berkeley's orders—he stated, "I know of no such men as you describe." The American very much hoped this assurance, along with his word as a fellow officer, would satisfy Captain Humphreys.

Lieutenant Meade was rowed back to the *Leopard,* letter in hand. Barron noted the open gun ports of the *Leopard*, through which the muzzles of her guns were visible. He quietly ordered that his ship be readied for action. The gun deck was crowded with lumber, pork barrels, casks, a forge and anvil, a grindstone, and other items still to be stowed belowdecks. Even if the gunnery area could be cleared, the guns themselves were not in a state of readiness, as they were lashed down for heavy weather, many without sponges and rammers, and none had powder at hand.

When the letter reached him a few minutes later, Captain Humphreys scanned Barron's refusal, then hailed his opposite number. He warned the American to comply with the demand for inspection. On board the *Chesapeake* Barron understood that if his ship was to have a chance in an exchange of fire, his sailors needed more time. He attempted to delay matters, shouting back that he could not hear what Humphreys said. Humphreys hailed again, but Barron's reply ("I do not hear what you say") was the last of the spoken dialogue. Moments later, gunners on the *Leopard* fired a shot across the bow of the *Chesapeake.* A second warning shot boomed a minute later. After another interval, the air roared with the ear-splitting booms of a full broadside.

Solid shot ripped into the hull of the American frigate. Canister shot—small balls of lead and iron packed in sawdust—poured down on the Americans, as did cordage and great splinters from shattered rigging. The Americans were unable to return fire because their guns were unprimed and the red-hot iron loggerheads used to light the charges were not yet heated. Meanwhile the British reloaded, and a second broadside blasted the *Chesapeake*; a third followed. With his ship unable to defend itself, Barron had no choice but to order the colors struck. The men on the gun deck finally managed to get off a single shot. Lit by a coal from the galley, it discharged at almost the same moment the descending flag reached the taffrail.

The battle lasted less than fifteen minutes. Some seventy-five charges fired by the *Leopard* left three men dead and eighteen wounded on the *Chesapeake*. The American ship took on water through twenty-two round-shot holes in its hull. Its masts were damaged, its sails perforated, and Commodore Barron was among the wounded, flying slivers having lodged in his thigh.

Captain Humphreys dispatched two boats to the *Chesapeake*. British officers ordered all able-bodied members of the crew—there were 329 seamen and 52 marines aboard—to muster on deck. Any likely-looking sailor with an accent deemed British or Irish might have been fair game, but the boarding party returned to the *Leopard* with just four men. Three were Americans, two of whom were free black men, while the fourth was Jenkin Ratford, found skulking in the coalhole. The British ship soon set sail, leaving the *Chesapeake* to mend her rigging, pump the three and a half feet of water from her hold, and limp back to Hampton Roads in disgrace.

WORD OF THE ATTACK ON THE DEFENSELESS *CHESAPEAKE* had reached Washington rapidly. Despite its Republican perspective, the *National Intelligencer*, which was also the nation's paper of record (it posted government notices), probably spoke for Republicans and Federalists alike when it reported "the late ATROCIOUS OUTRAGE offered to *the honor and rights of our country.*"[15] The news made its way from port to port, and in Norfolk, the militia had to be summoned to control crowds of angry seamen. Many Americans called for a Declaration of War, but opposition to war was among the basic tenets of President Thomas Jefferson's Republican Party. Secretary of State James Madison was among the first in Washington City to learn of the humiliation. He confided in President Jefferson that, "having effected her lawless & bloody purpose, [the *Leopard*] returned immediately to anchor with her squadron within our jurisdiction. Hospitality under such circumstances ceases to be a duty; it becomes a degradation."[16]

Madison worked intimately with President Jefferson; as John Quincy Adams described their partnership, "the mutual influence of these two mighty minds upon each other is a phenomenon, like the invisible and mysterious movements of the magnet in the physical world."[17] They decided upon a less-than-bellicose stand in the face of the world's most powerful navy. Instead of a war declaration, a frigate was dispatched to London with instructions to America's Minister to the Court of St. James's, James Monroe, to demand both punishment for those responsible and full restitution in the affair of the *Chesapeake*. Jefferson went further, issuing a proclamation that declared American waters off-limits to British ships.

As American anger simmered over the *Chesapeake-Leopard* affair in 1807, Jefferson and Madison worked to avoid war. They fell back on their belief that trade—specifically, the restriction of trade—was a weapon they could wield effectively in international affairs. During the revolutionary era, they remembered, the colonies had first expressed resistance to King George by defying the Stamp and Tea acts. Following the same logic, Jefferson and Madison devised a series of non-importation laws. Six months to the day after the attack on the *Chesapeake*, Congress passed the Embargo Act of 1807, which effectively banned trade between the United States and other nations. But the cure proved almost as unpopular as the disease.

During the preceding years, France and England had been at war, and American merchants had built more ships to supply the belligerents with the American agricultural products they needed, including tobacco, wheat, and cotton, and to bring back exports for the American market. With the fleet expanding by about 10 percent a year in the early years of the century, and with no war bills and few monies expended for military preparedness, President Jefferson, who had taken the oath of office for the first of his two terms in March 1801, saw his nation enjoy a burgeoning prosperity.

But the year before the *Chesapeake* debacle, an Order in Council issued by the British cabinet had decreed a blockade of Europe's north coast. Napoleon responded to the British policy with his Berlin Decree, which declared Great Britain to be in a state of blockade. Other Orders in Council were issued from London, other decrees from Paris. But it was the Americans themselves, with the Embargo Act, who caused exports to plummet. From their peak in 1807 of $108 million, they dropped in a year to $22 million. Farmers and merchants alike felt the economic pain, and the opposition Federalist Party, which had been losing influence, suddenly experienced a rebirth of popularity, especially in New England.

The resurgence wasn't enough to end the Democratic-Republican reign, as Madison was elected to the presidency in 1808, bringing to office a distinctly different style. Unlike Jefferson, a freewheeling philosopher who, in the eyes of Augustus John Foster, was a visionary (Jefferson "loved to dream with his eyes open," he observed), the man who stepped from his role as Secretary of State to become the nation's fourth President was a practiced parliamentary politician.[18] He was hard to read, a man who preferred quiet to company.

The Embargo Act was repealed in March 1809, the day before Madison was sworn in. It had failed to accomplish its purpose, which was to penalize the French and British and thereby persuade them to stop interfering with American trade. The non-intercourse act that took its place forbade trade only with Great Britain and France but the new law, along with additional non-importation acts later, had little impact in Europe. In his inauguration speech in 1809, Madison declared "scrupulous impartiality" and "sincere neutrality toward belligerent nations" as his goal.[19] In brief: He did not want war.

Even as Jefferson and Madison had attempted to remain bystanders as the French and British engaged one another, their new nation remained a pawn whose fortunes were determined by more powerful players. The Americans had put great stock in America's role as a neutral nation, which geography made plausible. The Atlantic Ocean was a broad buffer that separated the United States from the two entrenched rivals on the other side, but there were all-too-regular reports of the losses of American merchant ships and cargo, as neutral vessels were seized by the British on the high seas and goods of neutral merchants were confiscated by the French in continental ports. The American economy was based upon trade; Madison knew that the grievous harm wrought by British restrictions and seizures was a genuine threat to the young nation's economic independence.

Some nine hundred American merchant ships were taken in the several years after the attack on the American frigate; furthermore, diplomatic discussions between the Americans and the British regarding the *Chesapeake* affair yielded neither apologies nor reparations.[20] Even Jefferson, who avowedly hated war, had found his thinking coming about, having confided to a friend in 1811, "When peace becomes more losing than war, we may prefer the latter."[21]

In truth, the continuing outrages at sea had repeatedly reopened the bloody great gash in British-American relations torn by the HMS *Leopard*.

II.

Afternoon, June 18, 1812 . . . The Seven Buildings . . . Washington City

THOUGH BARELY INTO HIS THIRTIES, AUGUSTUS JOHN FOSTER thought himself a man experienced in the ways of the world. The haughty grandson of an earl, he knew Napoleon and Goethe and had been a habitué of the brilliant societies of Paris, London, Naples, and other European capitals.[22] Despite his upbringing in an aristocratic milieu, however, he prided himself on being adaptable to a place like Washington, a city just being born, which he described as a "skeleton city." He could even bring himself to see the humor in a tavern keeper who, as a guest in Foster's house, had emptied his bladder in a fireplace at a ball celebrating Queen Charlotte's birthday.[23]

British Foreign Secretary Lord Castlereagh hoped that, if any Britisher could, Foster would be able to deal with the Americans. The younger man had earlier served a three-year tour of duty as secretary to the British Legation in Washington, traveling widely, visiting the likes of Madison at Montpelier, his home in central Virginia, and Jefferson at his plantation home, Monticello. After his return to the United States in late June 1811, Foster was pleased to report that he found there were "many sensible worthy men in Congress."[24] He took up quarters at the northwest corner of Nineteenth Street and Pennsylvania Avenue, and, though Foster's Washington City digs were hardly up to London standards (he condescended that the setting reminded him of "a small street of Edinburgh or Dublin"), he did manage to combine three adjacent row houses into one grander house, despite the fact they were of different heights, at four, three, and four and a half stories.[25]

Foster entertained often, recognizing "how important it was, when party spirit ran so high and questions of peace or war were debating almost every day, to keep a constant and friendly connection with as many Members of Congress and public men as possible."[26] In particular, he found much in common with the men of the East, the New England Federalists. Though in the minority in Congress, they were monied coastal merchants who favored a commercial economy and shared a close cultural affinity with British society. In particular, Foster found the Connecticut delegation congenial, not least because they were uncompromising opponents of the ruling Democratic-Republicans.[27] He found the Republicans more of a mystery: He observed a blend of agrarians, who put great stock in the educated and independent yeoman farmer as the ideal citizen, and of "War Hawks," a newly emergent faction, many of whom hailed from the country's western frontier.

On this day, however, it would be Mrs. Madison's turn to welcome guests. She had often been hostess for the dinners the widower Jefferson held for select groups during his presidency, but after James's election, she changed the tone. As her husband went about the "public business," she regularly threw open the doors of her home to all comers, transforming the President's house into the city's social center. Along with men of political influence and power, she welcomed a great variety of others with little claim to social prominence (as one Englishwoman complained, "many of [the men] come in boots and perfectly undone and with dirty hands and dirty linen [and] stand mostly talking with each other in the middle of the rooms").[28] Mrs. Madison's Wednesdays were far from invitation-only affairs; announcements of her first Drawing Rooms had appeared in the papers, and to attend, one needed only an introduction to Mr. or Mrs. Madison. Between the hours of three and five o'clock on any Wednesday when Congress was in session, a crush of guests enjoyed food and drink offered by servants carrying large japanned trays called *waiters*. On a warm day in June like this one, there might even be ice cream, a new specialty of Mrs. Madison's.

As England's Minister to America, Foster thought the presence of the hoi polloi was a bit too "democratical," but Washington was a new city with no traditions, no hidebound social rules, and few elders to pass judgment. It was a company town, but, rare in America, its focus was

Dolley Madison looking surprisingly youthful near the close of James's second term in a portrait painted by Joseph Wood. *Virginia Historical Society*

neither commerce nor agriculture. In the absence of a monied merchant class, politics rather than trade was the lingua franca for people who came from all regions of the country.

Today's Drawing Room would be filled with diplomats, Washington City social lions, politicians of all parties, and many of their wives, but one person who would most certainly not be there was a Frenchman who called himself the Comte de Crillon. As a man who prided himself on knowing nobility when he saw it, Foster, upon first laying eyes on de Crillon in January 1812 at the Madisons' dinner table, had "at once [been] persuaded from his personal appearance that he was an imposter."[29]

Now, six months later, it was a small satisfaction that his instinct had proved prescient. He might wish that other people had been as wise as he; if they had, the burden of worry he carried about an impending war might have been very much lighter.

THE COMTE ÉMILE ÉDOUARD DE CRILLON had stepped ashore on Boston's Long Wharf on Christmas Eve 1811, arriving from London on the Boston merchantman *New Galen*. During the transatlantic journey he had come to know another passenger, Captain John Henry. Though they had been passing acquaintances back in England, it was aboard the *New Galen* that Captain Henry unburdened himself, telling de Crillon of his travails. The count listened with care to Henry, who he thought possessed "an air of melancholy showing some secret trouble."[30]

A younger son of Irish gentry, Henry had first come to America at twenty-one to seek his fortune. Nearly six feet tall, his eyes hazel and hair brown, he was strikingly handsome. On his arrival, he sought out a rich uncle in New York and, by 1798, secured a military commission as a captain of the artillery in the U.S. Army. He became a naturalized American citizen, married the well-connected daughter of a Philadelphia family, and, after his release from the army, resided for a time in Boston. "Perceiving that there was no field for my ambition," Henry told de Crillon, "I purchased an estate in Vermont, near the Canada line, and there studied law for five years."[31] He doted on his two young daughters.

He also wrote increasingly pro-British articles for Federalist newspapers, and his outspoken opinions came to the attention of Sir James Craig, Governor General of Canada. Craig invited Captain Henry to Quebec, seeing something in the passionate young man—a military veteran, mannerly, and literary in inclination—that he thought could be put to good use.

Craig persuaded Henry to return to Boston via Vermont and New Hampshire, carrying letters of introduction that gave him access to many of the most powerful interests in the region. The journey had been "*a secret and confidential mission*," Henry confided to Crillon. His task, according to Craig's written instructions, was "to obtain the most accurate information of the true state of affairs in that part of the union." Without revealing that he was "an avowed agent" of the British, he was to take the measure of the Federalist desire "to bring about a separation from the general Union."[32] Henry was given a cipher for his future communications and adopted the code name A.B.

In a word, he became a *spy*. But the story that John Henry told his new French friend did not end there.

Captain Henry, who would also be known by the aliases John Adrien Henry and John St. Adrien, spent several months in Boston in the winter and spring of 1809. Arriving as he did after the Embargo Act had been in effect for more than a year, he heard many voices raised in discontent, as complaints poured forth from merchants whose fortunes suffered with their ships forced by Federal fiat to sit at anchor. He reported what he learned to Sir James, dispatching some letters in cipher, others by "private conveyance." He advised that "the common people" regard "the constitution of the United States with complacency"; that "[a]n unpopular war . . . [might] produce a sudden separation of any section of this country from the common head"; and that, should Mr. Madison seek to declare war, his "party will not support him in any manly and generous policy."[33]

Henry returned to Canada hoping to obtain a government job. Craig refused him. In 1811 he traveled to London to appeal to His Majesty's government to compensate him for his clandestine services but was again rebuffed. During their Atlantic voyage that December, having confided his secret to de Crillon, he confessed his bitter desire to "take [his] revenge against the British government." He also allowed as how he had in his possession "the instruments of [his] revenge," namely a sheaf of letters exchanged with British officials.[34]

As Henry talked and the count listened, a plan began to take shape, a means by which Captain Henry's need for money and his deep resentment might both be satisfied. Might not the Comte de Crillon benefit, as well, if he were to help his new friend sell his secret correspondence to the American government? Henry examined his scruples briefly and soon settled upon a justification for betraying Great Britain, namely, "the wrong of his native country, Ireland, inflicted by the British government."[35] A partnership was formed.

IN JANUARY 1812, A LETTER HAD ARRIVED ON PRESIDENT MADISON'S DESK. The Governor of Massachusetts, Elbridge Gerry, a Republican rarity in Federalist New England, wrote to recommend two men to Madison's attention. One, Gerry reported, was the "son of the celebrated duke who besieged Gibraltar." The French Count, Gerry continued, "came in company with Captain John Henry formerly of our army, . . . also a great military character and in every point truly respectable."[36] Such words held weight, coming as they did from a political ally and a patriot who had signed the Declaration of Independence.

The Comte de Crillon arrived first. He was an odd-looking man, short and bearlike with "monstrous thick legs" and a thick beard that obscured his facial features. His nearly hairless pate bore a conspicuous scar, frightening evidence, no doubt, of his military past as a colonel of hussars. Wearing the star of a knight of Malta, he quickly ingratiated himself in Washington society and made a firm friend of the French ambassador.

To Mr. Madison, the count confided privately that he possessed secret intelligence that New England Federalists were guilty of sedition. The president was quick to understand that the documents the Frenchman described could be highly useful in embarrassing what he saw as the disloyal opposition. Two months earlier he had called for increasing military appropriations in his State of the Union message; with the support of much of the country, he was readying for a war that almost daily seemed more likely. But the Essex Junto, as he referred to the most disaffected faction of the Massachusetts Federalists, was outspoken in opposing war. The secret papers, Madison confided to Jefferson, might offer "formal proof of the Cooperation between the Eastern Junto and the Br[itish] Cabinet."[37]

Madison delegated the task of procuring the documents to his Secretary of State, James Monroe. At their first meeting on February 1, the Comte de Crillon set the price at twenty-five thousand pounds. Such an exorbitant sum would pay for the construction and outfitting of two sloops of war, but Monroe remained keen, as he told de Crillon, "to make known . . . the full extent of the intrigues which have been carried on in this country by means of a certain secret mission."[38] When a deal had been struck, Henry was summoned from Baltimore. The understanding called for Captain Henry and his family to be given free passage to France, and Monroe promised that the letters would remain secret until they had left the United States. In return for his cache of correspondence with his British handlers, Henry would receive two checks from the U.S. government, totaling fifty thousand dollars, a sum equal to the secret service funds budgeted for the year.

An agreement having been signed, the documents and monies changed hands. As a parting gift, Henry offered gratis his counsel for putting the forty handwritten pages to use. "Reserve them a short time for the promotion of some great object," he wrote the Secretary of State. "With those papers you have in it your power *at any time*, *or upon any emergency*, to extinguish everything worth the name of opposition to the Government."[39] On March 7, Henry sailed for France on the sloop of war *Wasp*.

Two days later Madison delivered the documents to Congress, along with a disingenuous letter from Henry explaining that they had been given over voluntarily. When a congressional clerk read the papers to the assembled body, a New Hampshire Congressman observed signs of nervousness among his Federalist brethren (one "looked pale," another suddenly sweated profusely, a third "began to kick and *squirm*").[40] Almost overnight, *Henryism* became a shorthand term for treason.

The documents were real enough; that was indisputable. But Boston Congressman Josiah Quincy was suspicious of how the administration had come by the letters. Searching through Treasury Department warrants, he soon found evidence of the fifty-thousand-dollar purchase price. A close examination of the papers also revealed that Henry named no New Englanders; in fact, not a single name was cited, as the papers had many omissions, emendations, and rows of asterisks that effectively blacked out sections of the documents. When the Federalists demanded to interview Henry, they were told he had left the country. The Comte de Crillon was deposed, but, being little more than the messenger, he had no new information to offer.

There was general outrage among Federalists at the outlandish price paid for what was little more than a weather report regarding political discontent; in a contentious Congress, this was no great revelation. With a presidential election forthcoming in the autumn, the publication of the documents by Madison, Monroe, and the Republicans was decried as "a most pitiful electioneering Manoeuvre."[41]

The Comte de Crillon departed Washington City on April 1; from New York, he sailed for Spain in May. Soon after he left, however, a letter from America's minister to Paris, Joel Barlow, brought the astounding news that de Crillon was not at all who he said he was. His real name was Soubiran; neither knight nor nobleman, he had a long record as a swindler.[42]

If Henry's documents failed to prove the perfidy of the New England Federalists (Foster, for one, had dismissed them as "lies" and "invention"), Madison nevertheless read British intentions as "intrigues, having [as] their object subversion of our Government, and dismemberment of our happy Union."[43] By the time word arrived that, upon his arrival in Bayonne, Sobiran had been arrested for impersonating the real Comte de Crillon, events had marched on and the Frenchman ceased to be a man of importance in Washington City. But he had done grave damage to British-American relations.

III.

Afternoon, June 18, 1812 . . . Mrs. Madison's Sitting Room . . . The President's House

NOT EVERYONE IN WASHINGTON HAD READ THE SIGNS, but Dolley had long since calculated their import. A full month earlier she wrote to a trusted friend, "War! Yes—that terrible event is at hand."[44]

On June 1, as a first step to making it official, Mr. Madison's secretary, Edward Coles, had traveled down Pennsylvania Avenue to deliver a "confidential Message" to the Speaker's table at the House of Representatives. The missive from the President had prompted the Speaker to order that all guests depart and, for nearly half an hour, the members listened grimly while the clerk read out Madison's detailed summary of Great Britain's hostile conduct toward the United States.

His text decried the "crying enormity" of impressment; the "avidity of British cruisers" in harassing American ships in American territorial waters; the blockades that violated the "neutral rights of the United States"; and the "secret agent" sent into their midst. The President advised that this litany constituted "a spectacle of injuries and indignities which have been heaped on our country."[45] The message was hardly a surprise to the members, since Congress had been debating military readiness and, in April, approved another embargo, this one intended to clear the seas of American merchantmen, which in the event of war would be easy prey for British warships. But the timing and tone of Madison's June 1 summary of events were those of a prosecutor's closing argument.

What the President left unsaid—but everyone in the chamber understood—was that this was a call to war. Years earlier, President Washington had sought to keep the United States clear of what he saw as the dangerous vortex of a serial war in Europe; but President Madison's dilemma was that isolationism no longer seemed to serve America's interests. The momentum toward conflict had been building, what with

James Madison in a circa-1816 oil portrait, a pendant to the one Joseph Wood made of Dolley. In hers, Dolley looks resilient; here James merely looks old. *Virginia Historical Society*

the *Chesapeake* affair, the machinations of Captain Henry, thousands of impressed sailors, the seizure of so many ships, and the confiscation of cargo on the high seas. Another shift of the fulcrum had occurred in 1811 when two new factors further altered the balance.

Mr. Madison cited in his call to war the role of Great Britain in "the warfare just renewed by the savages" in the Northwest Territory. A conflict had begun in the West when an Indian federation, led by the Shawnee brothers Tecumseh and Tenskwatawa (known to his people as "the Prophet"), refused to cede further lands to white settlers.* William Henry Harrison, Governor of the Indiana Territory, wanted the expansion of

* *Indians* was the term used to identify indigenous American peoples during the Federal era; today's preferred *Native Americans* did not come into common usage until the 1960s.

settlements to continue, and he persuaded the government to provide troops. Events reached a climax with a bloody battle at the confluence of the Tippecanoe and Wabash rivers the previous November, when Federal troops and local militia succeeded in pushing the Indians back. But widespread Indian attacks on frontier settlements had continued. Because the British maintained diplomatic and trading relations with the Indians, the *Lexington Reporter* told its Kentucky readers, "THE SCALPING KNIFE and TOMAHAWK of *British Savages, is now, again devastating our frontiers.*"[46] Former Senator Andrew Jackson of Tennessee also drew the connection: "[T]he blood of our murdered heroes must be revenged," he wrote, ". . . this Hostile band, *which must be excited to war by the secret agents of Great Britain must be destroyed.*"[47] Rumblings among the Creek Confederacy in the deep South added to the concerns of western settlers, and the general notion was that the British were to blame for the Indian unrest.

There was also a new dynamic in Congress itself. On convening the previous year, Congress had welcomed a group of young congressmen, mostly Westerners and Southerners, led by the man they soon chose as Speaker of the House. Henry Clay had ridden the wave of discontent to new influence, captaining the band known as the War Hawks. The central piece of their philosophy was simple: For years America's rights had been trampled by the tug-of-war between Napoleon and the British; henceforth the War Hawks wanted not trade laws or talk, but action.

Mr. Madison himself was no warrior. He was physically small, bookish, with a soft voice and a temperament ill suited to barking orders. Having been sickly as a young man, he had no military experience, but he understood the gut instinct that motivated the War Hawks' call for war. As Foster pointedly put it, "[I]n the opinion of the Speaker, Mr. Clay, and his friends [war] was as necessary to America as a duel is to a young officer to prevent his being bullied and elbowed in society."[48]

JAMES MADISON HAD COME TO THE PRESIDENCY uniquely prepared to manage the mechanics of government. Born on his father's plantation in Orange County, Madison, unlike many of his Virginia peers, attended the College of New Jersey.* He followed in the footsteps of a favorite tutor, then returned after graduation to help manage the family plantation. He had left again to help draft the Virginia constitution in 1776, then became the youngest delegate in Philadelphia, aged twenty-nine, at the Continental Congress in 1779.

Although he served four sessions in the Virginia House of Delegates in Richmond following the Revolution (1784 and after), Madison's chief labor of the mid-1780s had been a self-assigned research project. Closeted in the second-floor library in his father's house, he spent countless hours reading widely on the topic of government (one year he read four hundred books). His syllabus, which included many volumes sent to him by his friend Jefferson from Paris, approached the subject from a mix of historical and theoretical perspectives, studying modern and ancient models. But Madison's investigations were more than an intellectual exercise. As a son of the Enlightenment, Madison believed such a disciplined survey might produce a plan whereby man could control his destiny. He was looking, in short, for political solutions to self-government.

A new approach was required, he believed, because of what he termed the "imbecility" of the Articles of Confederation, which, having granted the central government few powers, left the nation unable to levy taxes, negotiate with foreign powers, or manage its economy. Madison was readying himself for an opportunity he soon facilitated, namely, the gathering of twelve states for a "Grand Convention." He and fifty-four other delegates spent seventeen weeks in Philadelphia in 1787, hammering out a new governing document for the nation, the U.S. Constitution.

After its 1788 ratification—which Madison helped accomplish as a co-writer (with Alexander Hamilton and John Jay) of the essays collectively known as *The Federalist Papers*—Madison was elected to the House of Representatives. There, as President George Washington's most trusted

---

* The College of New Jersey would become Princeton University in 1896.

ally in Congress, Congressman Madison guided the passage of the first ten amendments to the Constitution, colloquially known as the Bill of Rights. During his four terms in Congress, the never-married Madison, at forty-three, also met a young widow, Dolley Payne Todd, who, in 1794, became his wife.

MR. MADISON'S CALL TO ARMS ON JUNE 1 met with less than universal acceptance. Heated debate ensued on the floor of the House, with the Federalists mounting an impassioned opposition to what they called the "evil of a war with Great Britain," certain that it was to become a "dreadful scourge." The Federalists yielded the floor only when a rowdy member kicked one of the brass spittoons across the chamber, and the shocked Federalist who was speaking sat down in surprise.[49] By whatever means, a declaration emerged from committees in each body of Congress in a matter of days; the measure passed the House quickly by a 79–49 vote. Finally, after a long wrangle and unbeknownst to Augustus John Foster, the Senate had voted in favor of declaring war by a narrow 19–13 margin.

The *nays* in both houses came largely from Federalists, but that surprised no one, given long-established enmities dating from the presidency of George Washington. In the days after his inauguration in April 1789, the nation had moved into unknown terrain, led by the General and the counselors in his cabinet—chiefly, Secretary of State Thomas Jefferson and Secretary of the Treasury Alexander Hamilton—and the President's point man at the Capitol, Congressman James Madison. They blazed a trail of constitutional governance that, in retrospect, had been strewn with a thousand unexpected pitfalls.

At first, the new government had moved as if through fog, treading carefully along an uncertain path. Gradually, the journey had revealed that Washington was leading the nation along a great divide, from which two distinct vistas could be seen. To one side was Hamilton country, a growing and prosperous coastal megalopolis in which trade and industry flourished, where power was vested in a central authority run by bankers, large landowners, and men of business. The opposite view was of Jefferson country, an inland agrarian landscape of sprawling independent farms where yeomen controlled their own democratic destiny and expanded on a frontier that moved ever westward. But the vistas varied depending upon the point of view. When the Republicans regarded Federalist country, they saw the specter of a national bank accumulating a dangerous debt and an emerging social elite all too reminiscent of aristocratic and monarchic Great Britain, which represented to the Republicans vice, licentiousness, and corruption. From the reverse angle, the Federalists saw the Jefferson landscape as antagonistic to economic growth and shadowed by a cloud of French anarchy.

By the time the Congress took up Mr. Madison's war declaration, Hamilton was long gone, shot dead by Aaron Burr in their 1804 duel, but in the months and years leading up to June 1812, Federalists in the North had retained their intimate cultural associations with London. Even as Republican War Hawks from the West and South talked of the necessity for armed conflict with Great Britain, Federalists Josiah Quincy of Boston, William Hunter of Rhode Island, and virtually the entire congressional delegation from Connecticut had been fixtures at the British ambassador's Washington table.[50] The Republicans saw the approaching war with Britain as "a second war of independence"; the Federalists, with debate limited by Republican parliamentary maneuvers in Congress, said little but voted as a body, 39–0, against the war. A Federalist pamphlet was in the works that argued the Declaration of War was "a headlong rushing into difficulties, with little calculation about the means, and little concern about the consequences."[51] On the opposing side, a Boston paper, the *Independent Chronicle*, would soon cogently explain the justification to fight. The British had, by policies that threatened the American merchant, seaman, and frontiersman, "forced the United States . . . either to *surrender their independence,* or *maintain it by War.*"[52]

After years of reluctance to pursue a military solution, Mr. Madison sought a Declaration of War. He had brought himself around to seeing the inevitability of war, but even as a majority of the gentlemen of the Congress voted for it, both houses—like the populace they represented—were deeply divided as to its wisdom.

IV.

Early Evening, June 18, 1812 . . . The President's House . . . Washington City

UPON ARRIVAL AT THE PRESIDENT'S HOUSE, Augustus John Foster did indeed find all the players. Even after the Henry-Crillon affair, when the "affronted" Federalists boycotted Mrs. Madison's Drawing Room, they stayed away for only one week.[53] She had long since mastered the art of appearing politically neutral, and the society of "Mrs. M.," as many of her intimates called her, seemed more important than yesterday's political outrage.

As the British minister strode through the grand entrance hall with its tall columns, he entered "an immense and magnificent room, in an oval form."[54] It was decorated with a forty-two-piece suite of Grecian-style sofas and chairs, with yellow damask curtains and swags, all designed by the most gifted architect in the nation, Benjamin Henry Latrobe. As a young man from New England who visited just months earlier observed, "The President's house is a perfect palace."[55] Foster had dressed for the occasion; he favored tall starched collars and extravagant gold braid applied in military style to a fashionable short jacket. He composed his expression with care, too, confiding in his journal that he wished to appear "as if nothing extraordinary had happened."[56]

As always, the most visible personage in the Drawing Room was Mrs. Madison. Though her hair was black, Dolley's eyes were a deep blue and her "complexion was . . . fair and brilliant . . . in its perfect feminine beauty."[57] At forty-four, Dolley still had a bloom about her as she made her way around the room, a means of socializing that was a notable departure from her predecessors Martha Washington and Abigail Adams; they had waited, almost like royalty, for courtiers to approach them. In Dolley's world, as a friend explained, "few ladies ever sit. . . . The consequence is that ladies and gentlemen stand and walk about the rooms in mingled groups, which certainly produces more ease, freedom and equality than in those rooms where the ladies sit and wait for the gentlemen to approach and converse."[58]

Dolley's chef was one lure that drew people to the President's house—he was perhaps the best in Washington—but just as he sought to balance flavors and textures in his basement kitchen, Mrs. Madison had become mistress of the fine art of satisfying her guests' differing expectations. As she possessed almost total recall of names and faces, she greeted her guests by name. She often carried a book in order to have something to talk about. *Don Quixote* was one such, since Cervantes was regarded as suitable reading for a woman, unlike Shakespeare, whose works were thought by many to be coarse and improper.

At her Drawing Rooms, "Mrs. M" was no fading flower. Far from appearing thin and fragile, she had rococo curves that men and women alike admired. Washington Irving, a man who claimed pride of place as the first American to make his living as a writer, hadn't put too fine a point on it a year earlier when he confessed his admiration. "Mrs. Madison is a fine, portly, buxom dame, who has a smile and a pleasant word for everybody."[59] Her dresses were low-cut; she made no attempt to be willowy, and in the eyes of her admirers, she was perfect. Even a disapproving female observer—"she has been very much admired and is still fond of admiration . . . [Mrs. Madison] loads herself with finery and dresses without any taste"—could not help but remark upon the Presidentess's skin, which remained soft and smooth after a girlhood dressed in a modest Quaker sunbonnet, long gloves, and sometimes even a white linen mask to protect her fair skin.[60] "Her complexion is brilliant—her neck and bosom the most beautiful I ever saw—her face expresses nothing but good nature."[61]

In the Drawing Room, Foster soon spotted the animated Henry Clay, whom Dolley had long since made a particular object of her attention. They both were inveterate snuff takers, and the Speaker and Mrs. Madison famously shared the fine powder from her lacquered snuffbox. Another of the War Hawks was Congressman John C. Calhoun. A man who ordinarily kept his emotions in careful check, the elated South Carolinian was said to have performed a Shawnee war dance with Clay back at their rooming house.[62] As Foster watched these and other Republican partisans, their mood evidently ebullient, they were "all shaking hands with one another."

Another man nearby stood quietly. A stranger might not have guessed that the little man in the black suit, looking wizened and tired at sixty-one years, was the most powerful person in the room. President James Madison weighed perhaps one hundred and twenty-five pounds and was noticeably shorter than his five-foot-six-inch wife. As a man with no gift for back-slapping, Mr. Madison stood as if at a distance from the celebration, with the somber mien of a man who kept his own counsel. Augustus John Foster needed no introduction to the man some called the Chief Magistrate; he had seen Mr. Madison just ten days earlier in church, only the second time in seven months that the overworked Madison left the presidential grounds.* (The other had been the funeral of his Vice President George Clinton two months earlier.)

Foster went to him, and he and the President exchanged three courtly bows of greeting. Mr. Madison, thought Foster, "was remarkably civil" as they exchanged pleasantries concerning affairs in Europe.[63] But a proper diplomatic distance was maintained on both sides throughout the exchange, and the topics covered were of no particular moment.

Later, when Augustus John Foster departed the President's house, he had enjoyed another generous dose of Mrs. Madison's hospitality. Though he had heard no official word of war, the British Minister Plenipotentiary

---

* A familiar title in Federal America, "Chief Magistrate" was a term employed by, among others, George Washington; he used it to refer to the office of the President in his second inaugural address.

returned to his quarters that evening with little doubt in his mind that the olive branch had given way to the sword. He was unsurprised when, having been summoned into the presence of the Secretary of State the next day, he was advised by James Monroe that Madison's signature had made the Declaration of War a matter of law.

Although he was reluctant to admit it, Foster had misread events. In his secret report dispatched to Castlereagh, he justified his misjudgment by asserting that, in his estimate, 80 percent of the American people opposed the war.[64] He chose to console himself in these hours by diminishing Madison's demeanor, describing him as "white as a sheet." Speaking to posterity, he wrote in his diary that the President had the look of man who "very naturally felt all the responsibility he would incur." But the British minister was far from the only one to underestimate the man whom Dolley herself had called "the great little Madison."

BOOK I

America at War, 1812–1813

CHAPTER 1
The War Begins

[A]ll men know that war is a losing game to both parties.
—Thomas Jefferson

1.
June 19, 1812 . . . In the Company of the President

WITH THE DECLARATION OF WAR SIGNED, the *National Intelligencer* noted, "the veil is at length removed from the Secret Proceedings of Congress."[1] At last the public had confirmation of the worst-kept secret in Washington City.

Having affixed his name to the declaration, Mr. Madison ventured forth. "The President . . . visited in person," wrote one observer, ". . . all the offices of the departments of war and the navy." At the two-story building just west of the President's house, home of the Department of War, he shook hands and offered good wishes to his military advisers, but even as he did so, Congress had convened at the Capitol to wrangle anew about the embargo (the Federalists wanted it lifted). Money was at issue, too, as Congress had authorized the government to seek $11 million in loans, but thus far the bankers and other sources of cash had provided barely half that sum. Madison and his cabinet officers would have to deal with matters of customs duties and coastal security, but first the President wished to make a show of his personal support for the military. "[I]n a manner worthy of a little commander-in-chief, [he wore] his little round hat and huge cockade."[2]

DOLLEY AND JAMES MADISON HAD BEEN MARRIED ALMOST TWENTY YEARS. She had been a young widow, her first husband eleven months in the grave, when Aaron Burr, a sometime resident at her mother's Philadelphia boardinghouse, introduced Dolley Todd to Mr. Madison in 1794. Older by seventeen years, James seemed a confirmed bachelor; in the previous decade a brief engagement to the sixteen-year-old daughter of a congressional colleague had ended badly when she dismissed the statesman in favor of a much younger clergyman.

James was brilliant, studious, and, as the principal author of the Constitution, a world-renowned political philosopher; yet, when not plying his electoral trade in Philadelphia, he lived with his parents. Dolley's and James's attachment grew rapidly, and they married within four months of Burr's introduction. The match of the Congressman and the widow Todd seemed odd to some. After all, according to one old friend, Dolley was "the first & fairest representative of Virginia, in the female society of Philad[elphia]."[3] But over time, theirs had proved a remarkable partnership, one that had played a central role in the emergence of the new capital.

James's association with Washington City went even deeper than Dolley's, back to its very conception almost a quarter century earlier. On June 20, 1790, a meeting of three great minds had set the course. At Mr. Jefferson's invitation, Alexander Hamilton and James Madison joined the then–Secretary of State for dinner at his house at 57 Maiden Lane in lower Manhattan, then the nation's capital. Jefferson loosened his guests' political inhibitions and incompatibilities with bottles of his best Madeira, and Congressman Madison and Secretary of the Treasury Hamilton reached an understanding. Hamilton's Bill of Assumption would pass Congress, meaning each of the thirteen states would assume a share of the nation's debt from the War of Independence. In return, the Virginians won the location of the new Federal City for their region.

Soon thereafter President Washington personally selected the Potomac site and hired an engineer to survey it. When Major Pierre Charles L'Enfant rendered his vision of the future city onto paper in 1791, the closest existing settlement was the port of Georgetown, located on the northwest corner of the plat that L'Enfant drew. Another small river town, Carrollsburg, had been established by landowners on the southernmost edge, where the waters of the Potomac and its Eastern Branch divided.* In between was a rugged, undeveloped expanse.

Though little more than a meandering stream, a tributary to the Potomac known as Goose Creek led into the interior of the eleven-square-mile precinct. It drained a rambling, marshy countryside with a few scattered farmhouses and densely forested acres of old-growth oak trees. This raw landscape inspired a diverse set of opinions. One early visitor to the site saw nothing more than "a morass and forest, the abode of reptiles, wild beasts, and savages." Another observed, "It is scarcely possible to imagine a situation more beautiful, healthy, and convenient, than that of Washington."[4] As an aid to weaker imaginations, Goose Greek was renamed Tiber Creek, a bow to the Republic of Rome and a designation that seemed more suitable to L'Enfant's vision of a city that he dreamed would merit comparison one day with the great capitals of Europe.

When the government moved from Philadelphia a decade later, nothing in the new capital had been completed, not even the plasterwork in the President's bedroom. Signs of construction were everywhere: crowds

---

* Today, the Eastern Branch is known as the Anacostia River.

of workmen and builders' shacks; buildings covered with scaffolding; piles of brick, stone, and lumber. The President's house was surrounded by brick kilns and split-rail fences, and entry was gained by climbing precarious wooden stairs. The north wing of the Capitol was completed in 1801, but the south was still six years from completion. Construction of the grand dome that was to rise between them had not yet begun.

Dolley and James arrived in Washington City in 1801 to find that the major thoroughfare, Pennsylvania Avenue, was little more than a cart road lined by great stumps recently pulled from the earth. Plentiful game birds like snipe were still to be hunted in the town; wild partridges were sighted on the steps of the Capitol itself. The city grid consisted of six thousand acres dotted with fewer than three hundred buildings, only about one hundred of which were built of brick. The population was 973 persons.[5]

During President Jefferson's two terms, Pennsylvania Avenue improved in a manner reminiscent of a boulevard in his beloved Paris, where he had served as American Minister. Both sides of the widened thoroughfare were lined with Lombardy poplars. The four rows of trees added a formality to the rough-hewn landscape, but other roads in the district remained unimproved. Augustus John Foster, then in Washington on his first tour of duty as Secretary to the British Legation, thought it all very rough indeed. "[I]n going to assemblies one had sometimes to drive three or four miles within the city bounds and very often at great risk of an overturn, or of being what was termed 'stalled' or stuck in the mud when one can neither go backwards or forwards and either loses one's shoes or one's patience."[6]

In their dozen years living in the nation's capital, the Madisons observed changes in the city with every year and every season. If, by 1812, the city still did not live up to the grand plan L'Enfant had drawn, the Capitol and the President's house were now accompanied on the streetscape by a pair of two-story brick edifices, one each for the Treasury and State

Departments. The Post Office and Patent Office occupied generous quarters in what had been Blodgett's Hotel. Numerous block-long row houses—the Ten Buildings, the Seven Buildings, and the Six Buildings among them—lined some of the streetscapes, most of them in the vicinity of the President's house and Capitol. A few grand homes had been built, including a mansion designed by Dr. William Thornton, the designer of the Capitol, for Virginian John Tayloe, the richest man in the city. Many lots remained empty and city squares unfinished, but Washington had ceased to be what a Congressman from New Hampshire described not so many years earlier as a suitable setting "to do penance . . . a lonesome dreary place, secluded from every delightful or pleasing thing."[7]

Even Minister Plenipotentiary Foster, at least in his most liberal moments, had to squint only slightly to imagine that the vistas of the American capital were beginning to assume the "majestick aspects" that Major L'Enfant envisioned.

THE FIRST AMERICAN PRESIDENT TO LAUNCH A WAR, Madison possessed no military credentials. He did not pretend to be a tactician (he had generals for that), but he felt confident that the United States remained secure behind the immense moat of the Atlantic Ocean. The sheer breadth of the Atlantic would prevent a major invasion (after all, the British were deep into a larger war with their ancient foe the French) and the distance might actually be of advantage to the small American navy.

Facing the Royal Navy at all was daunting, of course, but, as Madison confided to his Secretary of the Treasury, Albert Gallatin, he was of the opinion that the American navy "would, on equal terms, prove equal to that of Great Britain."[8] In ship-to-ship contests, Madison believed, the American navy could hold its own, and orders were sent to naval Commodores Stephen Decatur aboard the USS *United States* and John Rogers on the USS *President*. A dispatch boat caught up with the frigate *Constitution* as it drifted down the Potomac, headed for Annapolis. After the crew was mustered and the war declaration read, they responded with three cheers.

The enthusiastic counsel Madison received regarding a land war with Canada also buoyed his martial confidence. The combative talk of Speaker Henry Clay over many months helped persuade both his congressional brethren and the Chief Magistrate of the need for war. Clay had long since established the first target: "I verily believe that the militia of Kentucky are alone competent to place . . . Canada at your feet."[9] Virginian John Randolph had announced on the floor of Congress that with "no expense of blood, or treasure, on our part—Canada is to conquer herself—she is to be subdued by the principles of fraternity."[10]

As an express rider raced northward with orders for William Hull and the North-Western Army of the United States in Ohio, the likelihood of battle increased by the day. If he hadn't gone to war by choice, at least Mr. Madison had the assurances of many that invading Canada would be a "holiday campaign."[11]

AFTER A LAPSE OF MORE THAN THIRTY YEARS, William Hull donned a military uniform once again. When the colonies fought for independence, his role in nine major battles earned him "the reputation of a brave & valuable officer."[12] After the Revolution, Hull served as a judge and senator in Massachusetts before becoming, at the pleasure of President Jefferson, Governor of the Michigan Territory. As the prospect of a new war had grown by the day, he seemed a most excellent choice to command the North-Western Army of the United States.

Bearing his new honorific *Brigadier General*, Hull had departed Washington for Fort Detroit just a few days earlier. Hull was privy to the prewar planning at the War Department. The goal would be to divide the American forces with an eye to conquering Canada. An assault on Montreal would be key to seizing Lower Canada, as the provinces along the Saint Lawrence River were known. That mission was to be undertaken by forces under the command of another officer, Major General Henry Dearborn. Hull's responsibilities would be to secure the gateway to the upper lakes, the territories west of Ohio, and to restrain the Indians there. He first instructions were to "proceed to Detroit with all possible expedition, prepare for defence and wait farther orders."[13]

Florid of face and stout of body, General Hull met up with the forces he was to command in Ohio. With his shock of uncooperative white hair, he looked more like an aging grandfather than a military man bound for the front. In truth, the fifty-nine-year-old general was both. Among the thousand or so citizens entrusted to his care at Detroit were his daughter, Mrs. Hickford, and a granddaughter.

His troops consisted of a mix of fresh volunteers and regular military. Three regiments of Ohio Militia, amounting to more than 1,200 men, were soon joined by the 430 men of the Fourth U.S Infantry, and General Hull led them northward from Dayton on a two-hundred-mile trek. Though the men were eager (some wore the slogan "Conquer or Die" on their caps), the journey was hard. Their route required cutting a road through forested terrain, and new bridges and causeways had to be built to cross Ohio's Black Swamp.

On June 26, a special messenger caught up with the slow-moving caravan of troops, artillery, and supply wagons. The rider brought word from Washington of the imminent war declaration. Leaving the heavy equipage to trail behind, Hull double-timed it to the southern shore of Lake Erie with most of the troops. There, to lighten the army's load further, he hired a lake schooner to ferry several dozen ailing soldiers, his quartermaster, three officers' wives, the army's medicines, hospital stores, his and his officers' baggage, and other heavy and unwieldy items.

The *Cuyahoga* set sail on July 1 and Hull's troops resumed their march along the shore. As the sun began to set, a courier caught up with them, bringing another urgent message from the War Department. Now it was official: War had been declared. Hull's thoughts quickly turned to the *Cuyahoga*. No longer an innocent ship, the packet, with the Stars and

Stripes flying, had become a potential military target. The general dispatched horsemen to warn the schooner's captain, but, sailing in familiar waters, the captain had already charted a course along the eastern channel of the Detroit River, well away from the American shore.

As the wind carried the vessel past the British post at Fort Malden, she was brought to by a gunshot fired from an approaching bateau. The commanding officer aboard the flat-bottomed longboat, aware that war had been declared, ordered the mainsails of the *Cuyahoga* lowered. Under the watchful gaze of six Canadian militiamen, the ship became the first prize of the war. When the captured goods aboard the schooner were examined, the army roster and official correspondence, stowed in Hull's trunks, provided the enemy with details of his orders, the size and condition of his force, and the army's supplies. The British gained insight into the man himself, too, as his journals revealed his unease about the Indians, whom he feared as "savages" who might "murder our citizens and butcher our women and children."[14]

General Hull and his troops marched into Fort Detroit four days later. The stronghold occupied high ground, its perimeter a square enclosure of earthen curtain walls that rose to a parapet eleven feet above grade, surrounded by a five-foot-deep dry ditch lined with a double row of cedar pickets. Protruding from slits near the top of the ramparts were the muzzles of seven 24-pounders, eight 12-pounders, and a mix of other smaller guns. The fort itself was sound, if not impregnable, but outside its walls was the village of Detroit, home to some eight hundred settlers. The settlement, though surrounded by a palisade, stood in the line of fire between the fort and enemy territory on the opposite bank of the Detroit River.

On July 9, General Hull received orders to move on Canada. Three days later, he led his men across the Detroit River to attack the British garrison at Sandwich. His army, which now included Michigan Militia and other volunteers and recruits, numbered some twenty-five hundred men. At Sandwich, the much smaller Canadian militia force quickly retreated south to Fort Malden. No shots were fired, and, as the politicians in Washington had predicted, the Americans were well received by the population in the town, a mix of Canadians and Americans. This first encounter suggested that Mr. Jefferson, in retirement at Monticello, might have been right when he observed, "The acquisition of Canada this year . . . will be a mere matter of marching."[15]

An elated Hull promptly issued a proclamation addressed to the "INHABITANTS OF CANADA." This war, he announced, was a consequence of "the injuries and aggressions, the insults and indignities of Great Britain." He offered Canadian citizens freedom ("You will be emancipated from tyranny and oppression, and restored to the dignified station of Freemen"). He also gave vent to his anxiety about the Indians. If "the savages [are] let loose," he warned, "THIS WAR WILL BE A WAR OF EXTERMINATION. The first stroke of the tomahawk—the first attempt with the scalping knife, will be the signal of one indiscriminate scene of desolation."[16]

Hull's orders from Washington were to lay siege to Fort Malden, but with the victory at Sandwich behind him, his enthusiasm seemed to fade. He decided his gun carriages needed rebuilding. He held war councils nearly every day but, to the frustration of his junior officers, weeks passed with no action. As one delay followed another, the dithering general gained a nickname; he became "the Old Lady." The guns were mounted and ready for action on August 7, but still Hull issued no order to move on the British fortification.

One reason was his shock at the fate of Fort Michilimackinac. The American outpost to the north occupied an island between Lakes Michigan and Huron. The fort had been taken, Hull learned, by a force of British regulars, Canadian militiamen, and more than four hundred Indians. Badly outnumbered and fearing slaughter at the hands of the native fighters, the fort's commander surrendered his sixty-one-man garrison. At Fort Detroit, Hull's men could see the effect the news had on their anxious general. As he explained to the War Department in a report, he greatly feared that the fall of Fort Michilimackinac meant "a large body of hostile Indians may soon be expected here from the north."[17]

Then the enemy cut Hull's line of supply. His confidence was further shaken by word that the notorious Tecumseh, whom the admiring

British called "the Wellington of the Indians," had joined forces with the British. Hull felt surrounded by a "Northern hive of Indians [who] were swarming down in every direction."[18]

On August 11, the day Hull had scheduled for the much-delayed assault on Fort Malden, he stunned his officers by ordering the detachment holding Sandwich to return to Fort Detroit. Hull then ordered the civilian population to withdraw into the fort for their own safety, and the small enclosure was soon crowded with women and children as well as military personnel. Although his dispirited officers recognized that fear was overtaking their commander, a petition to remove him from command was resisted by the ranking officer of the Fourth Infantry, who himself was prostrate with malarial fever.

On August 15, British gunners opened fire from an artillery battery they had established at Sandwich. For seven hours, two 12-pounders, one 18-pounder, and two mortars sent a cascade of cannon shot raining down on Detroit. A note arrived from General Isaac Brock, commander of the British forces, demanding surrender. Hull refused, but the carefully tailored words of his opposite number elevated Hull's anxiety. "It is far from my inclination to join in a war of extermination," Brock wrote, echoing Hull's own proclamation, "but you must be aware, that the numerous body of Indians who have attached themselves to my troops, will be beyond controul the moment the contest commences."[19]

When the bombardment resumed the next day, Hull ordered all the field troops at hand into Fort Detroit. With an impossibly dense mass of humanity within the walls of the fort, there was no room for military organization. Hull withdrew into his own thoughts. As one of his officers reported, "the General selected the safest place in the fort for his seat, on an old tent on the ground and leaned against the ramparts." Hull compulsively stuffed his mouth with tobacco, "putting in quid after quid [and] . . . spittle coloured with tobacco-juice ran from his mouth on his neckcloth, beard, cravat and vest."[20] He took on the look of a madman.

Word came that a British force of seven hundred men was crossing the river to the American side. When told of the enemy's approach, "[General Hull] made no other answer than . . . 'are they coming?' " Soon the British were within cannon range, but Hull issued no order to fire. One officer reported the obvious: "I thought him under the influence of fear."

The artillery bombardment from the Canadian shore continued. An 18-pound cannonball crashed into the officers' mess, leaving four Americans dead. The British troops closed in, now just seven hundred yards distant. With their Indian allies very much in evidence, the assault was too much for William Hull.

His voice trembled when he spoke, but, finally, he roused himself, and without consulting his officer corps, he ordered a white flag raised over Fort Detroit. When an officer, aghast at Hull's decision, questioned the surrender, the cowering Hull could only respond, "My God! What shall I do with these women and children!"[21]

He surrendered the entire North-Western Army of the United States. The American soldiers, some with faces streaked with tears of frustration and humiliation, stacked their arms. The British took their stores, which included much food and other provisions, along with five thousand pounds of powder and thirty-nine pieces of artillery. The victorious British were outnumbered two to one.

Among the guns the British gained that day was a 3-pounder fieldpiece. Though of minor military significance, the sturdy little brass cannon had been returned to duty after many years of peace, just as William Hull had been. An inscription on the barrel of the gun testified to its past: TAKEN AT SARATOGA ON THE 17TH OF OCTOBER, 1777. Ironically, the gun and the promising young William Hull, then a major at just age twenty-four, both served at the revolutionary battle just north of Albany, New York. The fight at Saratoga had been a turnabout confrontation, an important American victory that, when news of it reached Paris, helped persuade Louis XVI to offer military support to the United States. Unlike

1777, however, the outcome in 1812—a flag of surrender raised at ten o'clock, August 16—would be remembered differently. As one militiaman reported to Mr. Madison, "I think the whole course of proceedings [at Fort Detroit] the most weak, cowardly and imbecile that ever came to my notice."[22]

II.

December 8, 1812 . . . The Naval Ball . . . Tomlinson's Hotel

THE PRESIDENT STAYED HOME. Dolley excelled at public events; James did not. A Madison presence at the Naval Ball was important, but the Chief Magistrate had work to do. And he trusted the woman he addressed as "My Dearest" on the rare occasions when they were apart and he had to resort to his pen to communicate with her.

Differing from many men of his time, he long since had reached the conclusion, as he put it, that "[t]he capacity of the female mind for studies of the highest order cannot be doubted, having been sufficiently illustrated by its works of genius, of erudition, and of Science."[23] Dolley had been his chief case study, and he was confident she would represent him well as he watched her climb into the reddish-brown chariot with the yellow lace interior. The liveried driver clucked the horses into motion, and they were gone.

As the carriage made the one-mile journey to Capitol Hill, Mr. Madison returned to his papers. In the course of the evening, he might have a nap in his chair for a time, expecting a full report from the celebrants on their return. Then, as was his pattern, he would likely keep a candle lit all night, writing and reading until dawn. Mrs. Madison objected to his "consuming labors," but he insisted that the "pressure of the war business allowed him no alternative."[24]

The President would soon be inaugurated for a second term, since the electoral college had officially reelected him on December 3. But this renewal of trust placed in Madison by the citizens of the country did not lessen his burdens. As if the August debacle at Fort Detroit had not been enough, word reached Washington in October that an American force of 950 men near Niagara had been captured on Canadian soil. That surrender abruptly concluded the campaign on Lake Ontario. In November, Major General Henry Dearborn's assault on Montreal fell far short of its goal, ending in retreat and a terrifying exchange of fire between American units. Even from the sympathetic point of view of a Republican Congressman, "[t]he campaign of 1812 ended in total eclipse, without a gleam of consolation."[25]

The abject failure in Canada had led to the resignation of his Secretary of War, William Eustis, five days earlier. Now Mr. Madison worried the matter of whom to appoint to that essential office. His thinking was influenced by the realization that the men who led the Canada invasion were of a certain age; their military experience dated from their long-lost youth. That corps of antique generals had thus far succeeded only in demonstrating the truth of the observation, "Nothing can so easily be forgotten and with such difficulty acquired as a knowledge of the art of war, which depends almost entirely on practice."* Thirty-one years had passed since the nation's last meaningful battle, which had been at Yorktown, and the long period of inaction during peacetime was apparent.

Another Madison preoccupation was the troubling refusal of the men in the East to embrace the war—and their willingness to oppose it. No fewer than nine installments of a pamphlet called "Mr. Madison's War: A dispassionate inquiry" had been published at Boston, the author identified as "a New England Farmer."[26] The tracts urged state militiamen *not* to fight for their country. In the same vein, the Bay State's Governor had refused to commit his militiamen to the war effort. Well aware of

* Wise words, but note that the source was James Wilkinson, himself an incompetent military man and a onetime conspirator with Aaron Burr; after his death he was also found to have been a spy in the pay of the Spanish crown.

New England's sympathy for London's policy and its opposition to war, Great Britain encouraged the Federalist opposition, exempting the coast north of Newport, Rhode Island, from its blockade of shipping, meaning that New England merchants continued their profitable trade with the enemy. It was reported that the Royal Navy had worked out a code with the coastal settlements of Massachusetts: A Spanish flag hoisted atop the mizzenmast on a good-weather day meant water and supplies were needed, in foul weather that a pilot was requested.[27] Treasury Department Comptroller Richard Rush worried, "Massachusetts and half New England I fear is rotten."[28]

For Madison, whose first principle was always *Save the Union*, this behavior met the standard for sedition. Yet he did not resort, as John Adams had done during his presidency, to restricting individual rights. He circulated no legislation of the ilk of the Sedition Act of 1798, which had made behavior adjudged treasonable a "high misdemeanor." Nor had Yankee resistance altered his firm belief that the indignities of impressment justified going to war, that human life was more precious than lost trade and profit. To him, the Federalists' view seemed out of balance. But he was deeply worried at their decision, in effect, to cooperate with the enemy. "The way to make [this war] both short and successful," he had written to a friend, "would be to convince the Enemy that he has to contend with the whole, and not a part of the Nation."[29] The Federalists were not helping the cause.

Yet such hard thoughts were softened somewhat by news from the sea. When war was declared, the tiny American navy had no large ships of the line and a paltry seven frigates, rated at between twenty-eight and forty-four guns. Three of the frigates had been laid up in port, in need of extensive work to be rendered seaworthy. The U.S. Navy appeared to be a negligible threat to the Royal Navy, which was said to consist of almost a thousand ships; even if the count was exaggerated (and it no doubt was), the British had at least 175 ships of the line rated for 64 or more guns. In the North American station alone, the enemy had almost 40 warships, compared to the American sum total of 19, most of which were sloops, brigs, and unrated vessels.*

But tonight's ball, with or without Mr. Madison, was to celebrate the unexpected.

THE USS *CONSTITUTION* HAD SET SAIL FROM ANNAPOLIS IN JULY, under orders from Secretary of the Navy Paul Hamilton to proceed with "the utmost dispatch to reach New York."[30] The ship and its 450-man crew were to join the USS *United States*, *President*, and *Congress*, the other three U.S. Navy frigates ready for active service. While the cabinet in Washington City debated whether the best strategy would be to protect American shipping or to deploy the small navy to disrupt British convoys, the *Constitution* sailed out of Chesapeake Bay and tacked northward.

Captain Isaac Hull had chosen a different path into government service than had his uncle William Hull. At fourteen he had shipped out on a Connecticut merchantman and, twenty-five years later, his skin leathered by years at sea, he knew his 204-foot-long ship very well. In 1798, as a freshly recruited navy lieutenant, he was aboard the *Constitution* on her maiden voyage and, after earning the rank of captain on lesser vessels, he returned a dozen years later to the decks of the Charlestown-built frigate. He had sailed her to Europe and back, then supervised a just-completed overhaul.

The freshly coppered, cleaned, and recaulked *Constitution*, though rated a 44-gun frigate, was fitted with fifty-six guns, including thirty 24-pounder cannons on her single gun deck, twenty-two 32-pounder carronades on the spar deck, and four chase guns, two each at the stern and

* There are significant disagreements among historians about the size of both the Royal and U.S. navies in 1812. While scholarly estimates range from 15 to 23 for the Americans and 500 to 750 or more for the British, there is unanimous agreement that the American navy was vastly overmatched.

bow.* With war now declared and many new men on board, Captain Hull drilled his gunners daily. "[W]e shall have nothing to fear," Hull wrote to Hamilton, "from any single deck Ship."[31]

With a slight headwind and a contrary current, the ship made slow progress toward New York, but, midway up the New Jersey coast, the lookout on the masthead spied topsails on the afternoon of Friday, July 17. Captain Hull changed his tack to sail in the direction of the nearest of the ships. With the war a month old, he was wary. The Royal Navy would be deploying ships along the United States coast from their station at Halifax, but Hull decided that the five distant vessels at the horizon line were more likely to be the friendly U.S. Navy squadron he had been assigned to join.

As darkness approached, Hull identified the closest ship as a fellow frigate. By ten o'clock the ships were half a dozen miles distant, and the *Constitution* hoisted its signal lanterns to confirm the other vessel's country of origin. When the other ship failed to reply to the coded signal, Hull ordered his ship brought about. The *Constitution* had been sailing directly into a squadron of enemy ships.

The crew of the American ship spent the night at battle stations only to find at first light on Saturday morning that the situation was even more dire than they feared. Two British frigates were downwind, almost within cannon range. Some five miles astern was a third, and in its wake was

* Both cannon (more precisely, "long guns") and carronades were mounted weapons intended to fire heavy projectiles. Both consisted of cast-iron tubes mounted on wooden carriages. Distinguished by their longer barrels, long guns differed also in that they were mounted on four-wheeled carriages; when fired, the carriages absorbed the recoil. Carronades had stubby barrels mounted on slides in carriages that were typically bolted to the deck of the ship.

Each design had its advantages. A new 32-pounder carronade (they had first been produced in Carron, Scotland, in the late eighteenth century) weighed in at roughly the same tonnage as a 12-pound long gun; since a ship's deck could bear only so much weight, a greater weight of metal could be fired at an enemy ship by carronades. Furthermore, they required less than half the powder to fire and half the crew to man, and took up less space on a ship's deck. A carronade could fire a cannonball only about a third of the distance a long gun could, and, because they were fired at lesser muzzle velocity, carronade projectiles consequently had less penetrating power. On the other hand, they were thought to produce more deadly splintering. According to tradition, carronades were not counted when rating a ship.

the rest of the fleet, consisting of a battleship, a brig, a schooner, and a fourth frigate. The flotilla included the frigates HMS *Shannon*, *Belvidera*, *Aeolus*, and *Guerrière*; the ship of the line *Africa* with its two gun decks; and a captured American brig, *Nautilus*.

The British firepower amounted to five times the guns aboard the *Constitution*. As Hull considered the odds—to try to fight his way out of this would be tantamount to suicide, he realized—his situation suddenly worsened. "Soon after Sunrise, the wind entirely left," Hull wrote in his report three days later, "and the Ship would not steer." The becalmed *Constitution* could neither fight nor flee. To Hull, it "appeared we must be taken, and that our Escape was impossible."[32]

In the coming hours, he set about proving his own prediction wrong. To regain steerageway, Captain Hull ordered two boats lowered to tow the ship. With the oarsmen straining to pull the fully loaded 2,200-ton ship, the *Constitution* began to move ever so slowly away from her pursuers. The British put out their own oarsmen, ganging the boats from several ships to tow the frigate *Shannon*. They soon began to gain on the United States vessel. Seeking whatever advantage he could, Hull ordered his ship's casks of freshwater emptied over the side to lighten the load. American and British gunners tested their cannon, but the distances remained too great for the guns to be effective.

Since they were in shallow waters, the Americans next tried kedging, a method more often used in port for close maneuvering. An anchor was rowed ahead of the ship in a small boat, dropped to the bottom, then its cable hauled in using the capstan. By alternating the action using another boat and a second anchor, steady forward progress was achieved. The *Constitution* began to pull ahead but the British again imitated the Americans' technique. When a breeze rose in the afternoon, the *Constitution* set its sails, although the wind proved intermittent. The towboats were in and out of the water for many hours.

On Sunday morning, first light again found two British frigates dangerously close. Hull ordered the sails wetted, an arduous task for an exhausted crew that involved hoisting buckets of seawater high into the rigging. Mother Nature then intervened on the American side: The wind increased in the course of the day, and by nightfall, Hull watched as the distance between the *Constitution* and her pursuers widened to more than six miles. "At day light in the Morning," he reported, "only three of them could be seen from the Mast head, the nearest of which, was about twelve miles off directly astern."[33] The British Commodore, who only hours earlier had been so confident that the *Constitution* was to be his that he had chosen the prize crew that was "to have the honor of sailing the *Constitution* to Halifax," ordered his ships to haul off to the north.[34] The extraordinary two-and-a-half-day race was finally over. The *Constitution* escaped to Boston.

Once in port, the American ship refreshed its water supply and other stores, then headed back to sea, riding the tide past the harbor light on August 2. Hull chose not to wait for orders from Washington City. With a British blockade in the offing, he wished to be at sea and, furthermore, he wanted to depart before a more senior officer, Captain William Bainbridge, got his orders from the Secretary of the Navy. Given the Navy's strict seniority system, those papers would likely force Hull to relinquish command of the *Constitution* to Bainbridge. But he relished the prospect of trying his ship in battle.

AFTER A WEEK OF SEEING LITTLE IN THE FOGGY SEA-LANES off the Canadian Maritimes, the *Constitution* captured two British merchant brigs. Rather than sending them to port manned with prize crews drawn from his own ship, Hull ordered them burned; he wanted to maintain a full component of men in case the *Constitution* met up with a British man-of-war. Sailing toward Bermuda, Hull learned a few days later from the captain of an American privateer that the HMS *Guerrière* was sailing solo in nearby waters.

This time the *Constitution* was the pursuer. At two o'clock on the afternoon of August 19, masts were sighted and, at Hull's orders, "[a]ll sail was immediately made in chace."[35] The *Constitution* closed quickly and, by three thirty, Hull knew the strange ship was a frigate, her gunports visible through his spyglass. The drum beat the men to quarters, and, as the ship cleared for action, "the Gallant crew gave three cheers." At a few minutes after four o'clock the *Guerrière* hoisted her colors. Both captains were ready to fight.

For two hours, Captain James Dacres of the *Guerrière* and Hull maneuvered to gain favorable position. Two long-range broadsides fired by the British did little damage. Hull "ordered the Ensign hoisted . . . and . . . the Enemy continued wearing, and manoeuvering for about ¾ of an hour, to get the wind of" them.[36] The American guns were double-shotted, their muzzles packed with both round- and grapeshot. As the ships sailed closer, Hull withheld the order to fire until all his guns might strike his prey at close range. When the *Constitution* approached at a distance of "less than Pistol Shot, [they] commenced a very heavy fire from all of [their] guns." As one, the report of the guns sounded at five minutes after six.

The effect of seven hundred pounds of shot delivered at point-blank range caused the *Guerrière* to "tremble as though she had received the shock of an earthquake."[37] Her rear mast teetered, ready to topple into the sea. Her mainsail, its yard shot away, was useless amid a nest of shattered spars and cordage. The damage rendered the British frigate unmanageable in the rough seas, and the helmsman of the *Constitution* soon provided the American gunners with a raking line of fire. Riflemen and gunners alike emptied their weapons into the *Guerrière.* Belowdecks on the British ship, rivulets of blood poured through the hatches. Water gushed through dozens of holes in her hull, and the hold began to fill with seawater.

For a time the ships became entangled, the bowsprit of the *Guerrière* across the taffrail of the *Constitution.* Hull readied his men to board the enemy ship, but as he watched, his opponent's foremast collapsed, dragging the shattered mainmast with it into the sea. The ships separated, and, at Hull's command, the *Constitution* hauled off a short distance. Though the crew worked to repair its rigging, Hull's ship had sustained relatively little damage. Once again the American ship wore around to approach the *Guerrière*. What the Americans beheld was a dismasted hulk, a proud ship that, in less than thirty minutes, the *Constitution* had reduced to what Captain Dacres would term "a perfect, unmanageable Wreck."[38]

Dacres ordered the British flag to be struck. A boat sent to the *Guerrière* returned to the *Constitution* with Dacres aboard, and, when the British captain offered his sword, Hull refused to accept it. With the fighting over, a long night was spent ferrying the prisoners and wounded through heavy seas to the American frigate. Surgeons worked to save the wounded, but the toll was high. British casualties amounted to a third of the crew of the *Guerrière*, with twenty-three dead and fifty-six wounded.

A prize crew worked to save the damaged ship, but, in the light of the following morning, the frigate was deemed beyond salvage. Not a spar was intact, and the hull was riddled with holes. That afternoon, a fire was lit in the storerooms of the *Guerrière*, and the *Constitution* sailed to a safe distance of three miles. British and Americans watched as the smoking hulk burned, abandoned and helpless in the sea some 750 miles off Boston. The *Guerrière* was shrouded in smoke when a flash of brilliant white light was accompanied by a great roar of sound. The air around the wreck became suddenly alive with fragments of its quarterdeck, blown into kindling by the explosion of the powder magazine immediately below. The shock of the explosion split the hull, and, weighted by its cannon, the ship sank quickly to the bottom.

Echoes of that explosion soon reached around the world. After her return to Boston on August 30, the *Constitution* became headline news: *A British ship taken, dismasted, and burned!* Ironically, the same page of the *Boston Patriot* that announced the capture of the *Guerrière* also reported news of Isaac Hull's uncle and the "melancholy intelligence of the surrender of General Hull and his whole army."[39] Still, the story of the naval victory found a more permanent place in the collective imagination.

Another report soon saw print, telling of an 18-pound cannonball that had struck the hull of the sturdy USS *Constitution* and fallen harmlessly into the sea. In the first frigate action of the war, an American ship prevailed over the vaunted Royal Navy and, in doing so, gained the gallant name *Old Ironsides*.

DOLLEY MADISON TOLD HER HUSBAND prior to his election in 1808 as Chief Magistrate, "You know I am not much of a politician." That was but a half-truth, and Dolley knew it; in her very next sentence, she assured James that she was "extremely anxious to hear . . . what is going forward in the Cabinet."[40] In practice, her instinctive gift for political gesture served Mr. Madison extraordinarily well; her mere presence made him more formidable. As his Federalist opponent in the election, Charles Cotesworth Pinckney of South Carolina, was heard to remark, "I was beaten by Mr. and Mrs. Madison. I might have had a better chance if I had faced Mr. Madison alone."[41]

On March 4, 1809, the occasion of Mr. Madison's inaugural, Dolley had alighted from her carriage at Long's Hotel on Capitol Hill. Four hundred invitations had been sent out and additional tickets sold for the Inauguration Ball, but Mrs. Madison was the most conspicuous person present.

She simply wasn't the linsey-woolsey sort—no homespun for her—and one admirer observed on the evening of her husband's swearing-in, "She looked a Queen." Dolley wore "a pale buff colored velvet, made plain, with a very long train, but not the least trimming, and a beautiful pearl necklace, earrings, and bracelets." Mrs. Madison had adopted the Parisian fashion of wrapping a strip of silk fabric, three or four feet in length, about her head. Decorating her turban that evening were two bird-of-paradise feathers that arched toward the ceiling.[42] James, who admitted to having slept poorly the night before, looked pale and exhausted, but Dolley, affable to everyone, presided happily.

Born to wear a Quaker bonnet, she had been read out of her Philadelphia meeting upon her marriage to the deist Madison. Thereafter Dolley shaped her own manner during a social apprenticeship spent in Philadelphia while her husband served his final two years in Congress, then four more that she enjoyed at the Madison mansion, Montpelier, during James's temporary withdrawal from government life while John Adams was President. When their friend Mr. Jefferson was elected, she came into her own, and invitations to the Madisons' home became the most coveted in the city. That she had learned her protocol lessons well was evident on inauguration night in 1809. The ministerial representatives of both France and Britain were in attendance, and a ticklish problem offered itself at dinner: Who would get the honor of sitting next to Dolley? The lady assumed a seat between them, flattering both and offending neither.

That had been the Madisons' night, with the newly composed "Madison's March" performed for the first time. But the Naval Ball on December 8, 1812, was to belong to the heroes of the U.S. Navy, among them Isaac Hull. Long's Hotel had changed owners and names in the interim, but as Edward Coles helped her from her carriage at what was now Tomlinson's, Dolley knew just where to go. As he watched her enter the hotel, Edward Coles understood Dolley's role in the nation's affairs as well as anyone.

A second cousin on her mother's side, he knew her as only kin can; as the President's private secretary, privy to the secrets of the Chief Magistrate, he saw her as Mr. Madison's confidante, a role that Dolley, as "a strong-minded woman, [was] fully capable of entering into. . . . [T]here is little doubt that he owed to her intellectual companionship, as well as her ability in sustaining the outward dignity of the office."[43]

The Naval Ball had been Edward Coles's idea. A bill of appropriation was pending for the construction of new ships for the U.S. Navy. In the weeks preceding, Congress debated the relative merits of commissioning 74-gun ships of the line and more 44-gun frigates, but the bill's passage remained uncertain. Isaac Hull and several other naval captains were in town to aid the lobbying effort, and their presence had given rise to Mr. Coles's notion: *Why not honor the naval heroes*—Congress had already voted that medals be struck—*as part of the effort to win congressional votes?* The city and the nation, dispirited by the bad news from the northern border, could use something to celebrate.

Adding to the evening's air of expectancy, a rumor had come to town just hours earlier. The report had it that Captain Stephen Decatur and his frigate the *United States* had captured a great prize off the Morocco coast south of the Azores. The *National Intelligencer* rushed an extra to press; it appeared at five o'clock announcing "ANOTHER BRILLIANT NAVAL VICTORY." As the handbills circulated, citizens throughout the city put candles in their windows and lit celebratory bonfires, making "the Avenue . . . very brilliant on [the] way to the Capitol Hill."[44] Yet as Dolley's company climbed the stair to the assembly room, a fresh rumor was passed. Doubt was cast on the first, as no official word had arrived of Captain Decatur's deeds.

ISAAC HULL WAS A SAILOR'S SAILOR. A man of few words, plain manner, and decisive action, he was a taciturn character with a heavy belly who was most content when staring silently at the sea. In contrast, Captain Stephen Decatur possessed the carriage of an actor ready to declaim—shoulders back, chest out—and an appetite for the hugger-mugger of politics. As commander of the Navy's Southern Department, he submitted memoranda outlining military strategy to the Secretary of the Navy. He was equally at home in the drawing room and the courtroom (he had served at the court-martial of Commodore James Barron of the *Chesapeake*, which settled the mantle of scapegoat on Barron, finding him guilty of a minor charge and suspending him from the U.S. Navy for five years). Decatur's dark eyes, tousled brown curls, and brooding good looks had won him an elegant wife, to whom he wrote love poems ("Love turns aside the balls which round me fly / Lest precious tears should drop from Susan's eye").[45]

The namesake son of a Revolutionary War Naval officer, Decatur abandoned his studies at the University of Pennsylvania to join the Navy at age nineteen. He distinguished himself during the Barbary Wars when, at age twenty-five, he sailed into the enemy harbor at Tripoli, his ketch disguised as a Maltese merchant ship. He stole aboard the captured American frigate *Philadelphia* and set her afire before escaping amid a torrent of enemy gunfire. That 1804 raid won him a reputation for daring and an appointment as the youngest captain in the U.S. Navy. He was clever and ambitious, and, as Secretary of the Navy Paul Hamilton reminded him in a letter shortly before war was declared, a man driven by his "love of fame."[46]

Since 1810, Decatur had commanded the USS *United States.* His connection to the ship began in the days when its keel was laid: He helped build the ship, one of the first of the six frigates commissioned by the U.S. Navy, when he worked in Philadelphia's Southwark shipyard as a lad. He served on board after being given his midshipman's warrant in 1798 and had come to know her well. Called the *Old Wagon* by some, the *United States* was not as speedy as her sister ships, but her gunnery included thirty-two 24-pounder cannons.

Decatur and his crew were cruising the waters off West Africa when, at sunrise on Sunday, October 25, 1812, the foremast lookout on the *United States* sent word to the captain that he sighted a tiny sail. Decatur studied the horizon where, a dozen miles away, a ship—*man-of-war or merchant?*—plied heavy waters in the stiff breeze. He ordered his ship's course shifted to intercept the vessel. Soon it became clear that the other captain had done the same, and the ships closed rapidly.

At a distance of three miles, the other ship, now recognizable as a frigate, ran up a British ensign. Decatur realized he knew the opposition at first hand; the warship he examined through his glass had been berthed next to the *United States* in Norfolk a few months before. "She is a frigate of the largest class," Decatur noted, "two years old, four months out of dock, and reputed one of the best sailors in the British service."[47] It was the HMS *Macedonian.*

Her captain, John Surman Carden, was an occasional companion of Decatur. The two navy men had dined together and swapped stories and even strategies. Carden had confidently asserted to Decatur in the days before the war that the British experience had demonstrated that 18-pounders were the ideal guns for arming a frigate. The tactician Decatur had taken note; on this day he might get the chance to test the hypothesis.

The American ship was rapidly overhauling the *Macedonian*, and Decatur ordered his helmsman to steer across the bow of the oncoming ship in an attempt to gain the weather gauge, the advantage of being upwind of the other vessel. But Captain Carden was quick to steer into the wind, leaving the two ships sailing the same tack.

As the distance between them narrowed, Decatur took care to maintain a calculated separation from Carden's vessel. At nine o'clock, the *United States* tested the range with its cannon, but its balls fell well short of the target. The *Macedonian* trailed the American frigate slightly; a faster ship, the British vessel gained on her. At twenty minutes past the hour, the separation having narrowed and with the *Macedonian* nearly abreast of the *United States*, the ships exchanged fire.

Aboard the American ship, the British 18-pound carronades did little damage, but the *Macedonian* lost her mizzenmast. Knowing his opponent had less ability to maneuver, Decatur turned into the wind, giving his gunners a raking position off his opponent's quarter. The synchronized firing of the American 24-pounders blasted the *Macedonian* at a rate almost twice that of the British gunners, and soon almost all the British vessel's standing rigging was shot away.

Dressed in their Sabbath best, the British found themselves under hellish fire with many of their guns disabled. "[I]t was like some awfully tremendous thunder-storm," wrote one Englishman, "whose deafening roar is attended by incessant streaks of lightning, carrying death in every flash and strewing the ground with the victims of its wrath: only, in our case, the scene was rendered more horrible than that, by the presence of torrents of blood which dyed our decks."

The powder one lad carried caught fire and "burnt the flesh almost off his face." When he raised his hands to his head, a cannonball ripped into his abdomen. His lifeless body fell to the deck, severed in two.

A single shot cut off a man's hands; at nearly the same moment, a second shot eviscerated him. The boatswain had "his head smashed to pieces by a cannon-ball."

In the midst of the battle, the dead were thrown overboard, while the wounded were carried below. Severed limbs were tossed into the sea. "[G]roans and cries . . . rent the air," and the "surgeon and mate were smeared with blood from head to foot: they looked more like butchers than doctors."[48]

The sea battle proved hopelessly one-sided and Captain Carden, despite the willingness of some of his officers to fight on, lowered his ship's colors. American casualties amounted to five dead and seven wounded, while the *Macedonian* lost a third of its crew, with thirty-six killed and sixty-eight wounded. Of fifty-two British officers, only nine remained standing. The *United States* sustained minor damage to her rigging. She had taken just nine shots to her hull, while the *Macedonian* was holed nearly a hundred times. Tossed about by the waves, her masts gone, the British frigate was, according to her captain, reduced to an "unmanageable log."[49]

John Carden took the burden of failure hard. British naval superiority seemed almost God-given, and he thought himself the first British naval officer to strike his flag to an American. When he was brought aboard the *United States*, the British captain told Decatur, "I am an undone man." Gracious in victory, Decatur assured him he was not the first of His Britannic Majesty's captains to surrender to an American ship. "You are mistaken, sir; your *Guerrière* has been taken by us, and the flag of a frigate was struck before yours."[50]

With the battle concluded, an inspection of the *Macedonian* found her seaworthy. Stephen Decatur had witnessed the citywide *Huzzah!* when Isaac Hull had brought the flag of the *Guerrière* into Boston Harbor. With his instinct for the dramatic, he imagined the thunderous welcome that would greet the return of the *United States* with the HMS *Macedonian* as its prize, and he soon wrote to Secretary Hamilton that he "deemed it important that we should see our prize in."[51] After almost two weeks spent patching holes in the hull, pumping out seven feet of seawater in the hold, and jury-rigging masts and sails that gave the *Macedonian* the look of a bark, the captor and captive began the two-thousand-mile journey back to the United States.

CONGRESSMAN SAMUEL MITCHILL OF NEW YORK was disappointed at how few of his colleagues turned up for the "ball in compliment of our naval heroes."[52] The event seemed to have taken on a partisan character with perhaps fifteen members of Congress present. Still, a party is a party, and, with the excitement surrounding the recent naval victories, the "assembly was crowded with a more than usual portion of the youth and beauty of the city."[53]

With Mrs. Madison at the helm, Washington City parties welcomed female guests, and her evenings became opportunities to show off the latest fashions. The previous generation favored layers of petticoats, corsets, and hoop skirts, with voluminous fabrics that camouflaged the female form. But in Dolley's Washington, such old-fashioned attire made its way to trunks in the attic; in its stead was a new style, all the rage in Europe.

The high-waisted Empire dress looked well on trim young women and was slimming to a matron seeking to disguise a thickening body. The long, loose skirts, derived from Greek and Roman images, were light and often diaphanous, rising from the floor to be gathered just beneath the breasts.

The material might also cling to its wearer's form, revealing her shape in a way that the more structured dresses of the previous generation did not. One of Mrs. Madison's friends, Elizabeth Patterson Bonaparte, had become somewhat infamous when she arrived in Washington City. The daughter of a Baltimore shipping merchant, she married Napoleon's youngest brother, Jerome, on Christmas Eve 1803; neither had yet reached age twenty, and both her parents and the French authorities on the American scene counseled against the match. The impulsive and beautiful young woman found the attention paid her in Washington intoxicating. While a few expressed shock at her revealing garb, others felt empowered to "take a look at her bubbies," as one woman reported.[54] The whole of her shapely form was on view, her pale muslin gown dampened. The look was Parisian, having been practiced by the circle surrounding Josephine, Napoleon Bonaparte's first consort.

On this evening a naval ceremony accompanied the music and dancing. Two British flags were unfurled, trophies of war. As Mrs. Madison, members of the cabinet, Supreme Court justices, and the assembled audience watched, American sailors presented the flags. Victorious Captain Isaac Hull of the *Constitution* was at hand to watch as the ensign of the HMS *Guerrière* was hung on the ballroom wall, along with the flag captured from the British brig *Alert*. The moment was dimmed for an observant few by the condition of Secretary of the Navy Paul Hamilton, who could barely stand, having consumed substantial quantities of drink. For the rest, "all was joy and gaiety, such as could scarcely admit of augmentation," reported the *National Intelligencer*.

"And yet," added the newspaper account, "it was destined to be increased."[55]

The ballroom was crowded with dancers when, shortly after nine o'clock, a commotion was heard from below. Pounding footsteps echoed on the stairs and excited voices interrupted the band. The men deserted their dance partners on the dance floor and moved toward the entrance. Some thought a fire might be about to engulf the building, but before panic could ensue, a young naval officer appeared, attended by the stocky Captain Hull, an honor guard of aging veterans, and the unsteady Secretary of the Navy Paul Hamilton. A silence fell over the large crowd.

The new arrival was Lieutenant Archibald Hamilton, son of the Secretary of the Navy. He had been traveling for four days from New London, where the ship on which he served, the *United States*, had docked the previous Friday. Captain Decatur dispatched young Hamilton to deliver a symbol of his prize, the flag of the HMS *Macedonian*. Looking exhausted from his journey and thin from his months at sea, Lieutenant Hamilton was soon surrounded and embraced by his mother and sisters; more than a few in the crowd shed tears of joy at the young man's safe return and his message of victory.[56] Senator Mitchill read the emotion in the room. "Mirth and jollity were suspended, and changed into the glow of patriotism and the rapture of applause."[57] The colors were then taken up by four navy men, one of them Captain Hull, and the flag was "marched like a Canopy around the room" to the strains of the national anthem, "Hail, Columbia!"[58] Arriving at the front of the room, the men laid the flag of St. George at the feet of Mrs. Madison.

For once, she was rendered speechless. "I saw her color come and go," one observer reported of the flush that came to Dolley's cheeks.[59] She was the admired face of the government, with or without James at her side. Inevitably, Mrs. Madison was the person the captains would honor with their symbol of naval and national success.

To understand her popularity, one had only to ask her "highly valued friend" the sandy-haired Speaker of the House Henry Clay.[60] "Everybody loves Mrs. Madison," he once remarked. Standing within earshot, she had an immediate riposte:

"That's because Mrs. Madison loves everybody."[61]

THE SPENT AND EXHAUSTED CELEBRANTS RETURNED to the President's house after midnight. Mrs. Madison had played her role perfectly, even as the drama changed before the actors' eyes. For all his planning, Mr. Coles never could have expected the extraordinary surprise of the arrival of a well-loved messenger with news of another momentous naval victory.

Having heard a full account of the evening's happenings, Mr. Madison added the Naval Ball and the victory of the *United States* to his mental ledger of the year's events. Since the war had begun, most of the entries added up to a hard history, one filled with battlefield failures and congressional calumnies. Certainly it was a relief to approach the New Year with a few ringing high notes.

CHAPTER 2

"A Distempered Imagination"*

Until the late alarm I have never been able to realize our being in a state of war; but now . . . I not only believe but feel the unhappy state of our country.
—Margaret Bayard Smith, July 20, 1813[1]

I.

June 1813 . . . At the President's Bedside

MRS. MADISON COULD NOT BRING HERSELF TO UTTER the dreaded word, but Louis Sérurier could. The French envoy to the United States reported back to his Paris ministry of the President's perilous health. "[H]is *death*," observed Sérurier, ". . . would be a veritable national calamity. . . . All good Americans pray for the recovery of Mr. Madison."[2]

Sickly even when young, Madison had confided in a fellow student

* On July 16, 1813, during Madison's prolonged recovery from a life-threatening fever, the editor of the *Maryland Gazette* observed that it was unfortunate that the "head of the government" was not a man like Rufus King, senator of New York and a staunch opponent of the war. According to the *Gazette*, King would be less likely to "pursue the phantoms of a distempered imagination."

at the College of New Jersey forty years earlier that a pattern of illness led him to conclude he ought not "to expect a long or healthy life."[3] His uncertain health led him to refuse an invitation from Thomas Jefferson to join him in France in 1785; then he had confided his belief that "crossing the sea would be unfriendly to a singular disease of my constitution."[4] In the years since, he suffered frequent bouts of fever, piles, and influenza, but now, with his health more delicate than ever at age sixty-two, the fever that came upon him on June 13, 1813, left him unable to rise from his bed.

For Dolley, James's feverish state was a nightmare revisited. In 1793, Dolley Payne Todd had lost her husband and younger son in a single day. The cause was the "malignant fever," as her friend and admirer President George Washington labeled it; for others in Philadelphia, however, the disease that yellowed the skin and often killed within a day of onset gained a more ominous name. To much of the panicked populace, yellow fever became "the plague." Though briefly ill herself, Dolley had survived, together with her one-year-old son, John Payne Todd. But the experience changed her. At twenty-five she donned widow's weeds, fought for her inheritance in a mourning city where nearly one out of five inhabitants died, and, within a year, left the Society of Friends to marry James. In the ensuing two decades, he helped raise Payne, as Dolley's son was called, and, together, the Madisons had come to rule Washington as they did one another's hearts. To Dolley, the loss of James was unthinkable.

James's health was a source of constant worry for Dolley. In truth, it was a rare week in his life when he did not experience some complaint, more often than not a "dysenteric attack." But the war added greatly to the pressures on the President, and in the last two years, Madison had spent barely a dozen days away from his office at the President's house. That had meant he spent very little time at his essential refuge, Montpelier, where in the past he had escaped the sickly summer air of the tidewater region to enjoy the refreshing breezes of the rolling hills of central Virginia. Unable to go to his native Piedmont, the enervated Madison this summer had fallen prey to his most serious bout ever of the ailment diagnosed by his three doctors as "bilious fever."*

A less serious malady had already taken one man from the President's house. In March, Madison's trusted secretary Edward Coles had fallen ill and, with Mr. Madison's blessing, departed for Philadelphia. Coles remained there, recuperating from surgery to treat a lingering case of the piles. For a time, Madison had relied upon Dolley's son, Payne, now twenty-one, to be his amanuensis, but the indulged lad proved as unreliable a scribe as he had a student (his days at the College of New Jersey ended in failure), and his mother assumed his duties as the President's secretary. Thus, on June 17, the task fell to her to write to a deputation of senators scheduled to call upon the President. "James Madison being too much indisposed to see the committee this morning," she told them, "[he] is obliged to postpone."[5]

With the letter written, she took up her post at his bedside. "I watch over him," she would confide in a friend, "as I would an infant."[6]

PRACTICE WAS REQUIRED TO LEARN THE ROLE OF CHIEF MAGISTRATE, and Madison had begun 1813 still honing one of the necessary skills.

When he was sworn in as President four years before, even Madison's enemies had to acknowledge that his experience was second to no one's in American government. Although he resisted the characterization "father of the Constitution" (that document wasn't "the off-spring of a single brain," he insisted, rather "the work of many heads and many hands"), he had crafted a great deal of the blueprint for the nation's government. As the General's man in Congress, he had drafted bills, coaxed

* Among medical historians, the consensus is that the term "malicious fever" in the Federal era was used to identify the acute infectious disease we know as yellow fever. In contrast, "bilious fever" was a less specific diagnosis, one that was applied to a range of medical conditions, varying from malaria to nonspecific ailments with symptoms of fever and vomiting of bile.

votes, and even written speeches for Washington himself; later, his eight years spent as Jefferson's Secretary of State had been a further apprenticeship in governance and foreign affairs.

The presidency, he found, posed different challenges, and one in particular had proved difficult. Though a dutiful son, a caring sibling, a devoted husband, and a constant friend, he had not learned an essential skill: the ability to delegate. As a legislator, committeeman, and Secretary of State, he was a collaborator, a partner, and a loyal subordinate, but as chief executive and commander in chief, he needed to be able to people his government with the best and most suitable men. At this task he failed. Of his original cabinet, the only man who had served him well was a holdover from Jefferson's administration, Albert Gallatin, Secretary of the Treasury.

Madison always examined, analyzed, and worried over a problem at length before reaching a reasoned decision. That approach had led him to name Robert Smith his first Secretary of State. His rationale was a mix of political pragmatism (he hoped to gain the support of Smith's brother, Samuel Smith, an influential senator from Maryland) and collegiality, as Robert Smith himself was an affable known quantity, after serving shoulder-to-shoulder with Madison as Jefferson's Secretary of the Navy and Attorney General. But President Madison found he was forced to do most of Smith's letter drafting for him, in effect functioning as his own Secretary of State. Smith proved to be a further liability as he repeatedly demonstrated a lack of diplomatic finesse, discretion, and even loyalty. As Mr. Madison reminded him on the day of his dismissal, too often Smith was guilty of making "disparaging remarks on my official character, & that of others in the Cabinet."[7]

Colonel James Monroe—his rank dated from his service as a Virginia cavalryman during the Revolution, when he served under George Washington—became Madison's second Secretary of State. He was a valued friend, occasional rival, and political ally of some thirty years' duration. Since taking the oath of office in March 1811, Monroe had proved a reliable counselor, particularly in the months leading up to the war declaration. As a former United States Minister Plenipotentiary to both France and England, Monroe brought international experience and a shared sense of outrage at the treatment the United States received from its European "friends." From his last posting at the Court of St. James's, Monroe returned, as he confided to a Washington City newspaperman, "thoroughly disgusted with the contemptuous manner in which the rights of the United States were treated by the belligerent Powers, and especially England." The experience left him convinced "that the rights of the U. States as a nation would never be respected by the Powers of the Old World until [the U.S.] Government summoned up resolution to resist such usage, not by argument and protest merely, but by an appeal to arms."[8] Unlike Smith, Monroe proved to be very much in Madison's camp.

With the coming of 1813, the President saw two empty seats at his cabinet table. One had belonged to Paul Hamilton, who, as Secretary of the Navy, had rarely been able to accomplish anything after the noon hour (thanks to his "too free use of stimulant potation").[9] At first, Hamilton resisted the President's request for his resignation, pointing to the notable successes of his warships. But Mr. Madison explained that Congress would approve no naval appropriations until the secretary was gone. In retrospect, however, Hamilton shouldn't have been surprised by his dismissal, since Mrs. Madison had already been dispatched to soften the blow. "[W]henever any of the *great state dependents are to be sacrificed*," the *New England Palladium* had reported, she functioned as her husband's advance guard. As someone who "knows everything going on" and who "moves many things," Mrs. Madison's especial "attention and civility" had of late been directed to Mrs. Hamilton. Though she would not have explained the reasons for her kindness, her attentions had preceded the falling of the axe.[10]

With Paul Hamilton gone, Madison's pick as Secretary of the Navy was William Jones. A Philadelphia merchant, former sea captain, and ex-Congressman, Jones arrived with the endorsement of his fellow Philadelphian Albert Gallatin, whose opinion carried great weight with Mr. Madison.

Filling the post of Secretary of War proved harder. After William Eustis's quiet departure following the autumn debacles in Canada, several early candidates refused the appointment, including James Monroe, who preferred to remain in charge at State. Finally Madison had turned to a Revolutionary War veteran, John Armstrong, recognizing that he "possessed . . . known talents [and] a degree of military information which might be useful." But the President also worried at what he called Armstrong's "objectionable peculiarities."[11]

His father had served with Colonel Washington in the French and Indian War. The younger Armstrong left the College of New Jersey to join the Continental Army during the Revolution, where his father's connections facilitated his rise to brigade major at age eighteen. Though he fought in the victories at Princeton and Saratoga, a shadow remained over his revolutionary service for his part in the infamous Newburgh Conspiracy.

Two anonymous letters—only later was Armstrong revealed as the penman—had given voice in 1783 to widely felt disgruntlement among Continental Army officers over years of undelivered back pay. Commander in chief Washington had quickly quelled the uprising; in his forthright way, the General addressed the officers and, famously, moved some to tears when, attempting to read a letter to them, he groped in his pocket for recently acquired spectacles and, donning them, remarked that he "had grown gray in their service, and now found himself growing blind."[12] Washington, the instinctive leader of men, conveyed the message that he, too, had sacrificed much during the eight years at war, and the mutinous resolve evaporated. But many remembered Armstrong's role in the little drama.

After the war Armstrong became secretary of Pennsylvania's Supreme Executive Council and adjutant general of the state militia (he liked the latter title, fashioning himself thereafter *General* Armstrong). After his marriage in 1789 to Alida Livingston, he relocated to his wife's native New York and, for a dozen years, contented himself with fathering children, reading Shakespeare, building a series of ever-larger houses for his family, and living as a gentleman farmer in the Hudson Valley, where he and his wife had been gifted with twenty-five thousand acres of the Livingston family's immense holdings.

In 1801, he arrived in Washington as Senator Armstrong of New York. He was immediately drawn to Madison and, especially, to Jefferson ("The nearer you approach Jefferson, the better you like him," he wrote).[13] The two Virginians appointed Armstrong American Minister to France, where he served for six years. Next Armstrong's strong New York connections led to his appointment as a brigadier general with responsibility for devising a defense of New York's harbor. He also published a small volume titled *Hints to Young Generals*, a gloss on a treatise he came across while in France by Antoine H. Jomini. Though the book appeared pseudonymously ("By an Old Soldier"), it sold briskly and the identity of its American author soon became known, adding to Armstrong's reputation as a man knowledgeable about things martial.

Madison hoped that Armstrong's New York residence—the state was on the verge of becoming the nation's most populous—might help counterbalance the angry congressional opposition from the East (even as Madison was deciding whom to appoint, Josiah Quincy of Massachusetts rose to his feet on the floor of Congress to hurl brickbats at him, terming Madison's cabinet "little less than despotic, composed, to all efficient purposes, of two Virginians and a foreigner").* Yet, Madison knew, Armstrong often feuded with his colleagues. He could be cutting ("This man," Ambassador Armstrong once wrote to Secretary Madison of one of his underlings, "really has not sense enough to feed turkies").[14] During his days as Minister to France, Armstrong even managed to anger the

* The reference was to Madison, Monroe, and the Swiss-born Gallatin, though the latter had been a naturalized American citizen for almost three decades.

emperor himself, as Napoleon, frustrated at Armstrong's peevish silences, complained that "he was morose, and captious, and petulant."[15] That Armstrong was ambitious for higher office was well-known, which also meant Monroe would be unhappy with his reappearance on the national scene, since Armstrong's rise to Secretary of War would elevate his status as a future presidential candidate and Monroe rival.

Despite his reservations, Madison offered the brash and confident Armstrong the job on January 14, 1813. Armstrong quickly accepted, but, predictably, approval from former colleagues in the Senate was slow in coming for the sometimes arrogant Armstrong. In the end, his nomination was narrowly approved by a vote of 18 to 15, and then only after an airing of the old allegations about the Newburgh letters.

At last, Madison's new team was in place to fight the war.

AT HIS SECOND INAUGURAL ON MARCH 4, 1813, Mr. Madison had tried to convey a sense of national confidence. "[T]he war with a powerful nation which forms so prominent a feature in our situation," he told his audience at the Capitol, "invites the smiles of heaven on the means of conducting it to a successful termination."[16] Certainly, he hoped his nation would prevail in the war he had declared, but for every flash of good news that came Mr. Madison's way in the first six months of 1813—and there were some—a new dark cloud was always to appear on the horizon.

In February, the newly appointed Secretary of the Navy William Jones had briefed the President on the sea battle that brought the year 1812 to a close. The USS *Constitution* had sailed with a new commander, Captain William Bainbridge (Isaac Hull was tending to the affairs of his brother, who had died unexpectedly). On December 29, the American vessel met up with a British frigate off the coast of Brazil. The engagement began badly. Bainbridge was twice wounded in the early moments, once in each leg, and cannon fire from the HMS *Java* splintered the

American ship's wheel. Though his breeches were crimson with blood, Bainbridge remained upright, shouting orders to men belowdecks who managed the rudder using cables. After an action of one hour and fifty-five minutes, with its fore and mizzenmasts gone and the mainmast a stump, the *Java* lowered its colors. The *Java's* captain lay dying belowdecks, and the British casualties were treble the American losses. Since the British ship was beyond salvage, its crew was brought aboard the *Constitution.* The British frigate was set afire and, as the victorious *Constitution* sailed toward the Brazilian coast, the powder stores aboard the HMS *Java* exploded in a fireworks display worthy of a New Year's celebration.

Although the U.S. Navy succeeded beyond anyone's hopes in 1812, the prospects of further victories at sea diminished in the new year. Reports had it that the British Admiralty ordered more vessels across the Atlantic and, by spring 1813, the British force in American waters added up to at least twelve 74-gun ships of the line, twice as many frigates, and dozens more gunships, brigs, sloops of war, and unrated vessels, a total of more than one hundred ships. But Madison's advisers could not know for certain the true number of British warships plying the American coast since the outnumbered American navy had to keep most of its vessels sitting quayside. In February, a Royal Navy squadron had chased the frigate *Constellation* into Norfolk harbor. In May the *United States* and the overhauled *Macedonian*, now a U.S. Navy ship, fled up the Thames River in Connecticut to escape a much larger British force on Long Island Sound. Two other frigates were moored in Boston—the *Chesapeake* and the *Constitution*—as a trio of British warships, the 74-gun *La Hogue* and the frigates HMS *Shannon* and *Tenedos*, sent taunting messages to shore via shore boats. Frustrating as it was for the newly confident American captains, they had little choice but to remain in the safety of port and, as spring gave way to summer, the U.S. Navy's presence on the high seas was limited to the *President* and the *Congress*, whereabouts unknown, which had slipped out of Boston Harbor shrouded by a dense fog.

Quite some time had passed since the last bit of happy naval news had arrived. On February 24 the sloop USS *Hornet* had met up with the HMS *Peacock* off the coast of Brazil. The gunners on the *Hornet* made short work of the *Peacock* in a bloody engagement that sent the British ship to the bottom, with nine hands still aboard. Still, news of a victory over a single 18-gun British brig in the South Atlantic meant little in the face of the British blockade that was squeezing American trade.

As for the land war, Madison was candid about the nation's military readiness in a letter he wrote in early April to an old Virginia friend who now resided in upstate New York, not so far from the border hostilities. War had been declared, he allowed, "at a moment when we were not prepared for it, and when it was certain that effective preparation would not take place."[17] It was no wonder, Madison explained, that the Americans fared badly on the battlefield. It wasn't an admission he could make publicly, but the Declaration of War had been a calculated gamble and Madison knew it.

He did offer his friend a note of optimism, though not of a military kind. There was now the prospect of peace talks. On March 7, word had arrived of an offer by Emperor Alexander of Russia to mediate between Great Britain and the United States (Russian trade, too, was hurt by the war). In response, Madison had promptly appointed a battery of Peace Commissioners. The Senate confirmed two of Madison's choices—one of their own, Senator James Bayard of Delaware, and John Quincy Adams, who was already abroad as minister to Russia. But even the prospect of peace proved a partisan issue, and a furious debate had ensued over the nominations of two others, Treasury Secretary Albert Gallatin and Jonathan Russell. Though the two had already sailed for Europe, neither Russell, a diplomat who had served in both France and England, nor Gallatin had been confirmed by Congress.

Madison's list of problems and political conflicts grew ever longer. Military recruitment was low. Provisioning the army in the north was a continuing problem, one that was heightened by competition from the

British military for American goods. Unlike the Americans, the Crown had money in hand to pay its bills, and northern merchants had proven mercenary, more than happy to profit from goods sold to the enemy, leaving American troops undersupplied. The Federal government was accumulating debt, but Congress was reluctant to raise taxes. The result was the March 1813 warning of Secretary of the Treasury Gallatin: "We have hardly money enough to last till the end of the month."[18] Mr. Madison's War was being fought with too few soldiers, too few dollars, and too many loud voices in opposition.[19]

SPRING 1813 HAD BROUGHT SOME GOOD NEWS REGARDING THE LAND WAR, but even reports of victory were troubling to the worried mind of Mr. Madison. In particular, the assault on York in Upper Canada brought an admixture of encouraging and disquieting news.

In January and February, the newly constituted cabinet devised a fresh plan for the Canadian front. Secretary of the Navy William Jones made the case for dominating the waterways; he told his commander on the Canadian border, Captain Isaac Chauncey, "The success of the ensuing Campaign will depend absolutely upon our superiority on all the Lakes."[20] To accomplish that goal, Secretary of War John Armstrong shaped a strategy that began with seizing Kingston, the principal British naval base on Lake Ontario.

Madison concurred, but when the plan was conveyed to the Canadian front, the region's commander, Major General Henry Dearborn, expressed reservations. Rumor had it that a reinforced Kingston now had troops totaling some seven thousand men, along with a new warship, and Dearborn worried that American forces might not prevail. Together with Captain Chauncey, he proposed a different first objective, namely "Little York," the capital of Upper Canada. York's defenses were far from impregnable, Dearborn argued, and he promised, "[T]o take or destroy the armed vessels at York will give us the complete command of the Lake."[21] Recognizing that capturing an enemy capital might also have important psychological and political benefits, Armstrong agreed. Since the military failures of the autumn left the American military in a "state of prostration," Armstrong wrote on March 29, "we [might] soon get on our legs again, if we are able to give some hard blows at the opening of the campaign."[22] Plain and simple, he wanted his tenure at the War Department to begin with a victory.

With the lake finally free of ice in late April, a flotilla of U.S. Navy ships sailed from Sackets Harbor at the east end of Lake Ontario. Twelve schooners and the brig USS *Oneida* accompanied the fleet's flagship, a newly launched, single-masted sloop bearing the President's own surname. Though armed with fourteen 18-pound cannon and eight 32-pound carronades, the USS *Madison* began the voyage as a troop carrier, with some 600 of the 1,700-man invading force aboard. The 112-foot-long corvette was so overcrowded that no more than half the men could squeeze belowdecks at a time. The soldiers were hard-pressed to stay out of the way of the 150-man crew as a fair wind carried the ships westward.

On the evening of Monday, April 26, after a two-day sail, Commodore Chauncey's armada heard the report of a signal gun from shore, as sentries atop Scarborough Bluffs warned the citizens of York of approaching ships.

At first light on Tuesday, the American vessels made their move. A spit of low-lying land, Gibraltar Point, with a blockhouse at the tip, protected the inner harbor. Rather than sail into the teeth of the Canadian defenses, which included two gun batteries, the fleet made for the site of an abandoned French fortification, Fort Tarento, about two miles west of York.* The Americans planned to land the soldiers in a clearing and, under the cover of artillery fire from the ships, assault the city. By seven A.M., the

---

* It is said—and oft disputed—that because the trees at York seemed to be standing in the water, Native Americans named the place *Tarontah* ("trees on the water"); thus the French Fort Tarento and, later, the anglicized name "Toronto."

two U.S. Navy warships, along with the converted merchantmen, dropped anchor a mile offshore, and men were clambering into a flotilla of small bateaux.[23]

At eight o'clock, the oarsmen were given the order to pull for shore.

Zebulon Montgomery Pike Jr. was in command. A newly brevetted brigadier general, Pike was young for his rank. But the thirty-four-year-old had followed his father into the army (Zebulon Pike the Elder served with General Washington) and had already spent eighteen years in uniform, much of it exploring the frontier. He had sought the headwaters of the Mississippi in Minnesota. On a trip to the Southwest in 1806, he charted a mountain previously unknown to Europeans, a summit already referred to by some as Pike's Peak.

The previous month Pike had marched his men through the snow for ten days, journeying from Camp Saranac on Lake Champlain. For soldiers dressed in cotton summer uniforms, the conditions of the march across upper New York were almost unendurable. As Pike reported, "One man was froze to death, last evening; and many wretches will lose their feet."[24] Now, as the moment of battle approached, one of the seamen rowing the soldiers ashore wondered at their readiness to fight. "They were mostly tall, pale-looking Yankees, half dead with sickness and the weather—so mealy, indeed, that half of them could not take their grog."

When the American force was within rifle range, British and Indian defenders half-hidden on the forested shore fired upon the troops. A regiment of U.S. Army riflemen fired back. As the shots rang out, the infantrymen "became wide awake, pointed out to each other where to aim, and many of them actually jumped into the water, in order to get the sooner ashore."[25]

A strong breeze had blown the landing party west of the clearing, so the American soldiers were forced to fight their way along narrow paths through a dense forest. With 12-pounder long guns on the schooners firing canister shot at the British defenders, General Pike led three companies toward the town, and, over the course of three hours of intense

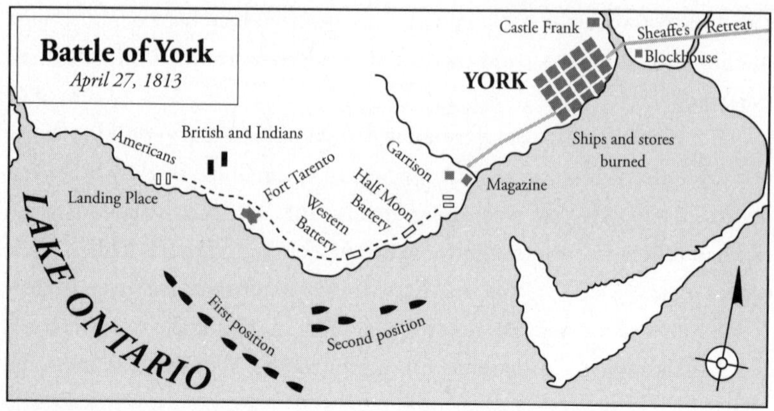

fighting, the smaller British force gave ground, with almost half their lead company of grenadiers killed or wounded.

When the American troops finally emerged from woodland cover, enemy cannon fire brought them to a halt. General Pike planned to assault the battery of guns facing him, but before he could marshal his men and artillery, there was a flash followed by a great, roaring explosion. An errant match had ignited a chest of spare cartridges within the British gun emplacement. "Every man in the battery was blown into the air," reported a boy in the town who was at hand, "and the *dissection* of the greater part of their bodies was inconceivably shocking." From the water, American seamen erupted in cheers. Dozens of British soldiers were killed or wounded and, at the field hospital, the lad reported, "a more afflicting sight could scarcely be witnessed. One man in particular . . . was brought in a wheelbarrow, and from his appearance I should be induced to suppose that almost every bone in his body was broken; . . . his cries and groans were of the most heartrending description."[26]

With the cannon at the redoubt dismounted and unusable, the survivors among the defenders retreated back toward the town. Canister shot from the ships' guns continued to fall on the enemy, and General Pike and his troops advanced to the town's abandoned garrison. When Pike stopped to interrogate a British prisoner, his interview was abruptly interrupted by an explosion even greater than the first. To the ship's surgeon aboard the *Oneida*, "It seemed that the heavens and the earth were coming together."[27]

The gigantic blast launched tons of debris into the air. Even at several hundred yards' distance, sailors on the schooners dodged boulders the size of small pumpkins that crashed to the decks. A cloud billowed skyward at the site of the explosion; it carried more than dust, smoke, and stone. To his horror, one observer reported that in the "awful black cloud" he could discern "objects in the air that I took for men."[28] This time, the casualties were U.S. Army.

At the order of Major General Sir Roger Hale Sheaffe, the retreating British had ignited a half-buried powder magazine near the water's edge, and the force of five hundred barrels of powder had blown skyward the roof and walls of the structure and a great quantity of rubble. The carnage on the scene stunned even the army doctor at hand. "My God!" Dr. William Beaumont exclaimed. "Who can think of the shocking scene where his fellow creatures lye mashed & mangled in every part, with a leg—an arm—a head, or a body ground to pieces."[29] Thirty-eight of Pike's soldiers were dead, another 221 wounded.

One of the injured was Zebulon Pike himself. With his back turned to the magazine at the time of the explosion, the general had been driven to the ground, struck by an airborne boulder. His spine and chest were crushed by the blow, but he still breathed. He was rowed to the USS *Madison*.

The surviving American soldiers entered the town to find the British regulars had marched into the woods, withdrawing toward Kingston. A fire at the shipyard consumed a ship in the stocks. When completed, the 30-gun HMS *General Brock* would have been the most powerful warship on the lake, and its capture would have tilted the balance of power to Commodore Chauncey's advantage. But as the fire burned itself out, a nearly completed frigate was reduced to smoking timbers, barely recognizable as the hull of a ship.

The Union Jack in the town was lowered, and the flag was brought to Pike. He murmured in recognition, asking that the ensign be placed beneath his head; by sunset, he was dead. Back on the shore, Dr. Beaumont spent the next forty-eight hours performing battlefield surgeries as he "waded in blood, cutting off arms, legs, and trepanning."[30]

Word of the battle at York reached Washington City more than two weeks later, on May 13. On first hearing, the news sounded very good indeed. Major General Henry Dearborn's report, dispatched from "*Head Quarters, York, Upper Canada*," conveyed the promise of victory even before the salutation. Yet as the grittier details of the events slowly emerged, the first significant American land victory of the war lost luster. The cost was great: Madison learned that Pike, a promising young general, would come home preserved in a hogshead of whiskey. Army casualties amounted to more than three hundred men killed or wounded. The enemy force and its commanding officer had escaped capture, and Armstrong scolded Major General Dearborn. "Battles are not gained," he wrote, "when an inferior and broken enemy is not destroyed."[31] No territory had actually been won, as the American forces abandoned York within days of taking it. Dearborn's promise of two captured ships went unfulfilled, since one vessel sailed out of York Harbor before the invasion, and the HMS *General Brock* was a charred hulk.

Another ill tiding was the report of widespread destruction of property, both private and public. After the explosion that killed General Pike, General Dearborn had come to shore to take command. Despite his presence and orders issued by General Pike before the attack, the invaders looted the town. Fired by liquor they found at York, sailors and soldiers alike plundered stores and homes, taking back to their ships tea, sugar, and whiskey. The rampage gained momentum, and on April 30 the looting gave way to the burning of public structures. The building that housed the provincial parliament, together with all the records it contained, was torched. Soon to follow were the Governor's residence, the courthouse, and the blockhouse.

Dearborn wrote to Armstrong, offering the justification that "a scalp was found in the executive and legislative chamber, suspended near the speaker's chair."[32] Many of the United States soldiers, sharing the common frontier fear of Indian massacre and outraged that the British would condone such "barbarous brutalities," set to burning Upper Canada's parliament buildings. But they hadn't stopped there, ransacking a library, emptying the treasury of twenty-five hundred pounds, and releasing prisoners from the jail.

The victory at York represented a notable military accomplishment, the first combined amphibious assault in the history of the U.S. Army and Navy. Still, a moment that should have been a cause for celebration was tainted by the burning and looting. Wise men could only worry at the risks of retribution: Might such egregious acts provoke an angry reaction at another time and in another place?

II.

June 1 . . . Aboard the USS Chesapeake

IN EARLY JUNE, THE FATE OF THE USS *CHESAPEAKE* WAS VERY MUCH IN DOUBT. With the latest dispatch from Boston in hand, Secretary of the Navy William Jones briefed Mr. Madison on June 6. "I am this moment told," Jones advised, "that a British Frigate came into Boston Bay—that Captain Laurence with the Chesapeake slipped his cables, went out, [and] brought her to action."[33]

Madison understood an ill portent when he encountered one: Word of a sea battle had reached shore, but the ship had not yet returned.

Insofar as was known, the action occurred on the first day of June. At high noon, the *Chesapeake* made sail from Boston Harbor under the command of James Lawrence, whom Madison had just elevated to the rank of captain. A well-liked fifteen-year navy veteran, "Captain Jim" had worked his way up through the ranks, rising from midshipman to lieutenant. He had skippered the schooner *Vixen*, the sloop *Wasp*, and the brig *Argus*, as well as the USS *Hornet*, which, under his command, had sunk the HMS *Peacock* in February. In celebration of that victory, he had been fêted in New York and, on arriving in Boston just ten days before as the newest officer on the captain's list, was given charge of his first frigate.

Spectators lined the decks of civilian yachts, schooners, and other boats in the bay at Boston, cheering as the *Chesapeake* headed for open water. The five consecutive American victories in ship-to-ship engagements had convinced the public, as well as Captain Lawrence, of the likely outcome. To those watching, Lawrence was an unmistakable presence, tall and broad as he strode the deck of the *Chesapeake*, "a very castle of a man."[34] The New Jersey–born Lawrence was fully uniformed in a blue coat with gold epaulets and a white vest. A black cocked hat rested atop dark, curly hair neatly braided into a queue, tied with a ribbon.

The *Chesapeake* had not been the thirty-two-year-old Lawrence's first choice of ship. He had written repeatedly in previous weeks to Secretary Jones, asking to remain aboard the *Hornet* or to be given the *Constitution*, also in Boston for refitting. Like every sailor in the U.S. Navy—a superstitious lot—Lawrence knew of the *Chesapeake*'s humiliating encounter with the *Leopard*. That bloody day left the ship with a reputation for bad luck that subsequent service did nothing to erase. She was notorious among navy men as a slow sailer, and on recent cruises to seek British merchantmen, she captured few prizes. But Lawrence was a man of duty. He was to proceed to the Gulf of St. Lawrence, where, Secretary Jones believed, "The enemy will not in all probability anticipate . . . our public ships of war [so] . . . the chance of captures upon an extensive scale is very flattering."[35] With the land war warming with the season, the goal was to interrupt the line of supply to the British troops along the Canadian border.

According to the sailors in Boston Harbor, however, Captain Lawrence weighed anchor for a very different reason.

By the last days of May, the freshly refitted *Chesapeake* had been ready to sail. Its crew had been remade as well. In the wardroom were four new lieutenants, two of them just promoted from the rank of midshipman. In barely ten days as its captain, Lawrence settled some lingering disputes about prize monies due from previous cruises, loaded in supplies, and added roughly one in four new crewmen. Some of the recruits were so new to the *Chesapeake* that their hammocks and bags were not yet stowed in quarters. With all the preparations, the *Chesapeake* had had just a single day's shakedown, and that within the confines of Boston Harbor. Captain Lawrence had yet to drill her gunners.

Lawrence's orders from Jones and the readiness of the *Chesapeake* were not the only considerations in his decision to sail; looming as large was the squadron of British warships that had blockaded the harbor for weeks. Although the USS *President* and *Congress* had used dense fog to escape unseen in early May, another period of prevailing fog and rain had just ended. Clear skies on the morning of June 1 revealed the HMS *Shannon* several miles from shore. Its captain, spotting the *Chesapeake* at anchor, ordered the *Shannon* hove to and one of its guns fired. Captain Lawrence himself climbed into the rigging with spyglass in hand to examine the silhouette of the solo British frigate; he ordered a gun fired in response to the *Shannon*'s. Having received the invitation, Captain James Lawrence reciprocated. Without further negotiation, the combatants stood out to sea, bound for a deep-water dueling ground.

Even as a light breeze filled the frigates' sails, a boat bound in the opposite direction carried a message from British Captain Philip Bowes Vere Broke. Entrusted to a discharged prisoner, Broke's letter offered a challenge; it was carefully couched, respectful and courteous, but pointed and provocative. "I request that you will do me the favour to meet the *Shannon* . . . ship to ship, to try the fortune of our respective flags." Broke described the armaments of his ship and the size of his crew; with some fifty guns each and over three hundred men apiece, the two ships were closely matched in almost every particular. The British captain promised to keep "all other ships beyond the power of interfering with us," and he appealed to Lawrence's sense of honor. "I entreat you, sir, not to imagine that I am urged by mere personal ambition for your acceding to this invitation: we have both noble motives."[36]

The challenge missed its intended recipient but arrived at the port of Marblehead some miles north of Boston and, the following day, was duly delivered to William Bainbridge, whom Navy Secretary Jones had rewarded with the command of the Charleston Navy Yard after his victory over the HMS *Java*. Commodore Bainbridge, in turn, forwarded the letter to the Navy Department. Certainly, it was the gauntlet thrown down, but Captain James Lawrence had needed no verbal persuasion to answer the call to fight. In fact, the battle was fought even before Bainbridge read Broke's words. Days later, when the letter reached the eyes of Madison and Secretary Jones, the outcome of events at sea was only to be guessed at.

BEFORE CLEARING THE DECKS FOR ACTION, Lawrence established the fairness of the fight, dispatching a boat to reconnoiter the nearby waters and confirm that the *Shannon* sailed alone. Then he ordered a large white flag run up the foremast that read "Sailors' Rights and Free Trade." This war, after all, was being fought in large measure on behalf of America's seamen.

The ship he was to meet was not one that inspired awe in the American commander, since the USS *Constitution* had outrun the *Shannon* the previous summer, with British cannonballs falling harmlessly into the Atlantic. Lawrence's orders were to proceed to the St. Lawrence. He understood that a ship-to-ship battle was to be neither sought nor avoided, and he also knew his navy could ill afford to lose one of its most precious vessels. But his confidence ran high. As he wrote to Secretary Jones that morning before setting sail, "An English frigate is now in sight from my deck; . . . I am in hopes to give a good account of her before night."[37]

Although Captain Lawrence was only just acquainting himself with his ship, his opposite number knew his own vessel intimately. Broke rose to his captaincy after the great naval battle at Trafalgar, and, in the intervening seven years, the *Shannon* had been his. During that span, few warships in the Royal Navy engaged in combat, as Britannia confidently ruled the waves and its sailors took her hegemony for granted. Yet, while other British captains rarely drilled their cannon crews, Captain Broke regarded gunnery as his particular hobby; he assembled a crew with care and drilled his men assiduously. From their skiffs and seaside cliffs, many New Englanders had watched in the preceding weeks as Broke drilled his men five days a week, with the forenoons and afternoons alternately devoted to small arms and the great guns. The exercises included shooting at floating beef casks mounted with four-foot-square pieces of canvas, three to four hundred yards distant. Each big gun had a sight, and each gun crew a quadrant for setting elevation. The ship's gun deck was incised with compass lines for precise aiming. According to one captain in the British North American fleet, "The 'Shannon's' men were better trained, and understood gunnery better, than any men I ever saw."[38]

A year earlier, Captain Broke might have shared the common belief that the "mere handful of ships" that was the U.S. Navy posed no threat to those that flew the Union Jack. But Broke recognized that the Royal Navy could no longer take its success for granted; the upstart Americans had earned new esteem. Embracing a common code of honor, the two captains sailed into battle, each confident his ship would prevail.

THE TWO GREAT SHIPS WERE WELL OUT FROM BOSTON HARBOR, under easy sail and luminous in the midday sun. On the tranquil sea, the *Shannon* led and the *Chesapeake* followed, but this was a pursuit in name only, as the captains had reached a tacit understanding that their ships would square off in a fair fight. At the stroke of four o'clock, with some seven miles separating the ships, the Americans fired a gun. Broke ordered the topsails reefed, slowing the *Shannon*'s progress.

By half past five, the *Chesapeake* was closing fast on the *Shannon*. Both ships steered into the wind. Moving barely fast enough to maintain steerageway, Broke watched as his opponent came down upon the *Shannon*'s starboard quarter at a speed of six or seven knots. For Broke, the moment was a nervous one, as Lawrence might have passed under the stern of the British frigate and opened fire, but the American captain chose not to attempt a raking maneuver. Again, the unspoken gentlemen's agreement honored, the two ships would fight on equal terms. This was to be an artillery duel at close range, with the ships sailing nearly side by side, separated by a mere fifty yards.

They were twenty miles east of Boston light when the *Chesapeake* ranged up on the *Shannon* at ten minutes before six o'clock. Lawrence barked, "Luff her!" and, even as she slowed, the ship entered firing range. Broke's standing order was for his crews to shoot when their guns bore on the second bow-port of the *Chesapeake.* Gun fourteen was first to fire, and a second report was heard from the British frigate before the gunners on the *Chesapeake* replied. Thereafter the air thundered, and, in the next six minutes, the ships exchanged three full broadsides. Dimly heard above the deafening booms of the cannon were the crackles and pops of small-arms fire from the muskets, rifles, and swivel guns.

The hellish cannon fire, aimed low, blasted into the decks and hulls of both ships. "Don't try to dismast her," Broke had told his men, "fire into her quarters; main-deck into the main-deck; quarter-deck into the quarter-deck and the ship is yours. Kill the men and the ship is yours."[39] On both ships, many men fell. A rifleman high in the rigging shot the helmsman of the *Chesapeake;* the man who took his place soon met the same fate. A round shot beheaded a lieutenant in an explosion of bone and brain. Two midshipmen were killed outright; another had his leg blown off. In the opening minutes of the action, the crew of the *Chesapeake* sustained at least a hundred casualties, a third of them dead where they fell. Aboard the *Shannon*, more than fifty men were dead or wounded.

Clearly visible from the tops, Captain Lawrence in his uniform made a pretty target, and a musket ball soon ripped into his lower leg. He could no longer stand without bracing himself, but he issued orders,

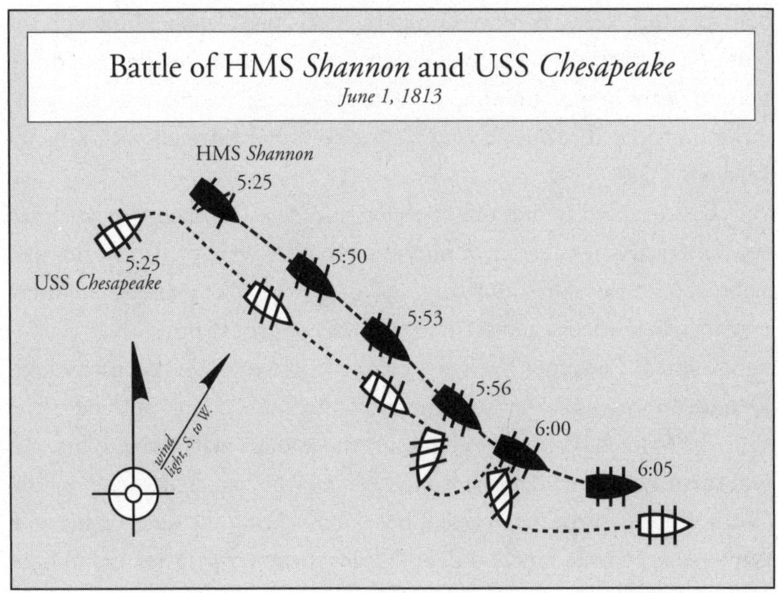

refusing to be carried below. As grape, canister, and solid shot sprayed her decks, the *Chesapeake*'s momentum carried her beyond where her guns would bear on the *Shannon*. Her headsails damaged, her sailing master dead and helm shattered by a cannon shot, she fell off her course and into the path of the *Shannon* as the British fusillade continued.

Captain Lawrence, blood pouring from his leg wound, called for a boarding party. But the British were quicker. As the ships collided, Captain Broke himself stepped from the railing of his ship onto the muzzle of a *Chesapeake* carronade then leapt onto the deck of the *Chesapeake*. Before Captain Lawrence could order a counterattack, another shot struck him, this one ripping into his groin. He staggered and fell, calling to his men, "Fire away, lads!"

Several American sailors met the British commander with force. The chaplain discharged his pistol but missed the British captain; Broke struck him in the face with his cutlass. Broke avoided the pike of a second assailant, but two other attackers drove him to the deck, one clubbing him with the butt of a musket, the other lopping off a section of Broke's skull, baring a portion of his brain. A marine came to Broke's aid and bayoneted the attackers; another Britisher bound the captain's head wound with a handkerchief.

Broke lapsed in and out of consciousness as his men overwhelmed the Americans in a matter of minutes. Another wave of British marines came aboard the American ship and drove the *Chesapeake*'s remaining crewmen belowdecks and secured the hatches over them.

Captain Lawrence had been carried below to the surgeon's cockpit. Despite his wounds, he still issued commands. "Don't surrender the ship," he ordered. When the ship's surgeon and his mate came to him, he sent them away to tend to the wounded men who had arrived before him. "I can wait my turn," he insisted, but upon hearing the quiet of his own ship's guns, he issued more orders. "Order them to fire faster and to fight the ship till she sinks."[40]

Even when another wounded officer was carried in, his head bleeding profusely from a saber wound, the news he brought didn't seem possible. "They have carried her," he reported. But Lawrence remained insistent. "*Don't give up the ship*," he ordered again and again. His exhortations were too late. A British lieutenant, his countrymen in full control of the deck, had already hauled down the *Chesapeake*'s colors and hoisted the British flag in its place.*

COMMODORE BAINBRIDGE PUT THE BEST POSSIBLE FACE on what he knew. Reporting to Navy Secretary Jones on June 2, he had written, "We have lost one frigate, but in losing her I am confi-

* Naval historians have long debated whether these well-remembered words were uttered by Lawrence or are merely patriotic apocrypha. However, the preponderance of contemporary reports, some of them from British officers reporting what they heard immediately after the sea battle, suggests that the words were among the orders Lawrence uttered as he lay belowdecks.

dent we have lost no reputation." That was all Mr. Madison knew when, a few days later, he drifted into the half-consciousness brought on by his malignant fever.

After the battle, the *Chesapeake* and the *Shannon* sailed in tandem for the British base at Halifax. The ships were, said one sailor, "charnel houses."[41] With total casualties numbering some 250 men, better than a third of those aboard the two ships had been killed or wounded. Twenty-six of Captain Broke's men were dead, and, by the time the ships docked in Nova Scotia on June 6, the death toll was almost sixty on the *Chesapeake*, including Captain Lawrence. He had lingered in the wardroom of his frigate for three days until infection in his gut finally killed him.

Only on June 23 did the brig *Henry* sail into Boston, carrying several officers and men from the *Chesapeake* to bear witness to the sea battle fought more than three weeks before. A full accounting of events from the pen of Lieutenant George Budd, dated June 15, was forwarded to Washington City, but rumors of the battle's outcome spread quickly.

"I remember at first the startling incredulity," reported one Treasury Department official of the arrival of the news. "I remember how the post offices were thronged for successive days, how collections of citizens . . . accost[ed] the mail to catch something by anticipation. At last, when the uncertainty was dispelled, I remember the public gloom."[42] The string of American naval victories was broken, and the shock at this turn of events was greatly compounded by the slaughter of so many American sailors on the *Chesapeake* in a mere fifteen minutes.

In some quarters doubts were quietly expressed at Captain Lawrence's strategy: *Should he have sought to fight? Could he have avoided a battle as the captains of the frigates* Congress *and* President *had done? Had his chivalrous avoidance of any tactical advantage damned his chances?*

Much louder voices extolled his heroism. Toasts were soon offered by the likes of Secretary of State James Monroe (in Washington) and the Society of the Cincinnati (in New York). Perhaps the most prophetic was spoken in Baltimore, where a celebrant intoned, "May the inspiring words of the illustrious Lawrence, '*Don't give up the Ship!*' be the eternal motto of America."

Lawrence's remains, though buried by the British in Halifax with high military honors as a brave and worthy opponent, were soon summoned home and reinterred on American soil in lower Manhattan. By then a just-completed brig on Lake Erie had been dubbed the USS *Lawrence* in his honor, and that ship, like many others in the U.S. Navy, would fly an ensign that bore his now famous phrase. A horrific loss begat both an American hero and a rallying cry for American forces.

III.

July 1813 . . . The President's Bedchamber

MR. MADISON'S FEVER CONFINED HIM TO HIS BED for one week and then another. The patient experienced chills and diarrhea, while his intense vomiting at times produced bile. As the President grew weaker, his doctors could do no more than name the cause. At his side, Dolley was deeply worried that her husband was dying.

Though out of office, Thomas Jefferson kept abreast of events, often exchanging letters with his enduring friends Madison and Monroe; with Madison ill, Monroe kept Jefferson posted. On the fifteenth day after the President took to his bed, Monroe wrote to Jefferson that James's "bilious fever . . . has perhaps never left him, even for an hour, and occasionally simptoms have been unfavorable." Word of the President's serious illness soon appeared in the pages of the *National Intelligencer* and other newspapers. With time, the story took on a life of its own, and, when it reached John Adams in Boston, the "afflicting Report" had it that Madison "lives by laudanum and could not hold out for four months."[43] Everyone worried.

Dolley believed her ailing husband was wracked not only by illness but by "the disappointments & vexations, heaped upon him by party spirit."[44] James's earlier hope that a peace might soon be negotiated grew dimmer due to vociferous opposition in Congress. "Nothing . . . has borne so hard," Dolley claimed, "as the conduct of the Senate in regard to Mr. Gallatin."

His old enemies in the Senate continued to fight Albert Gallatin's nomination as a Peace Commissioner. Swiss-born and -educated, Gallatin had seen in the American revolutionary experiment the realization of ideals he absorbed from the philosophy of Jean-Jacques Rousseau; at nineteen, he had emigrated to America believing that a democracy with fewer class restraints would produce a nobler society. But even after many years of service to his adopted land, Gallatin faced enemies who persisted in regarding him as a foreigner and sought to oust him from his post as Secretary of the Treasury, a move Madison had resisted. Another of Madison's choices for Peace Commissioner also faced harsh criticism, much of it from a freshman Federalist from New Hampshire, Congressman Daniel Webster. Webster made it his business to tarnish Jonathan Russell's reputation, alleging he had concealed diplomatic documents from the French in the lead-up to the war.

With the President sick in bed, there were no Drawing Rooms. During Madison's first term, even those who stubbornly opposed his leadership found themselves on Wednesday nights at the President's house talking to their opposition colleagues in civil tones, engaging in easy social discourse. Their hostess believed that the better you treated your guests, the better they would behave—and the formulation had worked.

But Daniel Webster was new in town. Armed with five resolutions from both legislative houses, he marched up the stone stairs at the President's house, demanding to deliver them personally to the man he and his friends gleefully dismissed as "the little occupant of the Great White House."[45] He found Mr. Madison still confined to his bed, at the depths of his sickness. The Virginian wore a nightcap on his head, despite the early summer heat; he was in no state to answer Webster's demands. On departing, Webster was undeterred, observing cruelly that Madison "will find *no relief* from my prescription." Writing to a merchant friend in New York, Webster promised with a certain glee that "the Senate . . . [is] not in a hurry to appoint any of Madison's Creatures."[46]

Only with the coming of July did James show signs of recovery. As Dolley advised Edward Coles on July 2, "For the last three days his fever has been so slight as to permit him to take bark every hour and with good effect."* She understood he was out of danger: "[N]ow I see he will get well."[47] On July 7, the *National Intelligencer* announced that the President was devoting his attentions once more to pressing public business. He would recover, it seemed, but his troubles—political, military, and otherwise—were far from over.

THE VISITORS WERE FATHER AND SON. Like Daniel Webster, they were New Englanders; unlike him, they received a warm welcome at the President's house.

Both bore the name Elbridge Gerry, and they hailed from Massachusetts. The older man was the new vice president. George Clinton of New York had died in office in April 1812, and the Republicans chose a man from the East in hopes he would win regional support for Madison's campaign that autumn. Gerry seemed a good choice, with an impressive political pedigree as a signer of the Declaration of Independence, a delegate to the Philadelphia Convention, and a former Governor of the Bay State. But not so many New England voters were won over. Aside from Vermont, New England voted as a block against the Madison-Gerry ticket. Even in Massachusetts, Gerry won only two of the state's twenty-two electors.

After taking his oath of office in Boston in March, Vice President Gerry had waited for the approach of the new session of Congress at the end of May to take the long coach ride from his home in Marblehead to

* When ingested, the salicin in white willow bark is metabolized as salicylic acid, a compound similar to aspirin.

Washington City. When he did, he was accompanied by his son, the youngest of the elderly Gerry's offspring. Young Elbridge delighted in the journey's many social intervals—and especially the young women he met—at New York, Philadelphia, Baltimore, and other cities. Now in the capital, the shy but sociable twenty-year-old was brought by his father to meet Mr. and Mrs. Madison.

Elbridge Gerry Jr. was ushered into Mr. Madison's presence on July 10. The President's convalescence was still precarious, and Gerry found him "reclining on a setee" wearing a loose nightshirt of flannel. Looking upon the Chief Magistrate, he thought the small man before him "pale and wan," but, as they talked, Madison soon impressed the young man as having "a very strong mind."[48]

Mrs. Madison was in attendance, too, and she paid young Gerry every kind attention. The two talked at length, and Gerry found his hostess "of elegant manners, accomplished and easy, and at the same time, possessed of that pleasing dignity which will always command the esteem and respect of every person." He was pleased that she treated him not like a political obligation, but "with friendly attention, and more like a son than a stranger."

By the time the Gerrys departed after nine o'clock (during the son's tête-à-tête with Mrs. Madison, his father conversed at length with Mr. Madison), the lad had been served refreshments and shown the house. He liked the tall windows and their "superb red silk velvet curtains." The price of the fabric—"4$ a yard"—impressed him, too.

He also examined the tall canvas of George Washington. The state portrait, said to be the work of Gilbert Stuart, held a place of honor in the dining room. In life, Washington's sheer physical presence had always impressed people; in death, from high on the wall, his portrait did the same. After looking up at the old hero that evening, Elbridge Gerry Jr. told his diary, "General Washington, is presented as large as life."[49]

He would return to the President's house several times in the coming days, but it would be yet another stranger, a man no one in the government wished to have set foot in Washington City, who would soon distract him and everyone else in town. As Gerry noted in his diary on July 15, "the city was alarmed by information, that the British were coming up the river with a large fleet, and were only 50 miles distant."[50]

BRITISH NAVAL FORCES HAD BEEN IN THE NEIGHBORHOOD FOR MONTHS. In February, two 74-gun ships of the line, the HMS *San Domingo* and the HMS *Dragon*, entered Chesapeake Bay. Fresh from a refitting, the USS *Constellation* nearly sailed into their path. A sailor in the tops spotted the enemy sails, and the American frigate escaped a confrontation only by sailing back up the bay to take shelter on the Elizabeth River above Norfolk. Three British battleships and two frigates in pursuit came almost within cannon range of the town. Although their desired prey was the *Constellation*, the British ships caused much of Norfolk's civilian population to flee in fear. In a matter of hours, the road to Richmond was jammed with wagons, livestock, and refugees.

In March, a British deserter warned that a Royal Navy squadron, including gunboats armed with incendiary devices called Congreve rockets, was sailing north from Chesapeake Bay. The destination, he claimed, was New York. The assault on Manhattan proved no more than a rumor or, perhaps, a deliberate falsehood, but the enemy strategy to harass and panic the populace and to worry Madison's government was surely working.

On April 1, Royal Navy ships penetrated deeper into the immense tidal waterway that defined eastern Virginia and Maryland. Making their way northward along the two-hundred-mile length of the Chesapeake, the squadron sailed past the mouths of the York, Rappahannock, Severn, and Potomac rivers, the largest arteries in a network of more than a hundred watercourses that flowed past the great cities of the region, including Annapolis, Baltimore, and Washington. On the first night a British cutting-out expedition captured six speedy Chesapeake schooners, as

British sailors on small boats slipped aboard the ships at anchor. A few days later, two American brigs and a half-dozen support vessels spotted several schooners approaching. The innocent-seeming vessels flew the U.S. ensign but to the utter surprise of the American seamen, one of the schooners raised the Union Jack. After a brief but fierce fight that left five Americans dead and ten others wounded, the British took possession of all the Yankee vessels.

Fear rose precipitously around the Chesapeake, an environment where fishing boats, river barges, pilot boats, and schooners were essential for commerce, communication, and food. In the month of May alone, at least seventy American merchantmen captured as prizes were sailed in flotillas to Halifax or Bermuda. Many oyster boats and other small craft captured by the British were unceremoniously burned or scuttled.

As news of the British sails sighted off Annapolis and then Baltimore spread, so did the name of the British commander behind the attacks. George Cockburn was new to the American war. His father's surname was that of an old Scots family (de Cockburn in Stuart times); his mother, the daughter of a prominent English churchman, had had her picture painted with her sons, including young George, by one of the leading portraitists of the day, Sir Joshua Reynolds. George had gone to sea at ten; by age fourteen, he was a junior officer and, at twenty, a lieutenant in the Royal Navy. A year later he was captaining a frigate and serving under England's great naval warrior Horatio Nelson, who remarked of his protégé that "his zeal, ability and courage . . . are conspicuous on every occasion."[51] Naval successes in the long war with Napoleon won Cockburn powerful friends in diplomatic and military circles. At a youthful forty, he had achieved the rank of Rear Admiral.

His ruthlessness won Cockburn a reputation among Americans as a "freebooter," a "fire-eater," and worse. At home, his surname was traditionally pronounced *CO-burn*, but, as he demonstrated a willingness to burn what was in his path, the British commander was soon disparaged in the American press as "*Cock-BURN*." He favored sneak attacks at night. An unabashed user of any *ruse de guerre* that came to mind, he also had the unusual distinction among his countrymen of holding a dual rank, as both a Royal Navy Admiral and a Colonel of the Royal Marines. For amphibious assaults he had a detachment of 180 seamen and 200 Royal Marines under his command. To many Americans, he became the most hated Briton, the man who brought the war to their soil.

As April ended, a flotilla of larger British ships plied the waters at the mouth of the Patapsco River and menaced Baltimore, while Cockburn, commanding a squadron of two frigates and a handful of smaller vessels, sailed north to the furthermost reaches of the Chesapeake and the mouth of the Elk River. There a landing party of marines overran the village at Frenchtown, Maryland, burning the 6-gun battery, the town's military stores, and a flour mill, along with five schooners in the harbor. On May 3, Cockburn attacked Havre de Grace on the Susquehanna River. A small force of the Maryland militia in the town had the temerity to resist Cockburn's assault, and he ordered an overwhelming display of power. A barrage of artillery shells terrified the townspeople, who "fled from their burning houses . . . carrying in their arms their children, clothing, &c."[52] Homes were put to the torch and pillaged, as was the Cecil Company foundry outside the town, the manufactory whence many of the cannon for the U.S. Navy had come.

Cockburn's depredations ashore did damage to vessels and towns but were also strategic strikes in a war where fear was an important weapon. As he had earlier written to his superior, his "excursions" were calculated to "set the whole country in a state of alarm."[53]

IN BALTIMORE, COCKBURN'S FAME led to the offer of a thousand-dollar reward "for the head of the notorious incendiary and infamous scoundrel, . . . or 500 dollars for each of his ears on delivery."[54] But in Washington City on July 15, there was no such bold talk, as the townspeople awoke to the news that Cockburn was coming their way.

The light frigate USS *Adams* was anchored in the Potomac for a refitting, and its commander dispatched a courier to William Jones. The messenger awakened the Navy Secretary at four A.M. with the news that a British squadron had entered the Potomac, and, further, given their knowing movements in the river's tricky waters, the enemy ships had good pilots aboard. Jones reported to Madison that he had his doubts that the British ships could make way further upstream, but, he promised the President, "I Shall set out this Instant for Fort Warburton in my sulkey."[55]

The news of the latest British assault in coastal Virginia was still fresh. Three days after a failed attempt to capture the *Constellation* at Norfolk, British forces had stormed the town of Hampton. Little more than an outport of Norfolk and of minor strategic value, the town and its seven guns were easily captured on the morning of June 25. But two companies of troops, rumored to be *chasseurs* (French prisoners from earlier battles who elected to join the British ranks in exchange for their freedom), went on a rampage through the countryside that lasted nine days.

Stories circulated in Washington City of outrages beyond "burglarious attacks" on ships and military stores. One correspondent had it that "Mrs. Turnbull was pursued up to her waist in the water, and dragged on shore by ten or twelve of these ruffians, who satiated their desires upon her, after pulling off her clothes, stockings, shoes, &c.").[56] A sick man was murdered in his bed, it was said; medicines from apothecaries were thrown into the streets. The pulpit and communion table at Hampton's Episcopal church were desecrated. The booty taken from homes included silver, clothing, and even slaves for resale in the Indies. "The town of Hampton, and the surrounding country," recorded one Congressman, "were given-up to the indiscriminate plunder of a licentious soldiery."[57] Writing to a sister a safe distance away in New Jersey, the Madisons' friend Mrs. Smith confessed, "The affair of Hampton . . . inspires us with a terror we should not otherwise have felt."[58]

At the President's house, the threat of a British invasion had an uncomfortably familiar sound. Before Madison's illness, an informant advised him that a plot was afoot "to seize your person & papers, & convey you to the [British] fleet."[59] The fame of Mrs. Madison's Wednesday nights made her a target, too, and she confided to her cousin Edward Coles, "[T]he Admiral (of Havre-de Grace memory) [has] sent me notis that he would make his bow at my Drawing room *soon*." Her fear was such that Mrs. Madison, "tho *a Quaker*," felt obliged to "keep the old Tunesian Sabre within [her] reach."[60]

With the news from the *Adams* of the British approach, the streets of Washington City echoed with the reports of alarm guns and the ringing of bells. The militia mustered quickly, and, Elbridge Gerry Jr. reported, "in a few hours 2 or 3000 troops were on their march to the fort, 14 miles distant."[61] Secretary of War of John Armstrong marched to Fort Warburton, too, together with two regiments of regulars. Yet another member of the cabinet, Secretary of State James Monroe, scouted the enemy himself, as he, together with a company of "gentlemen volunteers," ventured to Cedar Point sixty miles south. Colonel Monroe counted more than a dozen ships and found the British had landed a force of several hundred men at Blakiston Island. They were digging wells, probably in anticipation of establishing a base there.

Breastworks overlooking the Potomac were thrown up at Alexandria, Georgetown, and Washington. The militia drilled in front of the president's house. Civilians in the capital were enlisted to patrol the city on both horse and foot, and the youthful Mr. Gerry signed on. "Our duty was to hail every person," Gerry reported, "and if he could not give our countersign, or if he was not known to us, we must put him into the watch house until morn." Gerry encountered drunks and dogs but no invaders before retreating to his lodgings, where he and his fellow volunteers "drank port wine and ate cake until day light."[62] After an initial ripple of fear, as one well-informed citizen explained, the attitude of most of the inhabitants of Washington City: "It is generally believed impossible for the English to reach the city, not so much from our force at Warburton, tho' that is very large, as from the natural impediments; the river being very difficult of navigation. . . . We one and all resist useless anxiety and alarm."[63]

The British remained in the Potomac for a week. An American gunboat, the *Asp*, was captured, but even Admiral Cockburn turned back at Kettle Bottom Shoals. He had visited American waters before when, in 1803, he landed the new British Minister Plenipotentiary in Virginia. He understood the waters of the Chesapeake were tricky, with many uncharted sandbars that threatened the keels of his deep-draft ships. Even frigates had to be lightened to navigate the rivers. When he turned back, he had come no closer than within fifty miles of Washington. In the end, the well-informed Sarah Gales Seaton, whose husband and brother ran the *National Intelligencer*, dismissed the scare as a "tempestuous season of disturbance."[64] Like most others in the city, Mrs. Seaton chose to take comfort in the assurances of Secretary of War John Armstrong. As he had told the President upon the initial sighting of the British, "Neither the force nor the progress of the enemy indicates a serious attack on this place."[65]

After he sailed out of the Potomac that July, Cockburn's forces occupied a temporary base at Kent Island near Annapolis. The warm months passed and he ordered no assault on any of the major cities in the region; still, his crews remained busy, taking soundings wherever they went. Cockburn's sailors found that in some shallows the depth was but six feet, and, in countless places, they placed buoys to demarcate channels and obstructions. They mapped Watts, Tangier, and Smith islands, perhaps with an eye to establishing other island bases. The surveys of the winding rivers and shore led to the drafting of detailed charts, as the British came to know the undulating sands of the Chesapeake bottom as well as or better than the American commanders. If he was going to be stationed in the district, Admiral Cockburn wanted to base his movements on hard knowledge.

BY EARLY AUGUST MR. MADISON FELT WELL ENOUGH TO TRAVEL, though some said he had to be carried to his coach. In a private letter, he wrote of the "severe illness, from which I am now barely eno' recovered for a journey to the mountains prescribed by my physicians as indispensable."[66] Yet as their carriage delivered Mr. and Mrs. Madison to Montpelier in central Virginia, the disquieting presence of Rear Admiral Cockburn remained with them. With a new sense of fear in the air, the whereabouts of the President were kept secret for the first time since Madison took office.[67]

IV.
August and September 1813 . . . Montpelier

THE FOUR-DAY JOURNEY TO MONTPELIER PROVED EXHAUSTING. "The roads are very bad," President Madison wrote to James Monroe. "I bear the journey as well as I expected, tho' my influenza is no better."[68] Upon reaching his home, farmer Madison found his fields parched. "We are still without rain, and the prospect in our Corn fields [is] becoming desperate."[69]

With Congress out of session, Mr. Madison had the leisure to worry many things as he regarded the expanse of acres around his mansion. Not the least of them was the continued lack of military progress on the northern front. Daily letters from members of his cabinet kept him abreast of events along the border. General Armstrong had recently gone to the lakes himself to inspect the American forces and help shape military plans; as he advised Mr. Madison, his desire was "to give to the Campaign, a new & increased activity."[70] But the Canadian theater was immense, reaching from Fort Detroit in the Michigan Territory to Montreal some six hundred miles eastward. The contested area consisted of no fewer than four distinct zones, each defined by a body of water. In the east was Lake Champlain; moving westward was the St.

Lawrence River; Lake Ontario; and then Lake Erie. Armstrong made his way to a point near the center, the American base at Sackets Harbor, New York, on the eastern shore of Lake Ontario. There he watched the comings and goings of the region's largest fleet under the command of Isaac Chauncey.

The great lake seemed to have become the site of an immense waterborne chess match, as the navies on Ontario checked each other from a distance to avoid the risk of a fight. Navy Secretary Jones reported to Madison in his letter of August 23, "Chauncey still by every possible effort endeavored to bring the enemy to action. . . . The Enemy nevertheless sedulously avoided Battle." The British at the opposite end of the lake, reported Armstrong, visited "the neighborhood of the American installation of Fort George" near Niagara but did not invade.[71] It appeared to Armstrong that the British commander wished to "spin out the Campaign without either giving or receiving blows of decided character."[72] On the other side, Commodore Isaac Chauncey exhibited his own reluctance—despite plans to do so, he did not attack Kingston—and the Americans prepared no strategy to move downstream to attack the well-defended cities of Montreal and Quebec. Neither side had the advantage on Lake Ontario, and, despite his promise to the contrary, Secretary of War John Armstrong exhibited no tendency to boldness.

Back at Montpelier, Madison understood perfectly that Lake Ontario and Lake Erie were crucial. With few good roads amid the dense wilderness, the entire region could be controlled if command of the waters was to be gained. When word arrived on September 8 from Lake Champlain that the 11-gun USS *Eagle* and its sister ship the USS *Growler* had been captured, Madison acknowledged in a note to Armstrong that it was a painful setback ("The loss of our command of Lake Champlain, at so critical a moment, is deeply to be regretted).[73] With that, American military hopes in the region shifted to Lake Erie. There, at least, an opportunity for real military progress seemed at hand as a major confrontation was in the making.

As he gained strength and rode out daily to inspect his plantation acres, President Madison still could not advance the war; his lot was to wait for news. As a householder, though, Citizen Madison tended to matters long left in abeyance by his obligations in Washington City. On September 10, he updated his fire insurance certificate, revaluating his holdings in Orange County to the princely sum of fifteen thousand dollars. On that very day, some five hundred miles away, a dramatic battle was waged on the waters of Lake Erie.

WHEN THE WAR BEGAN, the U.S. Navy had no presence on Lake Erie. The only American military craft on the entire lake was an army supply vessel, the *John Adams*, which the British captured when Fort Detroit surrendered. On the opposite shore of the big lake, the well-established British shipyard at Amherstburg produced a potent flotilla of vessels. Even before the war declaration, the 18-gun HMS *Queen Charlotte*, the *General Hunter* (10), and the schooner *Lady Prevost* (12) had been launched. As the snows of 1813 melted, yet another ship, this one named in honor of the victory over William Hull's forces, was under construction. With nineteen guns and displacing 490 tons, the HMS *Detroit* would be the biggest ship on Lake Erie.

Isaac Chauncey, commander of all U.S. Navy forces on the Great Lakes, had been ordered by Navy Secretary Jones to embark on a building campaign and, at Sackets Harbor on Lake Ontario, the sound of shipwrights' hammers and saws carried across the bay that spring as the keels for a large sloop and a dispatch schooner were laid. Several converted lake schooners were armed and strengthened. To the west on Lake Erie, Master Commandant Oliver Hazard Perry arrived with the spring thaw to take charge at the newly established naval shipyard at Presque Isle Harbor, near Erie, Pennsylvania. He, too, was tasked with a building campaign. "Being so far separated from you," his superior, Commodore Chauncey, advised Perry, "I must necessarily leave much to your own judgment and discretion."[74]

That was just as Perry wished it.

He arrived from Newport, Rhode Island. Though he had previously commanded a flotilla of gunboats in coastal waters, he pined for the command of a big frigate. The order to Presque Isle, at the express request of Commodore Chauncey, gave him a chance to prove himself in war. It wasn't the captaincy of a frigate but an important and twofold responsibility to build a fleet of ships and then to command it in battle. At twenty-seven, newly promoted to Master Commandant, Perry brought shipyard experience from his native Rhode Island, the regard of his peers as an excellent sailor, and a reputation for "calm collectedness & decisive character."[75]

He arrived with one hundred men (some of them sailors, others ship's carpenters) and orders to build two 20-gun brigs. The construction of four gunboats was already under way (they would be launched as the USS *Ariel*, *Scorpion*, *Tigress*, and *Porcupine*), and within days of Perry's March 26 arrival, the frames of the brigs were rising in the Presque Isle shipyard. He managed the work closely, summoning supplies, sailmakers and other workmen, anchors, canvas, ammunition, cordage, and, of course, cannon. By the end of July, the new vessels were rigged and their guns mounted, but neither was yet on the body of the lake.

Between Presque Isle Bay and the main waters of Lake Erie lay a sandbar at a depth of less than six feet. The largest and proudest of Perry's ten-ship flotilla was the new 20-gun brig the USS *Lawrence*, named for Captain James Lawrence, the man so recently killed in the battle between the *Chesapeake* and the *Shannon*. But laden with guns and supplies, the *Lawrence*, along with its sister ship the USS *Niagara*, drew almost nine feet. To float the much smaller *Tigress*, *Porcupine*, *Scorpion*, and *Ariel* over the bar meant removing their guns, which were placed on timbers on the beach. Getting the *Lawrence* and the *Niagara* across would require more extreme measures.

New York shipbuilder Noah Brown, who had managed the construction of both brigs, devised a plan. Pairs of scows would be floated on either side and fastened by ropes to the ship to be raised. When a controlled volume of water was permitted to flow into these boats, which were also called "camels," the flat-bottomed vessels would rest lower in the water. Then the ends of large wooden beams, inserted through ports in the brig to be raised, could be positioned across the camels and rested on blocking that distributed the weight. When water was pumped out, the buoyancy of the camels would raise the ship clear of the sandbar.

That was the plan, but the practical work of crossing the bar would require many hours, and if Perry and his men were to attempt it with the Royal Navy in sight, the disarmed American ships would be defenseless targets. He could do little but wait for the right moment.

To his surprise, on the last of July no British sails could be seen off Presque Isle Harbor for the first time in weeks. Perry waited, wondering whether his opposite number was looking to trick him into trying to cross the sandbar. When no enemy ships were visible the next day, Perry ordered the camel crew to work.

The process proved even more arduous than expected, as the camels did not raise the keel of the *Lawrence* enough to clear the bar on the first try; the entire process had to be repeated. On the second attempt, the hull still got stuck in the sand, and the masts and yards were dismantled and removed to lighten the ship further. Finally, after more than forty hours of nonstop labor, the *Lawrence* slipped into Lake Erie on the morning of August 3. It was midnight before her armament was reinstalled. The other brig, the *Niagara*, remained in Presque Isle Bay.

When the cry "Sail ho!" was heard the following morning, the *Niagara* was in the midst of the process, its hull afloat over the sandbar, precarious and exposed. But a brief exchange of fire made it clear that the *Lawrence*, now outside the bar, was fully armed. Its cannon, along with the shore batteries, persuaded the British that this was not the moment to fight, and the Royal Navy squadron sailed away.

The intense labor of those hours with the camels launched an American fleet that was a match for the British. Still, as Perry complained to Navy Secretary Jones (and as the latter reported to President Madison on

August 11), the ships were "neither well officered or manned."[76] With his new ships ready for open water, Perry needed more sailors for the day when the two navies met in full combat.

Out on the American frontier, finding trained, able-bodied seamen was difficult. Roughly three in five of the men aboard Perry's flotilla were U.S. Navy regulars, but that was only after an earlier complaint to Chauncey that his crews were inferior (Perry described his men as "a Motley set, blacks, Soldiers and boys").[77] Chauncey had dispatched reinforcements, and the newly promoted Master Commandant Jesse Duncan Elliott had arrived; Perry promptly gave him command of the *Niagara*. Accompanying Elliott were eighty-nine men and several officers. When Perry confided his manning difficulties to Brigadier General William Henry Harrison, commander of the North-Western Army, Harrison provided more than one hundred men, many of them Kentucky sharpshooters, along with all the seamen to be found in Harrison's army. Yet Perry still worried that the crews on his vessels would be outnumbered.

LIKE HIS COMMANDER IN CHIEF, OLIVER HAZARD PERRY had been sick. The son of a sea captain and a veteran of the Barbary Wars, Captain Perry suffered periodic bouts that summer of a "severe Indisposition which confined me to my Birth." Many in Perry's command also experienced a recurrent bilious fever, "occasioned, it is supposed," wrote Perry, "by the water."[78] With more than a hundred of his men ill, on September 9 he ordered that all drinking water be boiled.[79]

For weeks, both Perry and his opponent, Lieutenant Robert Barclay RN, each tried to scout the other man's fleet, reconnoitering his ships, guns, and manning. On September 1, Perry tacked back and forth off Amherstburg and saw that the enemy fleet consisted of six vessels, including the newly launched HMS *Detroit*. Still, Perry held the advantage, as there were nine ships under his command. Counting the cannon and carronade was harder, but it appeared that, although the British had more guns (63 to 54), there, too, the Americans held the edge, as they could deliver a significantly greater weight of metal with their more numerous and larger-caliber carronades. Many were 32-pounders, of which the British had none.

The one-armed Barclay, who had served with Lord Nelson at Trafalgar, chose not to engage that day off Amherstburg. But both commanders understood that, despite the American advantage in both tonnage and firepower, a fight was inevitable. Effectively blockaded by the American force, the inhabitants of Amherstburg were growing desperate for food and supplies. What was available had to meet the needs of not only the townspeople and the combined British and Canadian military forces, but also an encampment of some ten thousand Indians. With the season about to change and a long Canadian winter ahead, the supply of flour, cattle, and other goods was rapidly diminishing.

Perry and Harrison devised a plan for an amphibious attack on Amherstburg. Perry established a new home base that he and Harrison scouted together, Put-in-Bay, a cove near the mouth of the Detroit River. In the lee of South Bass Island, the American flotilla anchored within twenty yards of shore. Perry's gun crews exercised their long guns regularly, improving their marksmanship, while the soldiers and marines practiced with their flintlocks and rifles. Harrison's troops began to assemble nearby.

In the early days of September, Perry met often with his officers, establishing strategy. He devised a line of battle for his ships to take best advantage of their firepower. In his plan of attack, he designated which U.S. Navy vessel would match up with which British brig or schooner. He issued instructions as to when to fire ("engage your designated adversary, in close action, at half cable's length."[80] Central to the plan of battle were the matchups between the two U.S. Navy brigs, the *Lawrence* and the *Niagara*, and the HMS *Detroit* and *Queen Charlotte*. It was a carefully assembled plan, as Perry tried to leave little to chance.

He also produced a flag, freshly sewn and never before flown. This was to be his fighting flag; when it was hoisted on the flagship *Lawrence*, the officers in his flotilla were to understand that the battle was to commence. The flag bore James Lawrence's words "Don't Give Up the Ship."

ON SEPTEMBER 10, EVEN BEFORE THE SUN'S RAYS reflected off the ripples of a calm Lake Erie, a voice from the maintop of Perry's flagship called down, "Sail ho!" Perry was summoned from his quarters and, by seven o'clock, the American squadron weighed anchor. In sight were the 19-gun HMS *Detroit* and the *Queen Charlotte* (17); the brig *General Hunter* (10); the schooners *Lady Prevost* (13) and *Chippewa* (3); and the sloop *Little Belt* (3).

Barclay had taken the initiative, sailing the previous day from Amherstburg for Put-in-Bay. As the day dawned, the British commander also found he held the weather gauge. To confront the British, the Americans were forced to sail directly into a southwesterly breeze of about seven knots. The captains of the British vessels, with the wind at their backs, could control the distance at which their ships engaged the enemy; if they could stand beyond reach of the short-range American carronades, their long guns could pound the American ships. But Perry was eager for battle and ordered sails set.

Until midmorning the American ships beat back and forth into the wind; despite their tacking, they made little headway. Then the wind died off. When it rose again in the next hour, the breeze was gentler—and from another direction. With the wind blowing from the southeast, the weather gauge shifted to the Americans.

As the ships grew closer, the crews prepared for battle. The guns were readied, cartridges packed, and powder pouches filled. Boarding weapons were positioned for use in hand-to-hand combat, whether against enemy attackers or to carry aboard an opposing ship. With all else in readiness, Perry brought forth the banner in honor of Captain Lawrence. Standing atop a carronade carriage, he addressed his crew. "My brave lads," he exhorted, "this flag contains the last words of the brave Captain

Lawrence. Shall I hoist it?" They gave three cheers as it was raised in honor of Lawrence, a man Perry had called his friend.[81]

The decks were sanded to assure footing and to absorb the blood that would be spilled. A ration of grog was given to each man, along with the midday meal. As the flotillas drew gradually closer, the crews manned their guns. Perry visited each station on his flagship, offering encouraging words.

According to one seaman, "There being only a light wind, we neared the enemy very slowly. . . . [W]e stood in awful impatience—not a word was spoken—not a sound heard, except now and then an order to trim a sail. . . . [T]he dart of death hung as if it were trembling by a single hair, and no one knew on whose head it would fall."[82] At eleven forty-five, the Americans heard a few bars of "Rule, Britannia" wafting across the water from the HMS *Detroit.* A bugle blast followed, then the report of the first gun. This ranging shot fell short, but five minutes later the first cannonball to strike the *Lawrence* sent splinters flying in all directions.

With the same determination Lawrence had shown aboard the *Chesapeake*, Perry's fleet sailed into enemy fire, the British long guns inflicting greater damage than could the Americans' outdistanced carronades. Yet no masts nor spars crashed to the American deck and, by twelve fifteen, the *Lawrence* sailed within carronade range. Perry ordered the sails of the *Lawrence* luffed. His 32-pounders commenced fire. The *Niagara* and several of the boats in Perry's line had fallen well back so that the *Lawrence* would be the focus of the battle.

With the *Detroit* and the *Lawrence* separated by barely three hundred yards, no ballistic calculations were necessary. With the cannon barrels leveled, the gun crews fired broadside after broadside. The same seaman who wondered where the "dart of death" would fall described the deck of the *Lawrence* as "one continued gore of blood and carnage—the dead and dying were strewed in every direction over it for it was impossible to take the wounded below as fast as they fell."[83] Those who did make it belowdecks to the care of the single surgeon on board found him so overwhelmed that he could do little as the battle raged. He stanched the worst of the bleeding by ligature or tourniquet and "in some instances division was made of a small portion of flesh by which a dangling limb that annoyed the patient was hanging to the body."[84] Of the hundred-odd men aboard that morning, twenty were soon dead and sixty wounded. There were compound fractures, head wounds, and a marine private took a wood splinter in the shoulder that penetrated the length of his trunk, all the way to his hip. Even the wardroom, where the surgeon worked, was far from safe, as cannonballs periodically blasted through the bulkhead, some of them further wounding the wounded.

Perry could see his ship was adrift, her sails tattered and her braces and bowlines shot away. One by one the guns on the *Lawrence* went out of commission; finally, the last working gun that could be aimed at the enemy fell quiet. But the *Niagara*, which Captain Elliott had doggedly kept to its place in the line, now sailed up to the windward of the *Lawrence.* Miraculously, to Perry's eyes, it appeared little damaged by the battle. Despite the sentiment of Lawrence's that flew on the pennant above him, Perry ordered that a small boat be lowered to the water. He climbed aboard the cutter and four unwounded sailors rowed him to the *Niagara.* He gave up his ship—the surviving officer in command soon lowered the colors of the *Lawrence*—but Perry still planned to win the battle.

Perry ordered the heading of the *Niagara* set for the middle of the British line. The British attempted to respond but the HMS *Detroit*, with rigging almost as riddled by shot as that of the *Lawrence*, collided with the *Queen Charlotte.* As the *Niagara* penetrated the British line, the gunports on both starboard and larboard flashed, delivering a double broadside. The battle continued for some minutes, but its outcome was all but decided at that moment.

When the guns were finally silenced after three hours of battle—the *Queen Charlotte* raised a white flag since the colors on the *Detroit* were nailed to her mast—Captain Perry quickly penciled a dispatch to Navy

Secretary Jones. He noted the time (four o'clock) and the ship on which it was written (the *Niagara*). The note was short and to the point: "It has pleased the Almighty to give to the arms of the United States a signal victory over their enemies on this Lake—The British squadron consisting of two Ships, two Brigs one Schooner & one Sloop have this moment surrendered to the force under my command, after a Sharp conflict."[85]

On September 23, a speeding messenger brought James Madison word from Secretary Jones of the "signal victory" on Lake Erie. The news was cause for celebration not only at Montpelier; as the gratified Jones told Perry, word of the victory met with "every demonstration of joy and admiration . . . as far and as fast as the roar of cannon and splendour of illumination could travel."[86]

Still, it was another note from Captain Perry, one containing a particularly artful turn of phrase, that would attach itself to the public memory of the decisive battle on Lake Erie. Even before writing to Jones, Perry had reused an envelope that came to hand to scrawl a report to General Harrison, who awaited word of the battle's outcome less than ten miles from the scene. In a moment of inspiration, standing on a deck saturated with blood from the battle just ended, Perry wrote in pencil, using his navy cap as a writing surface.

"*We have met the enemy*," he exulted, "*and they are ours*."[87]

V.

Autumn 1813 . . . Washington City

THE WEEKS AT MONTPELIER MADE HIM WELL. Upon Madison's return to the capital in late October, Comptroller Richard Rush told a political ally, "The little president is back, and as game as ever."

During his first week back in town, Congress shut its doors, since anyone interested in horseflesh would be attending the annual Washington race meeting—and that was almost everyone. At the Jockey Club Mr. Madison met up with other gentlemen of the turf, such as old friends Dr. Thornton (designer of the Capitol, a Commissioner of the Federal City, and a man with whom the President had once invested in a race-horse, *Wild Medley*) and the wealthy Mr. Tayloe, who owned a stable of coursers as well as the eccentric, six-sided mansion around the corner from the President's house. These men shared an avid interest in horseflesh and together they "saw a Virginia steed carry the day."[88]

In the days before and after his return, the daily flow of letters and reports brought mixed tidings from the northern front. Oliver Hazard Perry, whom Mr. Madison had promptly promoted from Master Commandant to *Captain* Perry, had written from Detroit on October 7: "I have the honor to inform you, that I . . . had the pleasure of witnessing the capture of the Brittish Army, and the defeat of their Indians, by the Army under Majr. Genl. Harrison."[89] A more detailed description of events arrived in the days that followed from William Henry Harrison himself.

Guarded by Perry's gunboats, Harrison's troops had been ferried to the Canadian shore. The British forces were already in retreat along the river Thames, since, with Lake Erie under American control, the British positions at Detroit and Malden became untenable. The American troops, most of them Kentuckian volunteers and riflemen, overtook the fleeing British after a daring charge by mounted riflemen. The British abruptly surrendered, giving the Americans the victory at the Battle of the Thames. Another rumor that arrived in the days after the battle had it that the charismatic Tecumseh, perhaps the enemy's most important Indian ally, had been killed in the action. That wasn't yet certain but, with the Detroit frontier in American hands, Madison could almost bring himself to believe that the smashing dual victories of Perry and Harrison signaled the end of the war in the Upper Lakes.

Yet he also understood that Harrison had done little more than regain what General Hull lost a year earlier, and the news from Lake Ontario was inconclusive. Commodore Chauncey, seemingly on the verge of routing the British fleet in the wicked winds of a gale near York, had been outsailed; the British flotilla, despite a badly damaged flagship, escaped to its anchorage at the east end of the lake. Another disappointment occurred well downstream in the waters of the St. Lawrence River, where a plan devised by Secretary Armstrong had failed. Instead of American troops marching victorious into Montreal as the Secretary of War had promised, they were driven from the field at the Battle of Chrysler's Farm, disordered and divided, many miles from their ultimate objective. They had abandoned Canadian territory altogether and set up winter camp back across the American border.

On the good-news side of the ledger, Madison heard early words of praise about a onetime senator turned military man, Major General Andrew Jackson. An experienced Indian fighter, Jackson had taken charge of the American forces in Creek country and beat a band of Red Stick Creeks near Talladega in the Mississippi Territory in November. Yet again, though, the reports were not entirely positive. Certainly, Talladega counted as a measurable victory—Indian casualties far outnumbered American losses—but the bulk of the enemy escaped.

One consolation was that military successes, such as they were, were proving dispiriting to the Federalist opposition. Maryland newspaperman and Federalist Alexander Hanson complained to a Massachusetts confederate, "Unless the British can gather sense and courage to strike some severe blows, the war by its own generative power will create the means for its support [and] . . . the administration will find more friends than enemies in this state by a great deal."[90] Madison employed the military momentum to pass an embargo on exports, aimed in particular at those New Englanders who were selling woolen and cotton goods, as well as rum, to the enemy. The measure sailed through Congress in December in a mere eight days.

More than a year of war had brought a mix of good news and bad as reliably as the tides; in his opening address to the new session of Congress the President listed the victories and acknowledged the hardships. But his conclusion was positive, whatever his private doubts. "[T]he war," he told the assembled Congressmen and Senators, "with its vicissitudes, is illustrating the capacity and the destiny of the United States to be a great, a flourishing, and a powerful nation."[91]

THE DOOR TO A NEGOTIATED PEACE SEEMED FIRMLY CLOSED as 1813 neared its end. The British cabinet rejected the tsar's offer to mediate, and, anyway, an obstreperous Congress had voted down two of Madison's nominees for peace negotiators. Then, in the wan light of winter, a thin wedge of sunlight pierced the darkness of the cabinet room.

On December 30, a letter addressed to Secretary of State James Monroe arrived at Annapolis on a British ship flying a flag of truce. The sender of the letter, dated November 4, was Robert Stewart, Viscount Castlereagh, the British Foreign Secretary. Its timing suggested—even if Castlereagh's text did not acknowledge it—that the communication was drafted after word of the dual American victories on the Upper Lakes reached Westminster.

The British minister offered "to enter upon a direct negotiation for the restoration of peace between the two States."[92] There were no broad promises; in fact, Castlereagh made reference to "established maxims of . . . the maritime rights of the British empire." For both sides, then, the crux remained the disagreement about British conduct on the seas.

Mr. Madison could hardly expect that Castlereagh's vague offering alone could make the war go away. No truce was proposed, and in no way could the document be read as a capitulation by the British. Yet a door seemed suddenly to have swung open to a negotiation that could, in Castlereagh's words, obtain a "conciliatory adjustment of the differences subsisting between the two States." At least the British were now willing to talk.

With alacrity, Madison seized the moment. In the new year he sent Congress a list of Peace Commissioners. This time the name that attracted everyone's attention was that of Henry Clay, the popular and powerful Speaker of the House. Madison hoped Clay's presence might be an antidote to the poisonous atmosphere that had prevailed, but the President also renominated the members of the team already abroad, including Albert Gallatin, James Bayard, and John Quincy Adams. Clay and the fifth Peace Commissioner, Jonathan Russell, were soon aboard the USS *John Adams*, bound for Europe, with a passport for safe passage signed by Royal Navy Admiral George Cockburn.

Madison had responded in kind to the British proposal, which the *National Intelligencer* characterized as "rather of a pacific character."[93] Dolley, whose son Payne had left for Europe months earlier as Mr. Gallatin's secretary, worried for her child and about the process of the negotiations, which she described as "our *particular occupation* in this Great City."[94] An ocean away from the negotiations, those in Washington City could do little but hope that the parties might, as Castlereagh suggested, find a means to "avoid an unnecessary continuance of the calamities of war."[95]

BOOK II

The Guns of August 1814

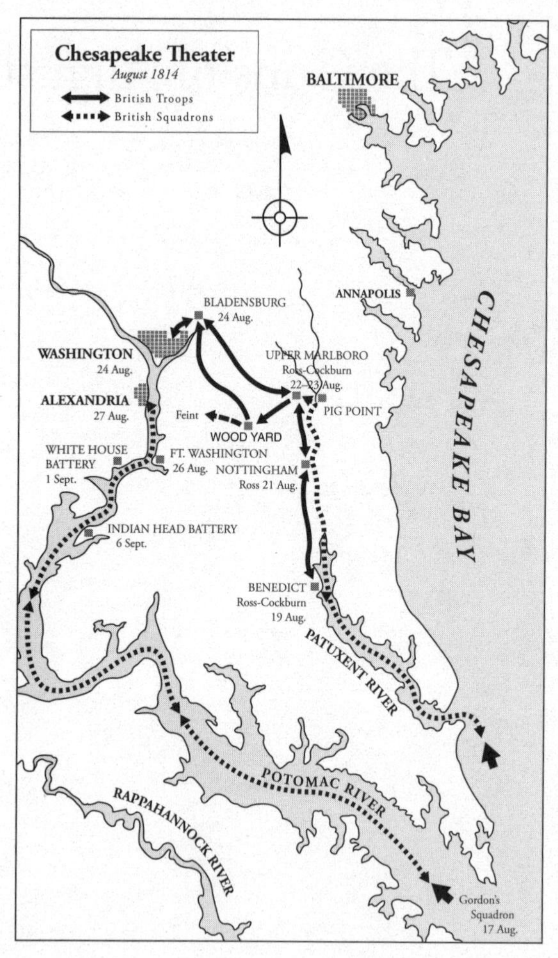
Chesapeake Theater
August 1814
British Troops
British Squadrons
BALTIMORE
ANNAPOLIS
CHESAPEAKE BAY
BLADENSBURG
24 Aug.
WASHINGTON
24 Aug.
UPPER MARLBORO
Ross-Cockburn
22–23 Aug.
ALEXANDRIA
27 Aug.
PIG POINT
Feint
WOOD YARD
WHITE HOUSE
BATTERY
1 Sept.
FT. WASHINGTON
26 Aug.
NOTTINGHAM
Ross 21 Aug.
INDIAN HEAD BATTERY
6 Sept.
BENEDICT
Ross-Cockburn
19 Aug.
PATUXENT RIVER
POTOMAC RIVER
RAPPAHANNOCK RIVER
Gordon's
Squadron
17 Aug.

CHAPTER 3

A Meeting at the President's House

I know not what it is to prevent Washington City, The Treasury office, the Presidents Pallace and the proud Capitol, from becoming the Head Quarters of British Principles.
—John Adams, writing to Richard Rush, January 7, 1814

1.

June 1814 . . . Mr. Madison's Sitting Room . . . The President's House

THE PRESIDENT'S HOUSE WAS IN SUMMER DRESS. The social season had ended in April, and, with the arrival of warm weather, straw matting was rolled out to cover the floors. With slipcovers protecting the furniture from dirt and perspiration stains, the advent of hot tidewater days reminded Mr. Madison how he longed to be at home, enjoying the cooler clime of central Virginia. But here he was, at work in his sitting room in the President's house, a letter from Peace Commissioners Albert Gallatin and James Bayard in hand. The letter changed everything. Europe was no longer at war.

That Napoleon's fortunes were falling was not news. Word of his military reverses had been dribbling in for months. A signal moment was the immense battle at Leipzig the previous October, a confrontation between combined Russian, Prussian, Austrian, German, and other coalition troops, which numbered more than three hundred thousand, versus some two hundred thousand French soldiers. Outmanned and outgunned, Napoleon was driven back over the Rhine. His southern army at the Spanish border met with similar setbacks in November and December, giving ground to British forces commanded by the Duke of Wellington. For the first time since 1793, French armies were confined to their own soil. Early in 1814, Secretary of State Monroe and President Madison learned that a humbled Napoleon had been driven still farther back into France, but even then most Republican partisans thought it no more than the ebb and flow of a war that had been going on for a generation.

The May 6 letter bearing Gallatin's signature was a stunning surprise. From London Madison's trusted friend wrote with double-barreled bad news. He began with the treaty negotiations: "No persons have as yet been appointed on the part of [the British] government," Gallatin wrote, "to conduct the negotiation."[1] The President's fond hope for a treaty to end his war was far from realization, since even the site of the talks remained undecided.

Yet the news was worse than that. Rumors of Napoleon's fall were indeed true. On April 11, he had abdicated unconditionally. The monarchy of Louis XVIII and the Bourbons regained the throne, while the erstwhile emperor sailed into exile to the island of Elba, a prisoner aboard a British frigate.

Madison didn't need Albert Gallatin to explain the cascading effects that might flow from the end of the French wars. It meant the two-decade demand for sailors to man British ships was over; the odds were that impressment on the high seas would cease, making one of the major causes of the American war a moot point. On the other hand, there was the prospect that, since the seasoned British army on the continent was no longer at war, it could now be unleashed, together with the full Royal Navy, on the only remaining declared enemy of the Crown. Madison's government had never been able to rely on the French as an ally, but their military presence in Europe had been a check on British power. And it no longer was.

From the streets of London, even the hearsay sounded ominous. "The complete success obtained by this country in their European contest has excited the greatest exultation," Gallatin wrote. "[T]his has been attended with a strong expression of resentment against the United States. . . . The popular feeling is evidently strong in favor of the prosecution of the war against us . . . and so powerful that it will be difficult for ministers to control it should they be disposed to peace."[2] The London press echoed the sentiments, reporting that many Londoners "talk with delight *of the sending of Lord Wellington's army to the United States*; they revel in the idea of *burning* the cities and towns, the mills and manufactories of that country; at the very least, they talk of forcing Mr. Madison from his seat, and new-modelling the government."[3]

More than a few of Mr. Madison's friends in high places began to panic. Virginia Governor James Barbour, who resided in a fine house a few miles from Montpelier that had been designed by their mutual friend Mr. Jefferson, wrote to Mr. Madison after he learned of Napoleon's abdication. "Great Britain if she wills, has now at her disposal an overwhelming force. Should she be disposed, she can with such a force, strike any part of our atlantic frontier with impunity. She can penetrate deep into our interior and the Capital itself must fall without some preliminary preparations."[4]

By early June, the British threat seemed all too near, and American and British naval forces clashed barely more than sixty miles from Washington in the Chesapeake Bay.

II.

June 1814 . . . St. Leonard's Creek . . . Patuxent River, Maryland

BIDING HIS TIME IN THE SHALLOWS, Commodore Joshua Barney had a chilling sense of presentiment. He and his "flying squadron" of barges had been forced to flee the deeper waters of the Chesapeake by the HMS *Dragon*, a towering 74-gun double-decker of such size it dwarfed the trees on Barren Island across the bay.

Barney had seen just about everything in his long career at sea. At age fifteen, he became the skipper of a merchantman when its captain (Barney's brother-in-law) died at sea. After commanding the *Sidney* to and from the Mediterranean, the young Baltimorean changed ships on his return home, volunteering to fight for his just-launched country. Commissioned a lieutenant in the infant Continental Navy in 1775, he sailed over the course of the next eight years on American frigates and brigs, at times captaining privateers that took numerous British prizes. After the war he set up as a merchant in Baltimore before donning an officer's uniform again as *Capitaine de Vaisseau Premier* in the French navy, once more fighting the hated British. He returned to his merchant business early in the new century but, in 1807, when the HMS *Leopard* opened fire upon the USS *Chesapeake*, Barney was among the first navy veterans to write to President Jefferson to offer his services. In March 1809, he dispatched another letter, this one to newly inaugurated President Madison, repeating his offer to "contribut[e] my feeble ability in any manner you please for the good of our country."[5] After the Declaration of War, he finally received Privateer Commission Number One in August 1812 for a schooner armed with twelve guns and a hundred seamen. He left his quiet retirement on his Maryland farm and, in just four months, he and the crew of the *Rossie* captured eighteen prizes.

By June 1, 1814, when the *Dragon* hove into view, he was Acting Master Commander Barney. The previous summer he had presented a plan for the "Defense of Chesapeake Bay &c." With Cockburn's marauders laying waste to shipping and coastal towns in the region, Madison's government adopted Barney's proposal as an inexpensive means of addressing an obvious defensive weakness. Barney set about constructing a fleet of barges of his own design, describing them as "a kind of . . . *Row-galley*, so constructed, as to draw a small draft of water, to carry *Oars*, light sails, and *One heavy long Gun*."[6] He planned to employ the small vessels, each manned by some seventy-five officers, men, and soldiers, to "[a]nnoy . . . the enemy in our Waters." After launching sneak attacks on the British, Barney's boats would seek cover upstream where the deeper-draft ships of the Royal Navy could not follow.

His new craft seaworthy, his crews mostly Chesapeake watermen, Barney had planned to attack the Royal Navy's Chesapeake staging area on Tangier Island, where the British were rumored to be training a battalion of runaway slaves. The American flotilla—consisting of the galleys, the five-gun cutter *Scorpion*, and two gunboats—had the wind gauge when a pair of becalmed enemy ships were spotted, a brig and the schooner HMS *St. Lawrence* (14). Barney's boats bore down on the two British vessels—only to have the *Dragon* sail into view. It was a trap. The American force was suddenly overmatched in the open waters of the bay, and Barney retreated up the Patuxent River. It was a near thing: A squall came up ("bad for *my boats*," Barney reported), and his gunners had to come about and exchange fire with the leading British vessels.[7] But Barney's flotilla had escaped intact.

In the days since, Commodore Barney had watched as the Royal Navy gained strength, with the *Dragon* and the *Lawrence* now accompanied by a sloop-of-war brig, the *Jaseur* (18); the *Loire* (38); and the frigate *Narcissus* (32). Barney saw that he was outgunned by a ratio of at least seven to one. In the face of such a powerful force (the British had fifteen barges, too), Barney moored his flotilla well upstream in the shady, sinuous flats of St. Leonard's Creek. He could defend his position, but he was mired in a watery cul de sac from which he could not escape. Meanwhile, the British patrolled and charted the Patuxent River.

~

ONE OF BARNEY'S REPORTS FROM ST. LEONARD'S CREEK arrived in Washington City accompanied by a most peculiar object. "I send you by express," the Commodore had written to Navy Secretary William Jones on June 9, "this letter & one of the *Rockets* which went into the ground and did not explode."[8]

On Pennsylvania Avenue, the men of the Navy and War Departments examined what appeared to be a sheet-iron tube about a foot in length and four inches in diameter. Welded to one end was a conical artillery shell, an incendiary warhead intended to explode on impact. The other end of the tube had been packed with propellant, perhaps ten pounds of powder that burned off. The rocket was attached by iron bands to a side stick, a fifteen-foot-long softwood shaft. Even with its fuel spent, the rocket weighed about twenty pounds.

Descriptions of such weapons had appeared in the British press ("carcass" rockets, the London papers called them). Sir William Congreve, a confidant of the prince regent and fellow of the Royal Society, had adapted fireworks for artillery purposes. His skyrockets had been used in Europe, notably at the siege of Copenhagen in 1807, and there had also been reports of their use by Admiral Cockburn's forces in the Chesapeake in the summer of 1813. Unlike cannon shot, the rockets required no heavy guns for firing; they were simply lit and fired from a ladder-like frame angled to the sky. Their range was considerable, up to two miles.

Barney's report to Secretary Jones advised that "[t]he enemy advanced a Barge which threw *Rockets*, but as they cannot be directed with any certainty they did no Execution." Even as he recognized that these projectiles were difficult to aim, the navy veteran still worried. "[T]hey can be thrown further than we can our shot; and [I] conclude from this Essay, this will be their mode of Warfare against the flotilla."[9]

Within days, his fears were realized. "One of the enemy's rockets fell on board one of our barges, and, *after passing through one of the men*, set the barge on fire—a barrel of powder, and another of musket cartridges, caught fire and exploded, by which several of the men were blown in to the water, and one man very severely burned—his face, hands, and every uncovered part of his body, being perfectly crisped."[10]

JOSHUA BARNEY WAS A FEW DAYS SHY OF HIS FIFTY-FIFTH BIRTHDAY, but he remained very much a man of action. His face weathered by decades at sea, his eyes were "a sparkling black—full, liquid, and . . . peculiarly expressive."[11] The handsome sea captain could claim a large circle of friends on both sides of the Atlantic, having known characters as varied as Ben Franklin, Marie Antoinette, James Monroe, and Mrs. Madison. His French connections had been the means by which Jerome Bonaparte entered American society and met his young wife, Betsy Patterson.

Whatever his social graces, this barrel-chested man of average height was afraid of nothing, most especially the Royal Navy. Three times he had been a British prisoner of war during the Revolution. His uniform hat and jacket had been pierced by musket balls in battle. All of that merely fed his passionate hatred of England, making him a decisive and dangerous opponent.

Following the first sighting of the HMS *Dragon*, Barney and his flotilla of small craft played cat and mouse with the Royal Navy. On June 6, small British vessels entered the waters of St. Leonard's Creek, but Barney, his ships moored in a defensive row across the creek, was ready. He ordered his men to row directly at the enemy, guns blazing; the British soon retreated and the HMS *St. Lawrence* ran aground. Barney returned to safer waters only when his flotilla came within the range of cannon larger than his. In another skirmish on June 10, an American barge was sunk, but after driving the British out of the creek once again, Barney and his men raised the barge and returned it to service.

Though his flotilla defended itself, Commodore Barney knew he could not escape without help. He wrote to Navy Secretary Jones requesting reinforcements. He needed artillery, marines, and militia. Jones ordered that aid be sent to St. Leonard's Creek, but even as men set out from Baltimore to bring cannon and munitions, Barney learned from a British sympathizer in his custody that Admiral Cockburn was also sending help to his blockaders. More British ships were en route to crush the small American force up St. Leonard's Creek.

While two warships blockaded Barney, other British forces resumed burning and plundering coastal villages as they had the previous summer. This year the raiding parties ventured further north on the Patuxent. On entering Benedict and Lower Marlborough, the latter less than thirty miles from the Capitol, the British to their surprise found both towns deserted. Abandoned stocks of muskets and other military equipment stood by, but the militia and the townspeople had melted into the surrounding woods (the militia in the region, Barney observed, "were to be seen everywhere but just where they were wanted—whenever the enemy appears, *they* disappeared").[12] The unavoidable conclusion for Cockburn was that Barney and his odd armada of river craft amounted to the entire opposition the U.S. Navy could offer in the Chesapeake.

Barney could do nothing as British vessels sailed quite unmolested past the mouth of St. Leonard's, carrying off tobacco, livestock, slaves, household furniture, and other captured goods to British ports of call.[13] Barney reported back regularly to Washington City. Secretary Jones read the news from the Patuxent with care; Barney's intelligence from the front raised ominous possibilities in Jones's mind. "If [the enemy's] force should be very considerable," Jones confided in Barney, "his apparent design upon the flotilla may serve to mask a rapid movement upon this City or Baltimore."[14] That danger seemed to grow day by day, as Barney learned from British deserters that large-scale reinforcements were coming from the British base at Bermuda, with troops said to number in the thousands.

Though many fewer in number, Barney's reinforcements were coming, too. In Washington City, the *National Intelligencer* reported that artillery and rifle companies were on the march to Benedict. On June 24, Colonel Decius Wadsworth, commissary general of ordnance, arrived with two 18-pounder long guns in tow, along with some smaller field pieces. A battalion of U.S. infantry and dragoons also moved to St. Leonard's Creek, bringing orders from both Jones and Secretary of War Armstrong. The plan, the men of the cabinet instructed, was to find "a commanding position to erect a Rampart" from which to fire upon the British ships. "If the enemy could be driven below the mouth of the Creek . . . [then] the flotilla could pass up the river."[15]

By the evening of June 25, Colonel Wadsworth had, without the enemy's knowledge, positioned his long 18-pounders on a high bluff overlooking the mouth of the creek. At sea level, Barney's men moved almost soundlessly downstream after nightfall. The Commodore ordered the masts on his boats removed and stowed, since Barney believed that British gunners used the uprights to sight their cannon. The flotilla's two gunboats had been scuttled; ineffective battle craft, they would only serve to slow the escape of Barney and his men. His thirteen barges, the schooner *Scorpion*, one little galley, and a lookout boat were in position. In the darkness before the dawn, Barney waited.

AT DAYBREAK, WADSWORTH'S MEN FIRED on the *Narcissus* and the *Loire*, the blockading frigates moored peacefully at the mouth of St. Leonard's Creek. The sound of cannon from the ridge was Barney's cue to order his men forward. They quickly stroked around a bend in the creek, bringing the British ships into view.

The creek was narrow, so Barney's armada presented a rank only eight barges wide, but the British surprise at being fired upon from above was all the greater when the dawn's first light was dimmed by the smoke from Barney's guns. Balls thudded into the British bulwarks from the boats, while others seemed to fall from the sky. The two British frigates raised anchor as their crews hurried to maneuver into firing position.

At a range of four hundred yards, the British ships soon opened fire, sending broadsides of grape and canister shot that foamed the water around Barney's little boats. The American 18-pounders on the bluff tore more than a dozen round-shot holes in the hull of the *Loire*, and the rigging of both frigates sustained damage from cannon shot ripping through the sails. Both sides had maintained a steady fire for nearly an hour when Barney observed that the cannonballs from the land battery on the bluff were now arching too high. The balls carried too far and splashed harmlessly well beyond the British warships; the repeated recoil of the guns had caused them to shift position off the acme of the hill, changing the inclination of their barrels. When the British recognized that Colonel Wadsworth's artillery posed no further danger to their ships, the cannon crews concentrated their fire entirely on the little flotilla at the mouth of the creek.

Barney was outgunned again. At just six A.M., he knew that to continue the fight into the long day ahead would be "an act of madness."[16] His little flotilla faced not only two frigates but a brig, two schooners, more than a dozen barges, and a rocket boat, all now engaged in the battle. But before Barney could retreat once again to the protected waters of St. Leonard's Creek, the British, almost as one, did what he least expected.

The Royal Navy did not advance on the Americans; rather, the ships "began to move and made sail down the river." The British were in retreat, and a stunned Barney realized that, against extraordinary odds, the British departure made his little fleet "Masters of the field."[17] One of the frigates had four pumps at work—certainly the American guns had inflicted damage—and before the sun was much higher in the sky, the enemy ships disappeared around Point Patience, bound for the waters of the Chesapeake.

The American flotilla made no pursuit; instead, Barney and his men made good their escape, moving up the Patuxent to find safe harbor at Pig's Point, near Upper Marlborough. As Barney wrote to his son the following day, "[T]hus we have again beat them and their Rockets."[18] In his written account to Secretary Jones, he reported one midshipman killed, another ten sailors dead or wounded. Jones responded promptly with his congratulations and a summons—now that he was free of the British blockade, Barney was to come to Washington.

News of the little victory was welcome. Yet when the outcome was considered in all cold candor, it was merely a withdrawal. It was Barney who had beat a full retreat upstream while, in the waters of the Chesapeake, enemy forces grew more powerful by the day.

III.

July 1, 1814 . . . The Cabinet Room . . . The President's House

TWO ALARM BELLS IN ONE WEEK: The reverberations from Mr. Gallatin's news of Napoleon's abdication had hardly died down when Commodore Barney's narrow and nearby escape signaled the need for a new strategy. Mr. Madison desired the consultation of his cabinet, and the heads of departments were asked to appear at the President's house at twelve o'clock.

One of those summoned was Attorney General Richard Rush, promoted earlier in the year from Comptroller at Treasury. The thirty-three-year-old Rush looked older than his years, his hair prematurely gray. He carried himself with patrician grace, but he was by far the most junior of the assembled cabinet officers and the man at the table with the least experience at this exalted level of government. He had succeeded William Pinkney just five months earlier as the nation's chief legal officer, having attracted the favorable attention of the President for his diligence, tact, and competence as Comptroller and Albert Gallatin's deputy at Treasury.

Rush had been honored by Madison's offer; as he had written to his father, "[The President] is a most enlightened man upon all subjects, . . . a great civilian, a great diplomatist, a great statesman, and a . . . pure and virtuous man."[19] He shared Madison's anger at the merchants up north, the men he described as "bedollared commercial delegates . . . [who] think [of] nothing but their codfish and skippers."[20] Rush especially cherished his connection to Madison's generation. After the death of his father the previous year, Rush valued anew his bond with the President as well as their mutual affection for a common correspondent, retired president John Adams in Quincy. Madison and Rush agreed that Adams's wise words on many matters "had the smack of rich and old wine."[21]

But Rush was worried by the challenges of his new office. Indeed, his first weeks as attorney general had proven a trial by fire, since he was possessed of little relevant legal experience after pursuing what he called a "low" sort of work as a young Philadelphia lawyer. He thought himself "blundering on in an agony of embarrassment and ignorance, doing the business of the court and not doing it."[22] He worried whether his reserved personal style was a disappointment in Washington City, whose citizens had filled the galleries at the Supreme Court to watch the witty and flashy Pinkney, a former Congressman, Annapolis mayor, and minister to Russia and Great Britain. Although the literate Rush had mastered Latin as a boy and, as an adult, studied history and literature ("I read the whole of [Samuel] Johnson's writing from beginning to end *twice*," he remembered, "with a constant and close attention to the structure of his periods, his syntax, his words"), he hurried to Philadelphia after the Supreme Court session. He had returned with "a stock of new law books, as I hope, by hard study, to lay in a stock of law knowledge."[23]

Whatever his shortcomings in the courtroom might be, Rush arrived at the President's house on July 1 possessed of something more valuable than legal experience or a barrister's high style. He had the President's trust. Rush's father was Dr. Benjamin Rush, a notable man even among the generation some were beginning to call the "Founding Fathers." A practitioner, lecturer, and prolific writer on medical matters, and a pioneer in investigating mental disorders, the elder Rush had been a signer of the Declaration of Independence, a regular correspondent of Jefferson and Adams, and the founder of one of the nation's first colleges.* When Benjamin Rush died in 1813, young Richard was poised to carry on the family tradition in the public sphere. Richard had earned himself a reputation of his own among fellow Philadelphians, who still spoke of the young man's resounding public orations, delivered on the occasions of the attack on the *Chesapeake* by the HMS *Leopard* in 1807 and the 1812 Declaration of War.

In their earlier passing acquaintance, Madison recognized the younger Rush as a political ally. Having been made welcome in Mr. Madison's inner circle, Mr. Rush knew why Madison had summoned them, even if all the others did not.

In the early days of the war Madison had advised Thomas Jefferson, "We do not apprehend invasion by land."[24] That had become accepted wisdom but, unburdening himself more recently to Rush, the President admitted in a private conversation that he now had worries. He told Rush he had come to "dwel[l] upon the probability of an attack upon Washington; enforcing [that] opinion on the grounds, among others, of its own weakness, and the eclat that would attend a successful inroad upon the capital, beyond the intrinsic magnitude of the achievement."[25]

With the danger to Washington City newly fixed in Mr. Madison's mind, he intended to do something about it.

AT THE APPOINTED HOUR ON JULY 1, the members of the cabinet arrived. In came the two military chiefs, Secretary of War John Armstrong and Navy Secretary William Jones, along with James Monroe from State. Of late, ill health had often kept Secretary of the Treasury George Washington Campbell from his duties but, to the surprise of the others, his fever abated, Campbell appeared to take his seat at the table. The cubical space in which they met had been partitioned off within the immense and still unfinished East Room that Jefferson had used for

* Dickinson College in Carlisle, Pennsylvania, chartered in 1783, which Rush graciously named after the state's Governor, John Dickinson.

storage. The room's ceiling seemed disproportionately high, even with the patterned paper that covered the walls.

The President opened with a warning. "If it fell within the plans of the enemy to send out troops for operations upon the Atlantic frontier this season," he told his advisers, ". . . the capital [will] be marked as the most inviting object of a speedy attack."[26]

Mr. Rush sat at the table at the invitation of the President. With no departmental territory to protect, he watched those around him from a unique vantage; he also saw the men in the fresh light of a notable shift in strategy.* To date, military planning had been concerned almost entirely with the northern border; now, given Madison's fear for the Federal City, the far-off focus was shifting. Madison wished to confront "the fierce aspect of military power" that *could*, and to Rush's way of thinking probably *would*, menace "the parts of our country most vulnerable to its immediate irruptions."[27]

This threat to the Federal City was news to Washingtonians. That very day, an anonymous writer in the columns of the *National Intelligencer* ("A VOLUNTEER") spoke boldly of the ability of the citizenry to protect themselves. "Whenever the enemy invades our territory, when he comes within twenty miles of us, . . . our citizens will, as one man, take up arms and follow their own commanders to the field."[28] Just the previous summer, many mustered along with Elbridge Gerry Jr. when word of Cockburn's deeds in the Chesapeake reached the city. Richard Rush himself had bought a musket and joined in the drilling.[29]

Yet Mr. Madison now laid before them his concern whether a spontaneous army of militiamen, really just citizen soldiers, could stop an invasion. He produced a specific plan. He wanted to position a force of some two to three thousand well-drilled regulars south of Washington City. Another, larger force of ten to twelve thousand militiamen was to be at the

---

* The Department of Justice was formally established in 1870 by an act of Congress; in earlier years, the Attorney General was a one-man department representing the interests of both the Chief Magistrate and the Congress.

ready for a call to protect the city and the district. These citizen volunteers would be drawn from the District of Columbia and the neighboring states. Convenient arms and military equipment depots would be established.

When Madison finished describing his plan, none of his advisers dissented. But as Mr. Rush looked about the room at these seasoned men, he knew they held strong views of their own, not all of which were necessarily in concert with Mr. Madison's. Anyone who looked at Colonel Monroe's perpetually set jaw could see his firmness and resolve; equally, everyone at the table was aware that he took a warm interest in the subject of defense. Monroe's strong feelings were well-known, and if anyone had been called upon to second the President's plan, Monroe's hand would undoubtedly have the been the first to rise.

On the other side, John Armstrong was perhaps the least likely to agree. Though aging, his white hair retreating up his forehead, his military bearing remained. Regarding the defense of Washington, he was known to be outspoken: He had said publicly on numerous occasions that he was certain Washington was not at risk. "What the devil will they do here?" he had been heard to ask. "No, no Baltimore is the place," was his answer.[30] When it came to Armstrong's thoughts on Colonel Monroe, a man he resented and envied for his access to the President, his dislike for the Secretary of State was easy to read.

Navy Secretary Jones held his tongue, as did Treasury Secretary Campbell. If both of those men lacked animation on the subject, perhaps it was because Jones, too, was skeptical of the danger, holding the view that there were targets that were "more exposed, less difficult of access, and more inviting to the enemy . . . than the metropolis."[31] As for Campbell, he soon withdrew to return to his sickbed.

Madison moved the discussion to troop levels, and Armstrong reported that only about a thousand regular troops could be assembled in the region. Recruitment levels remained low, although Congress earlier in the year had authorized a force of sixty thousand men; the ever-fluctuating ranks had only reached about half that number. Jones volunteered that he could provide between six and eight hundred seamen, consisting of Commodore Barney's force and some marines already stationed in Washington City.

Before the meeting adjourned, Armstrong spoke up, giving voice to his doubts about this defensive plan. First, he dismissed the possibility of an attack from the waters of the Potomac; he thought it unlikely and impractical. Moving on to the dangers from the Chesapeake, he explained that, should the British ascend the Patuxent to attack the capital, the enemy would have to embark upon a land march of some twenty miles through wooded country, "circumstances [that could] be turned to proper account against him."[32] Thus the risk of an attack from that quarter was also small. Armstrong's words were a harsh dismissal—hadn't he explained all this many times before?—but then people often remarked that Armstrong's general attitude, which seemed to vary from disapproval to disinterest, wasn't endearing.

General Armstrong's argument left Mr. Madison unmoved, and, whether he liked it or not, the Secretary of War was given clear presidential instructions. The following day, the War Department was to issue a general order creating the Tenth Military District, which was to consist of the state of Maryland, the District of Columbia, and adjacent northern Virginia. Brigadier General William Winder would be summoned from Baltimore to be its commander. Though a lawyer by training with scant military experience, Winder was a nephew of the Federalist governor of Maryland, and that state's militiamen would be essential to the defensive force.

Other fears, though left unspoken, charged the air. One worry was the Negroes. Some slaves had fled their masters to join the British, and Admiral Cockburn and his superior, Admiral Cochrane, actively encouraged runaways. Some of these "Cochrane Colonials" joined the ranks of the English; trained and uniformed for service, they were said to have their own unit.[33] A proclamation the British distributed in the South had reached the Chief Magistrate's desk; slaves there were invited to join the British, and a promise had been made to reward the them as "FREE settlers" in other British territories. To plantation owners like the Madisons, for whom slavery was both a social and economic fixture from birth, these calls for insurrection were unnerving and a grim reminder of their failure to address what Madison repeatedly called a "national evil."

Rush had said little at the meeting, watching and taking notes as Mr. Madison ordered a redeployment of forces. Rush was accustomed to living in someone else's shadow. As Madison had done for Washington and Jefferson, Rush served as other men's lieutenants, recently for Gallatin at the Department of the Treasury. He found Mr. Madison compatible; though Madison was twice his age, they shared many affinities. One was their alma mater, the College of New Jersey, another their common fondness for language and learning. In public manner, they both tended to be grave and serious; they shared a reputation for greater ease, wit, and companionability in private.

The Attorney General had long since noted his inclination to take Madison's side in most matters, and here he shared his mentor's hope that the plan promulgated would prove a sufficient response now that the war with France was over. Yet even as Mr. Madison took an unusually firm position, he had been met with John Armstrong's opinionated indifference. Further, as if Armstrong's reluctance was not worrisome enough, the simmering antipathy between him and Monroe surely didn't bode well for the government response if, in the coming days, the President's worry for the safety of the capital proved well-founded.

Richard Rush left the President's house worried that Mr. Madison's was a cabinet divided at a time when, in the judgment of some, the very security of the city was in jeopardy.

CHAPTER 4
A Sense of Uncertainty

I confess I do not admire contention in any form, either political or civil.
—Dolley Madison[1]

1.

July 28, 1814 . . . Mrs. Madison's Sitting Room . . . The President's House

MRS. MADISON HAD HER OWN CABINET. Her advisers could claim no official status, but Dolley's circle of female confidantes shared an intimate understanding of the Federal City and the business of government. Her sister Lucy was married to Supreme Court Justice Thomas Todd; their 1812 marriage ceremony was the first wedding ever held in the President's house. Younger sister Anna's husband, Richard Cutts, served as Congressman from the Maine district. Old friends from Philadelphia and cousins filled other seats when in town. From afar, letters kept other connections alive.

Whatever her bonds with the rest, however, Mrs. Madison's confidante in chief was Hannah Gallatin.

Like Mrs. Madison, Hannah Nicholson Gallatin had been a cabinet wife during the Jefferson years, arriving in a place that more nearly resembled freshly logged acreage than a city. To Hannah and Albert, cultivated city-dwellers that they were, the new capital was "far from being pleasant."[2] Hannah was a New Yorker, the daughter of a well-heeled Navy Commodore who had fought in the Revolution. On her arrival in 1801, she walked the muddy streets of Washington City with two young sons in tow, pregnant with another child.

The Gallatins rented a house on Capitol Hill, hard by the Bladensburg-Baltimore road. On hot summer days, Albert carried an umbrella to protect himself from the sun on his short walk to the Capitol, but Hannah, after one summer in the "miasmic heat" of Washington, chose to travel back to New York to spend the warmest months in her father's house.[3] This summer, with Albert across the sea, she was doing the same.

During Gallatin's able service as Madison's Secretary of the Treasury, Dolley and Hannah grew closer. Both were central players in the society of the city. Like the President's house, the Gallatins' home, given its convenience to the Capitol, had inevitably become a gathering place for members of the government. Staffing proved problematic (Hannah would own no slaves and relied upon white servants, most of whom she thought too fond of liquor). But as a hostess, Hannah Gallatin earned the respect of her husband's colleagues. One senator described Mrs. Gallatin as "by no means a pretty woman, but . . . a reading woman and a politician, unspoil'd by wealth."[4]

For the past year, Hannah and Dolley had shared their husbands' collective embarrassment at the hands of the Senate, which for so many months refused to consent to James's nomination of Albert as a Peace Commissioner. Dolley had written to her friend the previous summer offering solace at Albert's European absence (he sailed before the congressional contretemps began); in returning her kind words, Hannah signed herself "unalterably your sincere & grateful friend."[5] Hannah had sent words of comfort to Dolley during James's illness, and both women worried over the fate of the Peace Commissioners traveling to Russia and around Europe. Their strongest bond was their sons, as James Gallatin, now age seventeen, and Payne Todd, twenty-two, had gone along with Gallatin's delegation.

Dolley wrote to Hannah as July ended. There was some family news, what with the pregnancy of Anna Cutts (Dolley thought her "very *large*, & complaining"). She mused on what good might come of the boys' European adventure ("I hope we shall see our Sons highly benifitted by their Tour"). She reported that their mutual friend Lucretia Clay was "quite well & busy, in preparing a fine Gardin &c &c for her Husband." Lucretia's spouse, Henry Clay, was also far from home, keeping company with Albert as one of the other peace ambassadors across the Atlantic.[6]

Buried amidst the day-to-day ephemera, Mrs. Madison revealed a deeper vein of concern. She confided her underlying fears. "We have been in a state of purturbation here, for a long time," she wrote. For more than a year she had worried about Admiral Cockburn's threats; the news of Commodore Barney's narrow escape did little to relieve her sense of impending danger. "The depredations of the Enemy approach . . . within 20 miles of the City," she continued.

When meeting the public—Mrs. Madison ventured out daily to go calling and often received visitors at home—she took a confident line, offering assurances of the city's safety. To her son in Europe she wrote, "If the War should last 6 months longer the U.S. will conquer her Enimies."[7] She managed a note of optimism in her letter to Hannah: "I hope now, the worse is over & that I shall yet see you siting in your Sopha in *our own* circle—Adieu for the present." But even as she tried to convince others—and, perhaps, herself—she was deeply worried and, for just a moment, she let down her guard with Mrs. Gallatin, admitting, "I wish (for my own part) *we ware* at Phila[delphia]!"

II.

August 1, 1814 . . . The Tenth Military District

BRIGADIER GENERAL WILLIAM WINDER TOOK UP HIS NEW CHARGE to keep Washington City safe. In early July, he answered John Armstrong's summons to Washington City, where the Secretary of War issued his orders in person.

Armstrong instructed Winder that he was to arm and fortify the new Tenth Military District. Winder learned that no militia had yet been called to active duty, and the few hundred regulars at hand were already stationed at nearby Fort Warburton, the Navy Yard, and other sites. Winder asked Armstrong whether it might be wise to call the local militia to readiness, but the Secretary rejected the idea, insisting that "the most advantageous mode of using militia [is] upon the spur of the occasion, and to bring them to fight as soon as called out."[8]

As a general with no army to command, Winder decided he would do well to learn the lay of the land. Like an itinerant tinker, he resumed what of late had been a rather peripatetic existence.

Despite his rank, military matters were hardly second nature to the thirty-nine-year-old William Henry Winder (*Winder* pronounced like *finder*). His high repute at the Baltimore bar had won him his commission as colonel of that city's regiment when the war began, and in the officer shuffle after the Canadian setbacks in 1812, he was among the wave of younger officers promoted. A high rank being no guarantee of military expertise, Brigadier General Winder fared badly at the Battle of Stoney Creek near Niagara, New York. When awakened by a surprise British attack on June 6, 1813, he and his men attempted a rapid retreat but blundered directly into a British force half the size of their own. Pistol in hand, Winder came face-to-face with a British sergeant wielding a bloodstained bayonet. "If you stir, Sir," the grenadier threatened, "you die." Dropping both the pistol and his sword to the ground, General Winder replied, "I am your prisoner."[9]

His surrender began a year not of imprisonment but of travel. If he lacked the instinct to fight to the death, Winder did find his lawyerly negotiating skills useful. He persuaded his British captors to grant him a temporary parole, permitting him to shuttle back and forth between Quebec and Washington negotiating an exchange of prisoners (and, not accidentally, his own freedom). He had only recently returned home to Baltimore, once again a free man, when the summons from Secretary of War Armstrong found him on July 5.

He spent the rest of the month on horseback. Armstrong granted him not so much as an adjutant, so on his own he forded streams, surveyed fields, inspected dusty roads, and visited the several forts in the Tenth District. Winder was his own clerk, quartermaster, and scout as he traveled to Baltimore and Annapolis, as well as Washington, and ventured down the Patuxent for an exchange with Commodore Barney. On the Potomac he inspected Fort Warburton.

He came to understand that his command lacked transport, rifles, ammunition, provisions, forage, flints—and most especially men. His doubts rose once again at the wisdom of Armstrong's strategy of waiting for the British to make the first move, and he said as much to his superior in a letter he wrote on July 9. Winder worried that, after a "twelvemonth in the waters of the Chesapeake," the enemy knew the territory too well. Further, he feared they had already fixed upon an objective, even if he could not be certain which city it was. If British forces decided to move on Baltimore or Annapolis, he reasoned, they could muster an attack within hours of dropping anchor. Even the Capitol might be as little as a day and a half's march from debarkation. With such short notice, Winder held little hope of mustering a defense, explaining that he would be able to assemble no more than "a disorderly crowd, without arms, ammunition, or organization."[10]

The Secretary of War remained unpersuaded, and he left Winder's letter unanswered. Armstrong's attention was on the Canadian border, where confrontations on Lake Ontario and Lake Champlain seemed imminent.

General Winder was not alone in worrying about the absence of nearby defensive forces. While he crisscrossed the countryside, the city council of Washington City submitted to President Madison a unanimous resolution from "the Citizens of this City" concerning "their unprotected & defenceless state from menaced invasion." Their purpose was "to solicit respectfully of the President to take such means for their early & effectual relief."[11] Ten days later, one of the wealthiest men in town wrote directly to Madison concerning what he described as "the public wish" to summon "a battalion of the Militia of the District: to remain under Arms & in camp in the vicinity."[12] But the President left it to the military men to do their jobs.

During his travels, Winder wrote back to his betters in Washington City from Nottingham, Upper Marlborough, and Woodyard, each of them Maryland towns along the Patuxent. Armstrong seemed disinterested; when he finally did reply, his correspondence left Washington not by express courier but by regular mail. Three weeks were required for one of Secretary Armstrong's letters to reach Winder, having followed him around the countryside.

On August 1, Winder returned to Washington City. His constant movement of the previous weeks left him exhausted and bemused by the task before him. He planned now to set up headquarters in Washington, although he still had few men at his command. His uncle, Governor Levin Winder, was to have mustered thirty-five hundred troops; just one company was now at Bladensburg. William Winder learned that due to internal state politics, a promised force from Pennsylvania of five thousand men would not be coming at all. More than a month after Madison gathered his cabinet out of concern for the safety of the capital, the man delegated to prepare its defenses had not thousands but hundreds of soldiers at his command. A requisition for three thousand regular soldiers issued on July 4 had produced a total of 250 men. Winder, in fact, lacked not only personnel but also a plan. No ditches were being dug, no breastworks raised, no strategies developed.

One farmer near Bladensburg, Maryland, less than ten miles from the Capitol, saw Winder in these weeks. He reported seeing him alone, looking less like a general charting a battle plan than a lost traveler.

He observed Winder trying to reconnoiter the unfamiliar terrain around him with a map. "He'll be whipped," predicted the farmer, "because he's going to book-fight the British."[13] This man, at least, had no confidence in a general who needed a map to find his way home.

III.

August 4, 1814 . . . Patuxent River . . . Aboard the U.S. Cutter Scorpion

IN PEACETIME, JOSHUA BARNEY WAS UNLUCKY IN BUSINESS. In the 1780s, 1790s, and the first decade of the new century, his merchant enterprises ran aground. Defeated when he stood for Congress in 1810, he found playing the role of gentleman farmer on his wife's acreage in rural Maryland akin to being shipwrecked on a desert isle. At heart, the Commodore was a warrior, a man happiest, as he put it, when faced with "the point of the bayonet or the cannon's mouth."[14]

Yet this present situation, again cornered in a creek, was not a great deal better, even if he was at arms once more. Near the headwaters of the Patuxent River, Barney could only wait.

When he escaped from St. Leonard's Creek on June 26, Barney ascended the Patuxent some forty miles to the waters just north of Nottingham, Maryland. From the shelter of Pig Point, again in the shallows where no substantial British warship could follow, he attempted a few forays downstream but exchanged no gunfire with the British. He did everything he could to gather intelligence about the enemy's movements, all of which pointed to one conclusion: The British fleet, by fits and starts, was heading his way.

Early in July he had written to Secretary William Jones to report that a 74-gun ship of the line, the HMS *Albion*, was anchored at the mouth of the Patuxent. Grimmer still was the news that the big ship flew the flag of the dreaded Admiral Cockburn.

A week later Barney reported that a British frigate, together with two schooners and six barges, had sailed twenty miles upstream. British marines rowed to shore, where they burned a warehouse at Huntington and a courthouse in Calvert, marched into Benedict, and raided the surrounding countryside with impunity. "[T]he people are all frightened out of their senses running about the country like so many mad people," Barney told Jones.[15] Barney asked that he be provided with a swift, six-oared gig for scouting purposes. Secretary Jones obliged.

Barney learned from a deserter from the frigate HMS *Severn* that nine vessels were attacking the towns. The Commodore told Jones that "the Sole object of all the late expeditions . . . was *Tobacco & Negroes*, [and] some fresh provisions." No fewer than four great ships of the line and seven frigates were now afloat in Chesapeake Bay.[16]

From Washington City, Jones wrote back that other British warships sailing up the Potomac had raided towns along both the Maryland and Virginia shores. The Royal Navy also set buoys that marked a channel through Kettle Bottom Shoals, meaning the British might now negotiate that tricky passage, opening the way for substantial warships to sail up to Alexandria and Washington. Yet Secretary Jones saw no great reason for the cities to fear attack. "I . . . am myself of the opinion," he informed Barney, "that the principal object of the enemy at present is plunder."[17]

Barney kept his flotilla unseen and out of reach. In the tranquil upstream waters of the creek, the veteran warrior considered what he knew. The British were well-informed, since their raids gained them more than supplies and disgruntled slaves; the British read the newspapers they confiscated. They found traitorous citizens willing to talk. Strong rumors had it that Admiral Cockburn accompanied his men on the shore raids. Barney put no stock in the ability of the militia to fend off the likes of Cockburn and his marines. As he told Jones, the Maryland militia "gave way in every direction at the appearance of [the enemy]" or "according to custom appeared *after* all was over").[18]

Commodore Barney saw good reasons to disagree with Jones's assessment of British motives. His sources suggested that the British would not be satisfied with plunder but sought a much larger objective. "[Cockburn] has been heard to say that he could take the City of Washington," he wrote to Jones. What worried him in particular, he added, was the risk of a land attack. "[S]hould the enemy come up in force by *land* . . . in this quarter . . . they can march to the *Capitol* with as much ease and in as short a distance as from any place."[19]

For Joshua Barney, man of war, his problem was that there was very little that he could do to stop the British advance with his vastly overmatched flotilla.

IV.

August 19, 1814 . . . President's House . . . Washington City

FOR MR. MADISON, IT WAS A FORTNIGHT TO REMEMBER. Friday, August 5, had brought a dispiriting note from James Monroe. The Secretary of State had in hand dispatches from their men in Europe, among them one from Peace Commissioner Albert Gallatin. The news was not good, Monroe reported, with the British once again dominating French ports; that would make it much more difficult for American warships in European waters to take on water and supplies. Colonel Monroe thought it all very ominous and advised Madison, "We may therefore expect the worst and ought to be prepared for it."[20]

Secretary of the Treasury Campbell reported that the nation's coffers again were nearly empty. That meant the generals were unable to pay the bounties required to recruit new troops (the bounty had been raised from $16 to $124, the highest such price in the world). The northern commanders, the Navy, and even recruiters in Washington City found it difficult to enlist good men.

On Saturday, August 13, Mr. Madison finally gave vent to his frustration with the high-handed John Armstrong. Even if the man wanted to be president (did anyone doubt that he did?) Armstrong wasn't president quite yet. He just acted like it.

In a long and strongly worded letter, Madison reminded Armstrong how "the Secretary of War . . . acts under the authority and subject to the decisions and instructions of the President." Mr. Madison was civil—he knew no other way—but in his firmest manner he explained the whys and wherefores before enumerating ten specific areas where explicit presidential approval would henceforth be required. New regulations, courts-martial, officer promotions, and even resignations were to be "*previously communicated to the president.*"[21] In particular, Madison was irate at the Secretary's manipulation of General William Henry Harrison.

Some weeks earlier a disgruntled General Harrison had written to Armstrong threatening to resign. From his retreat at Montpelier, Madison, upon learning that his valued western commander might leave his post, promptly wrote to Armstrong instructing him to take no action until he returned to the city. But the Secretary of War wrote back, reporting that Harrison's resignation was already a fait accompli.

For Armstrong, Harrison's disappearance from the national scene was a plus; Harrison was a potential political rival now effectively banished (to many Americans, General Harrison's successes as an Indian fighter in the West had made him a hero). But he hadn't counted on Madison's meticulous review of the letters on his return to the capital; in his inspection of War Department correspondence, the President found clear evidence of Armstrong's duplicity. Madison uncovered a letter addressed to himself, from Harrison, that Armstrong had not sent on to Montpelier but had simply put in the files. In the letter Harrison clearly intimated that he could be persuaded to stay in the military; his irritation was at the "malicious insinuations" made concerning him in Washington. Madison was livid: Not only did his Secretary of War take every opportunity to burnish his own image, but he allowed—more than that, he had, in effect, encouraged—one of the nation's best generals to resign in a pique. By doing so, he hurt the war effort.[22]

Word also reached Washington of a new battle front. Beginning in August, the HMS *Ramillies* (74), *Pactolus* (44), and *Dispatch* (22), and the bomb ship *Terror*, had bombarded the Connecticut port of Stonington, where, the British suspected, a new infernal machine of war, the *torpedoe* (a recent invention of Robert Fulton), was harbored. The four-day bombardment caused few casualties, but the damage was considerable. The very fact of the attack added to Mr. Madison's worries.

Then, on August 14, a letter of warning arrived from Robert Stuart Skinner. Madison had appointed the young Annapolis lawyer to be the American agent for prisoners of war, thereby granting him the authority to negotiate with the enemy. Seeking a prisoner exchange with Admiral Cockburn under a flag of truce, he had gone aboard the HMS *Albion*, a fully rigged double-decker, 74-gun ship of the line.

Cockburn cut a fashionable figure in his uniform and bicorne hat with gold lace; his air toward Skinner was one of disdain. No American, it seemed, was worthy of his respect.

"Rear Adml. Cockburn inquired what our Ministers thought of peace," young Skinner reported to the President. "I told him we had recd. no recent communications from them."

In response, a smile had creased Admiral Cockburn's sunburned face.

"I believe, Mr. Skinner," said Cockburn, "that Mr. Maddison will have to put on his armour & fight it out I see nothing else left."[23]

FOR MORE THAN TWO YEARS, THE PACE OF THE WAR had been tediously slow. Reports from afar trickled in many days or weeks after battles ended. The news of negotiations in Europe, when it came at all, arrived even more slowly, at times requiring months to make landfall. If war was often the talk of Washington City, the action had always been somewhere else. But the President's internal barometer warned him of a change. Like the rising winds and darkling skies of an approaching storm, all the mid-August news from the Chesapeake presaged a military thunder of fearsome proportions.

On August 16, the largest British fleet yet sailed into the waters of the Chesapeake. Some of the ships had been in the region for months, but many were new arrivals. The armada consisted of many warships, including four ships of the line, numerous frigates, and an array of supply ships, rocket ships, and other vessels. The masts were so numerous as to be near to impossible to count from shore; most reports estimated fifty-one vessels, some accounts more. The British spent the night anchored at the mouth of the Potomac, whence the ships might sail upriver. They might continue up the Chesapeake to Annapolis, or they might ascend the Patuxent to destroy Barney's flotilla and then move on Washington. Or Baltimore. Whatever the British destination, the sheer firepower anchored off Point Lookout was unheard of in American waters.

Rumors flew that battle-hardened troops from the French wars were aboard. An informant writing from Halifax advised that the field commander was Major General Robert Ross, a veteran of the Peninsular War. The intelligence from Canada seemed in accord with firsthand reports from the Chesapeake that the big warships were accompanied by twenty troop carriers, meaning that, for the first time, a large force of foot soldiers was in the region. The sheer number of troop carriers almost made speaking the word *invasion* unnecessary.

The frigates HMS *Seahorse* and HMS *Menelaus*, along with two schooners, were the first to set sail, their northwesterly heading taking them up the Potomac River (see Chesapeake Theater map p. 114). The rest of the armada soon stood north on the Chesapeake, where at sunset they anchored at the mouth of the Patuxent. At dawn on August 17, a convoy tacked upstream toward Point Patience, revisiting Patuxent waters well-known to Admiral Cockburn's men from their earlier pursuit of Commodore Barney.

On the morning of August 18, James Monroe called on the President.

"Big Jim," as he was known to some, towered over the Chief Magistrate, who, in turn, some wags called "Little Jim." The President was grim, as a messenger had brought word of the approaching British.

"[H]e informed me," reported Monroe, "that the enemy had entered the Patuxent in considerable force." Though this latest British advance was news to the Secretary of State, he had a ready interpretation. "I remarked that this city was their object."[24]

Others in the government maintained their doubts. Navy Secretary Jones still dismissed the notion. "Appearances indicate a design on this place," Jones observed, "but it may be a feint, to mask a real design on Baltimore," which Jones regarded as of greater strategic value.[25] General Winder thought the port at Annapolis was the objective. Couriers were dispatched to muster militias in Virginia and Maryland, and seamen were summoned from New York and Philadelphia. Washington City was abuzz with rumor but the citizenry, receiving a mix of messages from their leaders, couldn't know whether to take the threat of invasion seriously. Even in the government no one had clear intelligence, not only as to British intentions but even their present movements.

"Big Jim" had no intention of running in place. As he had the previous summer, the Secretary of State volunteered to reconnoiter the enemy's position. Madison granted permission, and the next day, at one o'clock in the afternoon, Monroe and two dozen dragoons departed on a scouting mission, bound for the banks of the Patuxent. Colonel Monroe hoped for a firsthand view of the enemy as he and his escort disappeared in a cloud of dry dust.

A week earlier, Mr. Madison had published a summons to a special session of Congress. It instructed the nation's elected representatives, most of whom summered in their home states, to convene at the Capitol on September 19 to discuss the progress of the war. On returning, their task would be, in the President's words, to address "great and weighty matters." Now, however, the more immediate question, the one Colonel Monroe went off to investigate, was whether the British army might not arrive first.

CHAPTER 5

Reports from the Front

The Creator has not thought proper to mark those in the forehead who are of stuff to make good generals. We are first, therefore, to seek them blindfold[ed], and then let them learn the trade at the expense of great losses.
—Thomas Jefferson to General Theodorus Bailey, February 6, 1813

I.

Saturday, August 20, 1814 . . . A Hilltop Near Benedict, Maryland

As JAMES MONROE STUDIED THE PANORAMA BEFORE HIM, the details were hard to distinguish. A naval fleet filled the Patuxent River, but, from a distance of more than three miles, he could not be sure how many vessels there were. It was clear that one warship was anchored upstream such that its broadside guns overlooked the beach. Surely if a defender on shore chose to fire upon the flotilla, the brig's powerful cannon would readily return fire.[1]

Colonel Monroe had arrived at eight o'clock at the mill village of Acquasco.[2] After an entire night spent in the saddle, it had been a welcome relief to stand on his own two feet. Seeking knowledge of the enemy, he soon found that rumor abounded. One man reported that the

British army had marched into a nearby town, but that rumor soon proved unfounded. Only when Monroe made his way to the top of this, the highest hill between the mill and the Patuxent, could he make sense of the situation.

The invasion had begun.

Standing unseen amid the tall pines at the edge of a dense forest, Monroe watched the long line of ships. The mix of large vessels extended several miles downriver, and a flotilla of barges, bay craft, and smaller boats ferried men, stores, and matériel to the shore at Benedict. As the morning wore on, the veteran of another landing—James Monroe had crossed the Delaware in General Washington's army on December 25, 1776, as an eighteen-year-old lieutenant—made sense of the larger picture.

The British encampment on higher ground some two miles from the village of Benedict made clear the laborious embarkation had begun yesterday. A farmhouse with fences and barns partially obscured his view of the camp, but Colonel Monroe could make out an artillery installation on a ridge overlooking the Patuxent. Where the land in cultivation gave way to orchards and then dense softwood forests, sentries were on watch. He could spy no cavalry. The few horses would likely serve only the officers and artillery.

Even if they looked rather like ants from his vantage, the busy creatures below were unmistakably British. Monroe regretted very much the absence of his spyglass, but, having examined the scene as intently as he could, at one o'clock in the afternoon he wrote to Madison, dispatching his letter via express horse back to Washington. Aside from offering confirmation that the British had indeed landed and established camp, he could offer little. How large the force was, he could not say.

He added the conjecture that some around him conceived the notion "that Washington is their object." Whatever his personal opinion on the subject, he was a methodical man, given to careful conclusions. In his role as the President's eyes and ears, Monroe would go no further than to add, "of this I can form no opinion at this time."[3]

11.
Sunday, August 21, 1814 . . . Marching Toward Nottingham

THE SECRETARY OF STATE AND HIS CAVALRYMEN rose early the next morning at their bivouac near the Charlotte Hall School, a classical academy south of Benedict. They returned to monitor the British forces, but, upon ascending another hilltop, they found a surprise awaiting them.

In climbing to the summit overlooking the village from the opposite shore of Benedict Creek, they had hoped to reap a more detailed reconnaissance. Rather than the busy military base they viewed the previous day, however, Colonel Monroe and his men discovered they overlooked a "very tranquil scene."[4] The larger ships remained offshore in the Patuxent, and from this closer overlook Monroe counted twenty-three square-rigged vessels, including several frigates well downstream. But the entire force of British infantry had vanished, along with most of the smaller vessels. The surrounding landscape showed signs of plunder, with nary a head of cattle grazing in the pastureland before them. But Benedict appeared deserted.

Just one conclusion offered itself: The British had moved out the evening before and marched north. Along with his guard of grenadiers, Monroe set off in pursuit.

It would have been imprudent in the extreme to give the enemy a chance to take the nation's Secretary of State hostage, so out of caution they took an inland route. After a time they descended to the main road, where it was clear that no army had trudged.

Colonel Monroe recast his thinking. The enemy knew that Barney and his barges had escaped upstream, and, since Barney's cannons represented the main danger in the region, the British must have settled on the stratagem of eliminating Barney and his watermen once and for all. "[I]t [is] probable that a force by land and water has been sent against the flotilla," Monroe wrote to Madison in his midday dispatch.[5] Colonel Monroe redirected his men toward Nottingham, some fifteen miles upstream, where he knew Barney and his flotilla sheltered.

Traveling on horseback, Monroe arrived in Nottingham by midafternoon. He found no British. The river town consisted of two streets that paralleled the waterfront and two more at right angles. The streetscapes were lined with plain, wood-frame structures, which gave way to fields in tillage. Generous farmhouses could be seen in the distance set amid fields planted with tobacco. This year's crop stood tall and abundant.

As the afternoon wore on, Monroe's speculation about the British plan proved accurate. The speed of his horse had enabled him to arrive before the redcoats, but the British force soon appeared, having marched along a road by the river. The day was warm (people said it was the warmest summer in memory), and the British soldiers were heavily laden. Each man carried a knapsack containing clothes, a blanket, a haversack with provisions, and a wooden keg or canteen of water, along with his gun and ammunition. Monroe also spotted three barges on the water, at a distance of several hundred yards, and he began writing a dispatch to William Winder, proposing, "If you send five or six hundred men, if you could not save the town, you may, perhaps, cut off their retreat."

Before he could complete his note, Colonel Monroe realized his plan could not work. Another wave of British troops had marched into view. The first soldiers he had seen appeared to be no more than an advance guard. Three companies of infantry followed at a distance of a hundred yards. Next, at a similar distance behind the infantry, first one brigade and then another marched into view. The sea of soldiers now defied a head count.

Colonel Monroe watched the water, too, and soon added a postscript to his missive to Winter: "Ten or twelve more barges in view," he noted. At five o'clock he scrawled a final detail—"Thirty or forty barges are in view"—before he and his escort rode out. They exited Nottingham from one side as the enemy entered from the other.[6] They heard a few shots ring out as some American cavalrymen fired on the boats, but the arrival of the army vanguard brought the sparse fire to an end and the handful of American cavalrymen quickly retired. Colonel Monroe heard no further sounds of skirmishing as the British marched into Nottingham, unopposed.

III.

Midmorning . . . Monday, August 22, 1814 . . . The Road to Nottingham

ALTHOUGH THE MORNING BEGAN VERY EARLY WITH A CALL TO ARMS, the day proved a hurry-up-and-wait affair. At the American encampment at Wood Yard, twelve miles east of Washington City, the drumbeat of reveille roused every sleeper before one o'clock in the morning. With the tents struck and baggage wagons soon loaded, the men stood in readiness to march, but most of the militiamen merely watched as an advance force of some three hundred rifle corpsmen, light infantry, and artillerists departed at sunrise. Not until nine o'clock did the rest of the troops follow, and even then they proceeded only a mile toward the enemy before halting atop a rise. They overlooked the road from Nottingham, the better to watch for the British. Resting on their arms, they waited.

The previous evening the Secretary of State arrived at Wood Yard at eight o'clock. This was home base to General Winder's improvised army, and the American camp was a stark contrast to the tightly organized British operation Monroe had seen at Benedict. The King's regiments made camp along prescribed lines, their site carefully chosen, with pickets and artillery positioned at the periphery, and its rational scheme apparent even several miles away. While there was a practiced precision to the British camp, Wood Yard was on open ground, with bright fires illuminating a random sea of tents. Colonel Monroe entered its perimeter unannounced and unchallenged.

The exhausted Virginia colonel had immediately sought out General

Winder, who himself had arrived from his office in Washington City only the day before. Before retiring for a few hours of well-deserved rest, Monroe briefed General Winder on what he knew. On his journey he had met up with Colonel William D. Beall, another aging veteran of the Revolution and an officer in the Maryland militia. Monroe had observed the British troops from street level as they entered Nottingham, but Beall watched the enemy's column from a commanding height near the town. Pooling their knowledge, the colonels estimated the enemy at between four and five thousand men on foot, with another thousand sailors and marines on the barges in the river. Neither man saw cavalrymen; they noted few cannon. Taken together, their reports were reassuring but far from definitive, and General Winder could not entirely dismiss the hearsay that the invading force was more than double their estimate, at twelve thousand or more British troops.

General Winder possessed a better count of his own forces. On August 18, hearing of the British arrival in the Patuxent, he had dispatched more than a dozen letters to Maryland, Virginia, Pennsylvania, and Washington City, writing to governors, mayors, and militia commanders to requisition soldiers. Initially only a trickle of men arrived, as a draft of the local militia produced few troops, with many men already in service in response to recent alarms along the Chesapeake. Other militiamen stayed home to assume posts at Annapolis, Baltimore, and the capital, but a growing tide of men had poured into Camp Wood Yard.

By dawn on Monday, a company of regular U.S. infantry had arrived, as had a freshly trained cavalry unit from Pennsylvania. A thousand riflemen and artillerists with a dozen 12-pound cannon from Georgetown and the Columbia Brigade were at hand, along with some three hundred Maryland cavalrymen. Together with other arrivals, the force amounted to about twenty-two hundred men.

Accompanied by Colonel Monroe, General Winder led the advance force that departed Wood Yard at sunrise. Regarding the enemy's intentions, he possessed a new certainty: "[No] doubt," reported Winder, "was . . . entertained by any body of the intention of the enemy to proceed direct to Washington."[7] His mission that morning was to reconnoiter the enemy; the rank and file merely waited for their commanders to decide upon a strategy.

ALONG WITH HIS STAFF AND THE SECRETARY OF STATE, General William Winder watched and listened. The enemy had halted at a fork in the Nottingham Road less than a mile away in the midst of a thick forest. The decision to pause there posed a specific question: Would they march toward Wood Yard or would their next destination be Marlborough to the north?

General Winder pondered what might ensue. His deliberations with his advisers were heavy with uncertainties, a series of *if* or *when* possibilities based upon the enemy's moves, but accompanied by tactical questions concerning how he should deploy his forces, whether to "impede the march of the enemy" or to "retrograde and join the main body of the army."[8] Winder's army might, at best, deflect a British thrust. But he needed to gain an understanding of how Admiral Cockburn and General Ross, the British field commander, viewed the larger game board.

The man who first imagined Washington City two decades earlier, Major Pierre Charles L'Enfant, wanted to employ the Potomac River for its natural beauty. But as Winder considered L'Enfant's plat—a city with streets that aligned with the cardinal points of the compass and broad avenues that slashed diagonally across the rectilinear grid—his concern was defense. He looked to assess the strategic advantages and weaknesses of the topography.

A Royal Navy squadron was ascending the Potomac toward Fort Warburton. Reports had it that the 36-gun frigate *Euryalus* and 5 smaller warships had already negotiated Kettle Bottom Shoals and sailed well up the Potomac. The consensus among military men was that Fort Warburton was a poor excuse for a citadel; as one general who assessed its condition concluded the previous year, the structure was "a mere water battery of twelve or fifteen guns, bearing upon the channel in the ascent of the river, but useless the moment a vessel had passed. . . . [Its] octagonal block-house, . . . being calculated against musketry only, could have been knocked down by a twelve-pounder."[9] While a few guns had recently been added to the fort's armaments, Winder suspected a British naval force sailing up the Potomac could blast its way past, then have clear sailing to Washington City, which had no battlements or fortifications, not so much as a redoubt. Winder also had to weigh the possibility that the enemy army that paused less than a mile from him might march across the Maryland peninsula, bound for Fort Warburton, in order to join forces with the Potomac flotilla and launch a full-scale amphibious attack on the city.

Perhaps equally likely was a direct approach to the capital. Since L'Enfant's design nestled the new city into a fork in the river, where the waters of the Potomac flowed northwest and the smaller Eastern Branch northeast, an invading force that marched along the route through Wood Yard would, some twelve miles later, arrive on the bank of the Eastern Branch River. While it was not as wide as the Potomac, its breadth and depth offered the city protection: Since the enemy could not ford the river, the attacking force would have to cross the existing bridges to the city. These, Winder knew, might be defended or, failing that, destroyed.

The enemy's third choice was to march a similar distance north to Bladensburg, a small town where troops might ford the river, then descend on the city along the Baltimore Road. Or, perhaps, as Winder's own superior, Secretary of War Armstrong, had warned, the British might not move on Washington City at all but attack Baltimore.

The situation was altogether too perplexing, and Winder, as the noon hour approached, chose not to fight that day. He could not countenance ordering men, most of whom had been in service less than three days, to engage in a battle with experienced British troops. Though Mr. Madison's order called for "pelt[ing] the enemy from the start with light troops . . .

throwing in all sorts of obstruction in the routes," Winder would order no attacks from the cover of the surrounding woods.[10] Instead, as the British made a move toward Wood Yard, the soldiers in Winder's command were disappointed to hear that they were to retreat, destination Long Old Fields, another crossroads town that was half the distance to Washington.

As some among Winder's troops groused at the command to retreat, they heard in the distance "successive heavy explosions."[11] Brigadier General Winder guessed at the meaning of the blasts, which came from the direction of the Patuxent.

IV.

August 22, 1814 . . . Pig Point . . . Patuxent River

AS ADMIRAL COCKBURN'S SHIP EASED WITHIN SIGHT of the narrows beyond Pig Point, the elusive American flotilla came into view. At its head was the sloop-rigged floating battery, the USS *Scorpion.* Cockburn noted the ensign snapping in the breeze atop its mast. It was unmistakably the broad pennant of Commodore Joshua Barney.

Astern of Barney's flagship stretched a long line of thirteen barges and a gunboat. To Cockburn, this was a happy sight, an opportunity, at last, to do battle with Barney. The American mix of shallow-water craft had long since earned Cockburn's respect as the "formidable and So much Vaunted Flotilla," which had harried and distracted the Royal Navy in the Patuxent, all the while monitoring British activity and reporting back to Washington City.[12]

Cockburn ordered the sails of his fleet set to advance on Barney at all possible speed. This could be no fair fight, yet Commodore Barney's tiny armada had one last surprise in store.

The previous day Barney had learned from his scouts, freshly back in the fleet's swift gig, that the British barges approached Nottingham. The news prompted his departure: Barney, along with upwards of four hundred of his men, had pulled for Upper Marlborough, two miles away. On orders from Navy Secretary Jones, they went ashore and marched smartly inland to join the army at Wood Yard. Unbeknownst to Admiral Cockburn advancing on his quarry at Pig Point, the man in charge was not Barney but Second Lieutenant Solomon Frazier.

Some forty British vessels made for the *Scorpion*, launching a fusillade of cannon and rocket fire before them. Smoke began to rise from the deck of the USS *Scorpion*. Flames were soon visible and, as the ships of the Royal Navy neared, the powder stores on board detonated, blasting rigging, spars, decking, and Barney's pennant into the air. As shattered debris splashed into the water and black smoke billowed, a nearby barge exploded. A second, a third, and then another blew in quick succession. Cockburn saw that a fire had been set aboard each vessel and a train of powder laid down that guided the flames to the ship's magazine. Their demolition work done, Frazier and his skeleton crews had already abandoned ship. Men could be seen splashing into the bushes on the nearby shore, making a quick retreat.

In the next hour, one of the barges, in which the fire had fizzled, was salvaged by the British. A few escaping seamen were captured and some of the cargo schooners taken into service, though most were burned (though speedy, their light construction was poorly adapted to heavy cannon, limiting their military value). His flotilla no longer posed a danger to the invaders—but the resourceful Commodore Barney and his baymen had again eluded their would-be captors.

V.

August 22–23, 1814 . . . Camp Old Fields . . . Eight Miles from Washington City

EVEN THE FRENCH MINISTER KNEW THE BRITISH WERE COMING. This day the *National Intelligencer*, which had spilled more ink during the last week on the British bombardment of faraway Stonington, Connecticut, than on the growing enemy force in the Chesapeake, raised the temperature by titling its daily report "The Crisis." The editors possessed no more hard information than anybody else in Washington City ("Of the enemy's strength and movements," the paper reported, "we have as usual an abundance of absurd and contradictory rumors"). Fearing the worst, many residents of the town set about loading their valuables into wagons and preparing to evacuate.[13]

Penning a letter to his ministry at home, Louis Sérurier wrote, "[I]t was learned with fright this morning, that the English had left their ships and advanced boldly overland on Washington."[14]

At the President's house, Mr. Madison, despite daily reports from Colonel Monroe, was not satisfied with what he knew. He could vaguely hope that "the crisis . . . [would] be of short duration," but as the British drew nearer, the uncertainty of it all galvanized him to action.[15] Determined to see for himself, he would ride out to Long Old Fields.

Before departing, he needed a private word with Dolley. An anxious James had to ask her one of the hardest questions of their twenty-year marriage. The two were rarely apart; the only time they had been separated for more than a day or two had been almost ten years earlier when Dolley, recuperating from an ulcerated knee, remained in Philadelphia under the care of physician Philip Syng Physick; James, drawn by his duties as Jefferson's Secretary of State, had been compelled to return alone to Washington City. During those autumn weeks in 1805 husband and wife exchanged dozens of letters. He wrote that his happiness could "not be complete till I have you again secure with me."[16] She wrote to him and described a dream: "I saw you in your chamber, unable to move . . . I pray that an early letter from you may chase away the painful impression of this vision."[17] Both James and Dolley appreciated their especial affinity for one another.

On the morning of August 22, James asked her a question: With the streets fevered with fear, did she have the "courage, or firmness to remain in the President's house" until his return? He might arrange for her to travel to Virginia, to get her safely away from whatever danger the approaching military storm might bring, but his most valued partner offered a worthy and ready answer. She promptly assured him, "I have no fear but for [you] and the success of our army." She would stay.

James departed in the morning, though not before beseeching Dolley to tend to two important tasks. She was, he asked, "to take care of [her]self, and of the cabinet papers, public and private."[18] To help ensure her safety, he would arrange for a company of one hundred militiamen under the command of Henry Carbury to stand guard at the President's house. As James rode toward the enemy, Mrs. Madison remained where she was, organizing piles of documents, the written records of their lives and government.

AFTER A BRIEFING AT THE WASHINGTON NAVY YARD, the President pointed his horse across the river. The wooden roadbed of the bridge almost skimmed the surface of the fifteen-hundred-foot-wide Eastern Branch, which, like a broad natural moat, seemed to offer the endangered city a protective embrace. Accompanying Madison were Attorney General Richard Rush, Secretary of the Navy William Jones, and several aides, including Charles Carroll. Major Carroll, a friend of the Madisons and a man of "courtly manner and genial bearing," was one of the gentlemen soldiers whose social status, rather than military experience, had gained him an officer's rank in the Maryland militia.[19]

The sun set during the eight-mile ride that took the President and his escort within a mile of Long Old Fields. Madison found quarters for the night at a farmhouse, while the Attorney General and the Secretary of the Navy continued on to the main encampment. After midnight Mr. Rush conversed with General Winder in his tent, and, learning of the President's arrival, Winder ordered a guard posted at the Williams farm, where the President waited. Jones took shelter for the night in Joshua Barney's tent. Though he no longer commanded any vessels whatever, Commodore Barney, along with his baymen and their artillery skills, was a welcome addition to the American land force.

No one in the vicinity slept undisturbed that night. One of the sentinels raised the alarm at three o'clock, and the report of muskets fired by anxious sentries brought the entire camp awake. Men scrambled to rise, dress, and gather their weapons. It was a false alarm, its cause the noise in the nearby woods made by free-ranging cattle. But the air was alive with the worry that the British "would be upon [them] in the course of the night." As one officer noted, "[D]etermined to die like a trooper, I slept with my shoes on."[20]

Shortly after dawn Brigadier General Winder appeared before Mr. Madison, his countenance haggard after two months of unrelieved tension and sleepless nights. The alarm the night before had been more of the same, as the general felt required to "wade through the infinite applications, consultations, and calls, necessarily arising from a body of two thousand five hundred men, not three days from their homes, without organization, or any practical knowledge of service on the part of their officers." Only after "listen[ing] to the officious but well intended information and advice of the crowd," Winder reported, could he "lay down to snatch a moment of rest."[21]

General Winder briefed the commander in chief on what he knew. In attendance were Secretaries Armstrong and Jones, along with Attorney General Rush. The previous day he had ridden with a cavalry unit, Winder explained, observing the enemy near Marlborough and interrogating two British soldiers his cavalrymen had captured. The news was mixed: On the one hand, he told the President, the British appeared to be settled for the moment, perhaps waiting for the squadron that sailed up the Potomac. Further, they had almost no cavalry, with only a few dozen stolen horses for mounts, and they possessed fewer than ten cannon. More worrisome was their nearness: They camped less than four miles away. After a hot day of marching, the enemy occupied Marlborough, a village that, aptly enough, was named after a great British war hero of the previous century, the Duke of Marlborough.

Winder explained that he had made camp in Long Old Fields for tactical reasons. Situated at the junction of the two main roads to Washington, this spot represented a decision point for the British. If they were to march west, their destination would be the Navy Yard bridges over the East Branch; if they veered north, they were bound for Bladensburg, where they could either countermarch toward Washington City or proceed to Annapolis. Winder had divided his forces, massing roughly half at Old Fields, with another large force to the north in Bladensburg, and a third, smaller detachment to the south, in the event the British chose to march on Fort Warburton.

At eight o'clock that morning the presidential party rode to the Old Fields camp. The troops stood for inspection, and Madison passed among the units lined up for his review. The accumulating force now included four hundred cavalrymen, almost five hundred men from Barney's flotilla, more than a hundred marines, four hundred regular army from the Thirty-sixth and Thirty-eighth Regiments, and some eighteen hundred Maryland and Washington City militia.

Mr. Madison was buoyed by what he saw. He was surprised to find that many of Commodore Barney's men were Negroes, serving alongside white sailors and marines, but Barney spoke confidently of their ability to stand firm in the event of a British assault. "They don't know how to run," he told the President of these proven men, "they will die by their guns first."[22]

Mr. Madison exhorted the assembled officers "to be firm and faithful in their duty."[23] He also took a moment to write to Dolley, reporting that "the troops . . . are in high spirits & make a good appearance."[24] But he chose not to tell her that this was an army that had lost most of two nights of sleep; that they had insufficient tents; that some of the riflemen carried not rifles but outdated muskets, less accurate weapons with a shorter range. These ill-fed soldiers had a steady supply only of rumor and alarms; less predictable was the arrival of salt beef and musty flour. Even drinking water was, at times, muddy and hard to find. It went unmentioned, as well, that Winder had that day received a letter from a plantation owner in the district. The writer reported overhearing the braggadocio of British officers, who proclaimed that they soon "would be in Washington and have Mr. and Mrs. Maddison."[25]

The situation was uncertain, with the enemy's next movements unknown, and, as General Winder was frank to admit to one of his officers, "it was impossible . . . to decide how to act."[26] Before the President could return to Washington City, a scout galloped in with news of British movements. The rider gave the assembled brass the grave news that the British marched in the direction of Annapolis. General Winder immediately dispatched a company of men on horse to shadow the British force and report back on their movements.

Soon another scout who had been reconnoitering the enemy rode in, accompanied by two British deserters. A Georgetown dry-goods merchant until a few days before, Major Thomas L. McKenney reported that the British were not marching north—but directly toward Old Fields.

The President, looking to make some sense of the British plans, questioned the deserters himself. He asked who commanded their army. The two British soldiers said they didn't know.

The President asked what city the enemy held in its sights. Again, they could not say.

Mr. Madison asked about their army's strength—was it equivalent to the American forces around them? The men smiled and said they thought it was.

One who witnessed the exchange remained skeptical. Though he had largely absented himself from Winder's defensive decision-making,

Secretary of War Armstrong spoke with certainty of the British plans. He dismissed McKenney's belief that the British were marching westward toward Old Fields.

"They can have no such intention," Armstrong insisted. "They are foraging, I suppose; and if an attack is meditated by them upon any place, it is Annapolis."[27]

General Winder soon rode off to investigate the movements of the enemy and to coordinate with General Stansbury, the Baltimore brigade commander in charge at Bladensburg. Madison ate a hurried repast in the early afternoon back at the Williams farm before turning toward Washington City with the several members of his cabinet. He would return to the capital, possessed of less than perfect confidence in the defenses in place, his desire to know the enemy's likely plans unsatisfied.

CHAPTER 6

The British Are Coming!

The enemy are in full march for Washington. Have the materials prepared to destroy the bridges. . . . You had better remove the records.
*—James Monroe to James Madison, August 22–23, 1814**

1.

Tuesday, August 23, 1814 . . . The President's House

JAMES'S ABSENCE MADE THIS DAY DIFFERENT. But Dolley, as was her habit, rose early and went about her daily tasks, keys jangling at her side. Her usual outfit of plain gray, in the Quaker style with a white apron and kerchief, suited her morning ritual of tending to the domestic details of her household.

Yet there was nothing plain or ordinary about Mrs. Madison's home, which some in the city called the "Great House." Even as she planned her morning in her comfortable sitting room, she did so surrounded by

* Internal evidence suggests that this undated letter was written in two sittings, most likely Monday evening, August 22, and Tuesday morning, August 23. However, documents from the time that appear in *American State Papers* contradict one another as to its chronology.

high-back sofas and chairs upholstered in bright yellow satin. The sunflower-yellow curtains on the windows were damask, and a drapery cornice with silken fringe extended around the perimeter of the room. A ship model in a glass case was on display, too, commemorating the successes of the U.S. Navy. That the sitting room was the setting for occasional musical performances was evident from the presence of a guitar and pianoforte, but today no strains of Mozart would be heard here.

A foreign visitor once said of Mrs. Madison that she possessed "such discretion, impartiality, and kindliness, that . . . she gratified everyone"; on this day, with her gift for sensing the feelings of others, the Presidentess felt in her bones the turmoil that had overcome her city.[1] No more than a glance at the street outside was needed to confirm the rising panic of her fellow citizens. The streets were uncharacteristically congested with carts, most of them loaded not with the goods of day-to-day commerce but with people's most valued possessions. A disorderly flight from Washington City was well under way.

Honoring James's request on his departure that she tend to papers, presidential and private, Mrs. Madison duly ordered trunks brought from the attic. As she had done yesterday, she would spend much of the morning loading great stacks of letters, ledgers, and journals into the waiting wood-and-leather receptacles.

As she tended to the nation's precious documents, she wrestled with an almost overwhelming sense of personal regret. If the worst was to happen and she was forced to join the throng departing the city, she would have to leave behind the pianoforte and the guitar (for which the nation had paid $485 and $28, respectively), along with mirrors, Brussels carpet, marble mantels, china, and the latest oil lamps made of bronze with glass chimneys. A looming British invasion threatened her home and the life she knew here in Washington City.

Mrs. Madison's sitting room opened directly onto two other much larger rooms; taken together, the Elliptical Salon, the State Dining Room, and her Parlor had become the city's—and the nation's—social center; it was "at once the model of polished life, the dwelling of cheerfulness," and the setting for Mrs. Madison's squeezes.[2] At the core of the President's house, this suite of three rooms embodied Dolley Madison herself.

She had carefully chosen the instruments, the furniture, accessories, and decorations with the help of Benjamin Henry Latrobe. Even before his inauguration, President-elect Madison had, in February 1809, commissioned Latrobe to redesign the public interiors of the President's house. Everyone agreed that Latrobe, the first professionally trained engineer and architect to practice in America, was a man of the most sophisticated tastes. He already knew the executive mansion well, since President Jefferson, recognizing Latrobe's superior skills, had appointed him Surveyor of the Public Buildings. In that role Latrobe worked at the Capitol (which proved to be a seriatim argument with Dr. Thornton, whose original design Latrobe sought to alter), as well as the President's house, where he added wings to either side of the main block for support functions.

In the small world of Federal America's ruling class, the Madisons and the Latrobes were old friends. Dolley had known Mary Hazelhurst since girlhood in Philadelphia, long before Mary had become Mrs. Latrobe. Henry was fond of Dolley, whom he described to his brother as Madison's "very excellent and amiable wife."[3] He made the President's house more comfortable, installing the first bathtub, along with a newfangled Yarwood washing machine. More interesting to Mr. Latrobe was the commission to redesign the most important rooms in the mansion. In executing this task he found in Mrs. Madison a keen collaborator, one willing to embrace his theories of interior design.

To his way of thinking, guests shouldn't merely *visit* the President's house; they should *experience* the place. The colors, shapes, and light effects should change from one space to the next. As Latrobe put it, these aesthetic effects amounted to "scenery," and the experience was to be changing, pleasing, and surprising.[4]

Using the twenty thousand dollars Congress appropriated for the

Furniture Fund to improve the domestic arrangements at the President's house, Mrs. Madison and Latrobe created a mise-en-scène within which to welcome many and varied guests. While Jefferson had rarely entertained more than a dozen for dinner, Dolley Madison's table often accommodated thirty or more guests (the Madisons took care to invite each member of Congress to dinner during each legislative session), and her Drawing Rooms regularly attracted several hundred. "I never saw a Lady who enjoyed society more than she does," remarked one regular guest. "The more she has around her, the happier she appears to be."[5]

The grandest room was the Elliptical Salon. Latrobe himself designed its furniture in the new Grecian style, drawing upon recent archaeological findings about ancient Greece. Its appeal was in both its classical lines and the ancient ethos of *demos kratia* (literally, "the people rule"), which nicely complemented the new American experiment. He adapted the Greek *klismos* form with its sweeping saber legs, ordering fancy chairs that were "painted, gilded & varnished, with the United States arms painted on each."[6] Their cane seats were supplemented by red velvet cushions that matched the upholstery of the Grecian sofas and settees. Reaching nearly to the ceiling, the windows were voluminously curtained with the same red velvet, as were mirrored niches. Mrs. Madison and her architect friend envisioned a transformation of "a mere vestibule" (it had remained unfurnished during Jefferson's habitation). The sinuous curve of the walls, the reflections in the looking glasses, the brilliant colors, and the fresh forms of the furniture enriched a space that Washington Irving, one of the literati and wits of New York who came to visit, described as "the blazing splendor of Mrs. Madison's Drawing Room."[7]

As morning gave way to afternoon, a note arrived from James. A worried Dolley tore the letter open. Though it was written hurriedly in pencil from the Williams farmhouse near Old Fields, the small but finely shaped letters marched across the page in almost military precision.

James addressed her as "My dearest," but Dolley soon learned that he could offer her no assurances concerning his, her, or the city's safety. "The reports as to the enemy have varied every hour," he admitted. James promised to keep a messenger by his side, saying, "I might give you by him some final & certain information [when we] have something further from the camp concerning the Enemy." He further promised, whatever else were to happen, "I shall be with you in the course of . . . the evening."[8]

She would await further word, but she would not be idle. She pressed more papers into trunks, an accumulation that would soon fill a carriage bound for Virginia. But in her own mind, she reached a resolution regarding her own departure, one that she put on paper as she began writing a letter to her sister Lucy. "I am determined not to go myself until I see Mr. Madison safe."*

SEVERAL BLOCKS FROM THE PRESIDENT'S HOUSE, another sister, Mrs. Anna Cutts, scribbled a note to Dolley. Like most of the populace of Washington City, she was afflicted with a dread of impending attack. "Tell me for gods sake where you are and what [you are] going to do," she demanded. "We can hear nothing but what is horrible here."[9]

The approach of the British was altogether shocking. Until just days before, few serious fears were entertained for the safety of the capital. The Chesapeake raids the previous summer had been intimidating, but, in an odd way, they inoculated the city against the fear of an actual assault. Admiral Cockburn and his marauders threatened but never approached Washington City the previous summer; this year, the logic ran,

* Many of the details concerning Mrs. Madison's last days at the President's house are drawn from her letter to her sister of Tuesday and Wednesday, August 23–24, 1814. The original of this famous letter has been lost, but a version survives in Dolley's own hand that is thought to date from ca. 1834. Scholars have suggested that, in retrospect, she may have taken certain dramatic liberties in recounting events, but the document offers unique insight into the hours preceding the sack of Washington. For a cogent analysis, see David B. Mattern, "The Famous Letter: Dolley Madison Has the Last Word," *White House History* (1998), 228–33.

the same pattern ought to apply. That view now seemed naïve; if an overland assault on Washington had seemed preposterous just a day or two ago, now even the *National Intelligencer* warned of the British approach to the capital. Almost overnight, the entire city had begun evacuating. At noon on Monday a clerk at the House of Representatives got orders "to save such part of the books and papers . . . as he might be able to effect." In trying to impress wagons and carts, he found that virtually all were either in the hands of the army or were loaded with the personal possessions of citizens bound for Virginia or Maryland. Only by journeying to the surrounding countryside was the clerk able to requisition a single cart and four oxen.[10]

At the Department of the Navy, Secretary Jones had given his department a head start. At his instruction three clerks spent Sunday loading "all the books of record, papers, library, maps, charts, plans, stationary, trophies, various valuable instruments, paintings, prints, &c." Two city carts ferried the boxes and other articles to a pair of rented riverboats, which "proceeded up the river Potomac, and passed through the locks and canal to a place of safety."[11]

On Monday James Monroe instructed that his personal library and the stylish furniture he brought back with him from his days as Minister to France be carted far from the enemy's reach. Monroe himself would stay and fight, but he saw no reason to put his family at risk. Mrs. James Monroe was among the evacuees, departing with daughters Eliza and Maria for their farm in northern Virginia.

Colonel Monroe also ordered that State Department documents be made safe. A senior clerk, Stephen Pleasonton, purchased quantities of linen to be sewn into bags. Filling the newly fabricated bags were not only departmental records but precious historic documents, among them a scrolled Declaration of Independence and General Washington's resignation letter, delivered on December 24, 1783, at the close of the Revolution.

Pleasonton was at work packing papers into the coarse bags when

General Armstrong happened along the hallway bound for the War Department, which shared the building on Seventeenth Street with the Department of State. Before proceeding to his own office and assuming his seat in the red leather chair he favored, Armstrong paused a moment, watching Pleasonton at work. He told the younger man that, in his opinion, such labors reflected "unnecessary alarm." The Secretary of War still "did not think the British were serious in their intentions of coming to Washington."[12] But Pleasonton carried out his orders, and a small flotilla of flour boats soon carried the voluminous files across the Potomac. Thence the clerk saw to it that the papers were moved thirty-five miles inland to Leesburg, where, under lock and key, they were stored in an empty farmhouse.

All of Washington City was a-flurry with similar activity. The approach to the mile-long Potomac Bridge to Virginia was jammed with carts carrying all manner of goods. Its roadbed covered with planks of white and yellow pine, the bridge resounded with the hoofbeats of dray horses. Separated by a neat railing, a pedestrian way was thick with men, women, and children on foot, many laden with valuables they wished to save from the British. Every hackney cab in the city had been hired or put to use by its owner, and the operators, already widely known for disregarding the fares specified by the City Corporation, charged whatever they wished. As one young resident of Washington City reported, "[A]ll is hurry and panic, armies gathering, troops moving in all directions, the citizens trying to secure such things as are most valuable and easily transported, flying from their homes to the country."[13]

As banks relocated specie and militia drilled noisily in the open square nearby, Mrs. Cutts, like her sister, worried over the fate of her precious piano (Anna wanted her husband to load it into their carriage). The French minister, observing the helter-skelter retreat of Washingtonians, observed that the roads were "covered with them."[14]

II.
Wednesday, August 24, 1814 . . . The Navy Yard

THIS DAY BEGAN AS CONFUSEDLY for the military planners as the one before had ended. A dispatch arrived at the President's house addressed not to Mr. Madison but to General Armstrong. The President, who had ridden the nine miles back to Washington City the previous afternoon, was quite certain of "the urgency of the occasion," so he opened and read the letter. The sender, General Winder, requested "the speediest counsel."[15]

The players had been repositioned overnight. When Madison departed Old Fields, the American forces stood strategically poised in case of enemy attack, but on Winder's return from a nervous day monitoring British movements a few hours later, the general decided to remove his army. Winder still didn't know which way the enemy would advance—he just knew they were too close for comfort and darkness was falling.

He had reasoned, "[I]f an attack should be made in the night, our own superiority, which lay in artillery, was lost, and the inexperience of the troops would subject them to certain, infallible, and irremediable disorder, and probably destruction."[16] His fear was that, if the British made a bold move, he could lose his army. He issued orders, and the troops had fallen back toward Washington City. With their captains continually urging the men onward, "the march . . . literally became a run of eight miles."[17] Arriving around midnight, the soldiers "were so greatly fatigued, that they could scarcely stand by their guns."[18] The motley American army established a makeshift camp on the heights half a mile from the Eastern Branch bridge, back within the borders of Washington City.

After reading Winder's letter, Madison ordered it hand-delivered to General Armstrong's lodgings at the nearby Seven Buildings, a set of row houses on Nineteenth Street. It was not yet eight o'clock, and the

President rode directly to the brick house of the schoolmaster at the Navy Yard, which General Winder occupied as his headquarters.

The President was greeted by a man on the verge of collapse. Both of his horses being "exhausted and worn down," General Winder had spent much of the night on foot, wearing a path between the encampment at the Navy Yard and the Eastern Branch, where preparations were under way to blow up the bridges should the British approach. On his way back to the camp at three A.M., Winder had tumbled into a ditch in the darkness, emerging "considerably hurt in the right arm and ancle."[19] This morning, with less than two hours of fitful sleep, he was in a self-described "wearied and exhausted state" after six days and nights of "incessant application and exertion."[20]

The circle of advisers soon grew larger. Secretary of the Navy Jones was already there when the President arrived, but soon Colonel Monroe and Attorney General Rush joined the meeting. As they waited for General Armstrong, they could see Commodore Barney and his men working at gun emplacements on a hill overlooking the head of the lower bridge over the Eastern Branch. General Winder's orders were explicit: Barney and his men were to defend the bridge, but if the enemy gained ground, the American artillerymen were to destroy it. One boat with eight barrels of powder was already anchored beneath the bridge, along with other smaller boats also loaded with explosives. Fence rails and planks from a demolished tollhouse had been piled on the roadbed to fuel the blaze. Not far away, the only other means of crossing the Eastern Branch to the city, the rickety upper bridge, was already afire, kindled before dawn at Winder's order.

Even with these counselors at hand, the accumulated wisdom in the room didn't mean General Winder could decide upon a definite plan, and the deliberations continued to be subject, as one infantry surgeon recorded, to "a continual succession . . . of false reports and false alarms."[21] Dragoons who had been acting as scouts arrived every few minutes with the latest intelligence, some of which seemed to suggest that the enemy would "most likely move in a direction toward the Potomac, with a view to possess himself of Fort Warburton."[22] Plans and counterproposals were offered, but no decision was made to act. Every report of the enemy's movements seemed to contradict the last without diminishing the fear and expectation of attack.

At ten o'clock, a messenger arrived with news that changed the tenor of the discussion among these tired men. This report, soon confirmed, asserted "that the enemy had turned the head of his column towards Bladensburg."[23] At last, General Winder and his counselors were convinced that the British, at march since daybreak, had chosen the northern attack route. And it meant Washington City was in great danger. Winder quickly issued orders for the troops to march upriver to Bladensburg. Colonel Monroe, who in recent days had warned anyone who would listen that the danger to the capital was real, mounted his horse and raced toward Bladensburg to alert the commander there, General Stansbury. Before Winder could follow the Secretary of State to the front, General Armstrong strode in.

Though "impatiently expected" by Mr. Madison, he arrived a full hour after everyone else.[24] The usually impassive President could not hold his irritation in check, but even after a presidential reprimand, Armstrong was not contrite. It was his second dressing-down by Madison in barely a week, and he looked sullen, evidently irritated that Winder's letter to him "had been opened, and passed through other hands," and at what he saw as interference by Madison and Monroe.[25]

Mr. Madison asked him if he had any advice for General Winder. The Secretary of War demurred. He offered only the bitter observation that, if "the battle would be between [American] Militia and regular [British] troops, the former would be beaten."[26]

III.
Noon . . . August 24, 1814 . . . The President's House

MRS. MADISON HELD THE SPYGLASS TO HER EYE. From her architectural aerie high in the President's house, she scanned the faces of the refugees along the length of Pennsylvania Avenue, hoping to "discern the approach of [her] dear husband and his friends." Instead, she observed groups of soldiers who seemed to have no particular destination. To her, they exhibited "a lack of arms, or of spirit to fight for their own firesides!"[27]

Resorting to routine even in this extraordinary circumstance, Mrs. Madison went about preparing for a midafternoon dinner. The day before she had done the same, anticipating that James would return in the company of members of his cabinet and military officers. She had even dared to hope that one or another of their wives would appear, but that expectation evaporated when she received a note from Eleanor Jones, wife of the Secretary of the Navy, who most courteously sent her regrets. "My dear Madam," Mrs. Jones had written, "In the present state of alarm and bustle of preparation, for the worst that may happen, I imagine it will be mutually convenient, to dispense with the enjoyment of your hospitality today."[28]

A full day later, most all of Mrs. Madison's acquaintance was gone from town and most of the city's businesses shuttered; still, she ordered James's manservant, fifteen-year-old Paul Jennings, to prepare the table for dining.[29] The slave placed cider, ale, and open bottles of Madeira in coolers near to hand. But such small and familiar rituals offered little reassurance to Dolley.

The hundred-man guard assigned to protect the President's house had disappeared, melting away like so much of the city's population, but the household staff showed no sign of abandoning Mrs. Madison. Paul remained near at hand, as did her personal body slave and maid, Sukey.

Mrs. Madison even found herself having to rein in Jean-Pierre Sioussat. Though educated for the priesthood, "French John" had run off to sea at seventeen; then, after circumnavigating the globe in the service of the French navy, he jumped ship in New York in 1805, where he literally swam to shore. Eventually he made his way to Washington City, working first for the British Minister, then for Mrs. Madison, in whose service he rose to majordomo. He was wise in the ways of protocol, etiquette, and, as a child of the French Revolution, guns and gunpowder. He offered to spike the two 12-pounder cannon at the gate and "to lay a train of powder which would blow up the British."[30] Though warmed by his devotion to the cause, Mrs. Madison forbade him to do any such thing.

The kitchen staff downstairs readied dinner, per Mrs. Madison's order, to be served as usual at three o'clock. In the Dining Room, the table was set for thirty or more guests. Yet nothing seemed certain, not even in a room where James and Dolley had entertained so many of their neighbors, friends, powers of the town, political foes, and even foreigners, all under her socializing influence.

The well-lit room was another of Mrs. Madison's and Mr. Latrobe's joint accomplishments. He had purchased white-handled knives and forks and a china set to supplement the existing china. He installed an immense sideboard as well as the long table, which the servants now had moved to the center of the room in preparation for dinner. In its middle sat a silver platter that, after sundown, would reflect candlelight, illuminating the faces of the guests in a gentle, flickering glow. The young Elbridge Gerry had been impressed by this large corner room, calling it "very spacious, and twice the height of modern parlours and three times as large."[31]

The most important object in the room was not a Madison acquisition; the big portrait had arrived in 1800. In a day when the size of a canvas typically determined its cost, the purchase price for the eight-foot-tall painting of George Washington had been a substantial eight hundred dollars.

He stood the size of life, posed like an orator in a monumental setting between two columns, in a heavy gilt frame screwed fast to the west wall. Though the painting was perhaps not one of Mr. Gilbert Stuart's original Washingtons—Mrs. Madison had been told by her friend Mrs. William Thornton that Stuart "denies most pointedly having painted the picture in the President's house"—there was no mistaking the subject, who, unlike other Founding Fathers, remained universally honored.

Mrs. Madison and Latrobe had differed about the great portrait's placement. She favored the Elliptical Salon, but Latrobe argued that a grand mirror would serve that room better. With Mr. Madison's support, he persuaded her that the State Dining Room ought to be "the picture room, and . . . that not only the Gen[era]l.—but the succeeding Presidents should have a place there."[32] As a result, the big painting now hung in the well-lit corner room, a notable presence in a space with no elaborate curtains and fewer decorative elements than the Drawing Room or Parlor. George Washington, standing and gesturing as if delivering a speech, seemed to demand the attention of the room.

In the absence of her husband and their guests, with only the likeness of the General and her servants for company, Dolley sat quietly at her desk and picked up her pen once more. Yesterday she had begun a letter to her sister Lucy; it was a fits-and-starts letter, but then often her letters were. Her friends knew her as a diligent but often interrupted correspondent, and her letters reflected her distracted manner. She could write with great precision, but her handwriting tended to reflect her mood. When she was not in a hurry, her script had a graceful slant. When she had the most to say, her lines strayed from the strictly horizontal. They wandered, as if falling forward, spreading across the page, the careful elegance abandoned, the energy or passion apparent.

At this particular moment Mrs. Madison's elegant Italianate hand devolved to a "scrall," as she called it, expressive of her "unwearied anxiety."[33] Yet she was firm in her resolution and "so unfeminine as to be free from fear, and willing to remain in the *Castle*."[34]

CHAPTER 7

"The Bladensburg Races"

Tomorrow is the twenty-fourth,
And much indeed I fear
That then, or on the following day,
That Cockburn will be here.
—"The Bladensburg Races," anonymous

1.

Morning . . . Wednesday, August 24, 1814 . . . Bladensburg, Maryland

BLADENSBURG WAS A GEOGRAPHICAL ACCIDENT, a result of the pitch and yaw of the rolling countryside and the run of the river. Laid out in 1752, the village center occupied sixty acres along a curving main street lined with houses of brick and stone. Once a port of call for tobacco schooners, Bladensburg had seen its busy river trade fade as the plantations went south and silt raised the river bottom. Regular mail coaches still came through along the national thoroughfare that led to prosperous Baltimore, but the place had become a drowsy stopping place for travelers who crossed the Bladensburg bridge on their way elsewhere.

As Colonel Monroe urged his horse northward on the eight-mile journey to Bladensburg, the temperature rose above ninety degrees. The four hundred inhabitants of the town had, just the previous night, awakened to the sound of soldiers marching; with the report of Winder's retreat to the Navy Yard, the 2,150 militiamen commanded by General Tobias Stansbury had struck their tents and retired from their Loundes Hill bivouac east of town. The column of troops had snaked along Bladensburg's high street, crossed its bridge, and headed west along the turnpike road toward Washington City.

At sunrise Stansbury and his men halted a mile and a half from Bladensburg near a brickyard, and General Stansbury rode to the top of a nearby hill to examine their situation. When he rejoined his troops, an express rider awaited with orders from General Winder. Stansbury's forces were "to oppose the enemy . . . should he attempt a passage by way of Bladensburg."[1]

Even before Colonel Monroe brought the news that the British were in full march toward Bladensburg, General Stansbury knew what the British objective would be. If the two bridges at the Navy Yard at Washington City were destroyed, Bladensburg would become the only river crossing between the British and the capital. To the south of town, the Eastern Branch was too wide and deep to ford, and the dwindling stream to the north meandered into a rugged terrain of hills and forest through which marching would be difficult. The topography had anticipated the town; now its bridge, vital to the British advance, would be the center of the looming battle.

On his arrival, Colonel Monroe inspected Stansbury's order of battle. About 50 yards west of the bridge, the Georgetown Road angled away from the post road, and Stansbury had arranged his first line of defense in the fork's acute angle. Dirt flew on the rise that overlooked the river some 350 yards away as two companies of volunteer artillerymen from Baltimore, working with shovels and their bare hands, raced to complete an earthworks to shield six 6-pounders. In the bushes to the right of the battery stood 150 Baltimore riflemen, commanded by the former Attorney General Major William Pinkney. Two companies of Maryland militia

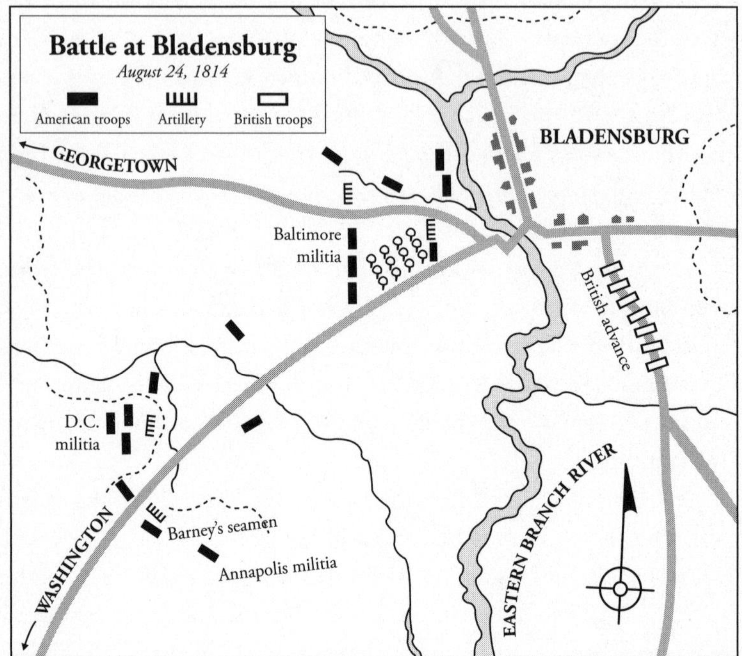

occupied the left flank near a tobacco barn on the Georgetown Road. Though positioned to act as riflemen, most of these men carried shorter-range muskets. A second and larger line of troops consisting of several brigades and a company of cavalry waited in the partial cover of an orchard, positioned to support the first line and to cover both the Georgetown and Washington roads.

Colonel Monroe immediately saw something he didn't like in Stansbury's configuration. Monroe believed "the left would be much exposed, as it scarcely extended to the rear of the battery."[2] He ordered one of the Baltimore regiments to a new station, 150 yards farther back to higher ground beyond the orchard. This position, though exposed, offered an expansive view of Bladensburg and the likely British advance. As these and other troops were shifted, Colonel Monroe met with Stansbury. Soon after, at about noon, Brigadier General Winder arrived.

Some eight hundred militiamen from Annapolis, commanded by Lieutenant Colonel Beall, marched across the bridge. The men had hustled sixteen miles that morning in the heat. Though dog-tired, they took a position anchoring a third line of defense atop a hill that looked down upon the Washington turnpike, several hundred yards behind the artillery breastwork and Pinkney's rifles. From the other direction, reinforcements began to arrive from the Navy Yard, and another gun emplacement of three 6-pounders was established on the Georgetown Road about five hundred yards from the bridge, manned by Captain Burch's volunteers from Washington City. Two more guns were set on the Washington road, their barrels directed at the Bladensburg pass. The scene was ever-changing, with the several commanders issuing orders that shifted infantry, artillery, and cavalry this way and that, not unlike sand on a tidal shore.

Though a member of no militia, William Simmons, a former War Department accountant, appeared at Colonel Monroe's side. Inspired by the alarm raised at the approaching British, he wished to offer "all the services in [his] power to oppose them." Simmons volunteered to reconnoiter the enemy as "no person appeared to be able to give any correct account of them."[3] With Monroe's approval, Simmons rode across the bridge to Bladensburg. Inquiring of militiamen in Ross's tavern what they knew of the British advance, he learned nothing. Regaining his horse, he rode east to the summit of Lowndes Hill, a rise less than half a mile from the town with an unobstructed view south along the river road. At first he could discern no sign of the enemy, but, after a short wait, he saw "at a considerable distance, a great cloud of dust." Though Simmons supposed it was the British "coming in great force," he continued watching.

Soon he spotted "a few horsemen, not in uniform, on the road, who appeared to be reconnoitering." Then a column of enemy troops began to fill the road behind the advance guard. The infantry marched "in close order, not less than twenty-four or thirty abreast in front." Simmons wheeled his horse and returned the way he came. As he recrossed the Bladensburg bridge, he saw the first British horsemen entering the streets and lanes of the town behind him.

Less than two months before, a War Department cartographer had surveyed Bladensburg. The man concluded that the town, with its long bridge across the river, offered the American defenders their best chance to stop an invading force bent on attacking Washington City.[4] He reported his findings to General Armstrong, but his recommendations had gone no further—Armstrong devised no strategy, made no plans. After all, President Madison had delegated the matter of defending the Tenth Military District to somebody else. To Armstrong's way of thinking, Bladensburg was General Winder's problem.*[5]

II.

Late Morning . . . Wednesday, August 24, 1814 . . . The Eastern Branch Bridge

AT HIS POST, GUARDING THE BRIDGE, Commodore Joshua Barney learned from a passing messenger of the British quick march on Bladensburg. Under orders from General Winder, Barney's seamen and marines were ready to defend and, if necessary, destroy the bridge if the enemy approached. But as Barney mulled over the new knowledge that the point of enemy attack would be miles away, he felt his ire rising.

Moments later Mr. Madison rode up, accompanied by militia officers and members of his cabinet, among them Secretary of the Navy

* Armstrong's inattention has been much discussed by historians, but surviving words of both Madison and Treasury Secretary Campbell describe a conversation the latter had with Armstrong in which the Secretary of War acknowledged he would be "taking no part on so critical an occasion." Madison bearded Armstrong twice that morning, once at the Navy Yard and later at Bladensburg; the upshot, in Armstrong's own words, was that he became "a mere spectator of the combat."

Jones. As an officer long known to the Chief Magistrate, Barney ignored the usual chain of command and pled his case directly to the President as Secretary Jones stood by. He hated the idea of being so far from the action, especially "with five hundred of the precious few fighting men." The Commodore argued that he and his men were being asked "to do what any damned corporal can better do with five."[6] His experienced artillerymen, he insisted, would be of far greater use at Bladensburg.

Madison quickly approved a new plan. A few men were detailed to remain at the bridge with two guns, and Commodore Barney rode off at speed on his bay horse, bound for Bladensburg. Pulling the rest of their great guns, his men followed at a trot, though many were without shoes and others "very much crippled from the severe marches . . . [of] the days before."[7]

Secretary Jones went in another direction, back to the Navy Yard, where preparations needed to be made to destroy military materials in the event the British broke through the American line. Vessels under construction, provisions, ammunition, powder, and other stores collected there must not fall into enemy hands. The ailing Secretary of the Treasury, visibly ill and unsteady on his feet, also rode off, bound for Washington City, but not before loaning the President a pair of large dueling pistols.

Thus armed, Mr. Madison rode north, hoping that his presence might help avoid any "embarrassing conflicts of authority" between Generals Armstrong and Winder.[8] After a short distance, his horse went unexpectedly lame, and, once again, the President relied upon the kindness of a friend, as Major Charles Carroll gave him his mount. Then, in the company of Rush and others, Madison rode toward Bladensburg.[9]

III.

12:00 P.M. . . . Wednesday, August 24, 1814 . . . The Orchard

THE GATHERING WAS PERHAPS THE ODDEST CABINET MEETING EVER. The men sat astride their horses, sunlight filtering through apple branches sagging with the weight of ripening fruit. Secretary of War John Armstrong attended, along with Secretary of State Monroe and Attorney General Richard Rush. The august body met almost within rifle range of the front line of Mr. Madison's War.

The meeting commenced. Together with General Winder, the heads of the departments and their aides discussed the distribution of soldiers and arms in the field around them. The President, whose borrowed horse bucked and dived, seemingly intent on throwing him off, heard little of the exchange as he wrestled with the reins. Behind them on the road just traveled, more of Winder's troops straggled in from the Navy Yard, "some fainting from loss of sleep, from hunger, fatigue [and] . . . the intensity of the heat."[10]

The number of American volunteers on hand rose toward seven thousand, but arranged on the ridge overlooking the water, the collection of different contingents appeared to be something less than an unified army. The regular soldiers in blue were far outnumbered by the militiamen, almost none of whom wore uniforms. They dressed in garb that ranged from plain black to ordinary shooting jackets and farming clothes. To the knowing eye, even those in the militias who had been issued guns and other military equipment remained "just what they were before, a parcel of inoffensive clerks or journeymen mechanics," many of them farmers called from their fields to war.[11] "[S]tanding, with muskets in their hands, on the brow of a bare green hill," the lines of American fighting men "might have passed off very well for a crowd of spectators."[12]

Within sight of this ragtag army, British dragoons, wary of American sharpshooters, explored the streets of the town. The main body of the British army paused at the outskirts of Bladensburg until the advance guard determined that the entire American force had abandoned the town for the far side of the stream. When no resistance was encountered, the red-uniformed infantry followed the vanguard into Bladensburg.

Though the American position atop the heights was advantageous, the British force the Americans looked down upon had an intimidating aspect. The longer one watched, the longer was the column that marched into Bladensburg from the Marlborough Road. With each collective step, His Majesty's army raised more dust through which their polished bayonets glittered, reflecting the sun, now at its zenith. Despite having marched some fifteen miles since first light, the soldiers in their bright red tunics maintained their rank and file. This was a disciplined, veteran army, aware and unafraid of the forthcoming combat.

Mr. Madison confided his plan in Colonel Monroe. He wished "to take a position, with the members of the administration in the rear of the line, that, looking to all the functions of the government, he might be able to act with their counsel according to circumstances."[13] Madison, like a puppet master, wanted to be able to monitor the imminent exchange, that he might exercise some control over what he expected would be a pitched battle. Though Madison lacked firsthand battle experience, he intended to fulfill his role as the nation's commander in chief.

Both sides now could see the Americans' artillery advantage. The British had almost no cannon, with just two or three small field pieces, while on the American side of the bridge the count was twenty and more, with some cannon entrenched behind the redoubt near where Madison stood. Farther back along the Washington road were Commodore Barney and his men, still arriving and working in haste to set their guns another three hundred yards from the bridge.

The spot Barney chose for his gun emplacement was a knoll that enabled him to sight his guns along the length of the Washington City road. He was flanked by another battery of guns on the left, as well as militiamen on both sides. Close to hand, some of his own marines and flotillamen were posted to act as infantry in protection of the artillery. Commodore Barney and his gun emplacement anchored the third line of defense; the British would have to pass through him if they wished to attack Washington.

Riding about the field, continually arranging and rearranging his forces, General Winder could not help but wonder how they would fare. By the time he rode over to inspect the 3-gun artillery installation on the Georgetown Road, he seemed resigned to an outcome that would not be to the advantage of his side. He remarked to a gunnery sergeant, "When you retreat, take notice you must retreat by the Georgetown road."[14] Others in the field held similar opinions. In concert, Joseph Sterett of the Maryland militia, Major Pinkney, and another officer recommended to General Stansbury that they fall back in order to better organize a defense.[15] With the British army marching toward them, splendid in their uniforms, the time for rethinking had passed. Looking down the Georgetown Road, General Winder pointed toward the Bladensburg bridge.

"[T]here is the enemy," Winder told Captain Benjamin Burch. "Take charge of your pieces."[16]

AS ONE O'CLOCK APPROACHED, both armies looked across the hundred-foot length of the bridge. The narrow roadbed, barely wide enough for three men to walk shoulder to shoulder, was entirely exposed to the array of American rifles, muskets, and cannon.

At General Winder's command, his forces opened fire as the first of His Majesty's forces charged across the bridge. The American cannon proved quick and well directed, with "bloody consequences" for the attackers.[17] Almost as soon as the charge began, an order to fall back was heard, and the British withdrew, seeking shelter in the town out of the line of fire. One Scotsman slumped onto the steps of a nearby house, his arm "shattered by a round-shot, . . . still dangling by a fibre to the stump."[18] Other British soldiers lay dead and wounded on the bridge.

From the American line, a cheer echoed across the stream.

The elation was temporary. After some minutes passed, a second wave of the British, this time led by an officer on horseback brandishing his saber, attacked at double-quick time. With a bugler sounding the charge, the bridge filled with redcoats. The forward battery of American guns played again, and in the renewed firing "almost an entire company was swept down." Though the riflemen and the musketry took a deadly toll, this time the British did not retreat. "[I]t was not without trampling upon many of their dead and dying comrades, that the light brigade established itself on the opposite side of the stream."[19]

In these early minutes of fierce fighting, the banshee-like wail of Congreve rockets added to the din. Resembling overscaled broomsticks with iron cylinders strapped to their tops, the devices whooshed harmlessly over the heads of the American defenders. Sitting astride their horses, Mr. Madison and Mr. Rush watched the enemy rockets arching high out of range. As he observed the unfamiliar elements of war—the British charge, the play of American artillery fire, the unpredictable movement of the battle—the President recognized that any notion he had of influencing strategy was unrealistic. He said as much to his companions, Rush, Armstrong, and Monroe. "[I]t would be proper to withdraw to a position in the rear," he observed, ". . . leaving the military movements now to the military functionaries who [are] responsible for them."[20]

The British officer who led the second charge had his horse shot from beneath him, but Colonel William Thornton, sword in hand, continued to lead the charge on foot. After a musket ball ripped into his thigh, he fell to the ground; his men lifted him to the roadside.[21] But the British advance continued. Just upstream from the bridge men were fording the shallow Eastern Branch as American militiamen near the tobacco barn above them emptied their muskets. The Americans were hard to discern in the tall grasses, dressed as they were in drab shades. Though the British sought cover in the thicket of willow and larch at the water's edge, more than twenty of the brightly uniformed men fell to the volleys of American fire. The British abandoned their knapsacks and haversacks to lighten their load and showed no sign of slowing as they pressed forward.[22]

More British infantrymen surged across the bridge. On reaching the American side, the well-drilled soldiers formed first one line of attackers, then another, and advanced on the center of the American force. Men continued to fall but fresh troops stepped up, "fill[ing] the voids thus created, without turning to the right or to the left to see whether their companions had lost a head, a leg, or an arm."[23] For a time, the defenders believed their cannon remained "manifestly destructive . . . produc[ing] hesitation and disorder in the enemy's ranks." But as the British neared, the American artillery fire began to carry over their heads. Behind their hastily built redoubts, the gunners were unable to lower the barrels of their 6-pounders to keep the charging British in the line of fire.

With bayonets bared, the British drove into the American line. When they rushed Major Pinkney's riflemen, few of whom were armed with bayonets, the Baltimore men retreated. The nearby artillery discontinued its fire altogether, and Pinkney himself left the field, seeking surgical assistance to treat a wound. A musket ball had splintered the bone in his upper right arm.[24]

A renewed barrage of rockets exploded overhead. After lowering the angle of inclination of the tripod bases from which the rockets were fired, the rocketeers had found the range. Suddenly the hissing rockets followed almost horizontal paths, showering sparks as they screamed over the lines of defenders and exploded at random. For men not hardened even to the sound of cannon, the din of the wildly wobbling rockets immediately overhead proved too much. Two of the regiments in the second line of defense gave way in a panic, breaking ranks and dispersing. Their departure left the gunners on the Georgetown Road unprotected, and General Winder ordered Burch and his artillerymen to "limber and retreat . . . as the enemy advanced so rapidly."[25]

The British soon outflanked the first American line of defense on both right and left; the supporting troops in the rear, already giving ground, were soon followed by the remaining men as a general order to retire was heard. There had been attempts by officers in the field to keep the ranks from breaking. Colonel Monroe was among those urging the men to fight and, "active in his efforts to aid the officers in the discharge of their duties, [Monroe] exposed himself to much danger."[26] General Winder did the same, ordering men to return to their lines and fight.

On the British side, an officer on a white charger rode to the top of the rise just vacated by the American force. Conspicuous by his gold-laced hat and the epaulets on his shoulders, Admiral George Cockburn looked as fearless as the men around him. He had little respect for the American military. For the past two summers his men had repeatedly bested the militiamen in skirmishes. When his fellow officer General Ross had expressed his doubts about an assault on Washington—as an experienced field commander, Ross knew his lack of cavalry and artillery could spell disaster—Cockburn made the case for striking the city. As recently as two weeks earlier, the admiral had ventured upstream on the St. Mary's River; his party of marines marched inland and destroyed "a building Manufacturing Cotton," then returned to the ships eighteen hours later. Their foray into enemy territory had been met by not "a single armed Person nor was one Musquet fired." Cockburn concluded that "the Inhabitants of this State Appear to have learnt that it is wiser for them to submit entirely to our Mercy than to attempt to oppose us in Arms."[27] Now Admiral Cockburn watched with satisfaction as, just as he predicted, much of the American force ran in terror.

But the danger had not altogether passed. As he surveyed the field where the fiery rockets landed amid the retreating Americans, "a musket-shot passed between the Admiral's leg and the flap of his saddle, cutting the stirrup leather in two, without doing any injury to him or to the horse." As a marine attempted to lash the severed strap together with twine, a round shot struck him, instantly dispatching the man "to the other world."[28]

Positioned a distance back from the line by Colonel Monroe, cavalry commander Lieutenant Colonel Jacint Lavall and his men had played little role in the battle. His view of the action was limited when the firing began, so Colonel Lavall rode forward "to judge better of the opportunity which might offer." The shower of rockets greeted him; then, as he watched, the American force before him seemed to disintegrate. "All of a sudden . . . a confused retreat appeared to be about in every corner of the battleground." Many ran in the direction of Georgetown—and Lavall and his men were in their path. "They poured in torrents by us; . . . an artillery company drove through . . . [and] several of my men were crushed down, horses and all, and myself narrowly escaped having my thigh broken by one of the wheels which nearly took me off my horse." Like most of the American troops at Bladensburg, Lavall found himself "in the midst of a confusion, the like of which I have never seen in a field of battle."[29] Men disappeared into the woods and a nearby swamp, while others retreated down the several roads that led away from Bladensburg.

Just after two o'clock, official word that "the battle was lost" reached Mr. Madison in a hastily scribbled note from General Winder. The President, accompanied by Mr. Rush, then "fell down into the road leading to the city."[30] Mr. Madison quickly penciled a warning to Dolley, which he entrusted to James Smith, a freeman of color in the President's service. Smith galloped off.

As the President joined the retreat to Washington City, surrounded by a sea of militiamen, many of whom hadn't even discharged their weapons, they rode past the last line of defense between Admiral Cockburn and his advance on the Capitol.

SINCE THE ONLY AMERICAN COCKBURN REGARDED AS A WORTHY OPPONENT that summer was Joshua Barney, it was only fitting that the Commodore and his flotillamen stood squarely in the Admiral's path.

Though he was accustomed to the deck of a ship, Joshua Barney's piece of terra firma was quite suitable for making a stand. From his gun emplacement he surveyed a small valley; the little flat was, he knew, Bladensburg's dueling ground, where gentlemen of Washington came across the line from the capital to settle disputes of honor by violent means.

Captain Barney and his mix of sailors and marines had barely unlimbered their guns when the first waves of retreating American soldiers streamed toward them. Barney expected they would halt and reform near his position, but he was "cruelly disappointed" when his countrymen swept past "with rapid step, in evident confusion and disorder."[31] But he stood his ground, his guns silent, waiting until "the enemy made his appearance on the main road, in force."[32] Unlike the army flooding past, Barney and his men were intimidated by neither the oncoming British nor their infernal rockets. They had faced both on St. Leonard's Creek.

The American front lines had evacuated in barely an hour, and by two o'clock the British began marching toward Barney's position. After the invaders proceeded a few hundred yards, Barney's heavy artillery came into view, directly in their path. Upon seeing the two 18-pounders and three 12-pounders, the British halted.

On the American side, Barney dismounted and sighted the guns himself before climbing back into the saddle. His men still held their fire.

When the British resumed their march, their rocketeers commenced throwing Congreve missiles at the Americans. In return, Barney ordered his expert artillerists to open fire. A full play of round and grapeshot had the desired effect, clearing the road of attackers. The British ranks soon reformed, but a second and a third move toward the American gun emplacement were met with grape and canister fire, and the enemy sustained heavy losses. The Washington road was strewn with enemy dead and wounded.

The British determined to take another line of attack, leaving the road to launch a flanking action. For a time, the Americans checked and even drove back the British assault, delaying their progress for nearly half an hour as the killing fire from Barney's cannon continued. But Commodore Barney could see the odds were against him. "By this time not a vestige of the American army remained, except a body of five or six hundred, posed on a height on my right, from whom I expected much support."[33]

The British tried yet another tactic, relying upon sharpshooters in advance of the main body of troops while dispatching two or three hundred men toward the remaining Americans on the hill. Barney's horse was shot from beneath him; it fell dead between two cannon. As he watched, to his "great mortification" the American troops to his starboard side "made no resistance, giving a fire or two, and retired."[34] He was outflanked. The desertion of their position by his own countrymen left one of the black sailors muttering contemptuously that the militiamen "ran like sheep chased by dogs."[35]

Barney and his men fought on, despite having "the whole army of the enemy to contend with." More than a dozen of their own lay dead and wounded nearby, but Barney's crewmen kept loading and firing. "[A]s fast as their companions and messmates fell at the guns, they were instantly replaced from the infantry."[36]

Several of his best officers were already among the casualties when Barney himself took a musket ball in the thigh. For a time, he managed to remain upright and in command, but with the flow of blood from his wound unstanched, he weakened. The fight began to seem truly hopeless. The supply of ammunition was almost exhausted since the drivers of the ammunition wagons had fled in the earlier melee. Finally, Barney told his men they must give up the fight. As he was too weak to ride or even stand, they refused to leave him. When he ordered them to quit the field, his men laid him on the ground a short distance from the battery and made good their retreat.

With Barney's guns no longer impeding their passage, the British swarmed over the American position. The Commodore lay prostrate and bleeding in the bushes to one side of the thoroughfare. A youthful-looking British naval officer wearing a short jacket was the first enemy combatant to approach him. Upon learning the wounded man was none other than Commodore Barney himself, Captain Wainwright quickly rode off, soon to reappear in the company of both Admiral Cockburn and General Ross.

Wounded and bleeding, his voice weak, Barney nevertheless offered the first salvo. "Well, Admiral," he said to Cockburn, "you have got hold of me at last."[37]

"Do not let us speak on that subject, Commodore," the Admiral replied. "I regret to see you in this state. I hope you are not seriously hurt."

Ross, too, addressed their prisoner respectfully. "I am really *very glad* to see you, Commodore," said General Ross.

"I am sorry I cannot return your compliment," was Captain Barney's retort. The fifty-five-year-old Revolutionary War veteran took no pleasure in becoming, for the fourth time in his military life, a British prisoner of war.[38]

A surgeon was brought and Barney's wound dressed. Four sailors arrived with a litter; they carried the Commodore to Ross's tavern in Bladensburg. On a day memorable for a lack of bravery on the American side, Joshua Barney became its most notable hero in the eyes of the uniformed men on both the American and British sides. For almost two hours his flotillamen, though vastly outnumbered and largely unsupported, had held the British at bay. But with Barney's guns silenced, no further obstacles stood between the four British battalions and Washington City.

IV.

Three O'Clock . . . Wednesday, August 24, 1814 . . . The President's House

"WILL YOU BELIEVE IT, MY SISTER?" Once again seated at her writing table, Mrs. Madison added to the letter that, at intervals, she had been composing since the previous evening. "We had a battle or skirmish near Bladensburg, and I am still here within sound of the cannon!"

Showing unusual candor, Mrs. Madison's jottings amounted to a dramatic monologue. It was both a cogent narrative of the changing circumstances at the President's house and a record of her own emotional journey. Her letter to Lucy Payne Washington Todd conveyed more, perhaps, than even its author knew.

The preceding two days had been an agony of waiting. Mrs. Madison occupied herself and her majordomo, French John, working at the packing of the Cabinet papers, transferring the contents of desks and cupboards into trunks and boxes. When Mrs. Madison put such distractions aside for a moment and picked up her pen, a range of emotions surfaced.

She felt fear for her husband. "Mr. Madison comes not," she told her sister, "may God protect him."[39] She knew frustration with the city's defenders and anger at the attackers. "If I could have . . . a cannon through every window; but, alas! Those who should have placed them there fled." Like the gray clouds that now filled the sky, she felt burdened by grief at the nation's plight. "[M]y whole heart mourn[s] for my country."[40]

When Dolley looked about her in the presidential mansion, her distress was magnified by a growing sense of personal loss. Before departing that morning, James gave her clear instructions that she should be prepared to flee directly if she received word that the battle went badly. Having readied the nation's papers for carting, she now surveyed her own goods with an eye to removing a favored few. Time and space would allow the packing and transport of token objects only, and, on an impulse, she ordered that the red velvet curtains from her Elliptical Salon be stowed. Some of her clothes, along with a few books, were packed. Perhaps it had been the approach of the dinner hour that prompted her to add to the road-ready goods a small bronze timepiece that had arrived with the first residents of the President's house, John and Abigail Adams.

Yet as she came to accept that she must bid her house farewell, she sought to maintain some semblance of normality. She could still vaguely hope that, as on more usual days, the chimes at three o'clock would mean dinner was served. Even as she wrote to Lucy, the cloth was still on the table, the Madeira cooling on ice, and some forty places had been set. But the arrival of the dinner hour did not bring the hoped-for return of James.

Instead, from a bedchamber window, her servant Sukey spotted another face known to the occupants of the President's house. James Smith, Madison's messenger, galloped into view. As he neared, Sukey saw him wave his hat.

When he came into earshot, he could be heard exclaiming, "Clear out, clear out! General Armstrong has ordered a retreat!"

In that instant, the pose of normalcy was exploded. The upset in the household, suppressed for hours, gave way to panic. "All then was confusion. . . . People were running in every direction."[41]

Mrs. Madison ordered her carriage be brought round, intending to obey James's instructions. On passing through the dining room, "she caught up what silver she could crowd into her old-fashioned reticule." Her string bag was now heavy with flatware.

The moment of departure was at hand. Charles Carroll appeared, returned from Bladensburg. "Our kind friend," Mrs. Madison noted, "has come to hasten my departure." But out of a deeply ingrained instinct for the public gesture, Dolley determined in an instant that one more task required her attention before she could abandon ship. It wasn't the papers. Those were gone, on their way to safekeeping out of town, as was most of the silver plate and the engravings and oil portraits of the Madisons.

Fond though she was of Mr. Latrobe's elegant Grecian furniture, that would not prevent her from retreating, nor would her remaining wardrobe of gowns and turbans. But one thing did.

Her departure would be delayed by a personage that Dolley had known in life and that her countrymen revered even in death; the unsmiling visage of the General could hardly be left behind. His painted expression was pinched, his false teeth by his own account "uneasy in the mouth" (they were made of animal and human teeth, mounted on lead plates).[42] George Washington, as rendered onto canvas almost twenty years before, looked down from his perch on the dining room wall. His likeness elicited from Dolley Madison a sense of obligation even in a moment of immense and growing danger.

CHARLES CARROLL'S PATIENCE QUICKLY GREW THIN. He was attempting to fulfill a duty to Mr. Madison; he was to escort Mrs. Madison away from Washington City, but, as the retreating army threatened to clog her avenue of escape, she refused to depart. The great portrait of Washington was still firmly fastened to the wall a few feet away. Until it had been secured, she would consent to go nowhere.

Two servants had set to the task of freeing the portrait for transport. Taller than any man and nearly an arm-span in width, the great picture was screwed to the dining room wall. But French John Sioussat was again proving his worth. With Mrs. Madison's permission, he and gardener Thomas McGaw hacked away at the decorative frame with a hatchet. With the gilt frame soon reduced to little more than kindling, the canvas on its stretcher came free and was lowered to the floor.

The British were rumored to be fast approaching, perhaps only a few squares distant. Two gentlemen of New York were at hand, having arrived on the heels of James Smith, offering their services. One was Jacob Barker, a ship owner and merchant who had brokered loans to provide the cash-strapped government the funds it needed to continue the war. A strong Madison ally, he had expressed his respect for another occupant of the President's house, naming one of his merchant ships *Lady Madison*. It was to Barker and his friend Robert G. L. De Peyster that the portrait was entrusted, and, at last, after issuing strict instructions, Mrs. Madison finally agreed to leave. "The Portrait I am very anxious to save," she told them. Equally, however, she said, it was imperative than they destroy the painting rather than allow it "to fall into the hands of the enemy, as [its] Capture would enable them to make a great Finish."[43]

Closing her letter at last, she wrote: "And now dear sister, I must leave this house, or the retreating army will make me a prisoner in it, by filling up the road I am directed to take. When I shall write, or where I shall be tomorrow, I cannot tell!!"

By three thirty, Mrs. Madison left the President's house for good.

JOINING MRS. MADISON IN HER CARRIAGE WERE MR. CARROLL, Anna Cutts and her three children, and Sukey. Richard Cutts followed in his carriage, which Paul Jennings brought from a stable on Fourteenth Street. Other members of the President's household took flight, too. The butler, John Freeman, lashed a featherbed to a coach and drove off with his wife, child, and servant.

Mrs. Madison's entourage rode west on Pennsylvania Avenue, then turned north onto Bridge Street. They crossed Rock Creek, entering Georgetown. On arriving at Belle Vue, Mr. Carroll's mansion, Mrs. Madison could look from the eminence of Georgetown Heights, surveying the city she had just abandoned.

The family of Navy Secretary Jones joined them, and Mr. Jones himself soon arrived. After five o'clock, the carriages sallied forth once again, bound for the Georgetown Ferry to make the Potomac crossing to Virginia.

AT THE PRESIDENT'S HOUSE, MR. MADISON'S RETURN was still anticipated. Having purchased the services of a cart, Barker and De Peyster returned as they promised Mrs. Madison they would. Aided by two servants, the two men loaded the portrait of the General, some large silver urns and other household goods, and two eagle ornaments that Mrs. Madison had taken from the walls of the Elliptical Salon at the last moment. While the two men waited for the avenue to clear of the troops retreating from Bladensburg, Mr. Madison arrived.

He had gotten little sleep and spent much of the past several days in the saddle, but, despite his exhaustion, he refused food, taking only a glass of wine. From his belt, he removed the dueling pistols Treasury Secretary Campbell had loaned him that morning. Still trying to understand what he had seen—the wholesale retreat of the militia—the President mused on the battle. He remarked to Barker that "he never would have believed in the difference between regular troops and militias, if he had not witnessed the scenes of that day."[44] Mr. Jefferson's oft-repeated belief that a citizen soldiery would fly to arms in defense of home now had a fearfully hollow ring.

As the troops passed, Barker and De Peyster "fell into the trail of the army and continued with it some miles." It was dark by the time they made their way through Georgetown, and other fugitives from Washington City saw the portrait in the cart highlighted by flashes of lightning. Well north of the city the men, "greatly fatigued, . . . sought shelter in a farm house."[45] Safely stowed in a barn, the portrait would not be a prize of war.

Soon Mr. Madison departed, observed by the watchful French minister Louis Sérurier. "The President, who . . . had displayed . . . a firmness and constancy worthy of better success," Sérurier wrote home to France, "coolly mounted his horse."[46] Impassive even in defeat, Madison made his way to Mason's Ferry at Georgetown. Paul Jennings, who had been left to make his own escape, was surprised to meet up with the

President, Mr. Rush, and others at the Potomac shore. Still astride their horses, they awaited the ferry. It soon returned, and the President's party went aboard and made the slow crossing to the Virginia side. The gentlemen of the government then rode into the hills.

The last to leave the President's house was French John, who banked the kitchen fires and locked the door behind him. He walked to John Tayloe's fine house on nearby Eighteenth Street, carrying Mrs. Madison's pet macaw in its cage. He entrusted the bird to the care of the household of one of his countrymen, Minister Louis Sérurier, before he, too, abandoned Washington City to the British.

CHAPTER 8

Washington in Flames

The large and elegant Capitol of the nation on one side, and the splendid national Palace and Treasury Department on the other, all wrapt in flame, presented a grand and sublime, but, at the same time, an awful and melancholy sight.

—The Federal Republican[1]

1.

Early Evening . . . Wednesday, August 24, 1814 . . . Washington City

WITH THE BATTLE WON AT BLADENSBURG, Admiral Cockburn and General Ross ordered a pause. Their officers had driven the troops since before dawn, and the twelve-mile march, followed by a three-hour battle, left the men exhausted. Overdressed for the hundred-degree temperatures in their heavy red jackets, a dozen infantrymen had simply dropped dead of heat exposure, their corpses bearing no marks of war.[2]

Total British casualties from the fighting amounted to 64 dead and 185 wounded, triple that of the American side (26 killed, 52 wounded). Certainly the defenders would have lost more men had they not, as one Maryland militia private put it, "made a fine scamper of it."[3] Fewer than 150 of the "runaways" had been taken prisoner.[4]

To Cockburn, the battle at Bladensburg amounted to a personal victory. Accepted military wisdom held that land fights were won by the strategic integration of artillery, cavalry, and infantry forces, but today's battle amounted to an extraordinary exception. Despite their superior field position on "rising Ground . . . well protected with Artillery" and their much larger force (Cockburn estimated the Americans to be "Eight thousand Strong"), the enemy had, Cockburn observed, "fled in every direction." Though he had not been the field commander, the strategy had been his, his arguments having won over General Ross the previous day. The Admiral could write with pride to his superior that "a Victory [was] gained by a Division of the British Army not amounting to more than Fifteen hundred Men."[5]

Gratifying as this was to Cockburn, he contemplated a still greater objective. For more than two hours, he and Ross permitted the dusty, thirsty, and battle-weary men to rest. Many lolled on the ground, while others buried the dead or carried the wounded into Bladensburg. But at six o'clock, the third brigade, consisting of Cockburn's seamen, Royal Marines, and the Twenty-first Fusiliers Regiment of Foot, began to march once more.

For the first mile, the British troops passed through a dense wood. A few American soldiers were spotted in the forest, but they withdrew as soon as they were observed. Then the road opened, and, though it was some five miles distant, Cockburn's objective came into view as the sun settled toward the horizon line. At eight o'clock, on arriving at a suitable area of open ground near the turnpike gate to the city, the troops were drawn up.

Less than a mile away, sitting atop the rise once known as Jenkins Hill, stood the Capitol, the tallest object in the fading light of day.

WHILE MOST OF THE BRITISH FORCE MADE CAMP, an advance guard of some one hundred and fifty men accompanied the two commanders and their staffs. At Ross's order, a parley was sounded as they entered the city on Maryland Avenue, but no one responded to the drum-roll summons. Most of the citizenry appeared to have fled, and those who remained cowered inside their homes upon seeing what one slave boy described as a "British armmy . . . [that] looked like flames of fier all red coats and the stoks of ther guns painted with red ver Milon [vermilion]."[6]

When the British reached the top of a small knoll at Second Street, musket fire rang out. Capitol Square was two hundred yards away, but to judge from the puffs of smoke, the shots came from a large brick house on the right and from Tomlinson's Hotel to the left. A volley might have come from the Capitol, too. In the crossfire two British corporals dropped to the ground, one mortally wounded. General Ross had to leap clear as his horse collapsed beneath him.

Although it wasn't *his* horse in its death throes, Admiral Cockburn took this musketry personally. As a brief cheer rang out from the American snipers, a familiar anger rose in Admiral Cockburn. A man who always carried himself ramrod straight, jaw set, his expression determined, he applied the same rigor and discipline to his military code. To maintain the respect and loyalty of his seamen, he adhered to a system of rules, one he made explicit for those who served under him. And of the enemy? He expected nothing less.

For George Cockburn, *guerrilla* tactics—the term was new, a coinage from the Spanish campaign—were a dishonorable violation of the rules of war. He made his position clear upon learning the previous summer "of our poor fellows being killed in a dastardly and provoking manner." He detested hidden shooters who fired from behind walls, behind haystacks, or the windows of their houses. To Cockburn, fair play forbade men to fire "whenever they thought they could get a mischievous shot at any of our people without being seen or exposed to personal risk in return." He made a widely published declaration that anyone who fired upon his men in such cowardly fashion would be treated as a combatant and that any property employed for such purposes would assume the status of a "place of arms."[7]

At Admiral Cockburn's order, a detachment of solders entered the barricaded house, but, finding no one, the British assumed the shooters had escaped to the rear. Other British troops broke into the hotel, where a store of weapons and ammunition was found. As he had done when fired upon in his forays in the Chesapeake, Admiral Cockburn ordered the two buildings burned in retribution. Congreve rockets soon lit the rafters. The house had been home to the Gallatins. Tomlinson's Hotel had been the site of the Naval Ball, where the captured flag of the HMS *Macedonian* had been laid at Mrs. Madison's feet. These were places known well to the Madisons and much of official Washington.

The two buildings, now "consigned to the flames [since] they had been appropriated to the uses of war," provided illumination as Cockburn and his men moved on.[8] Before they had gotten far, the earth moved beneath their feet; the quaking sensation was accompanied by ominous explosions.

Admiral Cockburn and General Ross looked around in wonder. The bright light of another inferno rose in the sky well to the south. It was an even larger fire than those they had set. The Navy Yard near the mouth of the Eastern Branch lay in that direction, but neither British commander had ordered its demolition, though great billows of flame now appeared and the explosions continued.

The only conclusion to be reached was that the Americans themselves had torched the Navy Yard to prevent its capture. Cockburn and Ross watched as the sky grew ever lighter as powder kegs, pitch, cordage, paint, warehouses, barracks, provisions, artillery, shops, wharfs, woodsheds, munitions, and two unfinished ships at anchor fueled the "irretrievable conflagration."[9]

II.

Nine O'Clock . . . Wednesday, August 24, 1814 . . . Washington City

LIT BY FIRELIGHT, THE UNFINISHED CAPITOL seemed to have been conjured out of the darkness. The building's two wings, one for the House of Representatives, the other for the Senate, were largely completed, but the main block at center remained little more than a low, hundred-foot-long unpainted covered walkway. One day, according to Dr. William Thornton's original plan, it would be topped by a tall dome, but this evening the massive silhouettes of the two flanking stone structures were merely dark shadows against the sky.

Once within easy range, the British troops formed a line, then fired a volley at the windows of the Capitol, a warning to any sharpshooters within. When no one returned fire, the doors were forced open and the invading force explored the nation's "Houses of Parliament."[10] To the surprise of some of the officers, they found a "beautifully arranged building; the interior accommodations . . . upon a scale of grandeur and magnificence little suited to pure republican simplicity." While the elegance of the interior finish surprised the invaders, one of them easily interpreted the symbolism. "Over [the presidential chair] was placed a handsome clock, surmounted by a gilt eagle with extended wings and ruffled crest, looking towards the skies, emblematical, it is to be presumed, of the rising greatness of the young nation."[11] Carved of stone, the eagle had a wingspan of twelve feet, six inches.

The men soon set to their task: burning the seat of the republic. Barely an hour earlier, rockets striking the nearby house and hotel had produced explosions that made "the rafters fly east and West." The Capitol proved a different matter since, at President Jefferson's instruction a few years before, architect Latrobe had installed a sheet iron roof. It proved impervious to the Congreve rockets.[12] When individual fires lit in some of the rooms also failed to set the building ablaze, Admiral Cockburn summoned one of his lieutenants, George Pratt, an expert in pyrotechnics.

Pratt improvised a technique that melded the old and the new. The troops made a great pile of the mahogany desks, tables, and chairs. Though the walls of the building were of freestone, the gallery stages and seats in the House chamber, as well as the central platform, were constructed of yellow pine timbers. This pile of dry wood, when fortified by Pratt with buckets of rocket powder, would burn very well indeed.

Meanwhile, Admiral Cockburn prowled the building. There were committee rooms, clerks' offices, and a chamber for the Supreme Court. In the President's Room, Admiral Cockburn's attention was drawn to a book in a three-quarter binding of sheepskin and marbled paper. It wasn't a volume of evident importance; on opening it, Cockburn found it was a ledger, one that detailed expenses for the year 1810. The business was quotidian, but many of the names were known to the Admiral, including Mr. Madison (his annual compensation of twenty-five thousand dollars was cited). There, too, were Albert Gallatin and Richard Rush. On its cover was a black leather label that, in gilt letters, bore the legend "President of the U. States." This volume Admiral Cockburn would take, a keepsake of the day.

The British were building pyres in the north wing, too, though the smaller body of senators meant less flammable matter was at hand. The soldiers set to removing window sash, paneling, shutters, doors, and wooden trim from the walls. Clerks' desks, other furniture, and records were piled in the center of the rooms.

Flames from a "funeral pile" soon licked at the great timepiece over the presidential chair in the House; reported one Royal Navy man, it "was lighted up as the clock told the hour of ten."[13] With both wings of the Capitol afire, the British exited the building through a vestibule lined with columns, which were topped with capitals of an American order. Mr. Latrobe's design incorporated corncobs rather than acanthus leaves, more usual in classical architecture.

As the British watched from the lawn, flames licked out of the windows and doors. The fire soon penetrated the roof. Inside, the intense heat melted the glass in the light fixtures and baked the carved stone columns around the perimeter. Before long the roof collapsed, and the rafters, joists, and interior structure fell to the cellars. The Library of Congress, a grand reading room eighty-six feet long with tall windows and a thirty-six-foot ceiling, burned quickly beneath its old shingle roof, its three thousand volumes consumed by the flames.

The national Capitol—the design of Dr. Thornton, the work of Mr. Latrobe, a passion of Mr. Jefferson—was rendered an ashen ruin.

III.

After Ten O'Clock . . . Wednesday, August 24, 1814 . . . The President's House

AS THE CAPITOL BURNED, the British marched up Pennsylvania Avenue to their next destination. The avenue had a paradoxical quality, an urban boulevard lined with four Lombardy poplar allées and a country streetscape on which grand buildings alternated with empty and undeveloped plots. Directly ahead was the largest and most elegant house in the nation, but one that, typical of the aborning Federal City, sat amid an unornamented landscape. The contingent of men, roughly two hundred in number, made their way, silently, by the light of torches.

They found the President's house abandoned, but, once they were inside, the beautiful presidential apartments were improbably welcoming. The cloth remained on the dining table and "a large store of super-excellent Madeira and other costly wines stood cooling in ice in one corner of the spacious dining room."[14] From the basement kitchen, cooking smells wafted up the twisting stair. Taking a tour of the dressing rooms, one officer, grimy from a long day of war, helped himself to a fresh shirt of "snowy clean linen . . . belonging to no less a personage than the chief magistrate of the United states."[15]

For soldiers nearing the end of a long day, the repast ready at hand met with approval. "[W]e found a supper all ready, which many of us consumed . . . and drank some very good wine also."[16] There were cut-glass decanters and plate warmers by the fireplace. "[I]n short, everything was ready for the entertainment of a ceremonious party."[17]

If the dinner lacked the thoughtful protocol of one of Mrs. Madison's evenings, the British guests did drink toasts to "the health of the Prince Regent and success to his Majesty's arms by sea and land." Admiral Cockburn drank a toast to his absent host, calling him "Jemmy," the dismissive nickname Cockburn favored. As a souvenir of Mrs. Madison he took her seat cushion, so he could "warmly recall Mrs. Madison's seat."[18]

While they amused themselves, a messenger arrived from the French minister. Word had reached M. Sérurier of the likely fate of the President's house. "I thought it best," wrote Sérurier, "to send one of my people to the general with a letter, in which I begged him to send a guard to the house of the Ambassador of France to protect it."[19]

The messenger found General Ross engaged in preparations for another bonfire, this one in Mrs. Madison's Drawing Room. Mr. Latrobe's gilded furniture, cushioned with red velvet and carved with the nation's coat of arms, would soon be set afire with every other combustible that came to hand. But General Ross promised that Sérurier's quarters at John Tayloe's house a few hundred yards west would be safe.

When the preparations for the fire were complete, the task of igniting the house was given to sailors and marines stationed at the windows, "each carrying a long pole to which was fixed a ball about the circumference of a large plate." When the command was given, the men simultaneously broke the windows and tossed in their torches, "so that an instantaneous conflagration took place." Almost at once, the entire building was on fire. Neighbors, slaves, the British, and other spectators "stood in awful silence . . . [as] the heavens redden'd with the blaze!"[20]

The Treasury building came next. There the invaders found no currency in the strong room. By midnight, the British marauders marched back along the length of Pennsylvania Avenue to rejoin the main force, leaving the Treasury offices another burning beacon in the night.

FOR THE BRITISH TROOPS BOUND FOR CAPITOL SQUARE, "dark red light was thrown upon the road, sufficient to permit each man to view distinctly his comrade's face."[21] To the people of the Federal City, the night's illumination was of "an almost meridian brightness," as one resident of Washington City wrote to her sister. "You never saw a drawing room so brilliantly lighted."[22]

From the heights of Georgetown several miles away, Dr. Thornton and his wife, Anna Maria, were guests at Tudor Place. The Thorntons had made their way north from their home on F Street to take refuge in one of Dr. Thornton's pet architectural projects, Tudor Place, a sprawling villa he had designed for Martha Washington's granddaughter, Martha Custis, and her husband, Thomas Peter. This grand house, still under construction, overlooked Washington City from a sloping hillside. Those assembled at the Peters' mansion watched from the Drawing Room, "witness[ing] the conflagration of [their] poor undefended & devoted city."[23]

Still further afield, Mrs. Madison sheltered at Rokeby, a friend's home ten miles along the Georgetown Pike into Virginia, across the Little Falls Bridge. She said nothing as she watched the fiery red sky over the capital.[24] Mr. Madison, on the move, stopped at a tavern in Falls Church, before finally reaching Salona, a home not far from Little Falls. The irony was not lost on the President that his war, which was supposed to open with a victory in Canada that was to be "a mere matter of marching," now reached its nadir. Unfortunately, the fates reversed themselves. It was the British military force that merely marched into America's capital.

IV.

Morning . . . Thursday, August 25, 1814 . . . The Patent Office

THE BRITISH FORCE BIVOUACKED ON CAPITOL HILL. They awoke the next morning to a violent thunderstorm that soaked the city in the wee hours before first light. At dawn, Admiral Cockburn, together with a body of sailors and soldiers, once more headed west on Pennsylvania Avenue.

They stopped at a house between Sixth and Seventh streets. It contained the offices of the *National Intelligencer*, the paper well-known for its support of the war. The building stood back slightly from the street, but the Republican paper most certainly stood out in the Admiral's memory. His men's shore forays had delivered him many issues of the *Intelligencer*, and Cockburn had grown tired of finding his name in its columns. The editor, Joseph Gales, himself English-born, repeatedly scorned Cockburn as a "British sarpent." At Gales's very door, Cockburn would repay the man's slanders: He ordered the building set afire. Before the command could be carried out, however, two ladies of the neighborhood pleaded with the soldiers to stop, saying that to burn the press would endanger their houses. Cockburn relented.

Although the building would not be put to the torch, Cockburn ordered the paper's quarters demolished. The offices were sacked, as books, papers, journals from various cities and countries, and other contents were tossed into a pile to the rear of the house; at the verge of the nearby canal, an immense bonfire soon burned. The presses were broken and the flammable parts added to the fire.

When the men began throwing type cases to the street from an upper story, Admiral Cockburn issued another order. "Be sure that all the C's are destroyed," he instructed his men, "so that the rascals can have no further means of abusing my name as they have done."[25] When the building was empty, Admiral Cockburn ordered a team of his blue-jackets to pull the house down. Stout ropes were looped around the piers between the windows. With the sturdy seamen pulling in unison, the roof soon crashed to the ground.

A FEW BLOCKS AWAY, DR. WILLIAM THORNTON WAS IN HIGH DUDGEON. His breakfast had been interrupted by the rumor that the British had resumed burning public buildings. The Patent Office, of which he was Superintendent, was to be among them.

Though trained as a physician in Edinburgh, the stocky Thornton had played many roles in Washington City. He had won the competition to design the Capitol; it was his architectural vision that lay a smoldering ruin. His design brought him to the new capital city in 1793, but his rambling curiosity led him in so many directions—not only various architectural projects but a steamboat and numerous other contrivances as well—that Mr. Jefferson had seen fit to appoint him Superintendent of the Patent Office in 1802.

He was also a man with a demonstrated capacity for outrage (hadn't he feuded interminably with Mr. Latrobe?) and he promptly rose from the well-appointed table, begged leave of his hosts, and rode down the Georgetown Heights. Along the way he encountered Charles Carroll, whom he persuaded to accompany him on his mission, as "one of the most respectable gentlemen of the District."[26]

As Thornton saw it, an assault by British troops at the Patent Office was an affront. He prided himself on the sheer variety of what his enlightened mind conceived, and he had recently added the craft of luthier to doctor, architect, educator of the deaf, watercolorist, poet, botanist, and other areas of expertise.[27] His current project was a musical instrument, a violin of a new sort. The prototype, as yet incomplete, lay within the walls of the Patent Office.

His was far from the only endangered invention. He had packed and evacuated many of the department's files to his Maryland farm in previous days, but the Patent Office was chockablock with examples of machines and innovations of all sorts that could not so easily be boxed and carted to safety. The spacious building, the former Blodgett's Hotel, had been designed by James Hoban, the same Irish undertaker who won the competition to design the President's house. Behind its classical façade, with pediment and six Ionic pilasters, were both the Patent and Post offices, and hundreds of what Dr. Thornton termed "the models of the arts."

Along with his clerk and Mr. Carroll, Dr. Thornton arrived in time to plead the case. The building's doors had already been forced by soldiers wielding axes, but Major Waters, the British officer in charge of the building's destruction, allowed that, as his orders did not include destroying private property, he would permit Dr. Thornton to remove his musical instrument. But, he warned, the building must still be burned.

Though not known for his speechifying—he tended to stammer—Dr. Thornton rose to the occasion with a rhetorical flourish. To burn the contents of the Patent Office, he said, would be "to burn what would be useful to all mankind, [and] would be as barbarous as formerly to burn the Alexandrian Library, for which the Turks have been ever since condemned by all enlightened nations."[28]

Blodgett's Hotel was spared.

~

SMOKE STILL ROSE FROM THE WAR OFFICE. Both ends of Long Bridge, which reached across the Potomac, were afire, one end lit by the British in anticipation of an American counterattack, the other by the Americans fearing a British advance.

A work party of four officers and two hundred British troops set fire to the ropewalks, which had survived the Navy Yard fire. The contents of dozens of tar barrels were spilt at the quarter-mile-long, roofed manufactories. When the accelerant was lit, the structures, along with the large stores of hemp and cordage, burst into flame, producing a dense, black, odorous cloud of smoke that "rolled over the captured city, obscuring the heavens from the view of its inhabitants."[29]

From the fortification at Washington City's southernmost point, an unexpected roar was heard. Accompanied by an earthen tremor, the blast occurred at the arsenal at Greenleaf Point. Having discovered more than a hundred barrels of powder, a detachment of British soldiers had been rolling them into a deep well near the fort's magazine. The casks of powder were so numerous that, as one cask followed another into the well, the level of the barrels rose above the water line. When a barrel hoop struck one of the stones lining the well, the resulting spark ignited the dry powder, producing an explosion that resulted in terrible carnage. A dozen men were killed instantly, and forty-four badly wounded British soldiers were carried back to Capitol Hill to a makeshift hospital.

An unexpected intervention came from the skies. At midday, an immense storm struck, a turn of weather that some in the city saw as God's wrath. As the sky grew suddenly dark, a prodigious wind blew men off their horses, ripped the roofs off houses, and dumped a great volume of rain, all in what seemed like an instant. Trees were broken and dismembered, chimneys blown down. More than two dozen British soldiers were killed, some of them when a building in which they had taken shelter collapsed, burying them in the rubble. Blodgett's Hotel, so recently saved from fire by Dr. Thornton, lost its roof in the hurricane-force winds.

The deadly explosion and the sudden gale were enough for General Ross, who chose to make an early departure from the captured city. He and his men waited until nightfall, then left their campfires burning as they marched quietly away from Washington. In the night they passed through Bladensburg, recrossing its bridge, before pausing to rest after seven A.M. After marching twenty-five miles in twenty-four hours, the invading forces arrived at Marlborough on August 26. They reached Nottingham the next day, and not so many hours later, the invading force was swallowed up by the four ships of the line, twenty frigates and sloops, and twenty transports that awaited them.

CHAPTER 9

The Exiles Return

To the great astonishment of the world, a handful of seven or eight thousand Englishmen were seen to descend in the midst of a state embracing of ten millions of souls, penetrate a considerable distance, seize the capital, and destroy all the public buildings,—results which history may be searched in vain for another example of.

—Baron Henri de Jomini, The Art of War, *1862*[1]

I.

August 28, 1814 . . . Sunday Morning . . . The Capitol

MR. MADISON RETURNED FROM EXILE. He wore his customary black coat along with matching breeches, tall boots, and stockings buckled at the knees. Powdered and pulled back in a queue, his white hair framed a face that was thin but round, the features small but well shaped. Like a carefully composed mask, the somber expression on the lined parchment skin betrayed little of the anguish of the preceding days.

The President's exile had been brief. He had witnessed his greatest fear come to life, as the British dragoons, their bayonets already scarred by decades of war with Napoleon, swarmed over the bridge at Bladensburg. His ears had rung with the booms of artillery, the report of hundreds of rifles, the screams of the wounded and dying, and the explosions of whirligig rockets overhead. The stinging cloud of smoke had been new to him, too, along with the pell-mell retreat of his army to the capital, where the entire United States government had been fleeing its offices, along with most of the town's eight thousand inhabitants.

Often during the long hours on horseback that followed the escape across the Potomac, Mr. Madison had looked back upon the city he left. The sight of the red-illumined sky was both beautiful and terrifying. As Mr. Rush described it, "the vivid impression upon my eye [was] of columns of flame and smoke ascending through the night from the Capitol, President's house, and other public edifices, as the whole were on fire, some burning slowly, others with bursts of flame and sparks mounting high up the dark horizon. . . . If at intervals the dismal sight was lost to our view, we got it again from some hill-top eminence where we paused."[2]

For the next two days, Madison and his companions had circled the northern districts of the city, concerned for their own safety, since the invading army would have been delighted to make the nation's Chief Magistrate their prisoner. The fugitives were uncertain where to take shelter but, finally, upon learning the conquering army had boarded its ships, Mr. Rush, Secretary of State James Monroe, and Mr. Madison returned to the city's streets, accompanied by a cavalry guard. This morning the men rode about Washington City, taking inventory of the damage done by the British assault and the fires they set.

They halted at the Capitol. The fire had burned intensely, stripping some sandstone columns of their fluting, reducing them to asymmetrical stacks of rubble. Some of the stone had been entirely consumed by the flames, burned to nothing more than a powdery residue of calcined pebbles and sand. Crystal ceiling fixtures, rendered into heavy lumps of glass, littered the cracked marble floor. Reduced to ash were the mahogany furniture, paneling, and even Congress's library. With the interior timber framing gone, some of the upper floors had collapsed into the

A contemporary engraving by architect William Strickland after a painting by George Munger titled "A view of the Capitol after the conflagration of the 24th August 1814." *Library of Congress/Prints and Photographs Division*

basement. On the exterior of the smoke-stained structure the onlookers could distinguish the ghosts of intricately carved decoration, grim reminders of its builders' vision of the Capitol as a great classical temple of democracy.

Mr. Madison's constant companion in those hours, Richard Rush, saw before him "the most magnificent and melancholy ruin you ever beheld."[3] But the President betrayed little in the way of sentiment. Only the day before, a family friend who had met up with him observed, "[Mr. M] was tranquil as usual, and tho' much distressed by the dreadful event . . . not dispirited."[4] Certainly, having watched his city burn from afar, Madison knew pity and terror; now, gazing at the ruins close at hand, he tasted anger and sadness at the defiling of the Capitol. Still he appeared unmoved, despite a charcoal scrawl on one wall that read, "James Madison is a rascal, a coward and a fool."[5]

As he regarded the smoking ruin, the President knew his country approached a dangerous crossroads—his challenge was to plot a way forward. He must decide what to do about the British forces, some of which remained dangerously near in ships a few miles south on the Potomac River. Mr. Madison worried, too, about how many of his fellow citizens he could count upon since, that very morning, he had been warned that a mob near at hand threatened his life. He understood that angry passions in New England would be running higher than ever; the burning of the Capitol could only fuel the outrage of the Federalists who had opposed and obstructed his policies since the war declaration two years earlier. Despite such burdens, no glimmer of regret surfaced, and nothing about this man with the large head and diminutive body conveyed agitation to those around him.

James Madison's brief exile had ended, but his ordeal was far from over. The disaster at Washington trebled his responsibilities, with the fate of his presidency, his nation, and his city entirely in his hands. Now that the war was being fought here, on his own ground, he could no longer dismiss as mere rhetoric the epithet the men of the East so often cast at him. Even he would have to admit that this truly had become *Mr. Madison's War.*

II.
Midday . . . Capitol Hill . . . Washington City

DR. WILLIAM THORNTON WAS ON A MISSION. Admittedly, it was a self-appointed task, but someone had to deliver a crucial communication to Mr. Madison. After more than twenty-five years of friendship, Thornton would be the man to bring Madison important news—bad news. Today, wearing one of his many hats as a justice of the peace, he was performing a civic duty, acting the messenger by bringing to the President what he saw as the will of the people.

The thunder of distant cannon was heard the evening before, echoing over the Potomac. That the British fleet was approaching seemed certain; as one hour of bombardment became two, the citizens of Washington supposed that the British navy had encountered the American guns at Fort Warburton, about twelve miles downstream on the Maryland shore opposite Mount Vernon, home of the late President

Washington.* The inhabitants of the Federal City hoped the fort would repel the invading force. But no one knew what to think when, after eight P.M., a tremendous explosion rent the air.

Though the sound came from a great distance, its reverberations were felt throughout the Federal City. At their home, Dr. Thornton; his wife, Anna Maria; and friends and neighbors wondered at the blast; nearby, where Mr. Madison had gratefully accepted Mr. Rush's invitation to take accommodation at his home, the President's meeting with several members of his cabinet came to a halt. They exchanged perplexed looks and words of wonder.

Hours later, news of Fort Warburton's fate arrived. In a shocking defensive failure, the drunken commander of the fort had spiked the guns, evacuated his sixty-man garrison, and ignited the magazine, filled with 3,100 pounds of cannon powder. The impact of the explosion not only rattled windows in Washington, it destroyed the fort's inner buildings. In his own defense, Captain Samuel T. Dyson, USN, could offer only, "The force under my command was thought not equal to a defence of the place."[6] In the face of British warships, he fled without firing a shot.

The hoofbeats of Dr. Thornton's horse drew Madison's attention. The President, Colonel Monroe, and Mr. Rush had resumed their survey of the damaged city. From Capitol Hill, they saw another result of last night's explosion: No longer threatened by the guns at Fort Warburton, the British had sailed north. Several barges were now visible on the Potomac, making their way toward Alexandria, six miles south of Washington City. A spyglass view affirmed a still more ominous fact: The flotilla of British ships coming into view included two frigates. The HMS *Seahorse* and the HMS *Euryalus*, 38 and 36 guns, respectively, were accompanied by 3 bomb ships that carried 2 mortars each, along with a rocket vessel, the *Erebus*. The capital had already been visited by an invading

* Though the name of the fortification established in 1807 was Fort Washington, it was popularly known as Fort Warburton after the manor house that had long stood on the property.

army; now a heavily armed naval force capable of a massive bombardment was within sight.

THE SMELL OF DISASTER FILLED THE CITY'S AIR. The whiff of wood smoke still rose from smoldering coals, mingling with the acrid odor of the immense, half-quenched fire. An even more pungent odor overlaid the others as the temperature rose in promise of an overheated tidewater day. This was the stench of carrion, rising from rotting carcasses nearby, the remains of dead horses that lay where they had fallen.

Yet Dr. Thornton's concern was the fear in the air, intangible but undeniable. He wheeled his horse to a halt and prepared to address Mr. Madison.

Dr. Thornton was a familiar figure in Washington. As the city had gradually been populated with politicians, speculators, and others drawn to the new seat of government, Dr. and Mrs. Thornton were among the most popular couples in the city's society. He was known as "a scholar and gentleman full of talent and eccentricity . . . his company the complete antidote to dullness."[7] He knew everyone, from presidents to painters, having designed town houses for George Washington and welcomed the painter Gilbert Stuart as his houseguest.

On most any day, Dr. Thornton was a formidable presence. Though he was a man of average size, his prominent chin, large nose, and steel-blue eyes conveyed confidence; his intellect and sense of rectitude intimidated many. On this day, Dr. Thornton was possessed by the redoubled confidence of a man who had done his duty when few others had. Returning to the city two days earlier to find that the mayor had fled and looters were helping themselves to unguarded goods and property, he ordered the gates of the Navy Yard closed, organized a citizen watch, and arranged for care of the wounded. He understood the mood of the city, and he felt honor-bound to tell the President.

The message for Madison was simple: "The people are violently irritated at the thought of our attempting to make any more futile resistance."[8] Just downstream, faced with the armada of British ships, the town fathers in Alexandria were in the process of surrendering their city; defenseless, they chose capitulation over bombardment. The people of Washington, reported Dr. Thornton, were "afraid of the landing of the British seamen who they thought were immediately bound for their city."[9] Believing any further resistance might put them in danger, he told Madison, "the citizens of Washington [are] preparing to send a deputation to the British commander for the purpose of capitulating."[10]

Dr. Thornton, his speech still tinged with the intonations of Lancashire and the burr of his days in Edinburgh, had the attention of Madison, Monroe, and Rush. But his words met with silence.

They all knew the facts. There was no organized American military force in Washington City. All the troops, both regular army and militia, had retreated north toward Baltimore. The man charged with the nation's military matters, Secretary of War John Armstrong, had yet to return; he was probably in Fredericksburg, Virginia, where the cabinet originally planned to reconvene. Washington City lacked fortifications, warships, troops, and military leadership. The odds were perhaps even less in the Americans' favor than three days earlier when a red-coated army overran the city from the east. Now ships from the world's most powerful navy threatened to the west.

Dr. Thornton looked upon what now constituted the government. For three days, not only the capital but the nation too had been headless, its leaders scattered and its offices burned. Whatever official documents and papers survived had been carried off in wagons, dispersed to a dozen different sites. These men around him had returned to take charge, but of what?

Through no fault of his own, Dr. Thornton brought a hateful message: He presented James Madison with the prospect of abject surrender, which would confirm the words a bitter Washingtonian had written on the wall of the burned Capitol. "George Washington founded this city after a seven years' war with England," read the charcoal scrawl. "James Madison lost it after a two years' war."[11]

With a lifelong reputation for taking a calm and deliberative approach, Mr. Madison, seated on his dapple gray mount, considered Dr. Thornton's words. As a friend wrote of him, "when the powers of his mind were called into action, . . . his brow was knit—deep and strong lines gathered on his forehead, and the stern expression of his countenance presented a contrast to its previous stillness and serenity, as striking as that of the lake whose smooth and glassy surface is suddenly roughened into furrows by the rising of the wind. Then, to the deep lines of thought thus developed, was added that air of unyielding determination."[12]

The President had not gone to war in anger: His declaration was born of his sense of national honor. In the same way, in this fulcrum moment, he expressed no outrage, though the threat to his country provoked him. He could not blame the messenger, a friend since 1787 when, as bachelors, he and Dr. Thornton roomed together in Philadelphia during the Constitutional Convention.

Emerging as if from the fog of regret, Madison was decisive. His response to his old friend Thornton was sharp and firm. James Monroe described it simply: "The President forbade the measure."[13] Madison told Dr. Thornton, "[I]t would be dishonorable to send any deputation, and . . . we [will] defend the city to the very last."[14]

Despite Madison's pointed words, Thornton objected that there was no force at hand to defend Washington City.

This time an angry answer came from Colonel Monroe, appointed acting Secretary of War a few hours earlier by Mr. Madison. The danger in his manner abruptly ended the discussion.

"If any deputation move toward the enemy," he warned, "it [will] be repelled by the bayonet."[15]

Colonel Monroe was soon issuing orders that called militiamen back to the city. He chose strategic sites with commanding views of the river for gun emplacements, and redoubts were speedily constructed of rubble, sand, and stone. Monroe established a new War Office in his home on Pennsylvania Avenue, between Twentieth and Twenty-first streets. He ordered that mounted sentries be established along the byways between Richmond and Baltimore in order to bring the War Office the latest intelligence regarding the enemy's movements.

As for Dr. Thornton, he understood the import of what he had been told. Mrs. Thornton would write in her diary that night, "Dr. T. came home & distressed us more than ever by taking his sword & going out to call the people & to join them."[16]

The President had decreed that there would be no surrender.

III.

Afternoon . . . F Street . . . Washington City

MRS. MADISON WAS NOT HERSELF. She felt out of sorts and out of place—she, too, had fled the city, barely ahead of the British invaders—and the shock of events shook even Dolley's usual unflinching equanimity. She did not even look like herself. A woman who set great store in her appearance, she dressed in disguise (James had been worried for her safety). She wore someone else's nondescript clothes and rode in another's carriage as she reentered Washington City.[17]

On his return the evening before, her husband was in the company of Monroe, Rush, and eleven uniformed dragoons, but Dolley's was a nearly anonymous figure, attended by a single bodyguard. A note Dolley received from James the day before informed her of his plan to return. "You will of course take the same resolution."[18]

Riding into her city, bound for her sister's house on F Street, she experienced an acute sense of dislocation. "I cannot tell you what I felt on re-entering it," she confided to an old friend. "Such destruction—such confusion." If James was a man given to collecting his thoughts in solitude and silence, Dolley was unabashed in expressing her reactions about the pain the sight of the ravaged city gave her. As she told her correspondent, "My whole heart mourned for my country."[19]

Any hopes of returning to the President's house vanished the first moment she laid eyes upon the remains of the big building. The finest mansion in the land, the home that she lovingly transformed into a social showplace for the nation, had been devoured by flames: "not an inch, but its crack'd and blacken'd walls remain'd . . . nothing but ashes."[20]

Together with their pet macaw, which survived thanks to the good offices of French ambassador Sérurier, Washington City's first family was homeless.

WHEN HE ARRIVED AT THE HOUSE ON F STREET, James found the woman he addressed as "My dearest" there to greet him. A few hours earlier, he had written to Dolley, advising her that since "the British ships with their barges" were in view downstream at Alexandria, "it would be best for [her] to remain in [her] present quarters."[21] But she had begun her journey before the letter reached her, and here they were, in her sister's house, a place where they themselves had lived during James's years as Secretary of State.

Dolley was still reeling from the week's events. For her, perhaps even more than James, the British assault amounted to a personal insult. From nearby windows she could see the fire-gutted ruin of the President's house two blocks away, its floors collapsed, walled but roofless, the sky visible through its tall windows. It was as if the attack had been on her person since Admiral George Cockburn had threatened that "the house would be burned over head."[22] When she learned of his threat a year before as Cockburn harried the people of the Chesapeake, the warning had sounded like overheated rhetoric; today, she could only wonder what might have happened if she had been at home when Cockburn and his troops came calling.

A matching aquatint to the image of the burned Capitol, this one of the President's house, was also engraved by William Strickland after a George Munger painting. *Library of Congress/Prints and Photographs Division*

Having now returned to an altered city, Mrs. Madison found refuge with her sister Anna and Anna's husband, Richard Cutts, a former Congressman from Massachusetts's Maine district, who had become superintendent general of military supplies for the federal government. The three-story Cutts home on F Street, with a cupola and dormered chambers on the top floor, was ample enough for a family, but it seemed modest indeed in comparison to Dolley's former home.

Her husband inhabited a world of documents, negotiations, and correspondence. His routine was to spend long days in conferences and at his desk, shaping the policy of the land. Dolley had acted as his gatekeeper; when he emerged from his sanctum to engage the world of Washington, he did so with her at his side. The public still expect that of

Mrs. Madison, as, for more than five years, Dolley's hospitality had played a central role in the business of the city, even in the governing of the country. But in the preceding days her stage had gone up in smoke.

WITH DOLLEY AND JAMES BACK IN TOWN and a temporary center of government established, people came calling. On Dolley's first afternoon back, the Smiths arrived. Samuel Harrison Smith came to see James, Margaret Bayard Smith to visit Dolley. Mr. Smith had been founding editor of Washington's *National Intelligencer*, and he was soon locked away with James and his secretary, Edward Coles; Attorney General Rush; and other members of the government who had come back to town.

Margaret Bayard Smith had described Dolley after their first meeting almost fifteen years earlier as possessed of "good humor and sprightliness, united to the most affable and agreeable manners."[23] But at tea that day Mrs. Smith observed a different Dolley; to Mrs. Smith, "Mrs. M. seem'd much depress'd." Yet Dolley soldiered through a full account of the events of the British arrival. "She was so confident of Victory," Mrs. Smith reported, "that she was calmly listening to the roar of cannon . . . when she perceived our troops rushing into the city, with the haste and dismay of a routed force." The recollections were painful, as Mrs. Madison "could scarcely speak without tears."[24]

Mrs. Thornton called in, too. She lived next door, and, during Dolley's earlier years in residence on F Street, theirs was a daily acquaintance. With Anna Maria, Mrs. Madison let down her guard. "She was very violent against the English—& wished we had 10,000 . . . men . . . to sink our Enemy to the bottomless pit."[25]

The ladies in the drawing room, along with the men closeted nearby in an improvised cabinet room, all held to the "hope . . . that the Enemy will not pay us a second Visit."[26] Certainly, the burden would fall to the gentlemen to see to the city's safety. With the nation's parliament and presidential palace in ruins, the young nation, proud of its bold beginnings, had been humbled, and a profound vision would be required to lead the nation back from this abyss.

That burden would fall to the Chief Magistrate; he understood that the Constitution he had engineered left the task in his hands. Yet as these men and women of the Washington ruling class knew better than anyone, Dolley would be at James's side, his most trusted confidante and adviser. The policies would be his, but her politesse would be essential as he sought to ensure the future of the Federal City, the presidency, and a nation at war.

BOOK III

Washington Regained

CHAPTER 10

A New Resolution

O! thus be I ever when freemen shall stand,
Between their lov'd home, and the war's desolation,
Blest with vict'ry and peace, may the Heav'n rescued land?
Praise the Power that hath made and preserv'd us a nation.
—*"Defence of Fort McHenry"*[1]

I.

Monday, August 29, to September 1, 1814 . . . Washington City

ALL PRESIDENTS AGE IN OFFICE, but never before had the nation's Chief Magistrate faced what Mr. Madison had in the preceding days. The country remained under siege as the President, his wrinkles deepening, called to order a cabinet meeting at noon on August 29, looking to reestablish the authority of his government.

Citizens on the opposite shore of the Potomac watched helplessly as seventy-one seized vessels were loaded with Alexandria's naval and ordnance stores, as well as tobacco, cotton, flour, and other goods. That very morning the gaping muzzles of more than one hundred guns aboard two British frigates, three gunboats, and a rocket barge had persuaded the mayor of the old Virginia city to capitulate, as he and his committeemen sought to avoid a fate like Washington's. The Royal Navy's next Potomac destination was unknown (might it be Georgetown?). Another worrisome uncertainty was the exact whereabouts of the deadly amphibious forces of Admiral Cockburn and General Ross.

With His Majesty's military still very much in the vicinity, the President's burdens grew no lighter. Yet he continued to act upon "his maxim that public functionaries never display, much less act, under the influence of passion."[2]

Although the President kept his feelings well hidden, many of the people of Washington returning from safe havens elsewhere gave vent to theirs. A sense of loss rose in the breasts of many who found their homes looted; that pain redoubled when they learned that the plunderers had been fellow citizens and not the British invaders, who, as Cockburn promised, left most private properties well enough alone. The widespread concern about a slave uprising had been unwarranted, but Madison was becoming acutely aware of a simmering passion that led to raised voices in taverns, coffeehouses, and homes all over his city.

The anger at what had befallen Washington City was termed by Colonel Monroe a "tempest of dissatisfaction at the late events here, [which] rages with great fever."[3] For some in the city, the outrage was directed at Madison, who that morning had met a delegation warning him that threats to his person were bruited about in certain quarters. But the President would not be deterred from the public path he chose to tread.

After meeting with his cabinet, Mr. Madison rode forth from his temporary quarters. As one who saw him wrote to Thomas Jefferson, "Our good President is out animating and encouraging the troops and citizens not to despair."[4] The President had lost no less than anyone else; he would show himself and, by example, model the strong and forward-looking behavior required under the circumstances. Colonel Monroe endorsed the strategy. He saw Madison's visibility as essential to the recovering city. "I am satisfied," Monroe noted, "that if . . . the President's return had been delayed [another] 24 hours, that a degree of degradation would have been exhibited here . . . of the most disastrous character."[5] The angry voices might not quickly fade away, and Edward Coles reported hearing Madison vilified as a "tyrant," "murderer," and "despot." But Madison himself refused to remain behind closed doors.[6]

Like an arrow falling back to earth, the fury in the air inevitably found another ready target: Secretary of War John Armstrong. That very afternoon Mr. Madison's daily tour of inspection took him to a militia encampment at Windmill Point. There the President encouraged the men as they constructed fresh fortifications to protect Georgetown. With the explosions at Fort Warburton, the Navy Yard, and the arsenal at Greenleaf Point, few defenses remained along the Potomac. After a time, he turned his horse back toward the Capitol, missing by a few minutes the arrival at Windmill Point of General Armstrong, who was only then making his belated return to the city.

For days the troops had heard nothing from Armstrong, which did little for their already low opinion of him. As one militia major put it, "the impression had become universal that, as Secretary of War, he had neglected to prepare the necessary defenses; and that [due] to this neglect, the capitol had been desecrated, and the glory of arms tarnished." Armstrong's repeated refusal to recognize the danger to the capital in the weeks before the Battle of Bladensburg made him a logical target for the anger in the city. His tardy return added to his apparent culpability for the events at Washington.

On seeing the General ride into camp, Charles Carroll confronted him. After refusing to shake Armstrong's hand, Carroll loudly denounced the General's conduct. Mrs. Madison's friend was hardly alone, as the men at Windmill Point held an informal caucus. The officers presented their swords and the men at the batteries threatened to throw down their spades. Neither weapon nor tool would be employed, they swore, "if General Armstrong is to command us."[7]

A short time later, two militia officers caught up with Mr. Madison and Mr. Rush riding down F Street. The President learned that "every officer would tear off his epaulet if Gen[l] Armstrong was going to have anything to do with them."

That evening Mr. Madison rode alone to the Secretary of War's lodgings. The two men talked of the events at Bladensburg and Washington, and the President advised his Secretary of War of the rage in the ranks. Armstrong defended himself, insisting that the "excitement against [me], . . . the intrigues, [were] founded on the most palpable falsehoods." But Mr. Madison remained firm, explaining that, in his judgment, too, the General's preparations fell well short of what was necessary, even of what he himself ordered back in July. Finally, Armstrong agreed to Madison's suggestion that it would be wise for him to leave the city; he would set out in the morning to visit his family in New York.[8] Mr. Madison did not insist upon his resignation, and Mr. Armstrong did not offer it.

"HOW GLOOMY IS THE SCENE," WROTE MARGARET BAYARD SMITH. Mrs. Madison's social friend waxed pessimistic. "I do not suppose Government will ever return to Washington."[9] From their country home in Maryland, Catherine Rush inquired of her husband. "I feel very anxious to hear what are your plans for the winter—is Congress to meet at Washington, and where will they get a room large enough?"[10]

Even Mrs. Madison needed time to recover from the shock. For a time she remained sequestered in her borrowed quarters in the last of the Seven Buildings at the corner of Nineteenth Street. Reunited with her pet macaw, she was more often seen feeding and petting it in a corner window than making her usual morning calls around the town.[11]

For the denizens of the Federal City, regaining a sense of normality proved to be a day-by-day affair. "After an intermission of several days," according to its editor, the *National Intelligencer* resumed publication on August 30, printed on a borrowed press in a smaller format. The ruined Congress house remained the saddest sight in town. The few arches and vaulting that survived of the once grand elliptical hall in the south wing stood atop columns that might collapse at any moment. According to

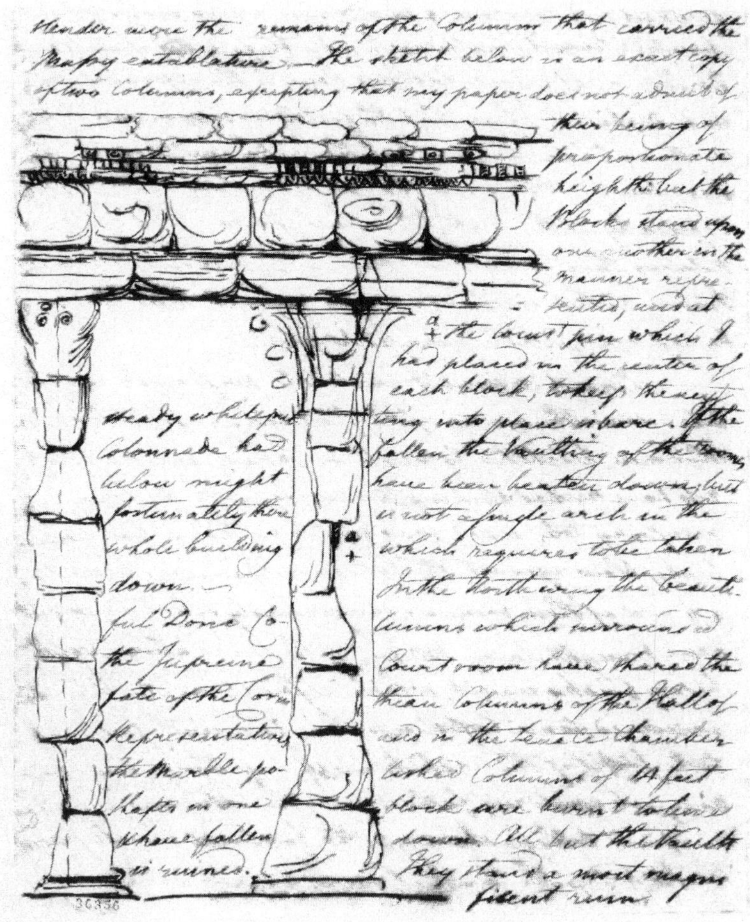

slender were the remains of the Columns that carried the massy entablature. The sketch below is an exact copy of two Columns, excepting that my paper does not admit of their being of proportionate height, but the Blocks stand upon one another in the manner represented, and at a+ the locust pin which I had placed in the center of each block, to keep them steady while putting into place where. If the Colonnade had fallen the vaulting of the room below might have been beaten down, but fortunately there is not a single arch in the whole building which requires to be taken down. — In the North wing the beautiful Doric Columns which surrounded the Supreme Court room have shared the fate of the Columns of the Hall of Representatives and in the Senate chamber the Marble polished Columns of 14 feet shafts in one block are burnt to lime and have fallen down. All but the vaults is ruines. They stand a most magnificent ruin.

When Latrobe wrote to his old benefactor Mr. Jefferson about the condition of the Capitol, he limned a quick drawing—quite literally, between the lines—to convey the dreadful damage. Note the tiny symbol—*a+*—indicating the point at which a stone split. Thanks to a locust-wood pin, the column remained standing. *Library of Congress/Jefferson Papers* one who knew the building intimately, the installation of scaffolding would risk bringing down "one hundred ton of the entablature, and of the heavy brick vault which rested upon it."[12]

The charred ruin did inspire Secretary of the Navy Jones to suggest a temporary solution. "I would recommend," he told Mr. Madison, "the instant removal of the patent and post-offices and the conversion of that building into comfortable Halls for the Senate and house of Representatives, with neat, plain furniture."[13] Heads nodded in agreement. Mrs. Thornton soon reported that her husband was officially notified by the Secretary of State that his "nick nacks and notions," as one wag called the patent models, were to be removed. The former Blodgett's Hotel, its roof freshly repaired from storm damage, would become the temporary Capitol.[14]

Other government offices took up temporary quarters elsewhere in the city. In the next week, the Department of State occupied the former residence of British Minister Augustus John Foster on G Street. Navy relocated to a house near the West Market. The War Office, the Post Office, Treasury, and other government departments set up shop in converted homes. Government staffers went back to work, and Congress would convene on September 19.

The arrangements were less than perfect. As one visitor would observe, the hall where Congress met was "a miserable little narrow box," but the progress was comforting.[15] Margaret Bayard Smith again spoke the minds of many when she wrote, "The city was capable of defence and ought to have been defended. But we will retrieve, yes I trust we will retrieve our character and restore our capital. This is not the first capital of a great empire, that has been invaded and conflagrated; Rome was reduced still lower by the Goths of old. . . . May a Roman spirit animate our people."[16]

RICHARD RUSH ALSO HAD AN IDEA. He wanted to foster a new resolution in the land, and he had a plan.

He puts his thoughts on paper for the consideration of Colonel Monroe. Rush proposed a bold public statement from the President. "[T]he more I have reflected upon the subject of a proclamation," he confided to the Secretary of State, "the more important . . . it strikes me. After an event so very marked in our public affairs and destined to be always prominent in our national history, I think some very marked notice should be taken of it."

This was an opportunity, he argued, to shape a historic moment. "We should be prompt to tell of the act ourselves and in our own way, without holding back as if from shame, and suffering our enemies alone to embrace it with nothing but their own malicious comments. The very dating of it so soon from Washington would be useful. . . . Such a proclamation should reach Europe contemporaneously with the account of the entry of the capital, thereby at once rejecting this idea, so prevalent there, that it carries with it the reduction of the country."[17]

In short, the United States should tell the story of the burning of Washington, characterizing it not as a sorry defeat but as an outrage to all civilized people. A firm statement would buoy the spirits of Americans at home and invite condemnation of the British from abroad.

With Madison's approval, Rush was polishing the proclamation when Colonel Monroe received an unexpected communication. The sender was the British North American commander, Vice Admiral Alexander Cochrane, and, although Colonel Monroe took receipt of the letter on August 30, it was dated August 18. The timing made no sense. The British had been everywhere in the district for more than two weeks and, if they wished, could have delivered it much earlier. But its message was even more peculiar.

The letter contained an explicit threat. "Having been called upon by the Governor General of the Canadas to . . . effect measures of retaliation against the inhabitants of the United States for the wanton destruction committed by their army in Upper Canada," wrote Cochrane, "it has become imperiously my duty . . . to destroy and lay waste to such town and districts upon the coast as may be found assailable."[18] Colonel Monroe showed the letter to Mr. Madison and Mr. Rush; all three read it with growing outrage. As Cochrane would have it, the Americans *invited* the events at Washington. In Cochrane's construction, the burning of the Capitol was retribution for the American sack of York in Upper Canada sixteen months earlier.

To Madison and his cabinet, the idea was risible, and made all the more so by the late date of the letter's arrival, weeks after the British began their march. All in all, it had the ring of a deceitful, after-the-fact justification, one based, in Mr. Madison's opinion, on entirely specious reasoning.

Mr. Rush's revised proclamation soon made that case for all to read. The analogue to events at York was, quite simply, false. The destruction of several wooden structures in a regional capital by a few American soldiers hardly justified a wholesale destruction of a nation's monumental public buildings. Furthermore, the American government had already disavowed the burning at York. British actions, they agreed, were entirely unjustified.

Addressed to "all the good people" of the United States, the proclamation was published on September 1. It produced the desired effect. As expressed by newspaper editor Hezekiah Niles, "The Spirit of the Nation is roused." Niles wrote from Baltimore, decrying the British "barbarian warfare" and bemoaning the risk of lost liberties.[19] Writers from other quarters echoed the response.

Colonel Monroe replied to Admiral Cochrane directly a few days later. He countered that the British burning of Washington City was "manifestly contrary to the usage of civilized warfare." He promised that the United States would meet any further attacks "with a determination and constancy becoming a free people."[20]

In his new role as Secretary of War, Colonel Monroe organized artillery emplacements along the Potomac below Alexandria, including a 10-gun battery at White House, a bluff on the Virginia shore, and more guns at Indian Head on the Maryland side. When the British at Alexandria set their sails for the Chesapeake once again (no offensive move would be made on Georgetown), the American guns took a toll on the enemy's ships as they sailed past (the British reported seven men killed and forty-five wounded). But the greater firepower aboard the fleet soon enabled the British to blast their way past the temporary gun emplacements and rejoin the other British warships in the Chesapeake.

Citizens of Richmond, Norfolk, Annapolis, and Charleston worried that their cities might be next. Indeed, just such an attack was contemplated but, after a few days at their base on Tangier Island, a combined Royal Navy armada that included the amphibious force of Cockburn and Ross moved on Baltimore.

II.

September 12, 1814 . . . The Mouth of the Patapsco River

STRANDED IN LEGAL LIMBO, THE THREE AMERICANS watched helplessly as the British invasion force went ashore. They were a dozen miles downstream from Baltimore as the pinnaces, cutters, and launches made for North Point. The sails of their own ship, the sloop *Minden*, had been confiscated, the vessel itself lashed to a 38-gun British frigate, the HMS *Surprise.*

The doctor, the purser, and the barrister were not prisoners of war. Nor were they free to rejoin their countrymen. These men in civilian attire had become the men who knew too much.

Beginning at two A.M., under a full moon and clear sky, more than three thousand British infantrymen commanded by General Ross and six hundred of Admiral Cockburn's seamen and marines, along with eight field pieces, went ashore. Having spent much of the week aboard British warships, the three American observers possessed knowledge of the larger plan afoot to attack Baltimore. In the wrong hands, such intelligence would cost English lives, so the three would remain confined under watchful British eyes.

Admiral Cockburn and General Ross headed the invading force once again. On their last sojourn on American soil they met Dr. William Beanes, one of the men aboard the *Minden.* Two weeks before, the British commanders had knocked at the door of Beanes's commodious mansion, Academy Hill, and availed themselves of his hospitality, enjoying his food and tobacco as well as wines from his celebrated cellar. They slept in his bedchambers. If welcoming them had been wise, a subsequent decision by Beanes proved ill-advised when, as the British returned to their ships after their destruction of the public buildings at Washington, Dr. Beanes and a few fellow townspeople arrested and jailed some British stragglers. The doctor may have been fortified by drink; perhaps the last, lingering invaders had been intent on plunder as they passed through Upper Marlborough. The story varied.[21] Whatever the details, upon hearing that some of his men were incarcerated in a country jail, an angry General Ross dispatched a detachment of soldiers to drag Beanes from his bed. Told he would be tried for treason in Halifax, the doctor was imprisoned with common seamen in the forecastle of the fleet's flagship, the HMS *Tonnant.*

Word reached President Madison via Dr. Thornton of the rough treatment given the sixty-five-year-old veteran of the Revolution, who had bandaged the wounded at the Battle of Brandywine and amputated the frozen feet of soldiers at Valley Forge. The President authorized John Stuart Skinner, the same navy purser and prisoners' agent who had warned him of Cockburn's threats a few weeks earlier, to seek Dr. Beanes's release. A prominent Georgetown lawyer, Frank Key, volunteered to help when he learned of his friend's plight. The two men's mission succeeded when the *Minden*, flying a flag of truce, met up with the British flotilla in the Chesapeake as it stood toward Baltimore. The American negotiators persuaded the British brass to parole Beanes. But the American deputation's timing also meant that they knew Baltimore had become the inevitable object of a British assault.

By eight A.M., three British brigades began marching. Soon the shallow-draft warships in the fleet that could negotiate the shoals of the Patapsco, including four frigates, the rocket ship HMS *Erebus*, and five bomb ships, weighed anchor and set sail up the meandering channel toward the city. The heavier ships of the line remained at the mouth of the river but the *Minden*, too, proceeded upstream toward Baltimore, still attached like a suckling calf to the HMS *Surprise*.

MAJOR GENERAL SAMUEL SMITH WAS RESOLUTE. Two mistakes made in Washington would not be repeated in his city. First, as commander of Baltimore's militia, he would put in place an effective defense. Second, having been given the job by Baltimore's Committee of Vigilance and Safety, he would not under any circumstances relinquish that command—especially to the man in charge of the Tenth Military District. Brigadier General William Winder was now a two-time loser, with his failure to defend the capital added to his earlier Canadian surrender. As a U.S. Senator, a veteran of the Revolution (he had risen to the rank of lieutenant colonel), and a Marylander, Samuel Smith intended to make sure the British did not capture Baltimore on *his* watch.

The intervention of Secretary of War James Monroe had been required to quiet the outraged General Winder, but since taking full command of the city defenses on August 26, Smith had worked to put Baltimore's strategic advantages to good use. The burgeoning metropolis had grown into the nation's third-largest city after New York and Philadelphia. As a center for shipbuilding, a hub for trade, and home to many mills, Baltimore prospered even in the face of embargoes and the war. Its seafaring population had adapted to life during wartime, and the city's privateers seized more than five hundred British ships, leading Admiral Cockburn to describe the city as a "nest of pirates."

Baltimore's downtown streets overlooked a protected bay. The key to General Smith's strategy was to keep the Royal Navy out of this inner harbor. He had the signal advantage of Fort McHenry, a brick fortress completed in 1802, which guarded the harbor's narrow entrance. Shaped like a five-pointed star with more than fifty guns mounted in the bastions at its points, the fortification enclosed a powder magazine and barracks. It was now home to a garrison of a thousand men, some of whom had served in Joshua Barney's flotilla. Under the command of Major George Armistead, the fort had in the preceding days been provisioned for a siege.

General Smith added to nearby shoreline protections. Batteries were thrown up outside the walls of Fort McHenry and at Point Lazaretto, which guarded the harbor entrance on the east with its own three-gun battery. Citizens of the city dug trenches at the perimeter of the town. Two redoubts were in place west of Fort McHenry at Fort Covington and Babcock Battery, near the west branch of the Patapsco. There were 18-, 24-, and 38-pounders in place, along with armed barges, redoubts, and a squadron of gunboats that patrolled the inner harbor.

As a final stroke, twenty-four ships and barges were being sunk at the entrance to the harbor. This barrier of half-submerged merchant vessels, their masts splayed at all angles, stood as an obstacle to any approaching ship.

In a gesture worthy of Mrs. Madison, Major Armistead had determined that something else was required. He commissioned a giant woolen flag. "It is my desire," Armistead had written to Senator Smith, "to have a flag so large that the British will have no difficulty seeing it from a distance."[22] A Baltimore flagmaker, the widow Mary Pickersgills, together with her thirteen-year-old daughter, Caroline, produced the giant ensign and submitted a bill for $405.90. Now, as preparations for a British attack proceeded, the three-story-tall flag waved atop the ninety-foot flagpole at Fort McHenry, its bold red, white, and blue geometry unmistakable.

FROM BALTIMORE'S FEDERAL HILL, the fleet of more than forty British vessels could be seen at anchor off North Point. That meant that part two of General Smith's master plan, his landward line of defense, would soon be tested.

General Smith recognized that the formidable British army might move to take the city on foot as it had at Washington. Even a cursory glance at a map of the region revealed that the logical line of attack on land would be along Patapsco Neck, the peninsula that extended to the point where the waters of the Patapsco River flowed into the Chesapeake Bay. At its tip, North Point offered a deep-water anchorage and a beach suitable for an amphibious landing. It was fourteen miles from Baltimore.

Smith's defensive plan took advantage of the terrain at Hampstead Hill, the tallest of a string of hills forming an irregular ridge overlooking the city. For almost two weeks, citizen work parties with pickaxes, shovels, and barrows worked to construct a series of palisaded redoubts linked to one another by breastworks. Cannon were mounted in semicircular batteries; to man the fortifications, miltiamen poured in from Pennsylvania and Maryland, reinforcing two U.S. infantry regiments. A contingent of seamen assigned to two new vessels under construction in the harbor, the 44-gun frigate *Java* and the 22-gun sloop *Erie*, were joined by the 350-man crew of the *Guerrière*, commanded by Commodore John Rogers, then blockaded in port in Delaware. These expert gunners mounted cannon on the hills, as well as at the shore. Smith's dual lines of defense at the water's edge and on the upland ridge could now claim more than twelve thousand men in arms.

With the British fleet at anchor off North Point, General Smith went on the offensive. At his order, a force of more than three thousand men under the command of General Stricker marched forth from Hampstead Hill. They established a forward line of defense of some seven miles along Long Log Lane, the road to North Point. Many of the defenders had been among those routed at Bladensburg, and, just as it was on that unlucky day, the main defense was arranged in three lines, roughly three hundred yards apart, ready to defend a narrowing on Patapsco Neck between Bear

Creek and Bread and Cheese Creek. But this battle would begin quite differently than that day at Bladensburg.

THE VANGUARD OF FOUR HUNDRED AMERICAN CAVALRY AND RIFLEMEN waited a mile in advance of the main defensive position. At ten A.M. on September 12, a company of soldiers came into view at a wooded turning in the road. Leading the British detachment of more than fifty men were Admiral Cockburn and General Ross.

The Americans opened fire. Despite being outnumbered, the British charged. Intimidated by the veteran fighting force, the defenders "fled to the right and left through the woods."[23] Yet it was the British force that sustained the greater loss.

Upon hearing gunfire, a young British officer just out of sight ordered his troops to move at double-time to join the skirmish. Moments later an officer on horseback raced past them, heading back the way they came. He was calling for a surgeon, and, even more worrisome, they could read "horror and dismay in his countenance."[24]

Then a second horse, this one riderless, galloped past, its empty saddle stained with fresh blood. The realization struck that the handsome white mount belonged to General Ross. Upon reaching the site of the skirmish, the infantrymen saw their commander under a blanket canopy to one side of the country road. After sustaining his terrible wound ("a Musquet Ball through his arm into his Breast"), Ross had toppled from his horse.[25]

Summoned from the second brigade, Colonel Arthur Brooke took command. The British closed on the main American force, which came into view on the other side of a large clearing, protected by a fence of upright, sharpened sticks. The Americans fired a sharp cannonade from behind the paling, clearing the road. British field pieces returned fire, while at Colonel Brooke's order, a British detachment moved to attack the left flank of the American line.

Admiral Cockburn, wearing his gold-laced hat and unmistakable on his white horse, rode along the line as it took shape on the British side. To the call of bugles, the British force, with machinelike determination, marched across the field toward the Americans at the tree line.

The American troops fired their cannon, and the balls "fell like a hailstorm" amid the British troops.[26] Despite the Congreve rockets fired over their heads, the American defense remained intact. The artillery continued to play upon the oncoming British, delivering "a dreadful discharge of grape and canister shot, of old locks, pieces of broken muskets, and everything which they could cram in their guns."[27]

The oncoming British troops held their musket fire; only when they were twenty yards from the American line did they fire as one before rushing forward to the palings, brandishing their bayonets. In the melee that resulted, the American line broke, and, by eleven o'clock, the British held the field. In the absence of a cavalry force, the invaders could not pursue the retreating army, and they set up camp for the night, establishing a temporary hospital and officers' quarters in a nearby meetinghouse.

The fight resulted in more than three hundred British wounded; the Americans lost half that number. Among the forty-six British dead was General Ross, whom no surgeon could save. Returned to the ships at North Point on a cart, wrapped in the Union Jack, his lifeless corpse was immersed in a hogshead of rum to preserve it for burial.

III.

September 13, 1814 . . . The Patapsco River off Baltimore

THE BRITISH FLEET COMMENCED THE BOMBARDMENT OF FORT MCHENRY at first light. Colonel Armistead ordered his artillerymen to return fire, and, for a time, the Americans maintained a brisk fire. Unfortunately, Armistead soon noted, "our shot and shells fell considerably short, . . . a most distressing circumstance as it left us exposed to a constant and tremendous shower of shells, without the remote possibility of our doing him the slightest injury."[28] The enemy ships, more than two miles from Fort McHenry, were out of the range of even the biggest American cannon.

For their part, the British kept up a relentless barrage from the decks of their bomb ships, firing ten- and thirteen-inch mortar shells at the rate of more than one a minute. Unlike solid cannonballs, each hollow projectile, some of which weighed up to two hundred pounds, was packed with a gunpowder charge. Launched from muzzle-loaded mortars that resembled large iron bowls, the shells flew in a high arc, remaining in flight up to thirty seconds. Many exploded in midair, scattering deadly shrapnel in all directions. Though the mortars were difficult to aim accurately, about a quarter of those fired rained down on Fort McHenry. With the immense booms and the long, slow trajectory of the big bombs, the morning passed slowly, a one-sided affair.

At about two o'clock in the afternoon, a shell registered a direct hit on an American 24-pounder cannon atop one of Fort McHenry's bastions. The lieutenant in charge of the gun was killed in the blast and four nearby soldiers wounded. The gun was dismounted, a wheel of its carriage shattered. Upon seeing a sudden commotion at the fort, three of the British bomb ships dared to sail closer. Observing the ships within range of the American cannon, Armistead ordered a barrage from every gun that would bear. The three British vessels soon slipped their cables, hoisted their sails, and fell back once again out of range of the American guns.

As the afternoon wore on, the sky grew gray and a torrential rain began to fall. But the bombardment didn't cease, continuing into the evening. Even in the dense blackness of the overcast night the bombardment went on, with rocket and shell explosions lighting the sky like fireworks.

Without warning, at one A.M. the firing ceased. With conditions on the water thick and hazy, the defenders could no longer distinguish the enemy, but a British landing force was soon observed when a boat supporting the attack fired Congreve rockets to illuminate the shore west of

Fort McHenry. The Americans at nearby Fort Babcock quickly replied with a blaze of artillery fire, driving off the attackers in their barges. The bombardment from the bomb ships resumed for several hours until, at about four A.M., the guns again went silent.

THE EERIE QUIET WAS MATCHED ONLY BY THE DARKNESS. Nothing could be seen of the blacked-out city, and aboard the *Minden*, the three Americans did not know what to think. One possibility was that Fort McHenry had surrendered. Or perhaps the British had abandoned the attack?

Employing the spyglass aboard the *Minden*, lawyer Frank Key had surveyed Fort McHenry the day before as artillery shells arched toward it. The brick fortress, the water, the sky graying as clouds moved in, and the smoke from the gunpowder explosions made a melancholy sight, and he had found his eye drawn repeatedly to the immense flag with fifteen white and red stripes, each of which was two feet tall. A field of blue in one quadrant contained fifteen large white stars. From his distant vantage he could not know it, but the woolen flag was a full forty-three feet across. But he did know that the flag was a beacon.

Early in the morning, in the silence after the firing ceased, he waited impatiently for the dawn to illuminate Fort McHenry. He and Skinner "paced the deck for the residue of the night in painful suspense, watching with intense anxiety for the return of day." They checked their watches, waiting for first light or word of the battle's outcome. "[B]efore it was light enough to see objects at a distance, their glasses were turned to the fort, uncertain whether they should see there the stars and stripes, or the flag of the enemy."[29]

Finally, with a soft lightening in the sky, Francis Scott Key, Esquire, saw the immense American banner. Upon seeing the giant flag, he put pen to paper.

Born on a Maryland plantation, Key had been educated at St. John's

College in Annapolis, then remained in Maryland's capital to clerk for a lawyer. He became not only a legal wordsmith, who, as a barrister, tried cases before the U.S. Supreme Court, but something of a literary man, too, with a taste for Jonathan Swift and Sir Walter Scott. He wrote occasional poems for his friends, and, in the night just passed, some poetical phrases came to him. With daylight, on the deck of the *Minden*, "in the fervor of the moment," as he told a friend, he noted them on the back of a letter he happened to have in his pocket.[30]

Before he could finish his composition, the *Surprise* made ready to sail. The sails for the *Minden* were handed down from the British frigate; Mr. Skinner, Dr. Beanes, and Mr. Key, along with the sloop's several sailors, were now free to go. The siege by sea was over. Once clear of the British warship, the one-masted *Minden* unfurled its sails and headed for shore at Baltimore several miles upstream. The men aboard watched as the invading fleet came about and retreated toward the Chesapeake Bay. Key kept scribbling, completing a draft of his ballad.

Once ashore, Key rented a room at the Indian Queen Hotel on High Street. There he made a fair copy of the lines he had written, complete with the phrases "rockets' red glare" and "bombs bursting in air." He composed them to the remembered strains of a popular drinking song (Key's four verses aligned with the melody of "To Anacreon in Heaven"). He showed his work to a friend, a well-connected Maryland jurist, and within a day a typeset version of the song came off the press at the Baltimore *American*, which had yet to resume regular publication after the siege. Key had left the piece untitled, but the small handbill—six and a half inches high, five and a half wide—bore the title his friend the judge had added. A few days later, the *Baltimore Patriot* published the poem, "Defence of Fort McHenry." Though the editors noted that the song was "destined long to outlast the occasion," no author was credited.[31]

The land assault on Baltimore had also ended. After receiving word from the harbor that the Royal Navy could not help them, Cockburn had held a long counsel of war to consider the entrenched Americans on

Hampstead Hill. At midnight, he decided to rejoin the fleet at North Point. In the rain and predawn darkness on September 14, the British army retreated.

IV.

September 19, 1814 . . . Blodgett's Hotel . . . Washington City

THE NEWS OF THE BIG VICTORY AT BALTIMORE could hardly have come at a more opportune time for Madison. It defused the elemental fear that the American army could not protect the homeland. The departure of the British fleet inspired a new confidence. As one Virginia barrister in militia service put it, "The struggle, I now believe, will be a short one. The invincibles of Wellington are found to be vincible."[32]

That did not mean that all the hostile voices in Washington City fell silent. As he prepared a message for the special session of Congress that was to convene that day, two months early, the President marshaled his arguments concerning the much-discussed proposal to relocate the capital. When word of the British invasion at Washington reached other cities, offers had poured in from Philadelphia and Lancaster, Pennsylvania, from New York and Kentucky, among other places, to host the seat of government. For people who had never been reconciled to the idea of locating the nation's capital in the South, this was an opportunity to reopen the debate. Mr. Madison would fight such a move, that was certain, both as a Virginian and as a partisan for Washington City, and so would Mrs. Madison. They held with the thinking of Congressman Nathaniel Macon that "if the seat of government was once set on wheels, there is no saying where it will stop."[33] It was nonsense to think of flying from the city; that would fulfill British desires.

Surely, too, there would be a motion from the floor to investigate the August events at Washington. Perhaps that was as it should be, with statements to be collected from the many participants. When all was recorded and analyzed, would the final report do more than recapitulate the event? Could blame be assigned to General Winder or Secretary of War Armstrong, or even to Colonel Monroe, who, at Bladensburg, had made free with his advice? Might the President himself be awarded blame? The outcome could not be known, but the investigation, Madison understood, was a certainty.

Yet he had even larger concerns. The nation was nearly out of money again, as less than half the monies to pay the year's war expenses were on hand, with none available for 1815, despite an unprecedented twenty-five-million-dollar loan authorized (but only half subscribed) in March. To make matters worse, on September 1, the New York banks, following those of Baltimore and Philadelphia, had suspended government specie payments.

This very day, however, the newspapers were filled with a new story. The events in question had unfolded well north, on the New York State shores of Lake Champlain, where for months the British had been preparing to exhibit their military strength. As Mr. Madison reviewed his address to Congress for the following day, the list of topics to be covered was considerable: the peace negotiations at Ghent, the battle at Baltimore, the nation's money worries, and the matter of the capital city. But he would also be obliged to devote a few lines to the outcome of a "recent attack by a powerful force on our troops at Plattsburg."[34]

V.

September 11, 1814 . . . Aboard the USS Saratoga *. . . Plattsburgh Bay*

THE COMMANDER OF THE FLEET'S FLAGSIHP knelt on the quarterdeck in the early autumn chill. With British warships two miles astern, their gunports open, the battle was imminent. But Master Commandant Thomas Macdonough—recently married, the father of one child with another on the way—offered a prayer to the Almighty, together with his officers aboard the USS *Saratoga*.

Even as a man of faith, the thirty-year-old Macdonough would not be relying upon divine intervention. Nor was he particularly afraid of what the hours to come might hold for him and the eight hundred and eighty-two men who crewed his ships. On the contrary, in the eight days since sailing into Plattsburgh Bay, he had plotted a careful strategy that played to American strengths and aimed to undercut those of the enemy. After two frustrating years as commander of the U.S. Navy force on Lake Champlain, he felt ready for this fight as he rose from bended knee.

The thirty-year-old Delaware native had spent almost half his life on the water. At sixteen, he shipped out as a midshipman to serve in the West Indies. During the Barbary Wars, he helped Stephen Decatur torch the captured frigate USS *Philadelphia* in Tripoli. He had been among the last to leap from the flaming vessel, and his bravery earned Macdonough a promotion to the rank of lieutenant. After Madison's Declaration of War, he briefly commanded gunboats defending the New England coast but, on September 12, 1812, he had been given command of the U.S. Navy fleet on Lake Champlain.

Not that it had been much of a fleet. Lieutenant Macdonough inherited two leaky gunboats and six unarmed trading sloops usable for little more than ferrying troops. At the time, the British could claim even fewer vessels on the lake, and shipbuilders in both Canada and Vermont raced to build warships of green pine harvested nearby. In early 1813, Macdonough gained three new armed sloops, only to lose his advantage over the Royal Navy on Champlain when two of them, in pursuit of enemy gunboats, were captured in Canadian waters.

In early 1814, the Navy Department dispatched a team of veteran boatbuilders to enlarge Macdonough's fleet. Noah and Adam Brown of New York, the men who had built the USS *Lawrence* and the USS *Niagara* for Commodore Perry on Lake Erie the previous year, set to work immediately on the 26-gun USS *Saratoga*; it had entered service that spring on Champlain. In August the balance of naval power shifted even more to Macdonough's advantage, with the launch of the USS *Eagle*. Built at President Madison's direct order, the 20-gun brig had been launched just nineteen days after the Browns laid her keel. Along with ten row galleys, armed with one or two guns each, Macdonough now commanded a fleet of four warships, including the *Eagle*, the *Saratoga*, the 7-gun sloop USS *Preble*, and a converted steam schooner, the *Ticonderoga*, reconfigured as a 17-gun warship.

Unfortunately for Commandant Macdonough, a subsequent launching, this one at the Isle aux Noix shipyard in Canada on August 25, had altered the balance of arms yet again.

THE AMERICANS HAD HELD THE ADVANTAGE FOR A MATTER OF DAYS, four ships to three, before the pendulum swung back. As Macdonough watched the British fleet approach, he fixed his gaze on the reason why—the HMS *Confiance*. The frigate was so fresh off the stocks that, barely an hour earlier, observers on Macdonough's guard boat reported that the ringing of hammers ceased only when the last work gang shoved off.

Whatever finishing touches it might have lacked on close examination, from afar the *Confiance* was an imposing ship, by far the biggest and most powerful on the lake. On its decks 37 guns were deployed, most of them long guns that possessed a much greater range than Macdonough's carronades. The accompanying HMS *Linnet* had a dozen more long guns, giving the British a decisive advantage in open water. In the broads of Champlain, the *Confiance* alone might destroy Macdonough's entire fleet. But this battle would unfold on his terms, within the relatively cramped waters of Plattsburgh Bay. There Macdonough waited patiently, calculating the disposition of his ships to best advantage.

While the danger loomed large for Macdonough and his men, word of what happened in the next hours at Plattsburgh might also have

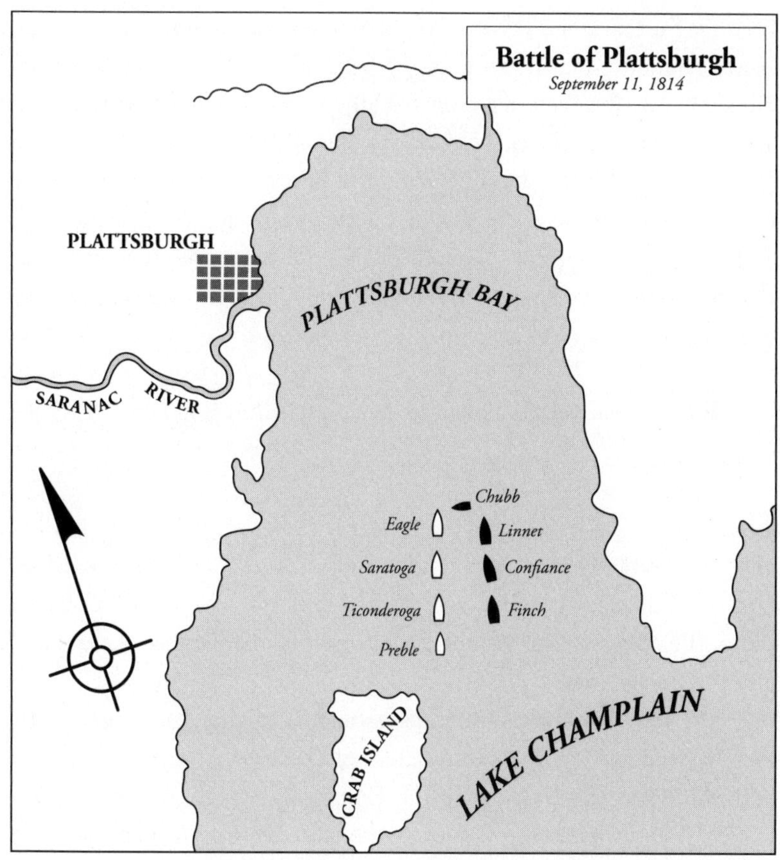

larger implications upon reaching London, Washington City, and even Ghent, where the peace negotiations had only just begun. On Lake Erie, Perry's big victory a year earlier had frustrated British aims; on Lake Ontario, neither the British nor the American fleet could claim any great advantage. But Macdonough had only to look over his shoulder toward the town to see that the enemy already held most of Plattsburgh. An invasion force of some eleven thousand men, many of them Wellington's troops fresh from conquering Spain, had marched south from the St. Lawrence. It was the largest invasion army ever to march onto American soil and, virtually unopposed, it had taken Plattsburgh on September 6. The American force, badly outnumbered, chose to retreat across the Saranac River. Now only a few blockhouses and fewer than 3,500 healthy soldiers stood between the British invasion force and the road south to Saratoga, Albany, and perhaps beyond. But Macdonough and his opposite number, Captain George Downie, held the key to the British progress. To keep their land force supplied, the British needed a victory on the water to accompany what looked to be a sure success on land.

The invasion, Macdonough understood, had to stop here.

THE BATTLE HAD BEEN IN THE MAKING FOR DAYS, and everybody knew it. As the morning sun rose over Plattsburgh Bay, farmers watched from the surrounding hilltops. On the Plattsburgh shore, the opposing armies north and south of the Saranac River could glimpse the two fleets.

The four American warships waited at anchor, sails furled, almost motionless on the calm waters of the bay. At the head of the battle line was the *Eagle*, with the *Saratoga* next, followed by the *Ticonderoga* and the *Preble*, with the gunboats covering the gaps between the warships.

Approaching off the starboard quarter was the British fleet, led by one of the captured American sloops, renamed the HMS *Chubb* (11). A 16-gun brig, the HMS *Linnet*, came next, with the *Confiance* third, followed by the second of the captured sloops, the *Finch* (11). Bringing up the rear were eleven smaller craft carrying one or two guns each. At least within the confines of the bay, the navies were well matched.

Soon after eight o'clock, Macdonough sighted the first gun aboard the *Saratoga*, aligning its barrel with a chosen spot on the hull of the *Confiance*. The moment after its report echoed across the bay, its 24-pound ball crashed through the hawse-hole of the *Confiance*.[35] Other American guns unleashed balls and canister shot, but the British frigate held her fire. Only after coming to and securing his ship's anchors did Captain Downie order the gunners of the *Confiance* to fire upon the Americans. As one, His Majesty's gunners unleashed a double-shotted broadside of all the port guns.

The opening broadside killed or wounded one-fifth of those aboard the *Saratoga*. The sheer shock of a third of a ton of airborne metal crashing into the wooden ship knocked men to the deck. The gunners on both sides worked their guns in spite of the murderous fire, swabbing, ramming, heaving in and out. The resultant cannonade was deafening and nonstop. The destructive fire tore holes in the hulls and ripped up rigging. One spar that crashed down struck Macdonough a glancing blow, driving him to the deck, dazed.

Fifteen minutes into the battle, the British suffered a shocking casualty. It happened in a single frozen moment as the crew of one of the long guns prepared to fire its 24-pounder. Standing at the breech, Captain George Downie was sighting along the cannon's length when a ball fired in an almost flat trajectory from the *Saratoga* scored a direct hit on the muzzle of the British gun. The barrel of the cannon was suddenly airborne, driven completely off its carriage. It crashed into Downie's groin, and he went to the deck with the gun on top. Though there was no external bleeding, the several tons of iron crushed bones and organs, leaving Downie unable to speak. In a matter of minutes, the fleet commander's heart ceased to beat.[36]

The decks of both ships were awash with blood. Musketry and grapeshot took a toll, with dozens dead and wounded; some were taken below, some merely tossed aside. Macdonough was knocked down again, this time when a cannonball severed the head of one of his gun captains, and the skull struck Macdonough a blow across his cheek.[37]

The smaller vessels ceased to be factors in the fight. The HMS *Chubb*, her sails and rigging damaged by heavy fire from the guns of the *Eagle*, drifted helplessly through the American line before hauling down her colors. The HMS *Finch* on approach had failed to keep near enough to the wind and never reached the position where she was to fire upon her assigned foe, the USS *Ticonderoga*. Adrift in a falling breeze, the *Finch* went aground at Crab Island and also struck. Both the USS *Preble* and the *Ticonderoga* were attacked by British gunboats. The *Preble* cut her moorings and floated off toward Plattsburgh. Though the *Ticonderoga* maintained her position, the battle had become a four-ship contest.

At about nine thirty, with most of her guns out of commission or no longer able to bear, the *Eagle* cut her cable, then ran down the line. She anchored by her stern south of the *Saratoga*, where she opened her unscarred larboard guns to the battle, delivering a destructive fire upon the *Confiance*.

Aboard the badly battered *Saratoga*, under almost continuous fire from the *Confiance* and now raked by the guns of the *Linnet*, the last of Macdonough's starboard artillery went out of commission when a carronade flew off its carriage and crashed down the main hatch.[38] The gun deck of his principal opponent, the *Confiance*, was also littered with dismounted and unserviceable cannon. Nearly two hours into the contest, the two flagships resembled punch-drunk pugilists, neither of whom possessed the strength to deliver a knockout blow.

But Macdonough's well-considered battle calculus left him with a surprise tactic: He would wind his ship, literally turning it one hundred and eighty degrees. The bow cable of the *Saratoga* was cut and the stern anchor released. The men then hauled the heavy hawser rope from a starboard kedge anchor astern. By means of the capstan, the port-quarter hawser was hauled under the bow and carried aft to the starboard quarter, thereby pivoting the ship on another kedge. In the process, first one then another new gun was brought to bear on the enemy, each one stuffed with handspikes. The renewed fire had a tremendous effect aboard the *Confiance*. "Where it had been black with men the moment before," observed one American seaman, "scarcely one man could now be seen."[39] When the turning maneuver was complete, an entirely new broadside brought fresh guns to the contest.

With these weapons now delivering deadly fire, the battle became a one-sided affair. Though the *Confiance* attempted a similar winding maneuver, she succeeded only in opening her stern to a raking fire from the *Saratoga*, and the *Confiance* was forced to strike her colors. After the *Saratoga* redirected her fire at the *Linnet*, the last British ship surrendered. The battle had lasted two hours and twenty minutes.

WITH THE GUNS SILENT, THE COSTS COULD BE CALCULATED. Fifty-two Americans were dead out of 110 total casualties; the British losses were perhaps twice as great. The *Confiance* had taken fully 105 round shots to her side, the *Saratoga* 55. A grand new ship barely a week in the water, the *Confiance* listed precariously. Only by running her guns to port did her crew prevent the ship from sinking, so perforated was her hull below the waterline.

The Governor General of Canada, Lieutenant General Sir George Prevost, had taken personal charge of the invasion and, watching from Plattsburgh, saw his ships go down in defeat. Thereby deprived of an essential means of communication and supplies, he made a hard but necessary decision. Before daylight the following morning, leaving stores and equipment in their wake, the British brigades abandoned Plattsburgh, retreating toward the Canadian border.

In Washington a few days later, the express messenger from Captain Thomas Macdonough arrived in Washington City, carrying a dispatch addressed to Navy Secretary Jones. A more detailed report would follow, but on the day of battle, just one sentence offered all that Macdonough felt needed to be said. "The Almighty has been pleased to Grant us a signal victory on lake Champlain in the capture of one Frigate, one Brig and two sloops of war of the Enemy."[40]

VI.

November 2, 1814 . . . The Tayloe Mansion . . . Washington City

MENDING THE SPIRIT TAKES TIME. At first, Mrs. Madison met the trauma of August 24 with tears and anger. Having been on the receiving end of Admiral Cockburn's threats, she could hardly help but apprehend the actions of the British as an almost physical insult to her person.

As she aged, Dolley Madison had become subject to blinding headaches and rheumatism, but in the days after the assault on Washington, an unfamiliar numbness came over her. Her pen went uncharacteristically quiet, and she wrote few letters in the aftermath of the burning. She had difficulty coming to grips with her "losses." It was months before she could write to her friend Mary Latrobe of the damage done. "Our own valuable stores of every description, a part of my clothes . . . etc., etc. In short, it would fatigue you to read the list." Even after making such an admission, she could only manage to describe her anguish and sense of violation in the third person, referring to those feelings as the "particular distresses of your acquaintance."[41]

Mrs. Madison did gradually recover herself, and the first essential step in regaining her usual grace and ease came with the offer of Mr. Tayloe's fine house.

John and Anne Ogle Tayloe occupied the top rank of the Washington City social echelon. She came from an old and powerful Maryland family; he had succeeded to the largest estate in his native Virginia. The city's richest residents, with holdings that included iron foundries, tens of thousands of acres, and John's stable of racehorses, they had been among the new city's first arrivals. George Washington himself suggested they build a town house (as the general was doing), and the Tayloes commissioned a grand dwelling. They took possession in 1800, the same year President John Adams and his government arrived in the Federal City.[42]

Most recently their three-story brick mansion had sheltered the French minister (the Tayloes only occupied it for the winter season, spending most of the year at their country seat, Mt. Airy, on Virginia's Northern Neck). After the events at Washington, M. Sérurier relocated the business of the French government to Philadelphia, and a mutual friend of the Tayloes and the Madisons stepped in.*

Dr. William Thornton had designed the house and, during construction, become a staunch friend of Mr. Tayloe; armed with a reserve of goodwill with all parties, he felt enabled to broach an understanding. Mr. and Mrs. Madison needed a place to live. Even if the Tayloes were unabashed Federalists, they shared the Madisons' commitment to the aborning city. They understood how essential was a suitable presidential domicile, not to mention the resumption of Mrs. Madison's Drawing Rooms. Her squeezes amounted to a shared social milieu upon which elected officials, the local gentry, and men of business had come to rely. The city needed a place where political and social differences meant little, where they could meet friends and political foes, the powerful and the ambitious, the amiable and the eligible, "even the shoemakers and their wives."[43] The Tayloes' house, second in size only to the now-ruined President's house, was the obvious choice, as the only private home with the elegance and scale for grand entertaining. An agreement made, the President had the finest house in the city at his disposal for six months for the sum of eight hundred dollars.[44]

On September 8, the Madisons had moved into the grand house. Even if her red velvet curtains were too tall for the windows, Mrs. Madison found the rooms fully furnished and well appointed. The Tayloes themselves entertained often, though Mrs. Madison immediately ordered additional china and glassware. Her more democratic squeezes could

---

* Precisely how the Madison occupancy of the house known today as the Octagon came to pass is not entirely clear. A Tayloe son asserted in 1872 that the idea had been his father's; other claimants for the plan included Sérurier and Thornton. Given Thornton's character and his peripatetic nature, among other factors, it seems almost certain that he played some role.

be expected to draw larger crowds than attended the Tayloes' invitation-only parties.

For Mrs. Madison, the move to the corner of New York Avenue and Eighteenth Street signaled a resumption of her patterns, of the life that, for almost fifteen years, she had made for herself and her city. Not everyone cheered, as there remained some who did not wish her to resume her Drawing Rooms. According to the *Washington City Gazette*, "The destruction of the President's House cannot be said to be a great loss . . . as we hope it will *put an end* to drawing-rooms and *levees*; the resort of the idle and the encouragers of spies and traitors."[45] But if the British couldn't stop her, no anonymous newspaper voice would either.

AS MRS. MADISON PREPARED TO WELCOME WASHINGTON CITY SOCIETY, Mr. Madison settled into his new office. He had chosen the cylindrical chamber over the vestibule, an elegant round room with curved windows and doors to match. Hung over a circular desk at center was a magnificent glass chandelier. As if in echo of his new space, he settled into his task of reestablishing Washington City's central role in governing the country.

In rebuilding the city, he found he could count on the help of many of his neighbors, who, like the Tayloes, having invested in the city's future, wished to see the capital remain in the Federal District. Local landowners had gotten a subscription together to underwrite a temporary building for the government. The glorious Capitol would take years to rebuild, but a temporary structure (the "Brick Capitol," they were calling it) might soon provide Congress a home for the interim that better suited its needs than Blodgett's Hotel.

The first cost estimates were in hand for rebuilding. Restoring the President's house, Madison learned, would cost a great deal of money, perhaps $295,000.[46] A report was due to be delivered by the Office of the Superintendent of the Public Buildings regarding reconstruction at the

Capitol and the public offices; the promise was of even greater sums. Better news came from Mr. Latrobe, who lately had written from Pittsburgh letting it be known he would accept a draft to rebuild the Capitol.

Before any advance could be made on these matters, Congress would have to concur. The new session had seen a resolution pass in the House of Representatives that ordered the appointment of a committee "to inquire into the expedition of removing the Seat of Government."[47] To no one's surprise, a vigorous debate ensued, but within a week, a majority on the committee submitted to the House another resolution stating "[t]hat it [was] inexpedient to remove the Seat of Government at this time from the City of Washington."[48] It proved to be well less than the last word on the matter.

A floor vote was taken; the result was a tie. The House then resolved into a Committee of the Whole, and the entire body invested two more weeks in debate before again counting yeas and nays. The final tally was 83 to 74 in favor of keeping the capital in Washington. Yet the discussion still wouldn't be concluded until the Senate seconded the resolution. To Madison's frustration, what might have been resolved in days or even hours looked as if it would require months.

The President also faced the nation's continuing money problems. The militiamen summoned into service in recent months had been an immense expense that exceeded all budget allowances. According to Treasury Secretary Campbell's report to Congress, even before allotting any money for rebuilding, the outstanding appropriations of some twenty-five million dollars exceeded anticipated revenues by more than eleven million dollars. To meet budget in the new year, higher direct taxes and internal duties would be required. To make Madison's job more complicated, the ever-ailing Campbell had resigned the very day his report was filed with Congress. Furthermore, William Jones would be departing, too. The reliable Navy Secretary advised Madison that his personal finances required that he invest his energies in his family and fortune.

The news from abroad remained uncertain. British newspapers

reported that after the news of Washington's capture reached London, guns at the Tower were fired in celebration three days in succession. Only as the details of the capture became generally known did the joy of victory take on the taint of outrage; there was a growing shame at what some termed a return to "the times of barbarism." The *London Statesman* saw the episode as embarrassing to Britain. "Willingly," its editors reported, "would we throw a veil of oblivion over our transactions at Washington. The Cossacks spared Paris, but we spared not the capital of America."[49] If Madison harbored hopes that this augured well for the peace negotiations, he faced a rude shock. His Majesty's government exhibited no remorse, at least to judge from Gallatin's latest dispatches, which arrived on October 8. The British negotiators at Ghent were taking a hard line, making demands of the American negotiators as if they represented a conquered nation.

One welcome letter did arrive on Madison's desk from Monticello. His old friend Jefferson offered personal words of encouragement, expressing his "sympathies" concerning "the late events at Washington." He offered assurances to his old friend James. "Had Gl. Washington himself been now at the head of our affairs, the same event would probably have happened." He added congratulations for the late news from Plattsburgh.

Buried in the closing paragraph, almost as an afterthought, was Jefferson's mention of the possibility of a grand patriotic gesture. "I have long been sensible that my library would be an interesting possession for the public," wrote Jefferson, "and the loss Congress has recently sustained, and the difficulty of replacing it, while our intercourse with Europe is so obstructed, renders this the proper moment for placing it at their service."*

The offer by his oldest ally was an extraordinary surprise. As a regu-

* Thomas Jefferson to James Madison, September 24, 1814. Jefferson's gesture was both generous and civic-minded; he believed strongly in the importance of books and education to his country. As a man deeply in debt, he also badly needed ready cash and eventually he would be paid $23,950 for his 6,487 volumes.

lar guest at Monticello, James knew how attached Jefferson was to his books; it was suspected he liked them rather more than people, and Jefferson himself had once confessed wryly that he "labored grievously under the malady of Bibliomanie."[50] This seeming addiction to acquiring books had produced the finest personal collection of books in the country, one double the size of the library the British destroyed.

To part with his cherished library would be an act of patriotism and of intellectual generosity and, perhaps most of all, an expression of confidence in Washington City. Jefferson volunteered to ship the thousands of volumes immediately, offering "immediate use of [my collection], as eighteen or twenty wagons would place it in Washington in a single trip of a fortnight."[51] If not everyone believed in the future of Washington City, Mr. Jefferson certainly did.

AS DOLLEY PREPARED FOR THE FIRST DRAWING ROOM of the season (the date was set for November 2), James faced a new challenge. For perhaps the first time in a presidency with many low moments, he found himself unable to maintain his stoic mask with a visitor.

His guest was known to him. A fellow resident of Virginia, William Wirt had practiced law in Charlottesville during Madison's brief retirement from public life at the close of the last century. Though he now lived in Richmond, Wirt had come to Washington before, when President Jefferson appointed him prosecutor in the Aaron Burr treason trial in 1807. Having returned to town two days earlier, he inspected the ruin of the President's house, which he described as a "mournful monument of American imbecility and improvidence, and of British atrocity."[52]

A tall, barrel-chested man, Wirt looked younger than his forty-one years, with light hair and intense blue eyes. Calling on Madison this October day, he seemed to tower over his friend in both body and spirit. He found the older man "miserably shattered and wo-begone." As he wrote to his wife, "he looked heart-broken."

The explanation, Wirt found, wasn't the "unroofed naked walls" of the President's house but an imminent gathering of Federalists. "His mind," reported Wirt, "was full of the New England sedition."

Mr. Madison recounted the story. Some thought the Federalist antipathy to the war would soften with the British invasion of Lake Champlain on the very borders of New England. Or that a nationalist instinct might arise in the region after British forces seized the upper third of coastal Maine, as they had done, virtually unopposed, in early September. Yet no instinct to national unity showed itself in the region; in fact, as yeoman farmers continued to smuggle livestock across the Canadian border for sale to British quartermasters, leaders in Massachusetts, including Harrison Gray Otis, publicly called for a New England convention that was to move toward "a radical reform of the national compact."

When Madison read these words in the hours before Wirt's arrival, he hadn't needed a translator to understand the Federalists: It was an open secret that some in their ranks were advocating withdrawal from the union. They were talking of a separate peace, one that New England might negotiate with Great Britain. Madison thought such divisive talk in wartime was madness, especially when, as Attorney General Rush put it, "If New England would only *threaten* to invade Canada and make some bustle, it will go far towards . . . scaring [Britain] into a peace."[53]

The more Madison thought about it, the more morose and angry he became. When Wirt attempted to change the subject, Madison "took the first opportunity to return to it, and convinced me that his heart and mind were painfully full of the subject."[54]

Otis and company had scheduled a gathering that they were so bold as to call the Hartford *Convention* for December 15. The very notion of it was exquisitely painful to Madison. He saw "the conduct of the Eastern States . . . as . . . the greatest, if not the sole inducement with the enemy to persevere in [the war]." He didn't blame the hoi polloi; it was the power-hungry elite. "The greater part of the people in that quarter have been brought by their leaders, aided by their *priests*, under a delusion scarcely exceeded by that recorded in the period of witchcraft."[55]

William Wirt politely declined an invitation to dine with the Madisons; he took his leave and went on to visit another old Virginia friend, Colonel Monroe, whom he found at the War Office. There, too, he talked politics.

This was a moment when the leverage was better than ever to end this war, but the men of the East, whom even the Frenchman Sérurier recognized as "a hostile faction at the heart of the nation," were an obstruction. As for Madison, his wish could be summarized simply. As he had recently enunciated it to Congress, he aimed for "peace and friendship on honorable terms."[56] Angry as his foes in New England made him, he had no choice but to be patient.

CHAPTER 11
Gloom or Glory?

Your anxious moments . . . will now be fewer; your labors abridged; your friends, more than ever, gratified; an unmanly opposition more than ever confounded; the nation, in your day, advanced anew in prosperity and glory.
—Richard Rush to James Madison, February 15, 1815

I.
January 1815 . . . Washington City

GEORGE TICKNOR WANTED TO VIEW AT FIRST HAND the ravages wrought by the British assault. A small man, short in stature and narrow through the shoulders, he emerged from the plush comfort inside the Baltimore-to-Washington coach. In spite of the bitter January weather, he took a seat beside the driver, his dark eyes intense and observant. Hours later, writing to his father back in Boston, he recorded what he had seen.

"We crossed the bridge at Bladensburg by which [the British] had crossed, and saw on its right the little breastwork by which it was so faintly and fruitlessly defended. The degree and continuance of the resistance were plainly marked by the small mounds on the wayside, which served as scanty graves to the few British soldiers who fell. . . . These few mounds, which the winters' frosts and rains will quickly obliterate, are all the monuments that remain to us in proof of the defence of the capital of the country."[1]

The elegiac tone of his letter to his schoolmaster father, Elisha, was that of a man who aspired to be a belletrist. The younger Ticknor had already earned a college degree (from Dartmouth, at age sixteen); he had immersed himself in the classics for three years thereafter, then clerked for the law, earning admission to the Massachusetts bar at twenty-one. Now, at twenty-three, having the found the law did not engage his capacious intellect, he left its practice. His new plan involved the Universität Göttingen. There, he had been told, was a library of two hundred thousand volumes, one that dwarfed Harvard's mere "closetful of books."[2] He spent the previous summer teaching himself German by translating Goethe's novel *The Sorrows of Young Werther*, employing John Quincy Adams's personal copy of the German original. Ticknor now planned to embark on an odyssey that would take him to the vaunted scenes of Europe, but he was beginning with an American tour to see more of his own nation.

Despite his learning, nothing prepared George Ticknor for the sight he saw next. "I knew that it was now a ruin," he wrote, "[though] I had formed no conception of . . . the [Capitol's] desolate and forsaken greatness." But his intended destination in Washington City was not the gloomy Capitol; Mr. Ticknor was bound for another address. A day trip a month earlier enabled him to take good advantage of his Adams family connections, as he paid his respects to John Quincy's aging father. The result was the letters of introduction he carried, one of which, in John Adams's clear and unembellished hand, was addressed to James Madison.

THE PASSING MONTHS HAD BROUGHT JAMES MADISON NO RELIEF. He steeled himself for the worst when the delegates to the Hartford Convention disappeared behind closed doors on

December 15, but until January 5, the silence from the twenty-six Federalists seemed deafening. Even upon their emergence, another full week elapsed before the delegates' report was made public. In those anxious days Madison, consulting with Secretary Monroe, increased the guard at the armory in Springfield, Massachusetts, fearing the Federalists at Hartford would call for secession or even an alliance with Britain.

The uncertain days had ended only the week before. On January 12 the Hartford Convention released its report, which included a demand for seven constitutional amendments, most of which sought to restrict Madison's power and enhance that of the Federalists. In truth, it was a relief. Almost everyone in Washington City understood that none of the amendments had even a remote chance of passage, and that the much-anticipated report, little more than a recitation of New England grievances, was more disagreeable than dangerous. The *National Intelligencer* was quick to dismiss the Connecticut assembly as yesterday's news, characterizing the Hartford document as the work of "nothing more than the Federalists in the Legislatures of three states." Furthermore, the editor intoned in an unsigned editorial, "The acts of this convention possess precisely the same validity, and are entitled to the same respect . . . as the proceedings of the caucuses of either party in the Congress of the United States . . . which selects and recommends to their constituents . . . antecedent to an election."[3] At the President's house, the relief was palpable. Hartford was pure politics, not a call to rebellion.

With the fear of disunion behind him, Madison could soften his view of men from the East. With a fulsome recommendation in hand from one of his most respected allies in the North, Mr. Ticknor would be welcome at the Madisons' table. An invitation to dinner was duly dispatched.

As Dolley prepared to welcome dinner guests that Saturday, James could hardly relax: There was still a war on despite the recent spate of good news.

THE BURNED AND THE BEAUTIFUL: That is what George Ticknor saw on his arrival at New York Avenue and Eighteenth Street.

He had taken lodgings at a rooming house in Georgetown. Compared to Boston and the cities he had recently visited, which included New York and Philadelphia, Georgetown seemed little more than an overgrown village. On the ride southeast along Pennsylvania Avenue, he saw a wintry terrain of rolling hills and open spaces that seemed more like countryside than a capital. Even his destination, the tall Tayloe house, seemed out of place. With its stable, laundry, and other service buildings, the complex more nearly resembled a country plantation than a town house.

As Ticknor approached, he saw a starker reality visible in the middle distance—the crumbling, smoke-stained shell of the President's house two blocks away.

Ticknor climbed the stone steps to Colonel Tayloe's mansion. Once inside, standing on the checkerboard floor of gray and white marble, he was uncertain of the proper etiquette. Such things varied, he found, from city to city, but he made his way to the Drawing Room. There he observed an assembly of perhaps a dozen people, a mix of men and women.

The man who turned to greet him was not, as he expected, a secretary or another intermediary. Ticknor quickly realized it was the Chief Magistrate himself, who, with appropriate courtesy, introduced him to Mrs. Madison and to Sarah Coles, known as Sally, a handsome young kinswoman of Mrs. Madison who seemed to be about Ticknor's age. He thought Mrs. Madison surprisingly tall and dignified, even as he noted the awkwardness, perhaps even the shyness, of the President. He was taken aback at Madison's diminutive stature. After his interview with the courtly John Adams, he had expected a man with greater presence.

Soon left to his own devices in meeting the other guests—that was the accepted protocol, he learned—Ticknor watched the party grow to about twenty. Even the host didn't seem to know the names of all the guests. There were members of Congress as well as several army officers in dress uniform who appeared uncomfortable in such society.

Though the Madisons offered "one or two commonplace remarks," the company was far from easy or lively, and the conversation tended to drift into awkward silences. After a time, a servant bustled in, and Ticknor soon learned the explanation for the anxious air that infected his companions. A message whispered in his ear, the President abruptly left, accompanied by Edward Coles. They disappeared into the stair hall at the center of the house, where an oval staircase rose to the study and the family quarters above.

The light of the late afternoon could be seen slanting through the three tall windows that overlooked New York Avenue, but it was events a thousand miles to the south that preoccupied the company. As Ticknor noted later that evening, "It was mentioned about the room that the Southern mail had arrived." In Madison's absence, the company worried the fate of New Orleans.

THE BRITISH DESIRE TO CAPTURE LOUISIANA WAS NOT NEW. Months before war had been declared, Admiral Cochrane advised his superiors, "the Americans are vulnerable [in] New Orleans and Virginia."[4] Two and a half years later, having proved his point in the Chesapeake, Cochrane sailed south.

Like a sentry at the gate, New Orleans overlooked the Mississippi River just a hundred miles upstream from the Gulf of Mexico. Its possessor controlled maritime access to the western states and territories. The British Cabinet calculated that capturing New Orleans would give the Crown a decided advantage in peace negotiations, so in November 1814, Sir Edward Pakenham was dispatched to the region to replace General Robert Ross, killed at Baltimore. "A hero, a soldier, a man of ability in every sense of the word," Pakenham was a major general, having served with distinction in Spain under his brother-in-law, the Duke of Wellington.[5] Pakenham met up with Cochrane's forces later that month in Negril Bay, Jamaica, where he took charge of ten thousand troops.

His opposite number on the American side was Major General Andrew Jackson. Jackson's recent military exploits had raised him in the estimation of not only the War Department, but among many citizens, too. In the winter of 1813, he and his Tennessee volunteers had marched home through some five hundred miles of wilderness after an earlier British assault on New Orleans hadn't come to pass. Having given up his horse to a sick soldier, Jackson had marched side by side with his men; his grit and toughness gained him the new appellation "Old Hickory." Later that year, a massacre of white inhabitants at Fort Mims, Alabama, by a band of Red Stick Creeks had resulted in a Jackson-led campaign against the Indians. The culmination had been a big victory at the Battle of Horseshoe Bend in March 1814, which forced the Creeks to cede some twenty million acres for white settlement.

With General William Henry Harrison's departure, Andrew Jackson had been the obvious choice as commander of the American troops in the West. He had already repulsed one British attack at Mobile, Alabama, in September; in early November, he had driven the British forces from Pensacola, Florida. Then he had marched his motley array of regulars, militia, and Indians, amounting to some four thousand men, to New Orleans. He set about evaluating defenses and vulnerabilities in order to protect the region's biggest prize.

Settled in 1718 on a natural levee that had been an Indian portage between the Mississippi and Lake Pontchartrain, New Orleans was flanked by the river on one side and, on the other, a broad band of wetlands crisscrossed with creeks, rivers, and bayous that emptied into a saltwater lake. Jackson found little had been done to prepare the city for attack and that its people, most of whom were French or Spanish, refused service in the militia. But he made an emotional appeal, promising to "drive their enemies into the sea, or die trying." But even as he addressed the inhabitants of New Orleans, a disparate populace that seemed to take pleasure in their feuds, he began to understand how unfavorable the conditions were.

To protect the city from an assault from the Mississippi, Jackson ordered that batteries of 24-pounder guns be positioned downriver. After surveying the topography of the bayous to the north and east, he established more gun batteries along those swampy approaches. Supplementing the fixed installations were five gunboats, whose flat bottoms were well suited to the shallow waters.

General Jackson's preparations had to be speedy; scouts had reported that the British convoy approached. Admiral Cochrane seemed to have decided against exposing his ships to artillery shelling on the Mississippi River, and, as at Washington, the British would attack overland, assaulting New Orleans across the marshlands. An advance force of more than a thousand seamen and marines closed on the American gunboats on the morning of December 12. No match for the British force of forty-five barges and tenders, armed with forty-three guns, the American boats were in the enemy's hands by midday.

The capture of the gunboats was a stunning loss; now extraordinary measures truly were needed. Jackson declared the city under martial law and mustered what militia there was. He sought reinforcements from all quarters. From Baton Rouge he summoned Tennessee riflemen. Jackson welcomed the services of black troops, most of them refugees from Santo Domingo. He even enlisted the aid of a force of one thousand Baratarian pirates. Jackson had his doubts about the pirates, having, just weeks earlier, proclaimed them "hellish Banditti," but he needed the men along with their ammunition and artillery. Their leader, Jean Lafitte, who possessed an intimate knowledge of the boggy topography of the region, became one of General Jackson's aides-de-camp.

The British advanced. Despite possessing few shallow-draft boats capable of navigating the lowland marshes, a brigade of eighteen hundred men made their way up the Bayou Bienvenu on December 22. The next day they captured the plantation of militia Brigadier-General Jacques Villieré, which extended to the bank of the Mississippi just seven miles downstream from New Orleans. Villieré's son managed to escape and get word to Jackson of the British movements, but the Villieré plantation house became British headquarters. A steady flow of British forces coming upstream made camp nearby.

The reports reaching Washington City advised that a large British force, commanded by Admiral Cochrane, had begun its siege of the great American city. Further, dispatches said, the enemy were taking the backwater approach and, as the British had begun to make their way upstream, had quickly overwhelmed the first line of American defense.

To Madison, the news from New Orleans was beginning to sound ominously like the events of the previous August.

WHEN THE PRESIDENT RETURNED TO THE TABLE, Ticknor thought his countenance bore the look of "added gravity." Seeing his guests' expectant looks, Madison announced in his subdued manner that there was no news of General Jackson's progress. His words were greeted with silence. "No man seemed to know what to say at such a crisis," Ticknor observed, "and I suppose from the fear of saying what might not be acceptable, said nothing at all."[6]

With darkness falling outside, dinner was announced. The President took Miss Coles's arm while one of the military men, who Ticknor had learned was General Winder, escorted Mrs. Madison to her accustomed seat at the head of the table. Mr. Coles, the President's secretary, assumed a place at the opposite end. At a loss as to where to sit (he "looked very much a fool," he thought), Ticknor heard Mr. Madison himself summon him to join him and Mrs. Madison. He immediately deduced why. "This was unquestionably the result of President Adams's introduction."

To his surprise, he soon felt as if he were among friends. While Ticknor found Mrs. Madison dignified and occasionally amusing, he warmed particularly to Mr. Madison. "I found the President more free and open than I had expected, starting subjects and conversation and making remarks that sometimes savored of humor and levity." The aspiring writer would spend nearly three hours in their company, first at table, then, upon their particular invitation, at coffee back in the Drawing Room, where they talked of religion and other topics. Only when the conversation threatened to turn political did Ticknor hesitate. Given his Federalist origins, he was pleased when the topic soon moved on to Monticello and Ticknor's intended visit to Thomas Jefferson.

The tension of the early evening certainly eased, yet when he took his leave at eight o'clock, one powerful image he took with him was of Madison's visage. "His face," observed Ticknor, "was always grave." It seemed to the young man as if "an unsuccessful war was grinding him to the earth."[7]

II.

February 4, 1815 . . . Mrs. Madison's Parlor . . . Washington City

THE WAIT FOR NEW ORLEANS NEWS was excruciating, with all of Washington, according to the *National Intelligencer*, "held in awful suspense as to the fate of that city."[8] As January had drawn to a close, the President received status reports from American military outposts on the Canadian front, including Sacket's Harbor on Lake Ontario and Buffalo on Lake Erie, but no news came from the south. "Our anxieties cannot be expressed," Dolley wrote to Hannah Gallatin. "The fate of N. Orleans will be known [soon]—on which so much depends."[9]

Preliminary reports said General Jackson counterattacked on December 23. He moved against the enemy encampment at the Villieré plantation, marching a force of about two thousand men on foot and horseback, including two hundred freed slaves, within a mile of the British position. After nightfall, under the cover of artillery fire from the 14-gun *Carolina*, the Americans attacked, surprising the British as they huddled around their fires. In the smoky darkness, friendly fire took a toll on both sides, but, before withdrawing, the Americans inflicted substantial casualties and acquitted themselves well in a close battle

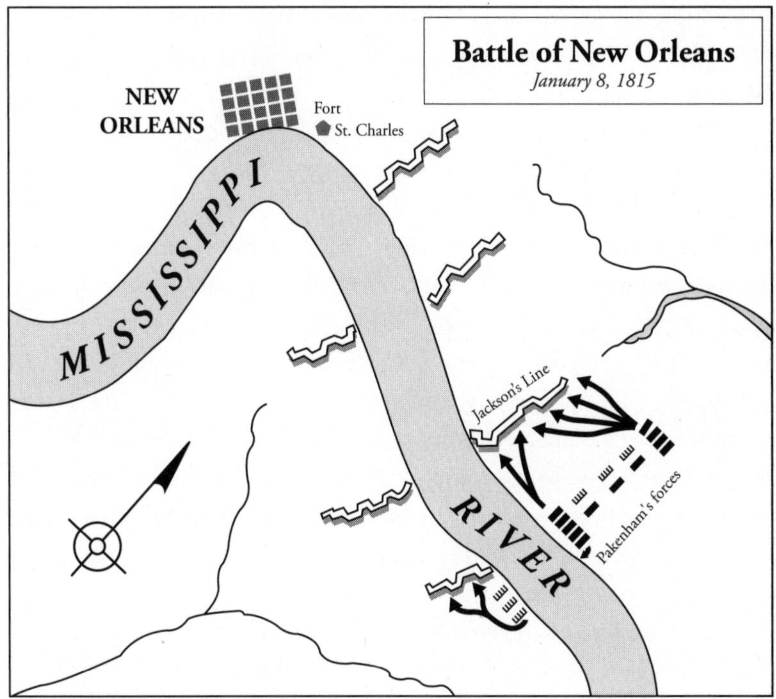

with experienced British soldiers wielding their feared bayonets and swords. In his report on the action dated December 26, Jackson reported, "The heavy smoke occasioned by an excessive fire rendered it necessary that I should draw off my troops, after a severe conflict of upward of an hour."[10]

Jackson's strategy was to delay the British advance, to buy enough time that his army could establish a strong defensive position. He chose the site of the Rodriguez Canal, a ten-foot-wide drainage ditch two miles from the Villieré plantation. The canal extended about fifteen hundred yards across an open field that linked a cypress swamp to the Mississippi. Jackson's men set to work constructing a five-foot-tall wall of earth and cotton bales, placing artillery batteries at intervals along its length. Thus fortified, the position would afford the American gunners and riflemen protection. Given the height of the wall and the four-foot-deep ditch at its foot, it also meant that attackers would need ladders to scale the parapet.

The British made an abortive attack on December 28, half-expecting the Americans to flee as they had done at Bladensburg. But Jackson's men drove them back with artillery fire. On January 1, Pakenham tested the Americans once again, this time with an artillery barrage aimed at compromising the American earthworks. But accurate American counterfire disabled at least a dozen British guns, some of which had been protected by casks of brown sugar. Unlike sand, the sugar was easily penetrated, and the British were forced to abort their attack in less than three hours. Jackson then ordered another American artillery battery constructed across the Mississippi and that two other lines be dug closer to New Orleans, just in case the main line was breached. Like General Smith in Baltimore, General Jackson was not going to repeat the defensive lapses at Washington.

By early January, Pakenham had perhaps six thousand soldiers in his camp, while Jackson's forces numbered more than five thousand. As the Americans worked to complete their fortifications on January 7, two regiments of the proud British army decided to have a parade. Within sight of the American line, recorded one British soldier, "[t]he music played, the sun shone brilliantly, and every member of the two regiments was in the highest spirits of his chance of being led forward to attack."[11]

The Battle of New Orleans would be fought the following day, but only on Saturday, February 4, did news of the outcome reach the capital.

~

THE FIRST REPORTS OFFERED SCANT DETAIL, but the headline in the *Daily National Intelligencer* said it in boldface: "**ALMOST INCREDIBLE VICTORY!**" The newspaper offered a summary of the events: "[T]he Enemy, attacking our entrenched Army on the 8th, beaten and repulsed by Jackson and his brave associates, with great slaughter."[12]

The news inspired a great celebration that night, even in advance of a full account of the battle. The sky was lit with flames from candles, torches, and celebratory rockets, the latter a strange reminder of August 24.

The first official report came not to James Madison but to Dolley. She had played a role in gaining Thomas Johnson his appointment as New Orleans postmaster, and on January 19 Johnson wrote describing the events. "Madam," his letter read, "the American army has gained immortal glory." Johnson continued, "The British, led by M^r. Edward Pakenham, attempted to storm our lines and to force a way to the city, at the point of the bayonet. . . . [F]ire from our guns and our musquetry opened on them, with such irresistible effect . . . leaving the ground strewn with dead and dying." It was "a spectacle of carnage" unlike any seen on American soil.[13]

The British master plan had called for an all-out attack. In the night, six hundred troops were to be ferried across the river to disable the American gun battery on the west bank of the Mississippi. In the morning, the main force, in three columns, was to make a frontal assault on the entrenched American position. A thick morning mist had covered the low-lying field as the American troops, who were unshaven and unwashed, a mix of regulars, pirates, militiamen, blacks, woodsmen, and farmers, watched British troops, who were dressed in their brilliant scarlet uniforms and marching in precise company order. The American artillery started firing grape and canister shot at the British at five hundred yards. At Jackson's order, drummers behind the American lines beat out "Yankee Doodle." At three hundred yards the riflemen opened fire. The British kept marching. At one hundred yards, the echo of American muskets added to the din. The British fired back, but the Americans, "without so much as lifting their faces above the rampart, swung their firelocks by one arm over the wall, and discharged them" into the sea of red uniforms.[14] One English soldier, a seasoned veteran of the war in Europe, called it "the most murderous [fire he] ever beheld."[15]

As he rallied his men, a musket ball penetrated Pakenham's thigh just above the knee and killed his horse. As he attempted to gain the saddle of another mount, he was struck again; after uttering a few final words, he died. Two other British generals were killed on the field of battle. All told the British lost two thousand men, with three hundred dead, twelve hundred wounded, and another five hundred captured.

The British asked for a truce to bury their dead. As one officer who surveyed the scene reported, "they were thrown by the dozens into shallow holes, scarcely deep enough to furnish them with a slight covering of earth." No less horrific was the sight of the wounded. As the same officer reported on visiting a field hospital, "It is here that war loses its grandeur and show, and presents only a real picture of its effects. Every room in the house was crowded with wretches mangled, and apparently in the most excruciating agonies. . . . Passing through the apartments where the private soldiers lay, I next came to those occupied by officers. Of these there were five or six in one small room, to whom little better accommodation could be provided than to their inferiors. It was a sight peculiarly distressing because all of them chanced to be personal acquaintances of my own. One had been shot in the head, and lay gasping and insensible; another had received a musket ball in the belly, which had pierced through and lodged in the back bone. The former appeared to suffer but little; . . . the latter was in the most dreadful agony, screaming out, and gnawing the covering under which he lay."[16]

As for Mrs. Madison's correspondent, he was in the midst of writing his letter from New Orleans when news arrived that he was quick to pass on: "[T]he British have evacuated the country." New Orleans had exploded in a paroxysm of joy. "The city is in a ferment of delight," wrote Johnson. "The country is saved, the enemy vanquished and hardly a widow or an orphan whose tears damp the general joy." The American casualty count at the Rodriguez Canal had numbered just seventy-one: thirteen killed, thirty-nine wounded, nineteen missing.

"All is exultation and jubalee," wrote Johnson.

In his closing, he also made clear to whom he thought much credit was due. In his eyes, it belonged to the Presidentess as much as to the

President. "Permit me to offer you my congratulation on this auspicious termination of our trials and dangers."[17]

III.

Saturday, February 11, 1815 . . . HMS Favorite *. . . New York Harbor*

WHAT A DIFFERENCE A PIECE OF PAPER CAN MAKE. Since the Declaration of War more than two and a half years earlier, Henry Carroll regarded every ship in the British navy as the enemy. Yet here he was on one such vessel, happy and honored to be aboard.

The crossing had begun on the first Monday of the New Year. As the well-fortified English port of Plymouth gradually disappeared astern, the *Favorite*, a sloop of war, had a new and surprising innocence. Barely a week earlier, Carroll's presence on this ship would likely have meant he was a prisoner of war. Today, both he and his British coequal, one Anthony St. John Baker, dined as honored guests of the ship's captain.

For everyone aboard, the 32-pounder long guns on the lower deck had a new quietude about them. As they crossed the North Atlantic, the crew of the *Favorite* no longer looked for American prey, since their higher mission was to get Messieurs Baker and Carroll promptly and safely to America so that they might complete their diplomatic assignments. The two men were secretaries to the Peace Commissioners in Europe, with Baker laboring for the envoys of the Crown. Henry Carroll had served the five Ministers Plenipotentiary and Envoys Extraordinary representing the United States government.

Young Mr. Carroll, now twenty-two years of age, had been invited to take his first journey beyond the borders of the United States in part because he was Charles Carroll's son. The elder Carroll, a man who assiduously cultivated his political connections, was a particular friend of Henry Clay. With considerable landholdings in the West, Charles Carroll had made a point of befriending the junior senator from Kentucky when Clay first arrived in Washington City. Much later, when the President asked Clay to serve as one of the Peace Commissioners, it seemed only logical for Henry Carroll to serve as Clay's secretary, since he knew the boy to be "a young gentleman of amiable manners, considerable acquirements in litterature & above all, commendable piety and regularity of life."[18]

Thirty-eight days had passed since the *Favorite* departed Devonshire, an elapsed time that certainly was slower than the record for the fastest Britain–to–New York crossing, set two years before by a trader, Jacob Barker's *Lady Madison*, at just eighteen days. But a storm had blown them off course so, for the crew of the *Favorite*, the transit time was unremarkable. As for young Carroll, the journey provided ample hours to muse on the months spent in the Netherlands city of Ghent, the neutral ground where the British and American negotiators met.

From Carroll's vantage, he could not help but see his mentor as the main actor in the drawn-out drama nearing completion. A tall man of easy demeanor, Clay could walk into a room of ten strangers and depart with as many friends. He was a man who, on his first day of service in the House of Representatives, was elected its Speaker. He liked his liquor, had been known in recent months to joke about making advances to a chambermaid, and enjoyed nothing more than bettering his fellows at the card table.[19] Although he arrived with the least diplomatic experience of the five American Commissioners, Henry Clay always appeared in Carroll's view and most everyone else's to be at the center of the action.

The peace process ought to have begun long before Clay and Carroll had arrived in Ghent in July 1814. Albert Gallatin and James Bayard had been abroad and ready to negotiate for a full year; they had joined a third American Peace Commissioner, John Quincy Adams, already abroad as United States Minister in St. Petersburg. But delays occasioned by London had repeatedly pushed deliberations back.

Mr. Madison's designation of Speaker Clay as a Commissioner surprised some Americans. The Kentuckian had been one of the strongest of the War Hawks; Madison's call for him to negotiate the peace seemed odd. But Clay had Dolley's as well as James's trust. He was a legendary debater, possessed a gift for seeing beyond immediate circumstances, and, for a politician, was a man of remarkable directness. When he and the fifth Commissioner, Jonathan Russell, arrived in Sweden in April, however, they discovered that none of the other American ministers were at hand and that the site of the negotiations was about to change. The British were playing a delaying game.

Napoleon's fall had changed the peace talks. Bayard and Gallatin, who had journeyed to London to try to advance matters directly with the British Foreign Office, witnessed firsthand the alteration in English attitudes toward the United States. The long war with France ended during their weeks in the British capital and, Bayard reported, "for an American," it was "a very inauspicious moment." The British regarded the American war declaration, he explained, as "an aid given to their great enemy at a moment when his power was most gigantic. . . . The government of England affect to despise us . . . [and] if they could crush us at the present moment they would not fail to do it."[20] To the patrician Bayard, aging and often ill, the altered European scene represented an immense danger to his country.

Carroll witnessed the frustration of the weeks that followed. Even after the talks moved to Ghent, the dispersed American Commissioners reached eastern Flanders slowly, with Adams traveling from Russia, Russell from Sweden, Gallatin from London, and Bayard from Paris. They could hardly have known that more months of waiting, frustration, British snobbery, and even infighting within their own ranks awaited them.

But that was over now, and Henry Carroll was charged with delivering a precious cargo that was safely stowed in a small but artfully crafted leather document box. The legal instrument within represented the outcome of the hard work of the Peace Commissioners.

The evening before, the *Favorite* had sailed past the Sandy Hook light, and the sight of the tall lighthouse meant the *Favorite* had entered the lower reaches of New York Harbor. Aside from Anthony St. John Baker, however, who carried another of the six copies of the document, no one else knew precisely what was said in the parchment with which Carroll had been entrusted.

Still, it was an open secret aboard the *Favorite* that Carroll was carrying words of peace back to his countrymen.

HENRY CARROLL KNEW FIRSTHAND HOW ARDUOUS had been the negotiations that led to the Treaty of Ghent.

Though appointed in May, the British delegation delayed making the brief sea journey to Ghent until August; for a full month, Clay, Adams, Gallatin, and company waited and worried about what impact the twenty thousand British troops said to be sailing to America might have on the war. There were daily reminders of Britain's military might, since the Americans shared the city with a garrison of British soldiers. At first, Henry Clay found the British uniforms unnerving, but soon he and the other Americans settled into the life of the city. They discovered the Lowlanders were none too fond of the British and, in turn, very curious about the Americans. Clay, Carroll, and the other ministers and secretaries were welcomed by the mayor and the people of their host city at public dinners, the opera, concerts, the city's fine library, and other public amusements.

When the British and American Commissioners finally met for the first time on August 8, His Britannic Majesty was represented not by a cabinet minister but by Lord Gambier, an admiral whose military luster had been tarnished by the notorious bombardment of Copenhagen in 1807. Gambier's seconds were Dr. William Adams, a man of the law whose expertise went to maritime matters, and Henry Goulburn, an Undersecretary of State for War with knowledge of Canadian affairs. None had a great deal of diplomatic experience.

At the first session, the British presented their demands, and, from the start, their manner seemed to John Quincy Adams "arrogant, overbearing, and offensive."[21] A sine qua non for any treaty, William Adams announced to the Americans, was the creation of an Indian buffer state between the United States and Canada. Though the United States envoys had no instructions on this point, they knew it was a nonstarter (not least because, as Gallatin pointed out, there were perhaps a hundred thousand American citizens living in the proposed Indian territory, which included parts of the state of Ohio, as well as land in the Indiana, Illinois, and Michigan territories). The British also wished to forbid an American military presence on the Great Lakes but insisted upon reserving the right to keep their own forts and naval forces there. Further, the British expressed a disinclination to discuss the blockade, the rights of neutral shipping, and impressment.

For their part, the Americans wanted to affirm their rights to fish in Canadian waters and to cure their catch on its unsettled shores. This was an issue of import to New Englanders in general and to John Quincy Adams in particular, since it was his father who succeeded in gaining the concession three decades earlier in the 1783 Treaty of Paris, which ended the War of Independence. The British also wanted full freedom to navigate the Mississippi. Henry Clay, a Westerner looking to safeguard the rights of his region, could never countenance granting the British permanent rights to his great river.

Aside from a seemingly vague desire for peace, the British appeared to have nothing to offer the Americans; with nothing to talk about, the peace negotiations seemed doomed. Yet as they began to draft their formal response, the American delegation was visited by a courier. He arrived at their quarters in the Hotel d'Alcantara carrying a coded dispatch from Secretary of State James Monroe. Adams, Gallatin, and one of the secretaries stayed up until one o'clock in the morning working to decipher it. What emerged was surprising: President Madison's policy on impressment had changed. The word from Washington City was, "On mature consideration, it has been decided, that . . . you may omit any stipulation on the subject of impressment, if found indispensably necessary to terminate [the war]."[22]

In short, "the Press," the hated practice that put a face on the British bully for many ordinary Americans, thereby justifying the war, was about to become a concession, vanishing with a few strokes of a State Department pen. The Commissioners recognized the rationale, of course. With the French war finally at an end, the British no longer needed a constant influx of new sailors; the impressment of American sailors would no doubt cease.

Looking back upon that moment, however, as he could do from the deck of the *Favorite*, Henry Carroll saw that with one large principle set aside, others could, and would, inevitably follow. He had seen exactly that happen.

Leaving impressment unmentioned for the moment, John Quincy Adams had begun drafting a response to the initial British demands. Adams was the most experienced diplomat, having accompanied his father to Europe at age eleven, become private secretary to the American minister to Russia at fourteen, and been a secretary to the American plenipotentiaries that negotiated the Treaty of Paris. He subsequently served as minister to Holland and Berlin and Commissioner to Sweden, as well as a United States Senator. To Adams, the language of diplomacy was a familiar art, and he assumed the lead role for the American Peace Commissioners.

He soon discovered his colleagues were unwilling to be silent partners. "I found," Adams confided in his diary, "that the draft was not satisfactory to my colleagues. On the general view of the subject we are unanimous, but in my exposition of it, one objects to the form and another to the substance of almost every paragraph. Mr. Gallatin is for striking out every expression that may be offensive to the feelings of the adverse party." The Switzerland-born Gallatin, who spoke with a French accent, was courtly by nature (to his embarrassment, one of the British ministers observed that M. Gallatin was more European than American).[23]

"Mr. Clay," Adams continued, "is displeased with figurative language, which he thinks improper for a state paper." Though less learned than Adams, Clay prided himself on his persuasiveness. "Mr. Russell, agreeing in the objection of the two other gentlemen, will be further for amending the construction of every sentence; and Mr. Bayard, even when agreeing to say precisely the same thing, chooses to say it only in his own language."[24]

Several days were required to hone the collective American response, but the end result to which they signed their names was pointed. "A Treaty concluded upon such terms [as you propose] would be but an armistice. It cannot be supposed that America would long submit to conditions so injurious and degrading." They went further, seeing no need to consult with their distant government, since the British demands constituted "an insuperable obstacle to a pacification."[25]

As a veteran chess player, Adams might well have observed that when a stalemate is reached, the board must be reset, supposing, that is, that the opposition wishes to play another round. In August 1814 in Ghent, that willingness was by no means certain.

SILENCE ENSUED. The British contingent was housed away from the bustle of the city at a former monastery, the Chartreux, or Charterhouse, and from the outskirts of Ghent nothing was heard for ten days. When a formal response did land in the laps of the Americans, it consisted largely of sputtering about the invasion of Canada. There was much talk in the written exchanges that followed concerning Indian territories, old boundaries and new, the American acquisition of Louisiana, and various diplomatic precedents established in centuries past. But for the better part of the next two months, the Peace Commissioners traded state papers full of detailed declarations, observations, propositions, and protocols that amounted to no real progress.

This had left Henry Carroll with the time to acquire a taste for continental fashion. Perhaps because he retained a soft youthfulness (his hair sat in curls on his head, his lips almost feminine), he affected the newest style, a forbiddingly tall white collar. The recent advent of starch made such neckcloths stiff indeed; his sat prodigiously high, encircling the neck and reaching his ears. He wanted the look to age him a bit, as he wasn't so far from those days when, at eighteen, he entertained the notion of joining the priesthood, only to have his father declare him too inexperienced to undertake such a commitment.[26]

In those weeks Carroll witnessed a second battle of wills, this one between two of the American ministers plenipotentiary. John Quincy Adams and Henry Clay proved to be the strongest willed of the team. While their regional loyalties differed, their unlike personalities and styles were perhaps even more responsible for the friction that developed between the two men.

In his diary, Adams outlined his regimen. "I [rise] . . . almost always before six, and without exception before daylight. Make my fire, read five chapters in the Bible, and write until between nine and ten. Breakfast in my chamber alone. Write, read papers, receive visits, and attend mission meetings until three, afternoon. Walk from one to two hours, dine at half-past four, and sit at table until six. Go to the theatre, concert, or party at a friend's house, or write in my chamber until eight in the evening. . . . [At] about ten at night return home and retire to bed."[27]

Mr. Clay's approach was rather different. He hadn't the intellectual inclination of Adams; though trained as a lawyer, he found early in his career that his gifts were for people and public life. His considerable charm won him allies, while his instincts for parliamentary maneuverings won legislative battles.

Clay's mouth was large, and it seemed as if anecdotes and amusing remarks were always falling from it. He was a master at cards. His late-night companions in those weeks of desultory negotiation included not only Henry Carroll but also Payne Todd, Mrs. Madison's son, who had traveled to Europe as secretary to Albert Gallatin. Todd proved to be unreliable over the many months of waiting, often disappearing for weeks at a time and drinking heavily (Paris became his chosen place to lose himself). Mrs. Madison's son showed some skill at cards and did win money that autumn from Jonathan Russell, but he more than met his match in Clay, to whom he promptly lost his winnings.

Adams and Clay met the day differently. On rising to his Bible reading, Adams grew accustomed to hearing "Mr Clay's company retiring from his chamber" after a long night of playing loo, brag, old sledge, or all-fours.[28] To Carroll and others who studied them, they looked very different, too. Henry Clay was tall, with a full head of light hair, a man whose charm couldn't quite hide his ambitions. John Quincy Adams, at five foot seven and balding, lacked Clay's dash. He tended to roundness and dressed carelessly. Though barely a decade Clay's elder, Adams had the demeanor of an aging but insistent churchman.

THE BRITISH COMMISSIONERS AT GHENT were empowered to do little more than state their demands, observe the American reaction, then report back to Whitehall. The Americans maintained a policy of firm and detailed written responses and sharp retorts in conference. But it would be happenings far from Ghent that gave the negotiations a new direction.

On October 1, news of the "distressing events" at Washington City reached the American Peace Commissioners. Predictably, War Hawk Henry Clay found his spirit rising in anger. "The loss of public property gives me comparatively no pain," he wrote. "What does wound me to the very soul is, that a set of pirates and incendiaries should have been permitted to pollute our soil, conflagrate our Capital, and return unpunished to their ships!"[29] John Quincy Adams's response was a sleepless night. But the men could do little until a new proposal arrived from the British a week later. Buried within much talk of other matters was a softened stance. The demand for an Indian buffer state had disappeared, as had the insistence on a British military presence on the lakes.

Word soon arrived of the American victory at Baltimore, then of the success at Plattsburgh. On October 21, the British altered their territorial demands. Dropping their previous insistence on retaining half of Maine and much of the south bank of the St. Lawrence River, they now required little more than a right-of-way across Maine's northern corner to ease transit between Halifax and Quebec. The principle of *uti possidetis* was also introduced (Latin for "as you possess," meaning that the land held by each side at ratification would remain with its possessor). The Americans rejected the proposal but began work on a draft treaty. In it Adams countered with *status quo ante bellum*, the restoration of boundaries as they had been before the war.

The new movement in the negotiations offered room for optimism. U.S. minister to France William Crawford offered his opinion to Adams. With his somewhat distanced view of the Ghent meetings and the military events in America, he wrote in early November, "We cannot fail to obtain an honorable peace, if we are true to ourselves."[30]

British Prime Minister Liverpool, in turn, was in correspondence with his man in Paris, the Duke of Wellington, now Britain's Ambassador to France. The nation's finest military mind chose not to tell his betters what they wanted to hear. In reply to an offer of the North American command, Wellington remarked that, in his opinion, there was little to be gained. "I feel no objection to going to America, though I don't promise myself much success there." He went further, offering an unsolicited assessment of the treaty talks at Ghent. "In regard to your present negotiations, I confess that I think you have no right, from the state of the war to demand any concession of territory from America. . . . You can get no territory; indeed, the state of your military operations, however creditable, does not entitle you to demand any."[31]

With pressures mounting among English merchants to bring the war to an end, it was only a matter of time before the notion of *status quo ante bellum* was adopted by the British. By December 2, the usually pessimistic Adams confided in his diary, "[I]t became probable that we should ultimately sign a treaty of peace."[32] Drafts were exchanged, meetings were held, alterations agreed to. New articles came and went, and the British and Americans grew closer to an understanding. But on the Rue des Champs, the Americans were arguing among themselves.

Adams was learned, well traveled, highly disciplined, intensely independent—and very difficult to like. He was quite aware that he was smarter than almost anyone else and unabashed about telling people what he thought, even when it hurt their feelings. He seemed to spare no one, not even himself. He confided to his diary with pained candor, "I am a man of reserved, cold, austere, and forbidding manners; my political adversaries say, a gloomy misanthropist, and my personal enemies, an unsocial savage." His diary also grew dense with references to Clay, who, according to Adams, regularly grew "peevish and fractious" and "lost his temper."[33]

Both possessed of a "dogmatical, overbearing manner," the two men behaved as if they were on opposing sides.[34] Neither was willing to negotiate on his pet issue. Clay's was British navigation of the Mississippi, while Adams drove his colleagues to distraction about fisheries in the North Atlantic. The man who found himself in the middle, Albert Gallatin, had to bring all of his considerable experience to bear. Born into the Swiss aristocracy, Gallatin had abandoned his prospects at home to emigrate to America. He had taught French at Harvard, worked as a surveyor, and accumulated contacts from Richmond to Maine before eventually settling in Philadelphia, then in Washington. With such a range of experience, he made an eminently reasonable and patient peacemaker.

Even the cigar-smoking Gallatin required weeks to quiet the conflicting voices around him. It was Adams who wrote to his wife, "I can scarcely express to you how much . . . Mr. Gallatin [has] risen in my esteem. . . . He has a faculty, when discussion grows too warm, of turning off its edge by a joke, which I envy him more than all his other talents; and he has in his character one of the most extraordinary combinations of stubbornness and of flexibility that I ever met with in man."[35] Gallatin's solomonic solution to the Clay-Adams contretemps was to omit all mention of the fisheries and the Mississippi in the final treaty. Like impressment, neutral shipping rights, and indemnities for spoliation, Adams's and Clay's hobbyhorses were soon relegated to the diplomatic storeroom.

THE ESSENTIAL SEALED DOCUMENT IN HENRY CARROLL'S LITTLE TRUNK was the "Treaty of peace and amity between His Britannic Majesty and the United States of America." On Christmas Eve 1814, the British and American Commissioners had arrived at four o'clock at the large but unadorned former monastery on the Place des Chartreux where the British Commissioners were housed. The Americans carried their three copies, which, upon being signed and sealed, would become British property. The British Plenipotentiaries brought handwritten copies in triplicate for the Americans.[36]

Carroll had watched and listened at the signing, which had been a surprisingly quotidian affair. His coequal Mr. Baker read aloud from one of the British copies, while other Commissioners followed along silently. A few discrepancies were noted—the Americans having rendered the year as *eighteen hundred and fourteen*, the British as *one thousand eight hundred and fourteen*—and a few minor mistakes were rectified.

The carillon at the Cathedral of St. Bavo tolled as the six true copies were laboriously signed and sealed by the three British and the five American commissioners. The bells rang by coincidence, but they suited the moment. In his usual solemn manner, Mr. Adams told his opposite number on the British side, Lord Gambier, that he hoped it would "be the last treaty of peace between Great Britain and the United States."

IV.
February 11–12, 1815 . . . New York En Route to Washington City

THE *FAVORITE* DOCKED WITHOUT FANFARE AT EIGHT O'CLOCK. The flag of truce it flew had gained the sloop of war safe entry to the harbor, and the guns mounted at the Battery on Manhattan's south tip remained quiet. No one in New York expected either Mr. Carroll or Mr. Baker, so no crowds cheered as the *Favorite* crossed the bay.

Almost as soon as the hawsers tied the ship to its mooring, Henry Carroll stepped ashore, his anticipation high, happy to be back on dry land after the weeks at sea. He headed north on Broadway, a route that took him within sight of Federal Hall, where George Washington had been sworn in as president in 1789. Two blocks north of Wall Street, he reached the new City Hotel, the city's finest hostelry, an imposing five-story structure with seventy-eight rooms.

Though night had fallen, the dark of the evening quickly gave way to a new illumination. Carroll's news traveled with the speed of a brushfire, bringing men with candles onto the streets. A sleeping city came fully back to life with calls of *Peace! Peace!* In a spontaneous outburst of joy, there was a cacophony of shouting voices, torches, and the general furor of celebration.

The precise terms of the treaty remained quite unknown, since Carroll's orders were to deliver the documents he carried directly into the hands of Secretary of State James Monroe in Washington City. But that didn't stop the maritime workers, who were quick to return to work, loading their ships with cargo and provisions, preparatory to setting sail.

By noon the next day, Carroll was on his way to Washington. A speedy post chaise carried the man and his news; the four-horse carriage proceeded at speed to cover the two-hundred-and-ten-mile distance to the capital. An express rider on horseback had already departed, galloping northward. In a mere thirty-two hours from the arrival of the *Favorite*, Boston would be the site of celebration, as were the towns along the route where the messenger, though racing to Boston, called out the glad tidings. Schools were closed, a general holiday proclaimed. American and British flags were hoisted, church bells rang out, and militia paraded.

ANOTHER RIDER HAD BEEN DISPATCHED TO THE SOUTH, visions in his mind of the thousand-dollar prize he had been promised if he reached Charleston by a specified time. Speculators eagerly anticipated news of the peace, hoping to make last-minute buys of cotton and tobacco at depressed wartime prices.

A hand-delivered letter reached a member of Congress late Monday afternoon with advance word of Carroll's approach. The rumor soon reached the ears of Senator Jonathan Roberts of Pennsylvania, a Madison supporter. He was seated at a formal dinner, his meal half-eaten, when a note arrived for another guest, a Navy clerk named James Paulding.

"News of the peace," blurted out Paulding on reading the message. The table fairly exploded in celebration, but Roberts quickly excused himself. "[H]aving a carriage to myself," Roberts reported, "I took leave & set out, before anyone else was ready. I drove to the President's."

To his surprise, he found the house at Eighteenth Street and New York Avenue still and dark. Upon entering, Roberts "found Mr. Madison sitting solitary in his parlor . . . in perfect tranquility, not even a servant in waiting."[37]

The winter had been a long one for Madison. In addition to worries about the war and the Hartford conspiracy, his health had once again been poor. "Mr. M. has not been well since we came to this house," Dolley had written to Hannah Gallatin. "[O]ur servants are constantly sick owing to the damp cellar in which they are confined."[38]

Senator Roberts visited Madison often as an important congressional ally who felt a strong affection for the Chief Magistrate and held him in high regard. "A truly great man," believed Roberts. "I never left him, without finding my mind cheer'd." On entering the long drawing room, he went straight to Madison's side. He apologized for intruding upon the President at home, but explained he had heard a rumor of peace.

"I apprehended it was incorrect," Roberts concluded.

Madison offered his visitor a seat. "I will tell you all I know."

The President continued. "I believe there is peace, but we have not as yet the information in such form, as that we can publish it officially."

Even in the face of words he devoutly wished to hear, Madison was methodical and measured. His demeanor, thought Roberts, was typical of Madison's "self command, and greatness of mind, [which] I witness'd on this occasion."

AS GEORGE TICKNOR HAD DONE, Carroll rolled through Bladensburg on his approach to Washington City. His route took him along Pennsylvania Avenue, past the masonry hulk that had been the Capitol. Though the storm clouds had finally cleared, a long week of rain left a muddy and rutted road, jouncing the carriage on its way to Colonel Monroe's.

Mrs. Madison had gone about her business that day, as she and Sally Coles had called upon friends, including Mrs. Thornton. But rumors of the imminent news circulated widely, leaving many in Washington City in a state of anticipation. When the carriage rolled to a stop at Monroe's doorstep, the Secretary of State quickly emerged. A gathering crowd cheered as the post chaise, with Monroe now a passenger, continued along the avenue to the Tayloe house.

When Carroll and Monroe arrived at the executive mansion, it was Mrs. Madison who met them in the entrance hall. This evening, perhaps more than any other in sixteen years at the pinnacle of public life in

Washington, she would demonstrate herself to be the nation's First Hostess.

V.

February 14, 1815 . . . The Residence of the President

THE TREATY OF GHENT MEANT A GREAT DEAL to the man who waited quietly in his study for the messenger to arrive. He could see that his reputation, his presidency, and even his legacy depended upon ending the war that bore his name. He knew full well that many Federalists still spat out the epithet—*Missssster Madison's War*—as they would a curse. What he could not know was whether the peace that seemed to be at hand could repair the damage done.

Perhaps he heard the commotion when Monroe and Carroll arrived, and he may have seen them from the windows that not only overlooked the streetscape at Eighteenth Street and New York Avenue, but took in a panoramic view of the growing city and the larger landscape defined by the broad Potomac River. He did not see Mr. Carroll bowing deeply to the lady of the house in the entrance hall below him, nor was Mr. Madison at hand to see his wife's expression, which conveyed that this was not the time for elaborate greetings. As the men removed their cloaks, she gestured simply, indicating the doorway to the rear of the round hall.

The men came into Mr. Madison's view as they climbed the last steps of the winding oval stair, which brought them to the study door. He welcomed them and, in particular, the contents of the lap-sized wooden box, its leather covering affixed with brass tacks, its dome top hinged and fastened with a cast brass lock set. Its heft suggested it contained more than one document.

Eager hands opened the box; it was most likely Madison's trusted secretary, Edward Coles, who did the honors. Inside they found a cover letter from Henry Clay. Addressed to Monroe, his immediate superior,

Clay's letter began with the all-important news. "Mr. Carroll carries a Copy of the Treaty of Peace, which was signed on the 24th inst." Having conveyed the main point in a mere sentence, Clay had chosen to take advantage of Colonel Monroe's attention to offer an endorsement of his young colleague Henry Carroll. "Throughout the Negotiation," Commissioner Clay had written, "he has enjoyed my entire confidence, and has invariably shewn himself worthy of it. . . . [I]f a Secretary should be appointed to the English or French Legation, Mr. Carroll's qualifications render him a person whom the government may employ with great advantage to its interests."[39]

While he understood this was not the time for that matter, Mr. Carroll might have allowed himself a short reverie about his future, since the coming months could well find him back across the Atlantic, assuming a position as first secretary to the American Legation in London or Paris. But that would be as it would be, all in due time. For now he needed to be nearby, just as he had been at the Hotel d'Alcantara in Ghent. He hoped to be able to answer the questions these gentlemen might ask of him, to offer them explanations as to how the treaty evolved.

Among the documents that emerged from the box were the position papers that the British and American envoys at Ghent exchanged during the talks, but it was the sealed treaty that drew all eyes. More of Mr. Madison's counselors began to assemble, and, with the wax seal broken on the treaty, the first task was to read out the terms to the assembled men. Not so much time would be required for the recitation. For an agreement that had required four months of negotiation, it was surprisingly simple, consisting of only eleven articles. But if the arrival of the treaty was a welcome event, before Mr. Madison and his counselors could allow a sense of relief to wash over them, they needed to know precisely what the Peace Commissioners had agreed to. They needed to analyze this final outcome to the war, if, indeed, it was to be that. The Chief Magistrate would sign it or not on the basis of careful and reasoned consideration. He would have to present it to the Senate for advice and consent. The treaty was merely paper until ratification, though everyone in the room hoped that the several precious sheets, simply bound by a length of green ribbon sewn into the left margin, contained the promise of an acceptable peace.

Nothing in the treaty was a shock. In Article the First, peace was declared: "There shall be a firm and universal Peace between His Britannic Majesty and the United States." To everyone's relief, it was soon abundantly clear that *status quo ante bellum* in regard to territories had become the guiding principle. That was consistent with Monroe's instructions to the peace envoys. Prisoners of war were to be returned; both sides agreed to seek peaceful relations with the Indians; and efforts would be made to end the slave trade. Several minor disputes concerning territories at the Canadian border, in particular several islands in the Bay of Passamaquoddy near the Bay of Fundy, were left to be resolved, but terms for establishing future commissions were specified.

What puzzled listeners was the utter silence on certain issues, several of which had been essential rationales for going to war in the first place. That impressment went unmentioned was unsurprising, as Monroe's instructions six months earlier gave the Commissioners permission to omit the matter if necessary. But silence also ruled when it came to the harassment of neutral trade, the fisheries, navigation of the Mississippi, and reparations. The treaty brought hostilities to a close, but it left many questions unanswered.

As they prepared to sign the document six weeks earlier in Ghent, the American Peace Commissioners worried that so very much had been left unsaid; Henry Clay had called the draft document before him a "damn bad treaty" before, reluctantly, agreeing that it was the best they could hope to achieve. In Washington, Mr. Madison, too, came to the realization that, though much was left for time to arbitrate, he could defend the document before him to the Senate and his fellow citizens.

The time had come to go public and, just after eight o'clock that evening, Joseph Gales, co-owner of the *National Intelligencer,* was summoned to the cabinet meeting. "Subdued joy sat upon the face of every one of them," he later reported. A one-paragraph summary that Gales might print in the following day's paper was drafted. It opened with the words, "We have the pleasure to announce that the treaty of the peace between the United States and Great Britain . . . was last evening delivered. . . . [W]e are happy to add that the treaty is thought, in all respects, to be honorable to the nation and to the negotiators."[40]

DOWNSTAIRS MRS. MADISON ORDERED THE DOORS to the mansion opened in welcome. The public rooms soon filled to capacity as all of Washington seemed to be arriving. "Among the members present were gentlemen of opposite politics," reported one in attendance, "but lately arranged against one another in continual conflict and fierce debate, now with elated spirits thanking God, and with softened hearts cordially felicitating with one another upon the joyful intelligence."[41]

Sally Coles, on learning Madison would sign the treaty, went to the head of the servants' stair and called down, "Peace! Peace!" Bearding butler John Freeman, she instructed him to break out the wine for the servants, too. Paul Jennings played "The President's March" on his fiddle. Jean-Pierre Sioussat set to drinking in earnest (he would remain intoxicated for two days). Everyone was "crazy with joy."[42]

The moment was Dolley's as much as it was James's, as one of those in attendance later reported. "The most conspicuous object in the room observed of all observers, was Mrs. Madison herself, then in the meridian of life and queenly beauty. . . . No one could doubt, who beheld the radiance of joy which lighted up her countenance and diffused its beam all around that all uncertainty was at an end, and the government of the country had in very truth 'passed from gloom to glory'. With a grace all her own, to her visitors she reciprocated heartfelt congratulations upon the glorious and happy change in the aspect of public affairs; dispensing with liberal hand to every individual in the large assembly the proverbial hospitalities of that house."[43]

ON FEBRUARY 15, MADISON TRANSMITTED THE TREATY, along with the conference protocols that had accompanied it from Ghent. The Treaty was read twice to the collected body.

On February 16, after a third reading, a motion was made to vote on the question, "Will the Senate advise and consent to the ratification of this treaty?" The vote was thirty-five yeas, none opposed.

On February 17, 1815, Anthony St. John Baker arrived in Washington City, via Boston and Norfolk, with a copy of the treaty signed by the Prince Regent (he had ratified it in place of his father, George III, who, a sleepless lunatic, was rumored to talk to trees of long-dead ministers). That evening, at the four-foot-round mahogany table in the center of the study at the Tayloe house, Mr. and Mrs. Madison's War came officially to an end.

EPILOGUE

The View from Montpelier

Their first war with England made them independent; their second made them formidable.
—London Times, *April 1817*

I.

April 17, 1817 . . . Potomac Wharf . . . Washington City

IN THE DAYS BEFORE JAMES MADISON'S PREDECESSOR left the presidency, he described his feelings. "Never did a prisoner released from his chains," wrote Thomas Jefferson, "feel such relief as I shall on shaking off the shackles of power."[1] On his own departure from office, in 1817, Mr. Madison's elation was evident.

Steamboat service on the Potomac had begun two years earlier. As he embarked on the first leg of his journey home, the former President seemed to have left the cares of office back on the Federal City quay. "During the voyage he was as playful as a child," reported James Paulding, a member of his traveling party. "[He] talked and jested with every body on board, & reminded me of a school Boy on a long vacation."[2]

Madison was not the only one in high spirits. In fact, a Boston newspaper would soon coin the phrase "era of good feelings" to describe the times.[3] Two years after the war concluded, its hardest days were receding into memory. Despite going unmentioned in the Treaty of Ghent, impressment of American sailors ended. Though the expected gain of Canadian territory had not come to pass, a westward boom was under way (on a visit to Ohio and the nation's newest state, Illinois, Madison's longtime secretary, Edward Coles, reported soaring land values, rapid population growth, and the appearance of new and substantial towns). Foreign trade and shipping were quite restored, with a new commercial treaty with Great Britain in effect and American ships departing daily for ports around the world.

As the boat churned southward on the Potomac, the hisses and clangs of the steam engine were a reminder of other changes. The war had compelled an expansion of American manufacturing. In the absence of imported goods, Americans set about making what they wanted. To facilitate such growth, Madison led a postwar shift from many long-held Republican positions. The nation's government now underwrote the construction of public roads and canals. After years of antipathy to the Hamiltonian notion of a national bank, Madison signed into law a bill creating the Second Bank of the United States and appointed as its president his former Secretary of the Navy William Jones.

The wartime successes of Jones's old department rendered obsolete the notion that the United States needed no permanent navy. America had become a naval power, with more new warships under construction and her prowess on the seas proven once again in the Mediterranean in a confrontation with the Barbary States of Tunis, Algiers, and Tripoli in 1815. The army college at West Point won added funding. Indian unrest was resolved, at least for the time being, with a series of treaties.

In Washington City, perhaps the most remarkable alteration was that no one was calling Mr. Madison insulting names. His popularity seemed almost universal, as even a lifelong enemy like John Randolph felt empowered to rise to his feet on the floor of Congress to allow that, as "his orb was sinking temperately to the West," Mr. Madison was to be described as "a great man."[4]

The steamboat journey covered forty-nine miles. The Madisons passed Mount Vernon, home of the man whose portrait Dolley so memorably saved from the British. They sailed within sight of Fort Warburton, a reminder of the many failures of the American military in the recent war, not a few of which had been rehashed in courts-martial. William Winder had been acquitted of blame, but General William Hull was found guilty of cowardice and sentenced to be shot for his failure at the Battle of Detroit. Mindful of Hull's honorable service in the Revolution, Madison pardoned the old man.

As the steamboat docked on the Virginia shore, it shared the waters of Aquia Creek with barges loaded with sandstone. A nearby quarry had been the source in the 1790s of the walling material for the President's house, and, once again, ashlar blocks were floated north to Mrs. Madison's former Great House, where reconstruction was well under way.

The rebuilt mansion wouldn't be ready for habitation until the autumn (with the life-size portrait of Washington once again on display), and its next occupant would be Colonel Monroe. He had won the office of Chief Magistrate in a landslide, with an electoral count of 183 to 34 over Rufus King. A few disgruntled Federalists in the East talked disparagingly of the "Virginia Dynasty," but in the wake of the Hartford Convention and the threats of secession, the Federalists had ceased almost overnight to wield any political power in Washington.

President Monroe took the oath of office at noon on March 4, but Dolley and James had remained in the city for a full month after the inauguration, a ceremony that Mrs. Madison, still the most visible person in Washington City, chose not to attend out of courtesy to her successor, Elizabeth Monroe. But both Madisons enjoyed many public moments in those weeks. During the day they worked at packing papers and other personal goods for their journey to Montpelier; night after night, they were fêted at balls and dinners held in their honor.

They had been showered with encomiums, but as they boarded the carriage that would take them the remaining ninety miles back to Orange County and Montpelier, Mr. Madison was permitted to contemplate that, for the first time in sixteen years, he might "indulge his relish for the intellectual pleasures of the closet, and the pursuits of rural life."[5]

If this journey seemed to possess an air of finality, time would prove it so. The former president, though he would live another nineteen years, never again visited Washington City.

MRS. MADISON'S LIFE AT MONTPELIER, now permanent and unchanging, was bittersweet. Much would be the same, with James to look after, her body servant Sukey to care for her, and her pet macaw, Polly, screeching out the French words taught it by John Sioussat. But this life would necessarily be circumscribed, and not only by the isolation of the five-thousand-acre plantation.

Washington City had been her town, and she would miss it. As Presidentess, she created and directed a great social enterprise that, as often as not, had political overtones. She could claim dozens of dear friends and hundreds of valued acquaintances back in the capital. She was accustomed to being at the epicenter of a culture that changed with every season and electoral cycle. At Montpelier she continued to be a gracious hostess, with visitors and family to entertain and feed. When the weather was warm and the roads passable, she could expect a dozen (or even dozens) of guests of an evening. Many members of James's extended family lived nearby; in fact, his aged mother would occupy her own quarters in the Montpelier mansion until her death at ninety-seven, twelve years into James's retirement. When the company were fewer, however, Dolley felt the absence of city energy. Two years into retirement she confided in a friend that her attachment to Washington was undiminished;

after four years, she complained of having spent what she called a "Norwegian Winter."[6] The chill was more than a matter of climate.

Yet to friend and stranger alike, the retired Madisons of Montpelier seemed the most settled and serene of couples. They lived a common, interdependent existence; they shared even a pair of spectacles. Mrs. Madison was forty-nine when James left office, her health good. Seventeen years her senior, James suffered from a growing miscellany of ailments. Dolley was his nurse and ever-sensitive to his needs ("I must go to Madison," she was often heard to say), and her own rheumatism, which particularly affected her ankle, came and went, along with his joint pains and bouts of bilious fever.

They took turns pointing the telescope on the front portico, employing it to monitor carriages approaching from afar; for both James and Dolley, the arrival of company—and fresh conversation—was a principal pleasure. For some years, they made annual trips to visit Monticello, and Mr. Jefferson was among Montpelier's visitors. Dolley maintained a busy correspondence with far-flung friends and family. She worried over her alcoholic son, whose gambling debts were an unneeded burden at a time when Montpelier's farming fortunes were falling. She threatened to visit Washington, Philadelphia, and relations in other states, but somehow she could not bring herself to leave central Virginia.

Together, Mr. and Mrs. Madison in those years took on an essential task. They worked at organizing and editing his papers, the very ones she had packed into trunks as the British marched on Washington. As important as she knew it to be, the work sometimes left Dolley feeling all the more tethered. After a long winter spent readying the papers for the press, she told a cousin, "Not a mile can I go from home." As she herself said, Dolley and James were "fixed" at Montpelier.[7]

MR. MADISON ALSO MAINTAINED CONTACT WITH THE OUTSIDE WORLD. Like his presidential predecessors Washington and Jefferson, he had ached to escape the seat of government, but, once home, he continued to be preoccupied with the nation's doings. For several years, President Monroe and his Minister to the Court of St. James's, Richard Rush, forwarded diplomatic dispatches to Montpelier. The Madisons heard regularly from the Gallatins in Paris, where Albert was

Near the end of Mr. Madison's life, several painters (including John G. Chapman and Asher B. Durand) came to record his likeness at Montpelier. Though he suffered from a range of chronic complaints, Madison, according to his many visitors, retained remarkable mental clarity to the end of his life, as is apparent in the intense gaze that J. B. Longacre recorded in this 1833 image. *Library of Congress/Prints and Photographs Division*

Minister to France, then in New York, where, like Jefferson, Gallatin was engaged in founding a college, the University of the City of New York.* News drifted in from abroad of Britishers. Admiral Cockburn had drawn duty as Napoleon's keeper after the Battle of Waterloo, accompanying Bonaparte on the seventy-two-day sea journey to St. Helena, then spent a year making sure the defeated emperor stayed there. Cockburn was knighted for his labors, while Augustus John Foster, after a long diplomatic and parliamentary career, was created a baronet in 1831. From Madison's second-floor room lined with the four thousand volumes in his personal library, he corresponded regularly with William Wirt, who had become Monroe's Attorney General, and with Henry Clay, once again Speaker of the House, whose ambition to rise to the presidency had stalled. Madison subscribed to many newspapers and read them habitually.

As one of the last surviving Founding Fathers and a central figure at the 1787 convention that produced the Constitution, Madison received probing inquiries from the likes of John Quincy Adams about the document's history and amendments. A printer trying to assign authorship to the individual essays in *The Federalist Papers* for a new edition sought his counsel. So did historian Jared Sparks, who was hard at work on his life of George Washington.

When his old friends Jefferson and Monroe died (on July 4, 1826, and July 4, 1831, respectively), Mr. Madison shared recollections and regrets with a range of friends and family. He remarked to Sparks, "Having outlived so many of my contemporaries, I ought not to forget that I may be thought to have outlived myself."[8] He proved longer-lived than many of the men who had served him. Commodore Oliver Hazard Perry succumbed to yellow fever in 1819 in South America, while Stephen Decatur, age forty-one, was killed in a duel at the Bladensburg dueling ground—by the former captain of the *Chesapeake* James Barron. Pistol fire killed

* The school of which Gallatin was founding president was renamed New York University in 1896.

Henry Carroll, too, in the Missouri Territory, and his father, Charles Carroll, followed him to the grave just three years later, though he was taken, according to the local paper, by "a tedious illness." Joshua Barney's physician attributed his death in 1818 to the wound he sustained at Bladensburg, as the bullet had been too deeply buried to be removed.

New acquaintances thought Mr. Madison warm and wise. On his visit in 1825, the Italian Count Carlo Vidua found him "a small, thin old man, but of a kindly and pleasant face; his bearing is very aristocratic, and without assuming the air of importance and dignity befitting one of his station, he displays an indescribable gentleness and charm. . . . I have heard few people speak with such precision and, above all, with such fairness."[9] As a member of the Board of Visitors and, after Jefferson's death, as Rector of the University of Virginia, Madison played a formative role in Mr. Jefferson's pet project, the "Academical Village."

During these years the old Virginian invested reams of paper and intellectual energy in the problem of slavery, and found that recolonization in Africa was the best solution he could offer. Soon, however, such visitors as General Lafayette (who used his American rank with pride) and Governor Coles (Madison's old secretary, Edward, risen to the governorship of Illinois) brought him to understand that colonization was a poor and impractical answer. Slavery was, in Madison's words, a "dreadful calamity." He went further: "The magnitude of this evil among us is so deeply felt, and so universally acknowledged; that no merit could be greater than that of devising a satisfactory remedy for it."[10] As the years passed, it was a profound sadness to him that slavery was a wrong he could not make right, and he worried at the nation's inability to crack the conundrum and what it might bode for the country's future.

The subject of his war inevitably arose from time to time and, with predictable courtesy and constancy, Mr. Madison answered questions put to him. In 1818, former Congressman Charles Jared Ingersoll wrote to say he was at work on a book about the war (three decades later it would appear as a four-volume opus bearing the title *Historical Sketch of the Second War between the United States and Great Britain*). Mr. Madison wrote back to his Republican colleague to express his confidence in Ingersoll's "talents" and "fairness of disposition." But he showed no interest in wading into muddy waters, offering Ingersoll little help. His private papers, he said, merely duplicated those already available from public sources.

The former president did volunteer one modest pronouncement. "If our first struggle was a war of our infancy," he told Ingersoll, "this last was that of our youth; and the issue of both, wisely improved, may long postpone, if not forever prevent, a necessity for exerting the strength of our manhood."[11] By implication, then, the war had been necessary, a national rite of passage. He would sound this note again a decade later when replying to a letter from legal scholar Henry Wheaton. "[T]he war," wrote Madison, ". . . so menacing in its aspect, led to exploits which gained for the arms of our Country a reputation invaluable as a guaranty against future aggressions."[12]

Madison also took pride in the fact that, despite great provocation from the men of the East, his administration had respected individual rights (unlike Adams and the Federalists, who had effectively outlawed political opposition by passing the Alien and Sedition Acts in 1798). As a Congressman, Madison had introduced the amendments that became the Bill of Rights on the floor of Congress in 1789; as a postwar president, Madison reminded the Massachusetts Legislature in 1815 that in wartime, despite "differences of opinion, . . . the rights of our Country [were] successfully maintained."[13] In looking back upon his war, Mr. Madison chose to go no further.

James Madison wrote no autobiography, but, at the request of a younger literary friend, the same James K. Paulding who had accompanied the Madisons on their last journey from Washington, he pulled from his files a few sheets.* Madison described the document as "too meager even

* New Yorker James Kirke Paulding was a writer, a sometime collaborator with his brother-in-law Washington Irving, and a government bureaucrat (Madison had appointed him in 1815 to the newly created post of secretary to the Board of Navy Commissioners). For an epigraph in his first novel, he would compose the immortal lines "Peter Piper picked a peck of pickled peppers, / Where is the peck of pickled peppers Peter Piper picked?"

for the name of a sketch," terming it an "abortive biography," one he said he drafted a few years earlier. At a mere fifteen handwritten pages, it seemed an odd document, and among its peculiarities was the subject's reference to himself throughout in the third person. Stranger yet, Madison devoted less than a single page to his presidency, and the war merited one inconclusive sentence.[14]

Though he spoke and wrote of the war rarely, its failures still irked him. When prompted, he remarked bitterly upon General Hull's "imbecility," which, said Madison, made Hull the "Mock Hero of Detroit." In his skeletal biographical notes, he also made pregnant mention of General Armstrong's deceptions.[15]

Mr. Madison's War was clearly not a subject that the former president enjoyed, and he let others speak of it.

MANY DID, AND DID SO WITH ALACRITY. Almost as soon as the Treaty of Ghent was signed, one of its negotiators, James Bayard, observed, "The war has raised our reputation in Europe and it excites astonishment that we should have been able for one campaign to have fought Great Britain single handed. . . . I think it will be a long time before we are disturbed again by any of the powers of Europe."[16]

Having become Minister to France, Albert Gallatin, with the dual perspective of a foreign-born convert to the American cause, observed, "[T]he war . . . has renewed and reinstated the national feelings which the Revolution had given and which were daily lessened. The people now have more general objects of attachment with which their pride and political opinions are connected. They are more American; they feel and act more like a nation; and I hope that the permanency of the Union is thereby better secured."[17]

In early 1816 a letter had been dispatched that, perhaps, Mr. Jefferson chose not to share with his friend, at least in toto. But as Madison's presidency drew to a close, the Sage of Monticello received a note from his devoted Braintree correspondent. John Adams had mused long and hard on the Madison presidency and, with the stringent sinews of his Yankee candor very much in evidence, wrote, "notwithstand[ing] a thousand Faults and blunders, [Madison's] Administration has acquired more glory, and established more Union, than all his three Predecessors, Washington Adams and Jefferson, put together."[18]

French Minister Louis Sérurier, writing home to his foreign minister, offered what proved to be a prophetic observation. "Finally the war has given the Americans what they so essentially lacked, a national character founded on a glory common to all."[19] The war would indeed engender a rich, patriotic mythology that gradually subsumed more nuanced characterizations of the conflict. Although James Lawrence's order "Don't give up the ship" would have led to an even greater massacre had it been obeyed, his words became the motto of the U.S. Navy and transformed Lawrence into a revered hero. A competing phrase uttered by Lawrence's friend Oliver Hazard Perry came quickly to the lips of schoolboys: "We have met the enemy and they are ours." The USS *Constitution* became perhaps the best-known ship in the world, at least by its nickname, *Old Ironsides*. An untitled song written by a man who had initially refused military service early in the war ("I shall not fight the poor, unoffending Canadians") was fast becoming the national anthem.[20] Because so many Tennesseans had come to the aid of their country, their home became known as the "Volunteer State."

Most memorable of all was the image of Mrs. Madison, who, as the British marched on Washington, refused to take leave of the President's house until the big portrait of Washington was dispatched to a safe haven. Her invasion-day story became one that everyone knew; her old friend Margaret Bayard, by then a novelist of some note (*What Is Gentility?* had been published in 1825), wrote a brief biography that recounted Mrs. Madison's brave stand at the president's house. During the war years, the term *Mr. Madison's War* had been a tarnish on her husband's good reputation; in the peace that followed it was her actions more than her husband's that

SAVING THE PORTRAIT OF WASHINGTON.

The legend—albeit one based on fact—grew. This image, published in 1879 in an engraving by Alfred Bobbett, represents one version (namely, that the canvas was cut from its frame) in a children's book of the era. More to the point, by 1947, a Washington social historian was saying of Mrs. Madison, "Next to Joshua Barney she was the bravest American soldier."

Americans chose to celebrate. In the nation's collective memory, Mr. and Mrs. Madison's War was better remembered for her role than his.

JUST WEEKS BEFORE JAMES MADISON'S DEATH, Charles Ingersoll came to Montpelier. He found Mr. Madison spending his days reclining on a sofa, suffering from a shortness of breath that made speaking difficult. Unable to walk without assistance at age eighty-five, the former president was emaciated, feeble—and very glad of stimulating company.

"Infirm as his body is," reported Ingersoll, "his understanding is as bright as ever; his intelligence, recollections, discriminations, and philosophy, all delightfully instructive." Given her husband's fragile condition, Mrs. Madison instructed Ingersoll to do most of the talking, but the conversation ranged widely, with Mr. Madison offering lengthy discourses on the past and future.

Several times the talk turned to armed conflict, and his guest was struck by both "Mr. Madison's abhorrence of the war" and, paradoxically, that it had been "his destiny to be President during the war." Madison himself broached the subject of "the worst stage of the war, just after the capture of Washington," a time when his life was threatened by some of his fellow citizens, and he was called "tyrant, murderer, despot."[21] Yet even two decades later, he refused to damn those who slandered him.

As usual, Madison's principal preoccupation was the preservation of the country he had helped create. As Charles Ingersoll reported of Madison's last public utterances, "His politics are as simple and lovely as his patriotism, peace and union. They are the whole system—to avoid war at almost any price, and to preserve the Union at all events."[22]

A few weeks later, on the morning of June 28, 1836, James Madison Jr. died. Sukey had brought him his breakfast and Paul Jennings waited to shave his master, just as he had done every other day for sixteen years.

As the two servants watched, "His head instantly dropped, and he ceased breathing as quietly as the snuff of a candle goes out."[23]

DOLLEY MADISON OUTLIVED HER HUSBAND BY THIRTEEN YEARS. At first, she felt his loss acutely, writing to her oldest and closest friend, "I have been as one in a troubled dream since my irreparable loss of him, for whom my affection was perfect, as was his character and conduct thro' life."[24]

Soon enough, financial woes drew her attention. On good authority Mr. Madison had anticipated that his papers would command a selling price of one hundred thousand dollars; he expected that sum to provide for the widow Dolley. But plans for commercial publication did not come to fruition (in part, the fault lay with Payne Todd, who self-importantly set off to sell his stepfather's papers but succeeded only in alienating the publishers with whom he met). The U.S. Congress eventually agreed to purchase the first lot for thirty thousand dollars, and three volumes appeared in 1840. The monies went little further than to pay off Madison's creditors. Dolley's debts grew increasingly unmanageable and, in 1844, Montpelier was sold. Its sale was both a wrench and a relief, as Mrs. Madison took up residence once more in Washington City.

She spent her last years in the capital. Though her threadbare wardrobe dated from the presidential years and her financial circumstances remained straitened, her many friends in Washington welcomed her return. Congress voted her a permanent seat on the house floor. The President granted her franking privileges, meaning her letters would travel at government expense. She resided in a row house near the large mansion that had come to be called the "White House"; her own modest domicile was referred to by some as the "little White House." She was a favored dinner guest around town, at the homes of both the old guard and newer arrivals.

When she sold the other four volumes of James's papers in 1848, the buyer was again Congress. The selling price was twenty-five thousand dollars, payable as an advance fee of five thousand dollars, with the balance put in trust. Income from the principal would be paid to her as it accrued, but the arrangement was a sad recognition that Mrs. Madison needed to be protected from her profligate son, Payne, who continued to undermine his mother's finances.

Back in the political and social culture she had helped sculpt, Mrs. Madison assumed a unique status. She had known all the presidents. She became such a revered figure that even a former antagonist of the Madisons, Daniel Webster, expressed his admiration, and he famously said of Mrs. Madison, "She is the only permanent power in Washington—all others are transient." (He had come full circle on James, too, characterizing him as "the wisest of our Presidents, except Washington.")[25] Webster also bought the devoted Paul Jennings in order to emancipate him and often sent the freed man to the little White House with baskets of food. For his part, far from resenting his former owners, Jennings contributed his own coins to the support of Mrs. Madison and said of his master, "Mr. Madison, I think, was one of the best men that ever lived."[26]

In 1848, Mrs. Madison engaged in a brief newspaper exchange regarding her final act at the President's house in 1814. When a descendant claimed credit for Charles Carroll, Dolley was both forthright ("The impression that Mr. Carroll saved Stuart's portrait of Washington is erroneous") and self-effacing (she characterized the story as merely a "little narrative").[27]

When Dolley Payne Todd Madison died on July 12, 1849, at age eighty-one, she was given a state funeral. Government offices were closed so members of Congress and the Supreme Court could attend, along with President Zachary Taylor (who was a second cousin of James's and a veteran of the war). At the time, Mrs. Madison's was the largest funeral ever held in Washington City.

~

ALTHOUGH THE WAR WAS INEXTRICABLY LINKED WITH HIS NAME, Mr. Madison never expressed regret nor claimed

Dolley Madison in a circa-1848 daguerreotype taken by Mathew Brady, more than thirty years after her departure from the President's house. Her style of dress, however, changed little since her days as the Presidentess, partly due to the fact that she lacked the means to buy new, stylish clothing. *Greensboro (NC) Historical Museum*

credit. He left no final defining words on the events of 1812–1815. Instead, he chose in the postwar years, as he had throughout his political life, to talk of *union.*

It was a word he used often, one in opposition to "disunion," which he saw as the direst of evils, akin to "the serpent creeping with his deadly wiles into paradise."[28] With each passing year, his conviction grew stronger that, above all, the states must remain united, even as the dual specters of slavery and "nullification" (the latter a notion he himself had broached in a very different context decades earlier) clouded his nation's future.

In his long life, Mr. Madison had seen his union tested. After the first War of Independence there had been an absence of a formal unifying national force; together with Washington and others, Madison masterminded the creation of the Constitution with which to govern the country. In his eight-year collaboration with Jefferson, they had sought to direct their satellite nation out of the orbit of Great Britain. Though they failed, in the aftermath of the resulting collision Mr. Madison managed to plot a new national course.

To Madison, the nation's life force was its appetite for liberty and thirst for independence; they were to be cherished and perpetuated above all else. Though he had played a central role in many "important transactions," he offered few summary judgments and no grand predictions. He admitted to puzzlement at the unfolding of "great events aris[ing] from little causes," but justifications and explanations did not draw his focus. He didn't seek to calibrate his contributions any more than he sought to predict what was to come.

As he had once explained to his young friend James Paulding, he accepted the simple truth that "history knows about as much of the Past as she does of the Future."[29]

ACKNOWLEDGMENTS

THE RESEARCH FOR *MR. AND MRS. MADISON'S WAR* TOOK ME to a great many destinations, most often libraries but also historic sites, such as the Madison home Montpelier (my thanks to Michael Quinn, Megan Brett, and Lisa Timmerman, as well as Sean O'Brien at the Center for the Constitution). At the Library of Congress, Kathy Woodrell and Emily C. Howie were the most welcoming of guides to the main reading room, as were Cheryl Fox in Manuscripts and Eric P. Frazier and Clark W. Evans in Rare Book and Special Collections. I much appreciated the patience and knowledge of Diann Benti at the American Antiquarian Society and, repeatedly, the help of Jessica M. Pigza, Rare Books Division, New York Public Library. I would be remiss if, in speaking of that midtown monument, it were to go unmentioned that, in a city of a treasures, it is one of the most essential.

My source of first resort being the Sawyer Library at Williams College, my thanks go to Rebecca Ohm, Lori Dubois, Jodi Psoter, and their colleagues. I also feel obliged to acknowledge James Phinney Baxter III (1893–1975), whose remarkable collection of early books on the War of 1812 resides at the college's library (he knew Gleig and James and the rest ever so long before I did). I visited the Waidner-Spahr Library at Dickinson College to learn of Richard Rush; my way was eased by William Durden, James Gerencser, and Maureen O'Brien Dermott, but especially by Ellen Kelley. I've asked pestering questions and found valuable materials at many libraries, including those at the New-York Historical Society Library, the Sterling and Francine Clark Art Institute, the University of Virginia Alderman Library, and the Chatham (New York) Public Library. I have regularly drawn upon the collective resources of both the Mid-Hudson Library System and C/W MARS, the central and western Massachusetts library system. Janet Bloom, Clements Library, University of Michigan, and Kym S. Rice, director, Museum Studies Program, George Washington University, also answered questions that others could not. Last but hardly least, my thanks go to Angela Kreider at the Madison papers project in Charlottesville and, in particular, to David Mattern for his counsel and goodwill and his reading of the manuscript.

Researching a book of this sort always involves learning from other historians, and I have come away from the process yet again with admiration for a goodly number of my fellow travelers in the past, both living and dead. If it were possible, I should like to shake the hand of Rear Admiral Alfred Mahan or have a conversation with Henry Adams; they helped make the recounting of the naval battles in this book a surprising pleasure. I would be delighted to have tea with Margaret Bayard Smith; above all others, her writings are essential to an understanding of Washington's social life circa 1812. I owe immeasurable debts to Irving Brant (regarding James); Catherine Allgor (on Dolley); John C. Stagg (for his analytical view of the War of 1812); and Donald Hickey (for an American view of the war's events) and John Latimer (for the British perspective).

I have whenever possible relied upon primary sources; thus the papers of Mr. and Mrs. Madison were invaluable, as were the Gallatin and Paulding papers (New-York Historical Society), various Adams papers (Massachusetts Historical Society), and the Mitchill, Rush, Augustus John Foster, George Watterson, Anna Maria Brodeau Thornton, Cutts, and Mrs. Smith papers (Library of Congress). National documents were also essential, many of which are electronic resources found online, not least being the *American State Papers* and the *Annals of Congress*. I remain happily amazed to discover that thousands of pages of governmental records are to be summoned to one's computer screen with no more than a few keystrokes.

This book would not have assumed the shape and form it has without the keen insights of Gail Hochman, friend, agent, and candid critic. Many thanks go to Peter Ginna, publisher of Bloomsbury Press, for the opportunity to wrestle with this unruly subject and for asking the essential questions at the right moments. My appreciation, too, to Pete Beatty, editor, for his thorough and thoughtful editing, and his willingness to tend to a thousand details. Kathleen Moloney, the literary equivalent of a short-fielder, was there to catch my many grammatical lapses; Jean Atcheson, valued friend, gave it the closest and most careful reading of all; and my thanks to Moacir de Sá Pereira for his clear and uncluttered maps.

I must thank some presidents, too, all of whom, in direct or not so evident ways, informed my understanding of James Madison and the chief executive's role. In no particular order, then, my thanks to Adam Falk, Thomas Jefferson, Walter J. Minton, George Washington, Woodrow Wilson, Joe Consolino, George W. Bush, and Barack Obama.

Finally, my love and appreciation go as always to Betsy, Sarah, and Elizabeth. The manner and sensibilities of the mother and her two daughters made it possible for me to envision Dolley Madison in a way I could not have done without them.

THE WAR OF 1812 TIMELINE

JUNE 18, 1812	President Madison signs into law the Declaration of War
JULY 17, 1812	British forces capture Fort Michilimackinac
AUGUST 16, 1812	Brigadier General William Hull surrenders Fort Detroit
AUGUST 19, 1812	USS *Constitution* defeats the HMS *Guerrière*
OCTOBER 25, 1812	USS *United States* captures the HMS *Macedonian*

DECEMBER 29, 1812	USS *Constitution* defeats the HMS *Java*
APRIL 27, 1813	American forces capture York, Ontario
MAY 3, 1813	Admiral George Cockburn's forces burn Havre de Grace, Maryland
JUNE 1, 1813	HMS *Shannon* captures the USS *Chesapeake*
SEPTEMBER 10, 1813	Oliver Hazard Perry and American forces prevail in Battle of Lake Erie
OCTOBER 5, 1813	General William Henry Harrison defeats British forces at the Battle of Thames; Tecumseh killed
APRIL 6, 1814	Napoleon abdicates
JUNE 27, 1814	Madison and Monroe authorize Peace Commissioners to drop demand that impressment cease
AUGUST 8, 1814	Peace negotiations commence in Ghent
AUGUST 9–11, 1814	Bombardments by the British of Stonington, Connecticut
AUGUST 24, 1814	Battle of Bladensburg, Maryland, and the burning of the public buildings in Washington City

AUGUST 29, 1814	Alexandria, Virginia, capitulates to the British
SEPTEMBER 1–11, 1814	The British occupy the Maine coast from Eastport to Castine
SEPTEMBER 11, 1814	Captain Macdonough and his flotilla defeat the British at the Battle of Plattsburgh on Lake Champlain
SEPTEMBER 13, 1814	Skirmish at North Point and the British bombardment of Baltimore begins
SEPTEMBER 14, 1814	The British withdraw from Baltimore
DECEMBER 24, 1814	Peace Commissioners sign the Treaty of Ghent
JANUARY 8, 1815	Andrew Jackson's forces rout the British at the Battle of New Orleans
FEBRUARY 16, 1815	Madison ratifies the Treaty of Ghent.

NOTES

Prologue

1. Thomas Jefferson to Tadeusz Kosciuszko, April 13, 1811.
2. *National Intelligencer*, June 6, 1812.
3. Louisa Katherine Adams, *Autobiographical Sketch*, Massachusetts Historical Society.
4. Senator Samuel Latham Mitchill to Catherine Akerly Mitchill, November 23, 1807, and January 25, 1808.
5. Foster, *Jeffersonian America* (1954), p. 140, 155.
6. Augustus John Foster to Robert Stewart, April 24, 1812.
7. Foster, *Jeffersonian America* (1954), p. 293.
8. Adams, *History of the United States of America During the Administrations of Thomas Jefferson* (1890), vol. 2, p. 12.
9. Vice Admiral Berkeley, quoted in Adams, *History of the United States of America During the Administrations of Thomas Jefferson* (1890), vol. 2, p. 3.
10. Perkins, *Prologue to War* (1961), p. 86.

11. Hickey, *War of 1812* (1989), p. 11.
12. Riddell, "Jenkin Ratford" (1916), p. 816.
13. Samuel Leech, *A Voice from the Main Deck* (1843), pp. 45–46.
14. Quoted in Perkins, *Prologue to War* (1961), pp. 84, 85.
15. *National Intelligencer*, July 1, 1807.
16. James Madison to Thomas Jefferson, June 29, 1807.
17. Quoted in "Introduction," Smith, *Republic of Letters* (1995), vol. 1, pp. 1–2.
18. Foster, *Jeffersonian America* (1954), pp. 155–56.
19. James Madison, "First Inaugural Address," March 4, 1809.
20. *American State Papers*, House of Representatives, 13th Congress, 3rd Session, Foreign Relations, vol. 3, pp. 332, 584.
21. Thomas Jefferson to William Wirt, May 3, 1811.
22. Foster, *Jeffersonian America* (1954), p. x.
23. Ibid., pp. 51, 55–56.
24. Augustus John Foster to Elizabeth, Duchess of Devonshire, January 2, 1812.
25. Foster, *Jeffersonian America* (1954), p. 18.
26. Ibid., pp. 86–87.
27. Ibid., p. 306.
28. Mary Bagot, "'Exile in Yankeeland': The Journal of Mary Bagot, 1816–1819" (1984), pp. 30–50.
29. Foster, *Jeffersonian America* (1954), p. 71.
30. Adams, "Count Edward de Crillon" (1895), p. 58.
31. Count Edward de Crillon, sworn testimony to the Committee of Foreign Relations, March 13–14, 1812, *American State Papers,* 12th Congress, 1st Session, Foreign Relations, vol. 3, pp. 555–56.
32. Herman W. Ryland [Secretary to Craig] to John Henry, January 26, 1809, in *American State Papers*, 12th Congress, 1st Session, Foreign Relations, vol. 3, p. 546.
33. John Henry to Sir James Craig, March 7, 1809; March 13, 1809; May 5, 1809, in *American State Papers*, 12th Congress, 1st Session, Foreign Relations, vol. 3, pp. 549, 550, 551–52.
34. Count de Crillon, sworn testimony to the Committee of Foreign Relations, March 13–14, 1812, *American State Papers*, 12th Congress, 1st Session, Foreign Relations, vol. 3, p. 556.
35. Ibid., p. 556.
36. Elbridge Gerry to James Madison, January 2, 3, 1812.

37. James Madison to Thomas Jefferson, March 9, 1812.
38. James Monroe to "Count de Crillon," February 2, 1812.
39. John Henry to James Monroe, February 13, 1812.
40. John A. Harper to William Plumer, cited in Hickey, *War of 1812* (1989), p. 38.
41. Judge Peters of Philadelphia to Timothy Pickering, March 18, 1812, cited in Morison, "Henry-Crillon Affair" (1950), p. 222, fn. 35.
42. Joel Barlow to James Monroe, April 14, 1812.
43. James Madison to Congress, June 1, 1812.
44. Dolley Madison to Ruth Barlow, April 19, 1812.
45. James Madison, "Special Message to Congress," June 1, 1812.
46. *Lexington* [Kentucky] *Reporter*, November 23, 1811.
47. Andrew Jackson to William Henry Harrison, November 1811.
48. Foster, *Jeffersonian America* (1954), p. 4.
49. Chiles, "Congress couldn't have been *this* bad, or could it?" (1995), p. 76.
50. Foster, *Jeffersonian America* (1954), p. 88.
51. "Address of the Minority to their Constituents," in *Annals of Congress*, 12th Congress, 1st Session, p. 2220.
52. *Independent Chronicle*, July 16, 1812.
53. Dolley Madison to Anna Cutts, March 10 and 27, 1812.
54. Gerry, *Diary* (1927), p. 180.
55. Ibid.
56. Foster, *Jeffersonian America* (1954), p. 100.
57. Louise Catherine Adams, "Autobiographical Sketch," Massachusetts Historical Society.
58. Smith, *The First Forty Years of Washington Society* (1906), p. 97.
59. Washington Irving to H. Brevoort, January 13, 1811, cited in Brant, *James Madison*, vol. 5 (1956), p. 239.
60. Clark, *Life and Letters of Dolly Madison* (1914), p. 13.
61. Few, "The Diary of Frances Few: 1808–1809," (1963), p. 351.
62. Chiles, "Congress couldn't have been *this* bad, or could it?" (1995), p. 76.
63. Foster, *Jeffersonian America* (1954), p. 100.
64. Augustus John Foster to Robert Stewart, June 21, 1812.

Chapter 1

1. *National Intelligencer*, June 20, 1812.
2. Richard Rush to Benjamin Rush, June 20, 1812.

3. Anthony Morris to Anna Payne, June 26, 1827, in *Records of the Columbian Historical Society,* vol. 15–45 (1942–1943), p. 218.
4. Dunlap, *History* (1834), vol. 1, p. 339; Warden, *A Statistical, Political, and Historical Account of the United States of North America,* vol. 3 (1819), p. 193.
5. Bryan, *History of the National Capital* (1914), vol. 1, p. 355.
6. Foster, *Jeffersonian America* (1954), p. 86.
7. Ebenezer Mattoon to Thomas Dwight, March 2, 1801. Dwight-Howard Collection, Massachusetts Historical Society.
8. Quoted in Brant, *James Madison*, vol. 6 (1961), p. 38.
9. Henry Clay, February 22, 1810, to Senate.
10. John Randolph, speech to Congress, December 10, 1811, in *Annals of Congress,* 12th Congress, 1st Session, p. 447.
11. Ibid.
12. James Madison to Henry Weaton, February 2, 1827.
13. *Report of Trial* (1814), p. 47.
14. Ibid., pp. 17–18.
15. Thomas Jefferson to William Duane, August 4, 1812.
16. *Report of Trial* (1814), pp. 17–18.
17. William Hull to Secretary of War William Eustis, August 1, 1812.
18. William Hull to Secretary of War William Eustis, August 26, 1812.
19. Hickey, *The War of 1812* (1989), pp. 83–84.
20. *Report of Trial* (1814), p. 40.
21. Ibid., p. 92.
22. Brigadier General James Taylor, quoted in Latimer, *1812: War with America* (2007), p. 67.
23. James Madison to Albert Picket, September 1821.
24. Preston, *Reminiscences of William C. Preston* (1933), p. 8.
25. Ingersoll, *Historical Sketch of the Second War,* vol. 1 (1853), p. 102.
26. John Lowell, "Mr. Madison's War," in Boston *Evening Post*, July 31–August 10, 1812.
27. Dudley, *Naval War of 1812*, vol. 2 (1992), p. 273.
28. Richard Rush to Charles J. Ingersoll, July 23, 1812.
29. James Madison to Samuel Spring, September 6, 1812.
30. Paul Hamilton to Isaac Hull, June 18, 1812.
31. Isaac Hull to Paul Hamilton, July 2, 1812.
32. Isaac Hull to Paul Hamilton, July 21, 1812.
33. Ibid.

34. Fairburn, *Merchant Sail*, vol. 2 (1947), p. 771.
35. Isaac Hull to Paul Hamilton, July 21, 1812.
36. Isaac Hull to Paul Hamilton, August 28, 1812.
37. Coggleshall, *American Privateers* (1856), pp. 26–27.
38. James Dacres, quoted in Fowler, *Jack Tars* (1984), p. 173.
39. *Boston Patriot*, September 2, 1812.
40. Dolley Madison to James Madison, November 1, 1805.
41. Carl Sferrazza Anthony, *First Ladies* (1990), pp. 80–81.
42. Margaret Bayard Smith to Susan B. Smith, March 1809.
43. Harriet Martineau, quoted in Clark, *Life and Letters of Dolly Madison* (1914), pp. 265–66.
44. Mary Elizabeth Hazelhurst Latrobe to Julian Miller, December 14, 1812.
45. Stephen Decatur to Susan Decatur, December 1804, quoted in Allison, *Stephen Decatur* (2005), p. 120.
46. Paul Hamilton to Stephen Decatur, April 4, 1812.
47. Stephen Decatur to Paul Hamilton, October 20, 1812.
48. Leech, *Voice from the Main Deck* (1843), pp. 80–82.
49. John S. Carden to John W. Croker, October 28, 1812.
50. Leech, *Voice from the Main Deck* (1843), p. 83.
51. Stephen Decatur to Paul Hamilton, October 30, 1812.
52. Dr. Samuel Latham Mitchill to Catherine Akerly Mitchill, December 10, 1812.
53. Seaton, *William Winston Seaton* (1871), p. 88.
54. Catherine Akerly Mitchill to Margaretta Akerly Miller, November 21, 1811; Anthony, *First Ladies* (1990), p. 83.
55. *National Intelligencer*, December 10, 1812.
56. Seaton, *William Winston Seaton* (1871), p. 89.
57. Dr. Samuel Latham Mitchill to Catherine Akerly Mitchill, December 10, 1812.
58. Benjamin Henry Latrobe to Henry S. B. Latrobe, December 9, 1812.
59. Seaton, *William Winston Seaton* (1871), p. 91.
60. Dolley Madison to Henry Clay, November 8, 1836.
61. Allgor, *Queen Dolley* (2006), p. 232.

Chapter 2

1. Smith, *The First Forty Years of Washington Society* (1906), p. 89.
2. Louis Sérurier to Hugues Bernard Maret, Duc de Bassano, June 21, 1813; italics added.

3. James Madison to William Bradford, November 9, 1772.
4. James Madison to Thomas Jefferson, April 27, 1785.
5. James Madison to William Hill Wells, June 17, 1813.
6. Dolley Madison to Hannah Gallatin, July 29, 1813.
7. James Madison, "Memorandum as to Robert Smith," April 1811.
8. "Joseph Gales on the War Manifesto of 1812" (1908), p. 308.
9. Samuel Latham Mitchill to Elizabeth Mitchill, December 22, 1812.
10. *New England Palladium*, January 19, 1813.
11. James Madison, quoted in Ketcham, *James Madison* (1971), p. 546.
12. Shaw, *Journals* (1847), p. 104.
13. Quoted in Skeen, *John Armstrong, Jr., 1758–1853* (1981), p. 45.
14. John Armstrong to James Madison, November 19, 1807.
15. Adams, *Memoirs of John Quincy Adams* (1874), pp. 150–51.
16. James Madison, "Second Inaugural Address," March 4, 1813.
17. James Madison to John Nicholas, April 2, 1813.
18. Albert Gallatin to James Madison, March 15, 1813.
19. Ibid.
20. William Jones to Isaac Chauncey, January 27, 1813.
21. Henry Dearborn to John Armstrong, March 16, 1813, in *American State Papers*, House of Representatives, 13th Congress, 2nd Session, Military Affairs, vol. 1, p. 442.
22. John Armstrong to Henry Dearborn, March 29, 1813, in *American State Papers*, House of Representatives, 13th Congress, 2nd Session, Military Affairs, vol. 1, p. 442.
23. Lossing, *Pictorial Field-Book* (1869), p. 487.
24. Hollon, "Zebulon Montgomery Pike and the York Campaign, 1813" (1949), p. 268.
25. Cooper, *Ned Myers* (1843), p. 45.
26. Cruikshank, *Documentary History of the Campaigns upon the Niagara Frontier in 1812–1814* (1902), pp. 208–9.
27. Dr. Amasa Trowbridge, in Trowbridge, *Trowbridge Genealogy* (1908), p. 537.
28. Cooper, *Ned Myers* (1843), p. 47.
29. Beaumont, *Formative Years* (1946), p. 46.
30. Ibid.
31. John Armstrong to Henry Dearborn, June 19, 1813.
32. Henry Dearborn to John Armstrong, May 3, 1813.

33. William Jones to James Madison, June 6, 1813.
34. James Fenimore Cooper quoted in Gleaves, *James Lawrence* (1904), p. 179.
35. William Jones in Mahan, *Sea Power and Its Relation to the War of 1812*, vol. 2 (1905), p. 131.
36. Philip Bowes Vere Broke to the commander of the U.S. frigate *Chesapeake,* June [1], 1813.
37. James Lawrence to William Jones, June 1, 1813.
38. Samuel Pechell, quoted in Mahan, *Sea Power and Its Relation to the War of 1812*, vol. 2 (1905), p. 134.
39. Broke, *Admiral Sir P.B.V. Broke* (1866), p. 167.
40. Gleaves, *James Lawrence* (1904), p. 204.
41. Cooper, *History of the Navy* (1856), p. 308.
42. Richard Rush quoted in Gleaves, *James Lawrence* (1904), p. 232.
43. John Adams to Richard Rush, September 6, 1813.
44. Dolley Madison to Hannah Gallatin, July 29, 1813.
45. Charles March to Daniel Webster, June 10, 1813.
46. Daniel Webster to Charles March, June 24, 1813.
47. Dolley Madison to Edward Coles, July 2, 1813.
48. Gerry, *Diary* (1927), p. 178.
49. Ibid., pp. 180–81.
50. Ibid., p. 188.
51. Horatio Nelson, quoted in Pack, *The Man Who Burned the White House* (1987), p. 24.
52. *Niles Register*, May 8, 1813.
53. George Cockburn to John Borlase Warren, March 23, 1813, quoted in Pack, *The Man Who Burned the White House* (1987), p. 148.
54. *Niles Register*, quoted in Pack, *The Man Who Burned the White House* (1987), p. 155.
55. William Jones to James Madison, July 15, 1813.
56. *American State Papers*, House of Representatives, 13th Congress, 2nd session, Military Affairs, vol. 1, p. 379.
57. Ingersoll, *Historical Sketch of the Second War*, vol. 1 (1853), pp. 197–200.
58. Smith, *The First Forty Years of Washington Society* (1906), p. 90.
59. Jonathan Dayton to James Madison, April 9, 1813.
60. Dolley Madison to Edward Coles, May 13, 1813.
61. Gerry, *Diary* (1927), p. 188.
62. Ibid., pp. 193–95.

63. Smith, *The First Forty Years of Washington Society* (1906), pp. 89–91.
64. Seaton, *William Winston Seaton* (1871), p. 111.
65. John Armstrong to James Madison, July 16, 1813.
66. James Madison to Henry Dearborn, August 8, 1813.
67. Brant, *James Madison*, vol. 6 (1961), p. 209.
68. James Madison to James Monroe, August 10, 1813.
69. James Madison to James Monroe, August 16, 1813.
70. John Armstrong to James Madison, July 25, 1813.
71. John Armstrong to James Madison, September 5, 1813.
72. John Armstrong to James Madison, September 1, 1813.
73. James Madison to John Armstrong, September 8, 1813.
74. Isaac Chauncey to Oliver H. Perry, March 15, 1813.
75. Quoted in Skaggs, *Signal Victory* (1997), p. 46.
76. Oliver H. Perry to William Jones, August 4, 1813.
77. Oliver H. Perry to Isaac Chauncey, July 27, 1813.
78. Oliver H. Perry to William Jones, September 2, 1813.
79. Oliver H. Perry, General Order, September 9, 1813, cited in Skaggs et al., *Signal Victory* (1997), p. 106.
80. Perry Order Book, September 4, 1813, quoted in Skaggs et al., *Signal Victory* (1997), p. 115.
81. Samuel Hambleton, *Diary* (1813).
82. Bunnell, *Travels* (1831), p. 113.
83. Ibid., p. 115.
84. "Surgeon Usher Parson's Account of the Battle of Lake Erie," in Dudley, *Naval War of 1812*, vol. 2 (1992), p. 563.
85. Oliver H. Perry to William Jones, September 9, 1813.
86. William Jones to Oliver H. Perry, September 21, 1813.
87. Lossing, *Pictorial Field-Book* (1869), p. 530.
88. Richard Rush to Charles J. Ingersoll, October 28, 1813.
89. Oliver H. Perry to William Jones, October 7, 1813.
90. Alexander Contee Hanson to Timothy Pickering, October 16, 1813, quoted in Brant, *James Madison*, vol. 6 (1961), p. 216.
91. President's Annual Message, December 7, 1813.
92. Lord Castlereagh to James Monroe, November 4, 1813. *American State Papers*, 13th Congress, 2nd Session, Foreign Relations, vol. 3, p. 621.
93. *National Intelligencer*, January 1, 1814.

94. Dolley Madison to Martha Jefferson Randolph, January 9, 1814.
95. Lord Castlereagh to James Monroe, November 4, 1813. *American State Papers,* 13th Congress, 2nd session, Foreign Relations, vol. 3, p. 621.

Chapter 3

1. Albert Gallatin and James Bayard to James Monroe, May 6, 1814.
2. Ibid.
3. From *Cobbett's Weekly Register*, May 7, 1814, reprinted in *National Intelligencer*, July 6, 1814.
4. James Barbour to James Madison, June 13, 1814.
5. Joshua Barney to James Madison, March 12, 1809.
6. Joshua Barney, "Defense of Chesapeake Bay &c," July 4, 1813, in Footner, *Sailor of Fortune* (1940, 1998), pp. 259–62.
7. Joshua Barney to William Jones, June 3, 1814.
8. Joshua Barney to William Jones, June 9, 1814.
9. Joshua Barney to William Jones, June 3, 1814.
10. Barney, *Biographical Memoir* (1832), p. 257.
11. Ibid., p. 299.
12. Ibid., p. 258.
13. Pack, *The Man Who Burned the White House* (1987), p. 173.
14. William Jones to Joshua Barney, June 10, 1814.
15. William Jones to Joshua Barney, June 12, 1814.
16. Barney, *Biographical Memoir* (1832), p. 260.
17. Joshua Barney to Louis Barney, June 27, 1814.
18. Ibid.
19. Powell, *Richard Rush* (1942), p. 38.
20. Ibid., p. 33.
21. James Madison, quoted in letter of Richard Rush to John Adams, July 11, 1814.
22. Richard Rush to John Adams, March 21, 1814.
23. Powell, *Richard Rush* (1942), p. 7; Richard Rush to John Adams, May 20, 1814.
24. James Madison to Thomas Jefferson, August 17, 1812.
25. Richard Rush narrative, October 15, 1814, in *American State Papers,* 13th Congress, 3rd Session, Military Affairs, vol. 1, p. 541.
26. Ibid.

27. Ibid.
28. *National Intelligencer*, July 1, 1814.
29. Powell, *Richard Rush* (1942), p. 44.
30. Armstrong quoted in Lossing, *Pictorial Field-Book* (1869), p. 918, fn. 1.
31. "William Jones narrative," October 31, 1814, in *American State Papers*, 13th Congress, 3rd Session, Military Affairs, vol. 1, p. 540.
32. "John Armstrong narrative," October 17, 1814, in *American State Papers*, 13th Congress, 3rd Session, Military Affairs, vol 1, p. 538.
33. Brant, *James Madison*, vol. 6 (1961), p. 270.

Chapter 4

1. Clark, *Life and Letters of Dolly Madison* (1914), p. iii.
2. Albert to Hannah Gallatin, January 22, 1801, quoted in Mannix, "Albert Gallatin in Washington, 1801–1813" (1971–72), p. 61.
3. Mannix, "Albert Gallatin in Washington, 1801–1813" (1971–72), p. 69.
4. Roberts, *Memoirs of a Senator from Pennsylvania* (1938), p. 239.
5. Hannah Gallatin to Dolley Madison, August 15, 1813.
6. Dolley Madison to Hannah Gallatin, July 28, 1814.
7. Dolley Madison to John Payne Todd, August 6, 1814.
8. "Narrative of William Winder," September 26, 1814, in *American State Papers*, House of Representatives, 13th Congress, 3rd Session, Military Affairs, vol. 1, p. 552.
9. Latimer, *1812: War with America* (2007), p. 145.
10. William Winder to John Armstrong, July 9, 1814.
11. Alderman and Common Council of the City of Washington to James Madison, July 18, 1814.
12. John P. Van Ness to James Madison, July 28, 1814.
13. Lossing, *Pictorial Field-Book* (1869), p. 919, fn. 3.
14. Footner, *Sailor of Fortune* (1940), p. 246.
15. Joshua Barney to William Jones, July 21, 1814.
16. Joshua Barney to William Jones, July 24, 1814.
17. William Jones to Joshua Barney, July 26, 1814.
18. Joshua Barney to William Jones, August 1, 1814, and August 4, 1814.
19. Joshua Barney to William Jones, August 1, 1814.
20. James Monroe to James Madison, August 5, 1814.
21. James Madison to the War Department, August 13, 1814.

22. For a detailed discussion of this brouhaha, see Brant, *James Madison*, vol. 6, (1961), pp. 260–61, 264–76.
23. John Stuart Skinner to James Madison, August 13, 1814.
24. James Monroe to R. M. Johnson, November 13, 1814, in *American State Papers*, 13th Congress, 3rd Session, Military Affairs, vol. 1, p. 536.
25. William Jones to Joshua Barney, August 19, 1814.

Chapter 5

1. Certain of the details of the British encampment have been drawn from [Gleig], *A Narrative of the Campaigns of the British Army at Washington, Baltimore, and New Orleans* (1821).
2. Hines, *Early Recollections of Washington City* (1866), p. 15.
3. James Monroe to James Madison, August 20, 1814.
4. James Monroe to James Madison, August 21, 1814.
5. Ibid.
6. James Monroe to William Winder, August 21, 1814.
7. "Narrative of William Winder," September 26, 1814, in *American State Papers*, House of Representatives, 13th Congress, 3rd Session, Military Affairs, vol. 1, p. 555.
8. "Report of R. M. Johnson," in *American State Papers*, House of Representatives, 13th Congress, 3rd Session, Military Affairs, vol. 1, p. 527.
9. Wilkinson, *Memoirs of My Own Times*, vol. 1 (1816), p. 735.
10. James Madison to James Monroe, August 21, 1814.
11. General W. Smith to R. M. Johnson, October 6, 1814, in *American State Papers*, House of Representatives, 13th Congress, 3rd Session, Military Affairs, vol. 1, p. 563.
12. George Cockburn to Alexander Cochrane, August 22, 1814.
13. *National Intelligencer*, August 22, 1814.
14. Louis Sérurier to Charles Talleyrand, August 22, 1814.
15. James Madison to James Monroe, August 22, 1814.
16. James Madison to Dolley Madison, November 6, 1805.
17. Dolley to James Madison, October 26, 1805.
18. Dolley Madison to Lucy Payne Washington Todd, August 23–24, 1814.
19. William Miller, quoted in McNamara, "Charles Carroll of Belle Vue" (1980), p. 5.

20. Williams, *History of the Invasion and Capture of Washington* (1857), p. 175.
21. "Narrative of William Winder," September 26, 1814, in *American State Papers*, House of Representatives, 13th Congress, 3rd Session, Military Affairs, vol. 1, p. 555.
22. Jennings, *A Colored Man's Reminiscences of James Madison* (1865), p. 51.
23. Barney, *Biographical Memoir* (1832), p. 264.
24. James Madison to Dolley Madison, August 23, 1814.
25. Benjamin Oden quoted in Brant, *James Madison,* vol. 6, (1961), p. 294.
26. George Peter to J. S. Williams, May 24, 1854, in Williams, *History of the Invasion and Capture of Washington* (1857), p. 360.
27. McKenney, *Memoirs, Official and Personal* (1973), p. 45.

Chapter 6

1. Harriet Martineau, *Retrospect of Western Travel* (1838), quoted in Clark, *Life and Letters of Dolly Madison* (1914), p. 265.
2. *The Port Folio*, fourth series, vol. 5, no. 22, February 1818, p. 91.
3. Benjamin Henry Latrobe to Christian Latrobe, December 4, 1808.
4. Fazio and Snedon, "Benjamin Latrobe and Thomas Jefferson Redesign the President's House," *White House History* (2000), p. 45.
5. Catherine Mitchell to Margaretta A. Miller, January 2, 1811.
6. Hugh Finlay invoice of September 16, 1809, quoted in Klapthor, *Benjamin Latrobe and Dolley Madison Decorate the White House* (1965), p. 158.
7. Irving quoted by R. L. Raley, "Interior Design by Benjamin Henry Latrobe for the President's House," *Antiques* (1959), p. 571.
8. James Madison to Dolley Madison, August 23, 1814.
9. Anna Cutts to Dolley Madison, August [23?], 1814.
10. *American State Papers*, Miscellaneous, vol. 2, p. 245.
11. *American State Papers*, Miscellaneous, vol. 2, p. 255.
12. Stephen Pleasonton to William Winder, August 7, 1848, in Hildt, "Letters Relating to the Capture of Washington" (1907), p. 65.
13. Quoted in Lloyd, *The Scorching of Washington* (1974), p. 158.
14. Louis Sérurier to Charles Talleyrand, August 22, 1814.
15. James Madison, "Memorandum," August 29, 1814.
16. "Narrative of William Winder," September 26, 1814, in *American State Papers*, House of Representatives, 13th Congress, 3rd Session, Military Affairs, vol. 1, p. 556.

17. "Mr. John Law's statement," November 10, 1814, in *American State Papers*, 13th Congress, 3rd Session, Military Affairs, vol. 1, p. 585.
18. "Captain Burch's statement," October 12, 1814, in *American State Papers*, 13th Congress, 3rd Session, Military Affairs, vol. 1, p. 574.
19. "Narrative of William Winder," September 26, 1814, in *American State Papers*, House of Representatives, 13th Congress, 3rd Session, Military Affairs, vol. 1, p. 557.
20. "Narrative of William Winder," September 26, 1814, in *American State Papers*, House of Representatives, 13th Congress, 3rd Session, Military Affairs, vol. 1, pp. 556–57.
21. "Dr. [Hanson] Catlett's statement", in *American State Papers*, House of Representatives, 13th Congress, 3rd Session, Military Affairs, vol. 1, p. 584.
22. Richard Rush to R. M. Johnson, in *American State Papers*, 13th Congress, 3rd Session, Military Affairs, vol. 1, p. 542.
23. "Narrative of General Winder," September 26, 1814, in *Annals of Congress*, 13th Congress, 3rd Session, p. 1615.
24. James Madison, "Memorandum," August 29, 1814.
25. "Letter of General Armstrong," October 17, 1814, in *Annals of Congress*, 13th Congress, 3rd Session, p. 1567.
26. James Madison, "Memorandum," August 29, 1814.
27. Dolley Madison to Lucy Payne Washington Todd, August 23–24, 1814.
28. Eleanor Jones to Dolley Madison, August 23, 1814.
29. Thornton, *Diary of Mrs. William Thornton* (1916), p. 175.
30. McCormick, John H. "The First Master of Ceremonies of the White House" (1904), pp. 170–94; Dolley Madison to Lucy Payne Washington Todd, August 23–24, 1814.
31. Gerry, *Diary* (1927), pp. 180–81.
32. Benjamin Henry Latrobe to Dolley Madison, April 21, 1809.
33. Dolley Madison to Hannah Gallatin, August 20, 1814; Dolley Madison to Lucy Payne Washington Todd, August 23–24, 1814.
34. Dolley Madison to Mary Latrobe, December 3, 1814.

Chapter 7

1. Tobias E. Stansbury to R. M. Johnson, November 16, 1814, in *American State Papers*, 13th Congress, 3rd Session, Military Affairs, vol. 1, p. 561.

2. James Monroe to R. M. Johnson, November 13, 1814, in *American State Papers*, 13th Congress, 3rd Session, Military Affairs, vol. 1, p. 536.
3. William Simmons to R. M. Johnson, November 28, 1814, in *American State Papers*, 13th Congress, 3rd Session, Military Affairs, vol. 1, p. 596.
4. William Tatham to John Armstrong, July 2, 10, and 13, 1814, cited in Stagg, *Mr. Madison's War* (1983), p. 412–13.
5. James Madison, "Memorandum," August 24, 1814; John Armstrong to R. M. Johnson, in *American State Papers,* 13th Congress, 3rd Session, Military Affairs, vol. 1, p. 539.
6. Ingersoll, *Historical Sketch of the Second War* (1849), p. 173.
7. Joshua Barney to William Jones, August 29, 1814, in *American State Papers,* 13th Congress, 3rd Session, Military Affairs, vol. 1, p. 579.
8. Richard Rush to George Campbell, November 2, 1814.
9. Ingersoll, *Historical Sketch of the Second War* (1849), p. 173.
10. *A Narrative of the Battle of Bladensburg* (1814), p. 5.
11. Williams, *History of the Invasion and Capture of Washington* (1857), p. 150.
12. Gleig, *A Subaltern in America* (1833), p. 67.
13. James Monroe to R. M. Johnson, November 13, 1814, in *American State Papers*, 13th Congress, 3rd Session, Military Affairs, vol. 1, p. 537.
14. "Mr. John Law's statement," November 10, 1814, in *American State Papers,* 13th Congress, 3rd Session, Military Affairs, vol. 1, p. 586.
15. Joseph Sterett to R. M. Johnson, November 22, 1814, in *American State Papers*, 13th Congress, 3rd Session, Military Affairs, vol. 1, p. 579.
16. "Captain Burch's statement," October 12, 1814, in *American State Papers,* 13th Congress, 3rd Session, Military Affairs, vol. 1, p. 574.
17. [Gleig], *A Narrative of the Campaigns of the British Army at Washington, Baltimore, and New Orleans* (1821), p. 121.
18. Scott, *Recollections of a Naval Life*, vol. 3 (1834), p. 286.
19. [Gleig], *A Narrative of the Campaigns of the British Army at Washington, Baltimore, and New Orleans* (1821), p. 122.
20. James Madison, "Memorandum," August 24, 1814.
21. Scott, *Recollections of a Naval Life,* vol. 3 (1834), p. 288.
22. *A Narrative of the Battle of Bladensburg* (1814), p. 8.
23. Barker, *Incidents in Life of Jacob Barker* (1855), p. 121.
24. William Pinkney to R. M. Johnson, November 16, 1814, in *American State Papers*, 13th Congress, 3rd Session, Military Affairs, vol. 1, pp. 573–74.

25. "Captain Burch's statement," October 12, 1814, in *American State Papers*, 13th Congress, 3rd Session, Military Affairs, vol. 1, p. 574.
26. Tobias E. Stansbury to R. M. Johnson, November 16, 1814, in *American State Papers*, 13th Congress, 3rd Session, Military Affairs, vol. 1, p. 562.
27. Morriss, *Cockburn and the British Navy in Transition* (1997), p. 104.
28. Scott, *Recollections of a Naval Life*, vol. 3 (1834), pp. 288–89.
29. Jacint Lavall to R. M. Johnson, November 3, 1812, in *American State Papers*, 13th Congress, 3rd Session, Military Affairs, vol. 1, p. 570.
30. James Madison, "Memorandum," August 24, 1814.
31. Barney, *Biographical Memoir* (1832), p. 265.
32. Joshua Barney to William Jones, August 29, 1814, in *American State Papers*, 13th Congress, 3rd Session, Military Affairs, vol. 1, p. 579.
33. Ibid., p. 580.
34. Ibid.
35. Ball, *Slavery in the United States* (1936), p. 362.
36. Joshua Barney to William Jones, August 29, 1814, in *American State Papers*, 13th Congress, 3rd Session, Military Affairs, vol. 1, p. 580.
37. Scott, *Recollections of a Naval Life* (1834), p. 291.
38. Barney, *Biographical Memoir* (1832), p. 267.
39. Dolley Madison to Lucy Payne Washington Todd, August 23–24, 1814.
40. Dolley Madison to Mary Latrobe, December 3, 1814.
41. Jennings, *A Colored Man's Reminiscences of James Madison* (1865), p. 52.
42. George Washington to John Greenwood, January 20, 1797.
43. Robert De Peyster to Dolley Madison, Februrary 25, 1848.
44. Jacob Barker to Daniel Carroll, February 8, 1843, reprinted in Barker, *Incidents in the Life of Jacob Barker, of New Orleans, Louisiana* (1855), p. 113.
45. Ibid., p. 114.
46. Louis Sérurier to Charles Talleyrand, August 27, 1814.

Chapter 8

1. Anonymous letter to the *Federal Republican*, quoted in Singleton, *The Story of the White House* (1907), p. 77.
2. King, "The Battle of Bladensburg" (1885), p. 446.
3. Tuckerman, *The Life of John Pendleton Kennedy* (1871), p. 201.
4. Scott, *Recollections of a Naval Life*, vol. 3 (1834), p. 295.
5. George Cockburn to Alexander F. I. Cochrane, August 27, 1814.

6. Shiner, *The Diary of Michael Shiner Relating to the History of the Washington Navy Yard 1813–1869* (2007), p. 6.
7. Cockburn, quoted in Morriss, *Cockburn and the British Navy in Transition* (1997), p. 92. See also Morriss's discussion of Cockburn's honor code, p. 10.
8. Scott, *Recollections of a Naval Life*, vol. 3 (1834), p. 300.
9. Thomas Tingey to William Jones, August 27, 1814.
10. Smith, *The Autobiography of Lieutenant General Sir Harry Smith* (1901), p. 200.
11. Scott, *Recollections of a Naval Life*, vol. 3 (1834), pp. 300–301.
12. Shiner, *The Diary of Michael Shiner Relating to the History of the Washington Navy Yard 1813–1869* (2007), p. 7.
13. Scott, *Recollections of a Naval Life*, vol. 3 (1834), p. 301.
14. Ibid., p. 303.
15. Ibid., p. 304.
16. Smith, *The Autobiography of Lieutenant-General Sir Harry Smith*, vol. 1, (1901), p. 200.
17. [Gleig], *A Narrative of the Campaigns of the British Army at Washington, Baltimore, and New Orleans* (1821), pp. 134–35.
18. Quoted in Latimer, *1812: War with America* (2007), p. 318.
19. Louis Sérurier to Charles Talleyrand, August 27, 1814.
20. Smith, *The First Forty Years of Washington Society* (1906), p. 111.
21. [Gleig], *A Narrative of the Campaigns of the British Army at Washington, Baltimore, and New Orleans* (1821), p. 132.
22. Mary Stockton Hunter to Susan Stockton Cuthbert, August 30, 1814.
23. Thornton, *Diary of Mrs. William Thornton* (1916), p. 175.
24. Alden, *The Flights of the Madisons* (1974).
25. Ingersoll, *Historical Sketch of the Second War*, vol. 2, (1849), p. 189.
26. William Thornton, "Letter to the Public," dated August 30, 1814, published in the *National Intelligencer*, September 7, 1814.
27. Lord, *Dawn's Early Light* (1972), p. 175.
28. William Thornton, "Letter to the Public," dated August 30, 1814, published in the *National Intelligencer*, September 7, 1814.
29. Scott, *Recollections of a Naval Life*, vol. 3 (1834), p. 312.

Chapter 9

1. Smith, *The First Forty Years of Washington Society* (1906), p. 115.
2. Richard Rush to John S. Williams, in Williams, *History of the Invasion and Capture of Washington* (1857), pp. 274–75.

3. Richard Rush to Charles J. Ingersoll, September 8, 1815.
4. Smith, *The First Forty Years of Washington Society* (1906), p. 105.
5. Pitch, *Burning of Washington* (1998), p. 163.
6. Samuel T. Dyson to John Armstrong, August 29, 1814, in *American State Papers*, House of Representatives, 13th Congress, 3rd Session, Military Affairs, vol. 1, p. 591.
7. Dunlap, *History of the Rise and Progress of the Arts of Design in the United States*, vol. 1 (1834), p. 336.
8. Thornton, *Diary of Mrs. William Thornton* (1916), p. 177.
9. *National Intelligencer*, September 7, 1814.
10. Monroe, "J.M.'s Notes Respecting the burning City in 1814," in *Writings*, vol. 4, (1901), p. 374.
11. Lord, *Dawn's Early Light* (1972), p. 216.
12. Smith, *What Is Gentility?* (1828), p. 154. Though nominally a novel, this anonymous work was written by Margaret Bayard Smith, wife of Samuel Harrison Smith, founder and former editor of the *National Intelligencer.* Mrs. Smith was a regular guest of the Madisons and wrote from firsthand experience and observation.
13. James Monroe, "J.M.'s Notes Respecting the burning City in 1814," in *Writings*, vol. 5 (1901), p. 373–74. The words "The President forbade the measure" do not appear in the printed edition of Monroe's "Notes" but are in the signed original in the Library of Congress.
14. Thornton in *National Intelligencer*, September 7, 1814.
15. Monroe, "J.M.'s Notes Respecting the burning City in 1814," in *Writings*, vol. 5 (1901), p. 374.
16. Thornton, *Diary of Mrs. William Thornton* (1916), pp. 177–78.
17. Ingersoll, *Historical Sketch of the Second War*, vol. 2 (1849), pp. 208–9.
18. James Madison to Dolley Madison, August 27, 1814.
19. Dolley Madison to Mary Elizabeth Hazelhurst Latrobe, December 3, 1814, reprinted in Clark, *Life and Letters of Dolly Madison* (1914), pp. 166–67.
20. Smith, *The First Forty Years of Washington Society* (1906), p. 109.
21. James Madison to Dolley Madison, August 28, 1814.
22. Dolley Madison to Edward Coles, May 13, 1813; Allgor, *A Perfect Union* (2006), p. 311.
23. Margaret Bayard Smith to Margaret Bayard Boyd, May 28, 1801.
24. Smith, *The First Forty Years of Washington Society* (1906), p. 110.

25. Thornton, *Diary of Mrs. William Thornton* (1916), p. 178.
26. Ibid., p. 179.

Chapter 10

1. Anonymous handbill published at Baltimore, September 17, 1814. Reproduced in Weybright, *Spangled Banner* (1935), p. 151.
2. Edward Coles to Hugh B. Grigsby, December 23, 1854.
3. James Monroe to William Winder, September 21, 1814.
4. John Barnes to Thomas Jefferson, August 29, 1814.
5. James Monroe to Joseph Nicholson, September 21, 1814.
6. Ingersoll, "A Visit to Mr. Madison at Montpelier, May 2, 1836" (1836).
7. McKenney, *Memoirs, Official and Personal* (1973), pp. 46–47.
8. James Madison, "Memorandum," August 29, 1814.
9. Margaret Bayard Smith to Jane Kirkpatrick, August 1814.
10. Catherine E. Rush to Richard Rush, September 3, 1814.
11. Clark, *Life and Letters of Dolly Madison* (1914), pp. 197–98.
12. Benjamin Henry Latrobe to Thomas Jefferson, July 12, 1815.
13. William Jones to James Madison, September 1, 1814.
14. Thornton, *Diary of Mrs. William Thornton* (1916), pp. 179, 180.
15. William Wirt to Elizabeth Wirt, October 14 [and after], 1814.
16. Margaret Bayard Smith to Jane Kirkpatrick, August 1814.
17. Richard Rush to James Monroe, August 28, 1814.
18. Alexander Cochrane to James Monroe, August 18, 1814, in *American State Papers*, Foreign Relations, 13th Congress, 3rd Session, vol. 3, p. 693.
19. *Niles Register*, September 3, 1814.
20. James Monroe to Alexander Cochrane, September 6, 1814.
21. Roger Taney cited in Weybright, *Spangled Banner* (1935), p. 110.
22. George Armistead to Samuel Smith, quoted in Lord, *Dawn's Early Light* (1972), p. 274.
23. Scott, *Recollections of a Naval Life*, vol. 3 (1834), p. 333.
24. [Gleig], *A Narrative of the Campaigns of the British Army at Washington, Baltimore, and New Orleans* (1821), p. 173.
25. George Cockburn to Alexander Cochrane, September 15, 1814.
26. Scott, *Recollections of a Naval Life*, vol. 3 (1834), p. 338.
27. [Gleig], *A Narrative of the Campaigns of the British Army at Washington, Baltimore, and New Orleans* (1821), p. 177–81.

28. George Armistead to James Monroe, September 24, 1814.
29. Roger Brooke Taney to Henry V. D. Johns, in Francis S[cott] Key, *Poems of the Late Francis S. Key* (1857), p. 25.
30. Ibid., p. 26.
31. *Baltimore Patriot and Evening Advertiser*, September 20, 1814.
32. William Wirt to Elizabeth Wirt, September 19, 1814.
33. *Annals of Congress*, House of Representatives, 13th Congress, 3rd Session, p. 313.
34. James Madison's Sixth Annual Message, September 20, 1814.
35. Skaggs, *Thomas Macdonough: Master of Command* (2003), p. 128.
36. James, *The Naval History of Great Britain* (1837), p. 344.
37. Roosevelt, *The Naval War of 1812* (1882), pp. 392–93.
38. Ibid., pp. 392–95.
39. Fitch, "Incident at the Battle of Lake Champlain" (1959), p. 6.
40. Thomas Macdonough to William Jones, September 11, 1814.
41. Dolley Madison to Mary Latrobe, December 3, 1814.
42. Tayloe, *Our Neighbors on La Fayette Square* (1872), p. 9.
43. Calvert, *Mistress of Riversdale* (1991), p. 334.
44. Bill cited in Hunt-Jones, *Dolley and the "great little Madison"* (1977), p. 51.
45. *Washington City Gazette,* September 19, 1814, cited in Arnett, *Mrs. James Madison: The Incomparable Dolley* (1972), pp. 249–50.
46. George Hadfield, "Proposals and Estimates," October 3, 1814, cited in Hunt-Jones, *Dolley and the "great little Madison"* (1977), p. 50.
47. September 26, 1814, in *Annals of Congress*, House of Representatives, 13th Congress, 3rd Session, pp. 311–12.
48. Ibid., pp. 341 ff.
49. *Annual Register for 1814* and *London Statesman* quoted in Williams, *History of the Invasion and Capture of Washington* (1857), pp. 254–45.
50. Thomas Jefferson to Lucy Ludwell Paradise, June 1, 1789.
51. Thomas Jefferson to Samuel H. Smith, September 21, 1814.
52. William Wirt to Elizabeth Wirt, October 14[and after], 1814.
53. Richard Rush to John Adams, October 23, 1814.
54. William Wirt to Elizabeth Wirt, October 14 [and after], 1814.
55. James Madison to Wilson Cary Nicholas, November 26, 1814. Italics added.
56. James Madison's Sixth Annual Message, September 20, 1814.

Chapter 11

1. George Ticknor to Elisha Ticknor, January 17, 1815, in Ticknor, *Life, Letters,* vol. 1 (1909), p. 28.
2. Tyack, *George Ticknor* (1967), p. 35.
3. *Daily National Intelligencer*, January 13, 1815.
4. Briefing paper drafted by Alexander Cochrane, April 27–28, 1812, cited in Latimer, *1812: War with America* (2007), p. 370.
5. Smith, *The Autobiography of Lieutenant-General Sir Harry Smith* (1901), vol. 1, p. 247.
6. George Ticknor to Elisha Ticknor, January 17, 1815.
7. Ticknor, *Life, Letters,* vol. 1 (1909), pp. 30, 347.
8. *National Intelligencer*, January 10, 1815.
9. Dolley Madison to Hannah Gallatin, January 14, 1815.
10. Andrew Jackson report of December 26, 1814.
11. Wheater, *Historical Record* (1875), p. 145.
12. *Daily National Intelligencer*, February 6, 1815.
13. Thomas Baker Johnson to Dolley Madison, January 19, 1815.
14. [Gleig], *A Narrative of the Campaigns of the British Army at Washington, Baltimore, and New Orleans* (1821), p. 330.
15. Smith, *The Autobiography of Lieutenant-General Sir Harry Smith*, vol. 1, (1901), p. 247.
16. [Gleig], *A Narrative of the Campaigns of the British Army at Washington, Baltimore, and New Orleans* (1821), pp. 300–301, 336.
17. Thomas Baker Johnson to Dolley Payne Todd Madison, January 19, 1814.
18. Bishop John Carroll, quoted in Warner, *At Peace with Their Neighbors; Catholics and Catholicism in the National Capital, 1787–1860* (1994), p. 247, fn. 20.
19. The chambermaid anecdote was recounted in De Witt Clinton's diary, cited in Dangerfield, *The Era of Good Feelings* (1952), p. 10.
20. James Bayard to Andrew Bayard, August 6, 1814, reprinted in *Letters relating to the Negotiations at Ghent, 1812–1814* in *The American Historical Review,* vol. 20, no. 1 (October 1914), p. 113.
21. Adams, *Memoirs of John Quincy Adams* (1874–1877), vol. 3, p. 51.
22. Secretary of State James Monroe to the Peace Commissioners at Ghent, June 27, 1814, in *American State Papers*, Foreign Relations, vol. 3, p. 704.
23. Dangerfield, *The Era of Good Feelings* (1952), p. 5.

24. Adams, *Memoirs of John Quincy Adams* (1874–1877), vol. 3, p. 21.
25. American Commissioners to British Commissioners, August 24, 1814, in *American State Papers*, Foreign Relations, vol. 3, p. 713.
26. McNamara, Robert F., "Charles Carroll of Belle Vue, Co-Founder of Rochester," in *Rochester History*, vol. 42, no. 4 (October 1980), p. 5.
27. Adams, *Memoirs of John Quincy Adams* (1874–1877), vol. 3, p. 136.
28. Ibid., pp. 32, 87.
29. Henry Clay to William Crawford, October 17, 1814.
30. William Crawford to John Quincy Adams, November 10, 1814.
31. Wellington to Castlereagh, November 9, 1814.
32. Adams, *Memoirs of John Quincy Adams* (1874–1877), vol. 3, p. 21.
33. John Quincy Adams, *Memoirs of John Quincy Adams* (1874–1877), vol. 3, (1874), p. 61.
34. John Quincy Adams to Louisa Catherine Adams, December 16, 1814.
35. Ibid.
36. Adams, *Memoirs of John Quincy Adams* (1874–1877), vol. 3, pp. 125–27.
37. Jonathan Roberts, *Memoirs* (1938), pp. 373, 377–78.
38. Dolley Madison to Hannah Gallatin, December 1814.
39. Henry Clay to James Monroe, December 26, 1814.
40. The quotations from Joseph Gales, originally published in the *National Intelligencer* (August 25, 1849), were reprinted in Ingersoll, *History of the Second War* (1853), vol. 2, pp. 63–66.
41. Though credited by Ingersoll in *History of the Second War* (1853) vol. 2, pp. 64–65, to Joseph Gales, the description here and after of Dolley Madison was the work of Margaret Bayard Smith. The story of the celebration at the Tayloe house, the details of which were recounted some decades after by several of the participants, differ as to whether the event unfolded on the evening the treaty arrived or the following day after it had been presented to Congress.
42. Jennings, *A Colored Man's Reminiscences of James Madison* (1865), p. 54.
43. Ingersoll, *History of the Second War*, vol. 2 (1853), p. 65.

Epilogue

1. Thomas Jefferson to Pierre-Samuel du Pont de Nemours, March 2, 1809.
2. James K. Paulding quoted in Ketcham, "An Unpublished Sketch of James Madison by James K. Paulding" (1959), p. 435.

3. *Columbian Centennial*, July 12, 1817.
4. John Randolph, *Annals of Congress*, 14th Congress, 2nd Session, p. 804.
5. Adair, "James Madison's Autobiography" (1945), p. 203.
6. Dolley Madison to Eliza Collins Lee, April 12, 1819; Dolley Madison to Elizabeth Coles, April 8, 1831.
7. Dolley Madison to Sarah Coles Stevenson, February 1820.
8. James Madison to Jared Sparks, June 1, 1831.
9. Carlo Vidua, quoted in Ketcham, *James Madison* (1971), p. 621.
10. James Madison to Francis Wright, September 1, 1825.
11. James Madison to Charles J. Ingersoll, January 4, 1818.
12. James Madison to Henry Wheaton, February 26 and 27, 1827.
13. James Madison to the legislature of Massachusetts, May 7, 1815.
14. Adair, "James Madison's Autobiography" (1945), pp. 191–209.
15. James Madison to Benjamin Waterhouse, July 13, 1825; Adair, "James Madison's Autobiography" (1945), p. 207.
16. James Bayard to Richard Henry Bayard, December 26, 1814.
17. Albert Gallatin to Matthew Lyon, May 7, 1816, quoted in Gallatin, *Writings* (1879), vol. 1, p. 700.
18. John Adams to Thomas Jefferson, February 2, 1817.
19. Louis Sérurier to Charles Talleyrand, February 21, 1815.
20. Francis Scott Key, quoted in Weybright, *Spangled Banner* (1935), p. 57.
21. Ingersoll, "A Visit to Mr. Madison at Montpelier, May 2, 1836."
22. Ibid.
23. *A Colored Man's Reminiscences of James Madison* (1865), p. 55.
24. Dolley Madison to Eliza Collins Lee, July 26, 1836.
25. Curtis, *Life of Daniel Webster* (1870), vol. 1, p. 224.
26. Jennings, *A Colored Man's Reminiscences of James Madison* (1865), p. 54.
27. Dolley Madison to Robert G. L. De Peyster, February 1, 1848.
28. James Madison, "Advice to My Country," 1834.
29. Paulding, *Literary Life of James K. Paulding* (1867), p. 75.

BIBLIOGRAPHY

Primary Sources

Adams, John Quincy. *Memoirs of John Quincy Adams, Comprising Portions of His Diary from 1795 to 1848.* Charles Francis Adams, ed. 12 volumes. Philadelphia: J.B. Lippincott & Co., 1874–1877.

Bagot, Mary. "'Exile in Yankeeland': The Journal of Mary Bagot, 1816–1819." David Hosford, ed. *Records of the Columbia Historical Society of Washington,* vol. 51 (1984), pp. 30–50.

Ball, Charles. *Slavery in the United States: A Narrative of the Life and Adventures of Charles Ball, a Black Man.* Detroit, MI: Negro History Press, 1970. Reprint of 1836 edition.

Barker, Jacob. *Incidents in the Life of Jacob Barker, of New Orleans, Louisiana.* Washington, 1855.

Barney, Mary, ed. *A Biographical Memoir of the Late Commodore Joshua Barney.* Boston: Gray and Bowen, 1832.

Bayard, James A. *Papers of James A. Bayard, 1796–1815,* Elizabeth Donnan, ed. In

American Historical Association, *General Report, 1913*, vol. 2. Washington, DC., 1915.

Beaumont, William. *William Beaumont's Formative Years: Two Early Notebooks, 1811–1821.* Genevieve Miller, ed. New York: Henry Schuman, 1946.

Booth, Mordecai. "The Capture of Washington in 1814." Ray W. Irwin, ed., in *Americana*, vol. 28, no. 1 (January 1934), pp. 7–27.

Bunnell, David C. *The Travels and Adventures of David C. Bunnell.* Palmyra, NY: J.H. Bartles, 1831.

Calvert, Rosalie Stier. *Mistress of Riversdale: The Plantation Letters of Rosalie Stier Calvert, 1795–1821.* Margaret Law Callcott, ed. Baltimore, MD: Johns Hopkins University Press, 1991.

Clay, Henry. *The Papers of Henry Clay*, James F. Hopkins, ed. Vol. 1. Lexington: University of Kentucky Press, 1959.

Coles, Edward. "Letters of Edward Coles." In *The William and Mary Quarterly*, second series, vol. 7, no. 3 (Jul. 1927), pp. 158–73.

Cooper, James Fenimore. *Ned Myers; or, a Life before the Mast.* New York: AMS Press, 2009. Reprint of 1843 edition.

Crowninshield, Mary Boardman. *Letters of Mary Boardman Crowninshield, 1815–1816.* Francis Boardman Crowninshield, ed. Cambridge, MA: The Riverside Press, 1905.

Fearon, Henry Bradshaw. *Sketches of America: A Narrative of a Journey.* London: Longman, Hurst, Rees, Orme, and Brown, 1819.

Few, Frances, in Noble E. Cunningham Jr., "The Diary of Frances Few, 1808-1809," in *The Journal of Southern History*, vol. 29, no. 3 (Aug. 1963), pp. 345–61.

Fitch, A. "Incident of the Battle of Lake Champlain." *Vermont Historical Society Notes and News*, vol. 2 (Sept. 1959).

Foster, Augustus John. *Jeffersonian America: Notes on the United States of America, Collected in the Years 1805–6–7 and 11–12.* Richard Beale Davis, ed. San Marino, CA: Huntington Library, 1954.

Gallatin, Albert. *Writings of Albert Gallatin.* Henry Adams, ed. 3 vols. Philadelphia: J.B. Lippincott & Co., 1879.

Gerry, Elbridge, Jr. *The Diary of Elbridge Gerry, Jr.* New York: Brentano's, 1927.

Gleig, G[eorge]. R[obert]. *A Subaltern in America; Comprising the Narrative of the Campaigns of the British Army, at Baltimore, Washington, &c., &c., During the Late War.* Philadelphia: E.L. Carey & A. Hart, 1833.

[Gleig, George R., attrib.] *A Narrative of the Campaigns of the British Army, at*

Washington, Baltimore, and New Orleans, Under Generals Ross, Pakenham, & Lambert, in the Years 1814 and 1815; With Some Account of the Countries Visited, by an Officer, Who Served in the Expedition. Philadelphia: M. Carey & Sons, 1821.

Hambleton, Samuel. *Diary: 1813–1832.* Maryland Historical Society. N.p.

Hildt, John C. "Letters Relating to the Capture of Washington." *The South Atlantic Quarterly*, vol. 6 (1907), pp. 58–66.

Ingersoll, Charles J. "A Visit to Mr. Madison at Montpelier, May 2, 1836." *Washington Globe*, Aug. 6, 1836.

Jefferson, Thomas. *The Papers of Thomas Jefferson: Retirement Series.* 5 vols. Princeton, NJ: Princeton University Press, 2004–2008.

———. *Thomas Jefferson, Writings.* Merrill D. Peterson, ed. New York: The Library of America, 1984.

Latrobe, Benjamin Henry. *The Correspondence and Miscellaneous Papers of Benjamin Henry Latrobe*, John C. Van Horne, ed. vol. 3. New Haven: Yale University Press, 1988.

Lawrence, Richard Russell, ed. *The Mammoth Book of Eyewitness Naval Battles.* New York: Carroll & Graf Publishers, 2003.

Leech, Samuel. *A Voice from the Main Deck.* London: Chatham Publishing, 1999. Originally published 1843.

Madison, Dolley Payne. *The Papers of Dolley Madison Digital Edition.* Holly Shulman, ed. Charlottesville: University Press of Virginia, Rotunda, 2008. http://rotunda.upress.virginia.edu/founders/DYMN

———. *The Selected Letters of Dolley Payne Madison.* Mattern, David B., and Holly Shulman, eds. Charlottesville: University Press of Virginia, 2003.

[Madison, Dolley Payne.] *Memoirs and Letters of Dolly Madison, Wife of James Madison, President of the United States, ed. by her grand-niece* [Lucia B. Cutts]. Boston: Houghton, Mifflin and Company, 1886.

Madison, James. *A Biography in His Own Words.* Merrill D. Peterson, ed. 2 vols. New York: Newsweek, 1974.

———. *James Madison's "Advice to my country,"* David B. Mattern, ed. Charlottesville: University Press of Virginia, 1997.

———. "James Madison's Autobiography," Douglas Adair, ed., in *The William and Mary Quarterly*, 3rd series, vol. 2, no. 2 (Apr. 1945), pp. 191–209.

———. *Letters and Other Writings of James Madison.* 4 vols. Philadelphia: J.B. Lippincott & Co., 1865.

———. *The Papers of James Madison*, Robert A. Rutland et al., eds. Charlottesville: University of Virginia Press, 1983–2008.

———. *The Writings of James Madison*, Gaillard Hunt, ed. 9 vols. New York: G.P. Putnam's Sons, 1900–1910.

McKenney, Thomas L. *Memoirs, Official and Personal.* Lincoln: University of Nebraska Press, 1973.

[Mitchill, Catharine Akerly.] Sung, Carolyn Hoover. "Catharine Mitchill's Letters from Washington, 1806–1812." *Quarterly Journal of the Library of Congress*, vol. 34, no. 3 (July 1977), pp. 177–92.

[Mitchill, Samuel L.] "Dr. Mitchill's Letters from Washington: 1801–1813," in *Harper's New Monthly Magazine*, Apr. 1879, pp. 744–55.

Monroe, James. *The Writings of James Monroe.* Stanislaus Murry Hamilton, ed. 7 vols. New York, 1898–1903.

[Officer of General Smith's Staff.] *A Narrative of the Battle Bladensburg; in a Letter to Henry Banning, Esq.* N.p., 1814.

Paulding, James K[irke]. *The United States and England.* New York: A.H. Inskeep, 1815.

Paulding, William I. *The Literary Life of James K. Paulding.* New York: C. Scribner and Company, 1867.

Peter, Grace Dunlop. "Unpublished Letters of Dolly Madison to Anthony Morris Relating to the Nourse Family of the Highlands." In *Records of the Columbia Historical Society*, vols. 44–45 (1942–43), pp. 215–32.

Preston, William C. *The Reminiscences of William C. Preston.* Chapel Hill: University of North Carolina Press, 1933.

Quincy, Josiah. *Speeches Delivered in the Congress of the United States.* Edmund Quincy, ed. Boston: Little, Brown, and Company, 1874.

Roberts, Jonathan. "Memoirs of a Senator from Pennsylvania, 1771–1854." Philip S. Klein, ed. *Pennsylvania Magazine of History and Biography*, vol. 61 (1937), no. 4, pp. 446–52; vol. 62 (1938), no. 1, pp. 64–97; no. 2, pp. 213–48; no. 3, pp. 361–409; and no. 4, pp. 502–51.

Rush, Richard. *The Letters and Papers of Richard Rush.* Wilmington, DE: Scholarly Resources, 1980.

———. *Occasional Productions, Political, Diplomatic, and Miscellaneous.* Philadelphia: J.B. Lippincott & Co., 1860.

———. "Some Unpublished Correspondence of John Adams and Richard Rush, 1811–1816." *Pennsylvania Magazine of History and Biography*, vol. 60, no. 4

(Oct. 1936), pp. 419–54; vol. 61, no. 1 (Jan. 1937), pp. 26–53; and vol. 61, no. 2 (Apr. 1937), pp. 137–64.

Scott, James. *Recollections of a Naval Life.* 3 vols. London: Richard Bentley, 1834.

Scott, Winfield. *Memoirs of Lieut.-General Scott, L.L.D. Written by Himself.* New York: Sheldon & Company, 1864.

Shaw, Samuel. *The Journals of Major Samuel Shaw, the First American Consul at Canton.* Boston: W. Crosby and H.P. Nichols, 1847.

Shiner, Michael. *The Diary of Michael Shiner Relating to the History of the Washington Navy Yard 1813–1869.* John G. Sharp, ed. http://www.ibiblio.org/hyperwar/NHC/shiner/shiner_diary.htm, 2007

Smith, Harry G. W. *The Autobiography of Lieutenant General Sir Harry Smith*, G. C. Moore Smith, ed. London: J. Murray, 1901.

Smith, James Morton, ed. *The Republic of Letters: The Correspondence Between Thomas Jefferson and James Madison, 1776–1826.* 3 vols. New York: W. W. Norton & Co., 1995.

Smith, Margaret Bayard. "'A Transcript of My Heart': The Unpublished Diaries of Margaret Bayard Smith," Cassandra Good, *Washington History*, vol. 17, no. 1 (Fall/Winter 2005), pp. 66–82.

———. *The First Forty Years of Washington Society.* New York: Charles Scribner's Sons, 1906.

———. "Mrs. Madison." In *The National Portrait Gallery of Distinguished Americans*, James B. Longacre and James Herring, eds. Vol. 3. New York: Herman Bancroft, 1836.

[Smith, Margaret Bayard, attrib.] *What Is Gentility? A Moral Tale.* Washington, D.C.: Pishey Thompson, 1828.

[Sparks, Jared.] "After-Dinner Anecdotes of James Madison: Excerpt from Jared Sparks' Journal for 1829–1831." "CC" [Mary Lucille] Proctor, ed. *Virginia Magazine of History and Biography*, vol. 60, no. 2 (1952), pp. 255–65.

Thornton, Anna Maria. *Diary of Mrs. William Thornton, 1800–1863.* Worthington C. Ford, ed. Vol. 10 (1907). Washington, D.C.: Historical Society of Washington, D.C., pp. 88–226.

———. *Diary of Mrs. William Thornton. Capture of Washington by the British.* W. B. Bryan, ed. Vol. 19 (1916). *Records of the Columbian Historical Society of Washington, D.C.*, pp. 172–82.

Ticknor, George. *Life, Letters, and Journals of George Ticknor.* 2 vols. Boston: Houghton Mifflin Company, 1909.

Trowbridge, Francis Bacon. *The Trowbridge Genealogy.* New Haven, CT: 1908.

Tuckerman, Henry Theodore. *The Life of John Pendleton Kennedy.* New York: G.P. Putnam's Sons, 1871.

[Watterson, George.] *A Wanderer in Washington.* Washington, D.C.: Washington Press, 1827.

[Watterson, George.] *Letters from Washington, on the Constitution and Laws; with Sketches of Some of the Prominent Public Characters of the United States. Written During the Winter of 1817–18. By a foreigner.* Washington, D.C.: Jacob Gideon, Junr., 1818.

Webster, Daniel. *The Papers of Daniel Webster: Correspondence.* Charles M. Wiltse, ed. Vol. 1. Hanover, NH: University Press of New England, 1974.

Wharton, Anne Hollingsworth. *Salons Colonial and Republican.* N.p.: Lippincott, 1900.

———. *Social Life in the Early Republic.* New York: Benjamin Blom, 1969. Reprint of 1902 edition.

Wilkinson, James. *Memoirs of My Own Times.* Vol. 1. Philadelphia: A. Small, 1816.

Wirt, William. *Memoirs of the Life of William Wirt, Attorney-General of the United States.* John P[endleton]. Kennedy, ed. 2 vols. Philadelphia: Blanchard and Lea, 1854.

———. *William Wirt Papers.* Maryland Historical Society, Baltimore.

Secondary Sources

Adams, Henry. *History of the United States of America During the Administrations of James Madison.* 2 vols. New York: Charles Scribner's Sons, 1890.

———. *History of the United States of America During the Administrations of Thomas Jefferson.* 2 vols. New York: Charles Scribner's Sons, 1889, 1890.

———. *The Life of Albert Gallatin.* Philadelphia: J.B. Lippincott & Co., 1879.

Alden, Robert Ames. *The Flights of the Madisons.* Fairfax, VA: Fairfax County Council of the Arts, 1974.

Allgor, Catherine. *Parlor Politics, In Which the Ladies of Washington Help Build a City and a Government.* Charlottesville: University Press of Virginia, 2000.

———. *Perfect Union: Dolley Madison and the Creation of the American Nation.* New York: Henry Holt & Co., 2006.

———. "Political Parties: First Ladies and Social Events in the Formation of the Federal Government." In *The Presidential Companion: Readings on the First Ladies*, Robert P. Watson and Anthony J. Eksterowicz, eds. 2nd edition. Columbia: University of South Carolina Press, 2006, pp. 35–53.

———. "'Queen Dolley' Saves Washington City." In *Washington History*, vol. 12, no. 1 (Spring/Summer 2000), pp. 54–69.

Allison, Robert J. *Stephen Decatur: American Naval Hero, 1779–1880*. Amherst: University of Massachusetts Press, 2005.

Altoff, Gerard T. *Among My Best Men: African-Americans and the War of 1812*. Put-in-Bay, OH: The Perry Group, 1996.

Ames, William E. "'The National Intelligencer': Washington's Leading Political Newspaper." In *Records of the Columbian Historical Society of Washington, D.C.*, 1966–1968, pp. 71–83.

Ammon, Harry. *James Monroe: The Quest for National Identity*. Charlottesville: University of Virginia Press, 1971.

Anthony, Carl Sferrazza. *First Ladies: The Saga of the Presidents' Wives and Their Power, 1789–1961*. New York: William Morrow & Co., Inc., 1990.

Anthony, Katharine. *Dolly Madison, Her Life and Times*. New York: Doubleday & Co., 1949.

Appleby, Joyce. *Inheriting the Revolution*. Cambridge, MA: Harvard University Press, 2000.

———. *Recollections of the Early Republic*. Boston: Northeastern University Press, 1997.

Arnett, Ethel Stephen. *Mrs. James Madison: The Incomparable Dolley*. Greensboro, NC: Piedmont Press, 1972.

Arnold, James Riehl. "The Battle of Bladensburg." In *Records of the Columbian Historical Society of Washington, D.C.*, vols. 27–28 (1937), pp. 145–68.

Barnes, James. *Naval Actions of the War of 1812*. New York: Harper & Brothers Publishers, 1896.

Barratt, Carrie Rebora, and Miles, Ellen G. *Gilbert Stuart*. New York: The Metropolitan Museum of Art, 2004.

Bell, Marian H. Graham. "Dr. William Thornton and His Essay on 'Teaching the Deaf, or Surd, and Consequently Dumb, to Speak,' 1793: Sketch of the Life of William Thornton." *Records of the Columbian Historical Society of Washington, D.C.*, vol. 20 (1917), pp. 225–36.

Belman, Laura Haines. *Dolley at Dumbarton*. Washington, D.C.: Dumbarton House/The National Society of the Colonial Dames of America, 1996.

Brant, Irving. *James Madison*. 6 vols. Indianapolis, IN: Bobbs-Merrill Co., Inc., 1941–1961.

Brighton, Ray. *The Checkered Career of Tobias Lear*. Portsmouth, NH: Portsmouth Marine Society, 1985.

Broke, Philip Bowes Vere. *Admiral Sir P.B.V. Broke, Bart., K.C.B., &c.: A Memoir.* Rev. J. G. Brighton, MD, ed. London: Sampson Low, Son, and Marston, 1866.

Bryan, Wilhelmus Bogart. *A History of the National Capital from its Foundation Through the Period of the Adoption of the Organic Act.* 2 vols. New York: The Macmillan Company, 1914–1916.

Busey, Samuel C. *Pictures of the City of Washington.* Washington, D.C.: Wm. M. Ballantyne & Sons, 1898.

Caroli, Betty Boyd. *First Ladies.* Expanded and updated edition. New York: Oxford University Press, 2003.

Carson, Barbara G. *Ambitious Appetites: Dining, Behavior, and Patterns of Consumption in Federal Washington.* Washington, D.C.: American Institute of Architects Press, 1990.

Chiles, James R. "Congress couldn't have been *this* bad, or could it?" In *Smithsonian* (Nov. 1995), pp. 70–81.

Clark, Allen C. *Life and Letters of Dolly Madison.* Washington, D.C.: Press of W.F. Roberts Company, 1914.

Coggleshall, George. *History of the American Privateers.* New York: 1856.

Colman, Edna M. *75 Years of White House Gossip: From Washington to Lincoln.* New York: Doubleday, Page & Company, 1925.

Cooper, J[ames]. Fenimore. *The Navy of the United States of America.* New York: Stringer & Townsend, 1856.

Côté, Richard N. *Strength and Honor: The Life of Dolley Madison.* Mt. Pleasant, SC: Corinthian Books, 2005.

Crawford, Mary Caroline. *Romantic Days in the Early Republic.* Boston: Little, Brown, 1912.

Cruikshank, E. *The Documentary History of the Campaign upon the Niagara Frontier in the Year 1813.* Part 1. Lundy's Lane, NY: Lundy's Lane Historical Society, 1902.

Cruikshank, E. A. *The Political Adventures of John Henry.* Toronto: The Macmillan Company, 1936.

Curtis, George Ticknor. *Life of Daniel Webster.* 2 vols. New York: D. Appleton and Company, 1870.

Cutler, Carl C. *Greyhounds of the Sea: The Story of the American Clipper Ship.* New York: G.P. Putnam's Sons, 1930.

Dangerfield, George. *The Awakening of American Nationalism.* New York: Harper & Row, 1964.

———. *The Era of Good Feelings.* New York: Harcourt, Brace & Company, Inc. 1952.

Davis, Robert Ralph Jr. "Diplomatic Plumage: American Court Dress in the Early National Period." *American Quarterly,* vol. 20, no. 2, part 1 (Summer 1968), pp. 164–79.

Drotning, Phillip T. *Black Heroes in Our Nation's History.* New York: Cowles Book Company, Inc., 1969.

Dudley, Wade G. *Splintering the Wooden Wall.* Annapolis, MD: Naval Institute Press, 2003.

Dudley, William S., ed. *The Naval War of 1812: A Documentary History,* 3 vols. Washington, D.C.: Naval Historical Center, 1985–2002.

Dunlap, William. *History of the Rise and Progress of the Arts of Design in the United States.* 2 vols. New York: George P. Scott & Co., 1834.

Ellet, Mrs. E[lizabeth] F[ries]. *The Court Circles of the Republic, or the Beauties and Celebrities of the Nation.* Hartford, CT: Hartford Publishing Co., 1969.

Engleman, Fred L. *The Peace of Christmas Eve.* New York: Harcourt, Brace & World, Inc., 1962.

Fairburn, William Armstrong. *Merchant Sail.* 6 vols. Center Lovell, ME: Fairburn Marine Educational Foundation, Inc., 1945–1955.

Farb, Peter, and Armelagos, George. *Consuming Passions: The Anthropology of Eating.* Boston: Houghton Mifflin Company, 1980.

Fazio, Michael, and Snedon, Patrick. "Benjamin Latrobe and Thomas Jefferson Redesign the President's House." *White House History* no. 8 (Fall 2000), pp. 36–53.

Foner, Eric, and Garraty, John A. *The Reader's Companion to American History.* Boston: Houghton Mifflin, 1991.

Footner, Hulbert. *Sailor of Fortune: The Life and Adventures of Commodore Barney, USN.* Annapolis, MD: Naval Institute Press, 1998. Reprint of 1940 edition.

Foster, John W[atson]. *A Century of American Diplomacy, Being a Brief Review of the Foreign Relations of the United States, 1776–1876.* Boston: Houghton, Mifflin and Company, 1900.

Fowler, William H. *Jack Tars and Commodores: American Navy, 1735–1815.* Boston: Houghton Mifflin Company, 1984.

Fredriksen, John C., ed. "'Plow-Joggers for Generals': The Experiences of a New York Ensign in the War of 1812." *Indiana Military History Journal,* vol. 2 (October 1986), pp. 17–27.

Freeman, Joanne B. *Affairs of Honor: National Politics in the New Republic.* New Haven, CT: Yale University Press, 2001.

Furman, Bess. *White House Profile: A Social History of the White House, Its Occupants and Its Festivities.* Indianapolis IN: The Bobbs-Merrill Company, Inc., 1951.

[Gales, Joseph.] "Joseph Gales on the War Manifesto of 1812." In *American Historical Review*, vol. 13, no. 2 (Jan. 1908), pp. 303–10.

———. "Recollections of the Civil History of the War of 1812." In *The Historical Magazine and Notes and Queries Concerning the Antiquities, History and Biography of America*. Series 3 (Apr. 1875).

Gay, Sydney Howard. *James Madison.* Boston and New York: Houghton Mifflin Company, 1912.

George, Christopher T. *Terror on the Chesapeake.* Shippensburg, PA: White Man Books, 2000.

Gillette, Howard Jr. *Southern City, National Ambition: The Growth of Early Washington, D.C., 1800–1860*. Washington, D.C.: George Washington University Center for Washington Area Studies and the American Architectural Foundation, 1995.

Gleaves, Albert. *James Lawrence, Captain, United States Navy.* New York: G.P. Putnam's Sons, 1904.

Goodwin, Maud Wilder. *Dolly Madison.* New York: Charles Scribner's Sons, 1896.

Green, Constance McLaughlin. *Washington: Village and Capital, 1800–1878.* Princeton, NJ: Princeton University Press, 1962.

Groene, Bertram H. "A Trap for the British: Thomas Brown and the Battle of the 'White House.'" *Virginia Cavalcade*, vol. 18 (Summer 1968–Spring 1969), pp. 12–19.

Hamlin, Talbot. *Benjamin Henry Latrobe.* New York: Oxford University Press, 1955.

Hickey, Donald R. *The War of 1812: A Forgotten Conflict.* Urbana: University of Illinois Press, 1989.

Hildreth, Richard. *The History of the United States of America*, vol. 3. New York: Harper & Brothers, 1852.

Hines, Christian. *Early Recollections of Washington City.* Washington, D.C.: Chronicle Book and Job Print, 1866.

Hoffman, Ronald; Sobel, Mechal; and Teute, Fredrika J., eds. *Through a Glass Darkly: Reflections on Personal Identity in Early America.* Chapel Hill: Published for the Omohundro Institute of Early American History & Culture, Williamsburg, Virginia, by the University of North Carolina Press, 1997.

Hollon, W. E. "Zebulon Montgomery Pike and the York Campaign, 1813." In *New York History*, vol. 30, no. 3 (July 1949), pp. 259–75.

[Hull, William.] *Report of the Trial of Brig. General William Hull.* New York: Eastburn, Kirk, and Co., 1814.

Hunt, Gaillard. "The First Inaugural Ball." In *Century Magazine*, vol. 69 (Mar. 1905), pp. 754–60.

———. *Life in America One Hundred Years Ago.* New York: Harper & Brothers, 1914.

———. *The Life of James Madison.* New York: Doubleday, Page & Co., 1902.

———. "Mrs. Madison's First Drawing Room." In *Harper's Monthly Magazine*, vol. 121 (June 1910), pp. 141–148.

Hunt-Jones, Conover. *Dolley and the "great little Madison."* Washington, D.C.: American Institute of Architects Foundation, 1977.

Hurd, Charles. *Washington Cavalcade.* New York: E.P. Dutton & Co., Inc., 1948.

———. *The White House: A Biography.* New York: Harper & Brothers, Publishers, 1940.

Ingersoll, Charles J[ared]. *Historical Sketch of the Second War between the United States of America and Great Britain*. Philadelphia: Lea and Blanchard, 1849.

———. *Historical Sketch of the Second War between the United States of America and Great Britain*, vol. 1. Philadelphia: Lippincott, Grambo & Co., 1853.

———. *History of the Second War between the United States of America and Great Britain*, vol. 2. Philadelphia: Lippincott, Grambo & Co., 1853.

[Ingraham, Edward Duncan.] *A Sketch of the Events which Preceded the Capture of Washington, by the British, on the Twenty-Fourth of August, 1814.* Philadelphia: Carey and Hart, 1849.

James, William. *The Naval History of Great Britain*, vol. 6, *1811–1827*. London: Richard Bentley, 1837.

———. *Naval Occurrences of the Late War.* London: T. Egerton, 1817.

Jennings, Paul. *A Colored Man's Reminiscences of James Madison.* Brooklyn, NY: George G. Beadles, 1865. Reprinted in *White House History*, vol. 1, no. 1, pp. 50–55.

Johnston, William Dawson. *History of the Library of Congress, vol. 1, 1800–1864.* Washington, D.C.: Government Printing Office, 1904.

Ketcham, Ralph. *James Madison: A Biography.* New York: Macmillan, 1971; reprinted by University of Virginia Press, 1990.

———. *The Madisons at Montpelier: Reflections on the Founding Couple.* Charlottesville: University of Virginia Press, 2009.

Key, Francis S[cott]. *Poems of the Late Francis S. Key.* New York: Robert Carter & Brothers, 1857.

King, Horatio. "The Battle of Bladensburg: Burning of Washington in 1814." In *Magazine of American History*, vol. 14 (Nov. 1885), no. 5, pp. 438–57.

Klapthor, Margaret Brown. "A First Lady and a New Frontier, 1800." In *Historic Preservation*, vol. 15 (1963), no. 3, pp. 88–93.

———. "Benjamin Latrobe and Dolley Madison Decorate the White House, 1809–1811." Museum of History and Technology, paper 49. Washington, D.C.: Smithsonian Institution, 1965.

Latimer, Jon. *1812: War with America.* Cambridge, MA: Harvard University Press, 2007.

"Letters relating to the Negotiations at Ghent, 1812–1814." In *American Historical Review,* vol. 20, no. 1 (Oct. 1914), pp. 108–29.

Lloyd, Alan. *The Scorching of Washington: The War of 1812.* Washington, D.C.: R.B. Luce, 1975.

Long, Orie William. *Literary Pioneers; Early American Explorers of European Culture.* Cambridge, MA: Harvard University Press, 1935.

Lord, Walter. *The Dawn's Early Light.* New York: W. W. Norton & Co., 1972.

Lossing, Benson J. *The Pictorial Field-Book of the War of 1812.* New York: Harper & Brothers, Publishers, 1869.

Luria, Sarah. *Capital Speculations: Writing and Building Washington, D.C.* Durham: University of New Hampshire Press, 2006.

Kennedy, Julia E. *George Watterston: Novelist, "Metropolitan Author," and Critic: A Dissertation.* Washington, D.C.: The Catholic University of America, 1933.

Magruder, Caleb C., Jr. "Dr. William Beanes, The Incidental Cause of the Authorship of the Star-Spangled Banner." *Records of the Columbian Historical Society of Washington, D.C.*, vol. 22 (1919), pp. 207–25.

Mahan, A[lfred] T[hayer] (Capt.). *Sea Power in its Relations to the War of 1812.* 2 vols. Boston: Little, Brown & Company, 1905.

Mahon, John K. *War of 1812.* Gainesville: University of Florida Press, 1972.

Mannix, Richard. "Albert Gallatin in Washington, 1801–1813." *Records of the Columbian Historical Society of Washington, D.C.*, vols. 71–72 (1971–1972), pp. 60–80.

Matheson, William. "George Watterston: Advocate of the National Library." In *Quarterly Journal of the Library of Congress*, vol. 32 (Oct. 1975), pp. 370–88.

Mattern, David. "The Famous Letter: Dolley Madison Has the Last Word." *White House History* no. 4 (Fall 1998), pp. 228–33.

McCormick, John H. "The First Master of Ceremonies of the White House." In *Records of the Columbian Historical Society of Washington, D.C.*, vol. 7 (1904). Washington, D.C.: Columbian Historical Society, pp. 170–94.

McNamara, Robert F. "Charles Carroll of Belle Vue, Co-Founder of Rochester." *Rochester History*, vol. 42, no. 4 (Oct. 1980), pp. 1–28.

Molotsky, Irwin. *The Flag, the Poet, and the Song: The Story of the Star-Spangled Banner.* New York: Dutton, 2001.

Monkman, Betty C. *The White House: Its Historic Furnishings and First Families.* Washington, D.C.: White House Historical Association, 2000.

Morison, Samuel Eliot. "The Henry-Crillon Affair of 1812." *Proceedings of the Massachusetts Historical Society,* 3rd series, vol. 69, pp. 207–31.

Morriss, Roger. *Cockburn and the British Navy in Transition: Admiral Sir George Cockburn, 1772–1853*. Columbia: University of South Carolina Press, 1997.

Muller, Charles G. *The Darkest Day: The Washington-Baltimore Campaign During the War of 1812.* Philadelphia: University of Pennsylvania Press, 1963.

Pack, James. *The Man Who Burned the White House: Admiral Sir George Cockburn, 1772–1852*. Emsworth, UK: Kenneth Mason, 1987.

Perkins, Bradford. *Prologue to War: England and the United States, 1805–1812.* Berkeley: University of California Press, 1961.

Plumer, William Jr. *Life of William Plumer.* A. P. Peabody, ed. New York: Da Capo Press, 1969.

Poore, Ben. Perley. *Biographical Sketch of John Stuart Skinner.* New York: John L. O'Connor, 1924.

Powell, J. H. *Richard Rush: Republican Diplomat, 1780–1859*. Philadelphia: University of Pennsylvania Press, 1942.

Raley, Robert L. "Interior Designs by Benjamin Latrobe for the President's House." *Antiques,* vol. 75 (June 1958), pp. 568–71.

"Richard Rush: Political Portraits with Pen and Pencil." *United States Magazine and Democratic Review,* vol. 7, no. 28 (1840).

Riddell, William Renwick. "Jenkin Ratford, Ordinary, Born in London." *Journal of the American Institute of Criminal Law and Criminology*, vol. 6, no. 6 (March 1916), pp. 815–19.

Roosevelt, Theodore. *The Naval War of 1812.* New York: G.P. Putnam's Sons, 1882.

Rutland, Robert A. *The Presidency of James Madison.* Lawrence: University Press of Kansas, 1990.

Seale, William. *The White House: The History of an American Idea.* Washington, D.C.: The American Institute of Architects Press/The White House Historical Association, 1992.

[Seaton, Josephine.] *William Winston Seaton of the "National Intelligencer."* Boston: James R. Osgood and Company, 1871.

Shulman, Holly Cowan. "Dolley (Payne Todd) Madison." In *American First Ladies: Their Lives and the Legacy,* Lewis L. Gould, ed. 2nd ed. New York: Routledge, 2001, pp. 21–36.

Singleton, Esther. *The Story of the White House.* New York: Benjamin Blom, 1907.

Skaggs, David Curtis, and Altoff, Gerard T. *A Signal Victory: The Lake Erie Campaign, 1812–1813.* Annapolis, MD: Naval Institute Press, 1997.

———. *Thomas Macdonough: Master of Command.* Annapolis, MD: U.S. Naval Institute Press, 2003.

Skeen, C. Edward. *John Armstrong, Jr., 1758–1853: A Biography.* Syracuse, NY: Syracuse University Press, 1981.

Stagg, J.C.A. *Mr. Madison's War.* Princeton, NJ: Princeton University Press, 1983.

Stearns, Elinor, and Yerkes, David N. *William Thornton: A Renaissance Man in the Federal City.* Washington, D.C.: American Institute of Architects Foundation, 1976.

Tayloe, Benjamin Ogle. *Our Neighbors on Lafayette Square.* Washington, D.C.: Junior League of Washington, 1982. Reprint of 1872 edition.

Toll, Ian W. *Six Frigates: The Epic History of the Founding of the U.S. Navy.* New York: W. W. Norton & Co., 2006.

Tucker, George. *The Life of Thomas Jefferson.* London: Charles Knight and Co., 1837.

Tucker, Spencer C., and Reuter, Frank T. *Injured Honor: The Chesapeake-Leopard Affair.* Annapolis, MD: Naval Institute Press, 1996.

Tyack, David B. *George Ticknor and the Boston Brahmins.* Cambridge, MA: Harvard University Press, 1967.

Warden, D[avid]. B[aillie]. *A Chorographical and Statistical Description of the District of Columbia: The Seat of the General Government of the United States.* Paris: Printed and sold by Smith, 1816.

———. *A Statistical, Political, and Historical Account of the United States of North America.* 3 vols. Philadelphia: Thomas Wardle, 1819.

Warner, William W. *At Peace with Their Neighbors: Catholics and Catholicism in the*

National Capital, 1787–1860. Washington, D.C.: Georgetown University Press, 1994.

Weller, M. I. "Commodore Joshua Barney: The Hero of the Battle of Bladensburg." In *Records of the Columbian Historical Society of Washington, D.C.*, vol. 14 (1911), pp. 66–183.

Weybright, Victor. *Spangled Banner: The Story of Francis Scott Key*. New York: Farrar & Rinehart, Inc., 1935.

Wheater, W. *Historical Record of the Seventh or Royal Regiment of Fusiliers*. Leeds, 1875.

Williams, John S. *History of the Invasion and Capture of Washington*. New York: Harper & Brothers, 1857.

Wills, Garry. *James Madison*. New York: Times Books, 2002.

Winter, Frank H. *The First Golden Age of Rocketry*. Washington, D.C.: Smithsonian Institution Press, 1990.

Wyeth, S[amuel]. D[ouglas]. *History of the Library of Congress*. Washington, D.C.: Gibson Brothers, Printers, 1868.

Young, James Sterling. *The Washington Community, 1800–1828*. New York: Columbia University Press, 1966.

INDEX

T

A NOTE ON THE AUTHOR

Hugh Howard's numerous books include *The Painter's Chair: George Washington and the Making of American Art*; *Dr. Kimball and Mr. Jefferson*; the definitive *Thomas Jefferson, Architect*; his memoir *House-Dreams*; and the classic *Houses of the Founding Fathers*. He resides in upstate New York with his wife and two daughters.